SELF DISCOVERY AND SOCIAL AWARENESS

EVERETT
OSTROVSKY

SELF DISCOVERY AND SOCIAL AWARENESS

JOHN WILEY & SONS, INC.
NEW YORK • LONDON • SYDNEY • TORONTO

Library of Congres Cataloging in Publication Data

Ostrovsky, Everett S
Self discovery and social awareness.

Bibliography: p.
1. Developmental psychology. 2. Self-perception.
3. Social perception. I. Title.

BF713.08 155.2 73-17333
ISBN 0-471-65714-X
ISBN 0-471-65716-6 (pbk.)

Set on Monophoto by Thomson Press (India) Limited, New Delhi-1

Printed in the United States of America

10 9 8 7 6 5 4 3 2 1

TO MICHAELA, RUTHY, AND NINA

FOREWORD

A foreword is often a formality, but this book requires a special introduction. As a teaching aid, it represents a new and different approach to the development in students of an increased awareness of their own experience as a foundation for understanding others.

Professor Ostrovsky has developed this collection of descriptive incidents to accord with a quite different approach to education. He is not presenting facts to be memorized or theories to be grasped and applied. Instead, he is trying to open up the perceptive faculties and the sensibility of students to the nature of life and experience.

This book belongs to a tradition that has ancient roots, but that only recently has been given respectful attention in Western culture. The intellectual, emotional, and spiritual disciplines of Buddhism have sought for centuries to free the individual from bondage to prevailing illusions. They help the disciple to become more fully aware of his complete "at oneness" with the world of nature. As Gordon Allport has written: "[The individual] blends with nature and he blends with society. It is only the merger that can profitably be studied." The experience of "satori," or liberation, enables the human personality to interact freely and spontaneously with the physical and social realities that form the "ground of his being."

In recent times, existentialist thinking has challenged men to accept responsibility for discovering what they are and for becoming what they want to be. Kierkegaard speaks of revealing to men "an inner picture too delicately drawn to be outwardly visible, woven as it is of the tenderest moods of the soul." It is precisely such an objective that Professor Ostrovsky has sought to serve.

An important current in American psychology converges today with the recent rediscovery of Eastern thought and with existentialism. Carl Rogers summarized, in the following statements, some of his learning during a lifetime devoted to trying to understand the troubled lives of clients.

"I find I am more effective when I can listen acceptantly to myself and can be myself."

"I have found it of enormous value when I can permit myself to understand another person."

"The touchstone of validity is my own experience."

"What is more personal is most general."

"I am at my best when I can let the flow of my experience carry me."

"I have come to feel that the only learning which significantly influences behavior is self-discovered, self-appropriated learning."

A similar movement of thought underlies the widespread use of what has been variously called "T-groups," "laboratory training in human relations," or "sensitivity training." Substantial research has demonstrated that adults who spend a week or two involved in this kind of personal learning usually emerge with new and deeper understanding of themselves and with such an improved perception of other people that their families and their co-workers notice significant differences in behavior. No comparable evidence supports the common assumption that knowledge about the findings of psychological research will result in better teachers, managers, or human beings.

At the Fourteenth Session of the International Congress of Applied Psychology (Copenhagen, 1961), Timothy Leary outlined the view that most human behavior is very much like playing a game. It reflects certain presented roles, rules, goals, rituals, language, and values. Some players get so lost in playing their assigned parts—child in family, pupil in school, employee in job, citizen in community—that they never discover the artificiality of these set games or the true nature of their own lives. "Most of our attempts to change behavior increase human helplessness. . .give more power to the few and less power to the many." Leary proposes to help us learn that "our own consciousness is infinitely greater than our little ego's and the ego-games into which we are so blindly caught up."

How is this made to happen? Professor Ostrovsky uses vignettes of child experience as starting points for a fresh and deeper understanding of our own living and relationships. These little episodes in print serve only as springboards. They become useful only if teachers and pupils are prepared to dive from them and swim on their own.

The significant task left to the teacher is to enable students to become more aware, more authentic, and more empathic. One may begin a class session with these fragments from the lives of children and adolescents, but important learning comes only as the discussion moves freely away from this starting point, toward recall and sharing of the students' own experiences. Indeed, it may be that after some weeks of learning how to do this, students will be able to bring into class discussions (preferably in small groups) "starter" items from their own daily living that can be used similarly.

When teachers such as Professor Ostrovsky have become more numerous, we shall see a new, more genuine, more perceptive kind of learning by students. They will relate to the children they teach more empathically and with more profound and constructive impact on the lives of youth.

Goodwin Watson

PREFACE

This is not the usual text. It combines various thought provoking devices. It includes episodes about children, adolescents, and adults, as well as articles, role-playing situations, proverbs, and quotations. It tries to instigate a wide range of personal responses by the questions it raises. It can be individually as well as collectively reacted to. It does not necessarily tell you what you ought to know. On the contrary, it helps you to find out what you feel, think, value, and want by exposing you to problems and situations in which you are asked to discover the answers for yourself. Your response to the questions should sensitize you to how you perceive yourself, the subjects under study, and your fellow students. In other words, what you derive from the book is not determined primarily by the contents of what is presented in the forthcoming pages. It essentially depends on how you relate to the subject matter and to classmates. Different facets of life are herein indicated. It is up to you to actively extract the meaning from them.

In the first part of the book, "Articles and Episodes," I combine professionally written statements by some of the foremost thinkers in education, psychology, psychiatry, and sociology together with my episodes. I personally developed the themes for these vignettes, although the actual content was inspired by my students, patients, and personal experiences. Whatever strengths and failings the episodes have as material for actualizing self discovery and social awareness, I alone am responsible, since the production of them is mine. The subject matter, however, might belong to all of us. They are intended to be written documentaries of what most of us have experienced directly or indirectly. They depict the human condition in a way that is different from what is generally presented in most texts that deal with human development and the behavioral sciences. They are not meant to be clinical descriptions. They permit you the opportunity to project your own life space into consciousness, and to share it actively with others. You will be confronted by the self you might have forgotten by the aid of these articles and episodes. The secret world of children, teenagers, and adults will be yours to unravel. You are the magician. You can bring into action your own experiential, empathetic and imaginative skills and props along with your critical thinking, and share them with your fellow students and teacher. No doubt you will be able to add your own versions and experiences to the episodes included here. This is as it should be. The questions that follow the articles and vignettes ought to help you become aware of your rich personal heritage. Much of what we take for granted about ourselves can be perceived anew, examined, appreciated, and used to broaden our scope of self discovery and social awareness.

The topics in Part One, "Articles and Episodes," were carefully selected in order to coincide with the current contents of the standard texts in Child and Adolescent Psychology, Developmental Psychology, and Human Development. These readings are no substitute for the objectively presented material of a primary text. They are, however, suggested as supplementary readings. The directness of the episodes and the questions that follow ought to provide you with a wealth of readiness to seek out further understanding of both yourself and the subject under discussion. The readings in Part One do not have to necessarily follow according to the sequence indicated here. Each division is complete onto itself even though it is dynamically related to all the others.

Since an introduction precedes each section there is no need to summarize its substance. A quick examination of the table of contents will alert you to the sequence. We start with "The World Of Play," which is followed by "The Family." From this source of development we highlight the significance of the child and adolescent's "Sex Awareness." This leads us to the area of the surrounding community of "School and Its Horizons." "Thinking and Creativity" precedes the next division, "Becoming and Being." This takes us through the general gamut of some of the healthy developmental areas. Then, in "The Disadvantaged" and the section that follows, "Confrontation and Aggression," we are exposed to the more atypical but current realities of youth and the immediate adult culture. In both the next two divisions, "Prejudice" and "Drugs," some of the pathological effects of our generation are discussed and illustrated. Finally, in "Values," we are given the opportunity to deal with the essential dilemma that confronts all of us.

In Part Two, "Role Playing," you are given the opportunity to find out what it is like to be someone else and still be yourself. This might seem to be a contradiction, but the significance of this statement will be appreciated and understood once you participate in a role-playing situation. The introduction to this section and the guide that follows it will prepare you for either task, that of observer or participator. In both cases, you will actively learn about yourself, the dynamics and the intricasies of the group process in action, how roles are perceived by players, and how human problems of conflict are confronted. This is a large order but a realistic one once you put yourself in someone else's shoes. Insight into the motives, fears, and hopes of others is aided by this invaluable experience of role playing. Understanding cannot take place in a vacuum, void of the quality of relationship we have with others. In role-playing we are inextricably part of a human problem; the adventure in learning takes place when we try to define it, and extricate ourselves from the dilemma by solving it. The intent is to help you learn something more about yourself and others as you role paly and reflect on the crises of children, adolescents, parents, and educators. Incidentally, the role-playing situations and short case study presentations are original; they are an outgrowth of my teaching and clinical experience.

In Part Three, "Proverbs and Quotations," a special type of reality is typified. Historical, moral, ethical, political, and social aspects of our heritage are introduced in the form of eclipsed statements of wisdom, banality, absurdity, truth, and witticism. The sayings are analyzed and interpreted according to our perceptions. The quotes are related to such topics as the child, parent, home, play, behavior, prejudice, war, peace, nature, solitude, love, cities, and imagination.

Through the use of the guide "How to Use the Proverbs and Quotations" you will learn how to approach and bring to consciousness your own symbolic meanings and traditions, stereotypes and folklore that you yourself have imperceptibly incorporated in the process of your socializations and education.

These sayings which represent the essence of what many men have felt and feel are significant and timeless. Your identification with the meaning of these quotes will help you bridge the 'generation gap' (the historical difference between what was and what is meaningful to you). You can project your own vision into them. The more that these sayings encompass and involve you, the more they are likely to tap the deeper recesses of your psyche. Your conception of the above-mentioned subject areas will be affected by what you attribute to and project into the quotes, as well as how you share these experiences with your fellow-students, and teacher.

Everett Ostrovsky

CONTENTS

PART ONE: ARTICLES AND EPISODES

PART THREE: PROVERBS AND QUOTATIONS

SELF DISCOVERY AND SOCIAL AWARENESS

PART ONE

ARTICLES AND EPISODES

How To Answer the Questions that Follow the Articles and Episodes

(Each article and episode is marked with numbers that correspond to questions at the end of its contents. You are asked to answer the questions as honestly and openly as you can. This is not a test. There is no right or wrong answer.)

1. Do you really believe in what you are saying?
2. How would your parents consider your answer?
3. How would your brothers or sisters respond to your answer?
4. How would your teacher react to your answer?
5. How would your best friend answer the same question?
6. How would the person you care least about answer the question?
7. Do you think there are any conditions that would make you answer differently?
8. What alternatives can you imagine to your answer?
9. Do you think you would have answered this question this way a few years ago?
10. Do you think you will answer this question this way a few years from now?
11. Are you saying what you really feel or is your answer the one you imagine is expected of you from your parents, teachers, and friends?
12. What would you be prepared to do about the answer you gave if you came across an answer that was completely the opposite of yours?
13. Can you give a rationale to support your point of view?
14. Can you imagine any situation that would support your argument?
15. Are you using words loosely or are you aware of their significance? Explain.
16. Suppose everyone thought the way you did. What would the result be?
17. How consistent is your point of view? (Look for any contradiction.)
18. Have you defined the problem connected to this question carefully?
19. What are some of the counterarguments to what you are saying?
20. Do you think all people should believe what you do?
21. What would the most ideal situation be between youngster and parent in regard to this question?
22. Are you willing to accept the feelings of others who feel differently than you do?
23. Does your answer make you feel wholesome?
24. Is your answer a defensive or protective one?

25. What are your motives for answering the way you do?

26. Have you given your answer much thought or was it the first thing that came to your mind?

27. Would you change your mind if you were put under pressure by your parents, teachers, friends?

28. Do you feel at home with what you are saying or are you saying what you would like to believe?

I

THE WORLD OF PLAY

So much of what we hope for, fear, and wish is best expressed through play. The child experiments with, explores, and tests reality and as a result learns about the boundaries of himself and the world. He discovers what it is like to win or lose, identify with others, release tensions, create, disguise or reveal his wishes, and adhere to and determine the rules of the game. Everything is possible: he can shoot his enemy dead without guilt, suffer a hero's torment and survive whole, be powerful as a giant and cunning as a weasel—the limits are not fixed. All subject matter can be translated or forged into play. Perhaps most important, it is fun. Life is less enjoyable without it. Now we must limit our discussion and turn our attention to the articles and episodes included in this section.

According to L. K. Frank, play contributes to the health of a child's growth and development. This theme is illustrated in the vignette "Dan and His Friends." What Roy experiences in the next episode might parallel what most children experience at one time or another. In the story "Street Scene," the children's activities and the grown-up world merge together as an intricate part of the whole environment. In a very concrete way, Alex, in the following episode, discovers something about trains and sounds and movement while he shuffles his feet through dry leaves. In the next episode, "The Bomb in the Nursery School," Toby illustrates how he becomes part of his dramatic play. Can we separate Toby, the child, from what and how he plays?

The Role of Play in Child Development

Lawrence K. Frank

Play provides occasions for children to exercise their varied capacities in spontaneous activities which are largely self rewarding and usually enjoyable. Today the constraints of urban living and the limitations of space, time and freedom are depriving children of opportunities and facilities for play essential for their normal wholesome development.

The many programs for organized play and more or less regimented exercises and physical training now being offered or required seem to overlook or deliberately reject the importance, if not the necessity, of play for wholesome growth and development and for the maintenance of bodily functioning.

A child, we should remember, is initially a young organism with all the "wisdom of the body," as Walter Cannon called these inherited capacities for self-organization, self-regulation and self-repair. The child inherits not only specific patterns from his parents and grandparents but also functional capacities evolved by his mammalian and premammalian ancestors. These give him the amazing potentialities exhibited only by humans.

The mammalian evolution occurred over millions of years during which organisms were in continual contact and were learning to carry on their intercourse with the environment, an environment with a variety of ever-changing impacts and demands: heat and cold, barometric pressures, wetness and dryness, and the constant pull of gravity. Against these impacts man early learned to develop and maintain an upright stance and bipedal locomotion.

The human child is a product of long experience in living in a natural environment requiring great flexibility and adaptiveness and in coping with the often hazardous and threatening situations that demand alertness and quick reactions and frequently sustained exertion for survival.

Physiologically Deprived

Today we are discovering that absence of these environmental demands may bring a progressive loss or impairment of functional capacities, since the various bodily processes must be continually exercised if they are to be efficient and capable of sustaining the many operations essential to wholesome living. Automobiles and buses, elevators and moving stairways, air conditioning, and many hours spent indoors at sedentary occupations are beginning to impose a "physiological deprivation" that may be as serious as the sensory deprivations of which recently we have been made aware.

The young child (even in infancy if given opportunity) likes to be alert and responsive to the world, engaging in a variety of activities. Except when asleep, he continually explores, manipulates and relates himself to the world physically and through his senses. By grasping, hitting, pulling, pushing, creeping and crawling, standing erect and walking, and then running, the young child learns what no one can teach him, as neuromuscular articulation and musculoskeletal coordination, for coping with the environment. At the same time the child is engaged in what is not overtly exhibited or easily observed; namely, maintaining his organism by the continual replacement of

"The Role of Play in Child Development," by Lawrence K. Frank. From CHILDHOOD EDUCATION, October 1964, Vol. 41, No. 2, pp. 70–73. Reprinted by permission of Lawrence K. Frank and the Association for Childhood Education International, 3615 Wisconsin Avenue, N.W., Washington, D.C.

cells, tissues, and the chemical constituents thereof, through these bodily activities that stimulate not only his incremental growth but this basic replacement growth.

Likewise, in his varied play activities, the child is fostering the progressive organization of his different organ systems and functional operations and learning how to maintain a dynamic stability that enables him to enlarge and reduce and to regulate all his bodily processes as responsive to his bodily movements and exertions. At the same time, these activities are developing his internal communications whereby the different bodily functions are synchronized and become more effectively responsive to the varying demands they must sustain.

The infant seems to act more or less randomly. But as he grows older and has opportunities for spontaneous, self-directed activities, he develops an increasing capacity for purposive, goal-seeking conduct. Unless obstructed and handicapped by others, especially in his play, he will show his own creative efforts to achieve what he individually projects ahead.

Play Essential to Health

If we deliberately ignore the psychological benefits of play, we can still say that play is essential to wholesome development of the young organism because in his play activities the child exercises these varied functioning processes essential to his health and well-being. But what is important is that the child does this spontaneously in his own individual way. He usually regulates the time, intensity and extent of his play activities by these inner regulatory processes that are difficult, if not impossible, for an observer to replace by external rules and regulations.

As children become increasingly subject to the constraints and demands of school they are more or less seriously deprived of the kind of bodily activities described above. By way of compensation schools offer greater or lesser opportunities for periodical play activities or prescribe formal physical training and participation in games supervised by adults. More recently schools have been requiring children to engage in a program of "physical fitness" in which spontaneous play activities are largely replaced by drills and training in skilled performances, as in gymnastics.

Since the usual elementary school program in largely emphasizing academic learning and performance imposes upon children the requirement of sitting quietly and refraining from conversation while focusing upon symbolic learning, as in reading, children may be said to be deprived physiologically of normal and healthy development. Not infrequently there is an acute discontinuity in the life of the child as he is required to relinquish his immediate interests and enjoyment of the actual world in which as an organism he has learned to relate by a variety of bodily activities and manipulations, to accept the insistent demand for symbolic learning, as in reading and writing and mathematics, with the further requirement of physical inactivity that may often create a hunger for movement.

Recess and Gym Not Enough

It is assumed that a brief recess and a period of physical training or organized exercise will be sufficient to satisfy this hunger, especially since children will have an opportunity for play after school. A careful assessment of recess and gym periods may show that many children are building up tensions not adequately discharged by these intervals or after-school play. Recess and gym periods are far from sufficient for large numbers of urban-dwelling children. The foregoing has given rise to serious questioning of the present conception of programs for physical fitness as not meeting the needs of the young child and the middle-aged child. Spontaneous play seems to be highly desirable—if not essential—to wholesome development and for relieving the stress and tensions of urban living and the increasing demands for intellectual achievement.

With the growing recognition of what has been called the "psychosomatic disorders and illnesses" and the realization that there is no functional separation of mind and body, there is a discrepancy between what we know is necessary for child development and what we are doing about it in our schools.

Advocates of a highly organized program for physical fitness apparently believe it possible, with only one or two hours a week of intensive training, to develop children's capacities for muscular exertion and endurance with little or no concern for what they may be doing the rest of the week in the classroom. A recognition of the "wholeness" of the child and of the importance of child development for our future national well-being calls for a critical examination of the assumptions and expectations of educators in all subject matter fields and academic programs. With the schools as primary agent for child nurture, education and conservation, the basic question is: What *can* and *should* they provide for the wholesome development of children at each stage in their sequential progress toward maturity? Known facts about children's needs and requirements, capacities and potentialities by various professions and disciplines studying children's growth, development and learning *can* and *should* be orchestrated into a coherent plan and program that will recognize and make operational two basic principles:

1. That there is a regular, orderly sequential path from infancy to adult life along which each child will move if given opportunities and encouragement; for negotiating these transitions he requires the teaching which is appropriate for each stage in this sequential development, at his rate of progress, to attain his own size and shape and exhibit the capacities of which he individually is capable.

2. That each child is a highly individualized organism-personality with his own cognitive style and with aptitudes, capacities and potentialities rarely so distributed that he can achieve equally well in all the different subject matter areas or modes of physical achievement.

Especially important is the recognition of the child's unique organism and what can be provided during childhood and youth that will enable him to grow up and face the problems of later maturity and aging. Today's children are likely to live longer than any previous generation in the history of the world.

Play—Outlet for Tensions

A conception of play that recognizes the significance of autonomous, self-directed learning and active exploration and manipulation of the actual world gives a promising approach to the wholesome development of children, who need the opportunities and facilities that permit full functioning of their organisms if they are to meet the many demands, restrictions, pressures and tensions which they must encounter as they grow and develop. Children need help to become capable of bearing the burdens of freedom, for living in a free social order and contributing to the development of an urban, industrial civilization to which, as a nation, we are committed. This is one way we can show our capacity "to love little children" more intelligently and compassionately. It is a way to translate into the education of children our long-cherished, enduring goal values, a belief in the worth of the individual personality, and a genuine respect for the dignity and *integrity* of the child.

Questions and Projects Related to the Role of Play in Child Development

1. In what way is play instrumental in the development of the young child?
   a. Of the adolescent?
   b. Of the adult?
2. What purpose does play serve in school?
3. What thinking processes are utilized in play?
4. What does the child learn about himself while he plays?
5. How do the play activities of today differ from those of your childhood?

Dan (7) : Dan and His Friends

The tall seven-year-old boy held the mottled green liquor bottle against his stomach and huddled himself around it as the other child, who was approximately his size but heavier and wearing a paper bag on his head, jumped on him and tried to grab the bottle out of his hands. They both rolled around in the withered grass and dust.[1] This wrestling match repeated itself; first one obtained the bottle from the other, then the other retrieved it. With each movement, the contents of the bottle, which was dirt, poured over one child then the other. Wherever they rolled or kicked and squirmed, the dirt followed them.[2]

Finally a larger boy called out, "Join sides—we're going to play war!" He was being followed by a company of four- and five-year-olds who were either wearing a hat or carrying a stick. This "war" announcement seemed to confuse the whole group because the children started to ask each other, "Which side is whose?"[3] The large boy with the red shirt and the pistol belt told them to be quiet and said, "You are to go with you, and you (he pointed quickly to some of the other children) are to go with I."[4]

Even though the children looked at each other—and tried to guess what was meant by "you" and "I," they fell into two groups by the very fact that one cluster of children started to veer toward a large collie that belonged to one of the children.[5] The red-shirted leader started to run, then charged the imaginary enemy. He then tumbled onto the ground. All the children followed his example, each running, charging with arms and voices held high.[6] Then each tumbled onto the ground while the dog just cantered watchfully next to the girl and barked when she fell. And after a moment they were on their feet again, charging, turning, falling, rising, and charging again, with their imaginary rifles and bayonets fixed toward their dust-filled enemies.[7]

Arguments developed in regard to who had killed whom, or whether it was time to be alive again.[8] When they heard the jingling of an ice-cream wagon, which was being pushed by an old heavy-footed man, they abruptly ended their game and ran to it, challenging each other that, "the last one there is a rotten egg."[9]

Case Questions

1. Can you remember ever having done this or something similar to this? Describe the experience.
2. If you were a parent of one of the children would you be upset by this wrestling? Explain your answer.
3. How did you choose sides when you were a child?
4. Is there something wrong about the logic of this sentence? Explain.
5. How else might have these children chosen sides? What are the factors to consider when a group breaks into two parts?
6. What do you think pushes children to imitate each other? Can you explain why these children followed the example of the leader?
7. What purpose might it serve to play such games?
8. Did you ever imagine situations in which you died and were revived again? What significance did it serve?
9. Do you have some of the same feelings now that you had when you were a child during a competitive situation?

Roy (9): Alone at a Merry-Go-Round

Neither the giant circling of the two crows that hovered over the thick-wooded area of the park nor the mechanical dronelike music that echoed from the smaller circling of the merry-go-round changed the drawn, compressed expression on Roy's face. He sat there on the hill, under a tree, and looked on at the scene below and above him.[1] Then he started—his mouth as immobile as his eyes. He seemed to be trapped in his own singleness and separateness, from the swirling, swelling groups and dwindling circles of both adults and children.[2] With his elbows on his knees, his finger against his chin, he began to revolve his head in small circles with a fixed expression on his face. At times, he bit the end of one finger, then another. At times, he pressed the side of his thumb against his lip. Once he stood up and looked around, walked to the top of the hill, returned to where he had been sitting, then sat down again with the same preoccupied look.[3]

The merry-go-round stopped. A new wave of children mounted the colorfully painted animals and the cycle of music and revolving commenced. A new line of eager customers formed behind the chained barrier and waited. The less patient pushed, but were shoved back by those who stood their ground. Some children ate ice cream, or popcorn, or hot dogs, while others drank cokes or from the water fountain. Baby carriages, bicycles, and tricycles skillfully maneuvered through the swirling crowd, while pinwheels, paper birds on strings, and balloons colored the air.[4]

He looked down at the scene. His mouth twitched; his eyelids quivered as he picked and rubbed his nose and bit his lower lip. With his body more deliberately bent over, his knees against his chest, he looked smaller against the tree behind him. A new surge of children crossed the unchained barrier, while the old group dismounted lions, tigers, horses, and camels. High and low voices called, laughed, cried, and cut through and blended into the ebb and flow of the music. The boy sat there, huddled over himself, as if he were trying to unlock himself but couldn't because he was bound.[5] He found an ice-cream stick and started to dig up the ground, his fist over one end. A squirrel scurried along a branch above him, then wound itself down the tree trunk. He followed the track of the animal impassively to the scene below, then continued to dig and stab the ground with the stick.[6]

A wave of children flowed over the hill and spilled out of sight. They wore improvised pirate hats and long sabers under their belts. When they disappeared, he rose and followed them down the hill without getting too close to them. When they charged past him, again, one boy called to him, "Hurry up, before they get you." Roy began to run with them. At first he trailed behind, then caught up to them. He added his own version to the excitement by saying, "YeaYeouuu." The vowels soared out and mingled with the exclamations of the other children. He ran with them, ran and stopped, fell, jumped up, then ran some more.[7]

By the time the children returned to where Roy had first observed them, the merry-go-round was no longer in operation. The attendants were in the process of boarding up the hex-shaped building. The food stand was closed. The pathways that led to and from the area were practically isolated. A few minutes later, the children were gone. Roy was once again alone, but this time his face was flushed, hair ruffled, clothes twisted about him, eyes bright and animated. He kicked an empty crackerjack box in front of him, then began to run in curves toward the underpass that led toward the big streets. He was heard whistling as he disappeared into the tunnel that led out of the park into the street.[8]

Case Questions

1. How important is it to describe the surrounding environment in order to understand Roy?
2. Is this a subjective analysis of how Roy feels about himself?
3. Why is Roy revolving his head, biting the end of his finger, and pressing the side of his thumb against his lips?
   a. What hunches might you have concerning Roy's preoccupied look?
4. Describe a merry-go-round playground or other place of activity where children play.
   a. Is there anything about the atmosphere here that might affect the way Roy feels?
5. What does it mean to you when you are emotionally "up tight," or contracted?
6. Do we use objects as a means of expressing our emotions?
7. Is Roy able to adapt easily to the other children's play?
   a. Do the exclamations add to the children's involvement with the game?
8. What can you learn about your friends during a recreational activity?

Street Scene

The overcast sky left a screen of maze over the houses and streets and foreshortened the possibility of seeing any great distance with clarity.[1] The combination of a humidity-laden air that bogged the grey atmosphere with a contamination of soot and dust made the activity on the street somewhat unreal to the passing observer, who was suddenly confronted with a team of construction workers and the games of children of all ages.

There was barely a foot in the whole living area that was not being utilized by both children and workers, as well as parents with their baby carriages, chairs, newspapers, and shopping bags. The children were playing lottos or feeding their dolls or calling to each other from the flower-potted, clothes-hanging firescapes to the streets below. One woman was leaning out of the window, her arms resting on a pillow. A hydrant was turned on by one group of children, who were defying the spray of water by rushing in and out of its pressured flow. Sometimes they blocked the water with their backsides or chests. Instead of using a wrench to turn the nut that opened the valve of the hydrant, they wound and twisted wire clothes hangers about the nut and used it as a wrench. The spray was fine, and the small and larger children not only actively ran through the spray, but some had found sticks and small cardboard matchboxes as well as cigarette butts to sail along the fast-moving stream of water that hugged the curb and emptied into the sewer.[2]

Some of the children were making grandiose bets that their ship or liner or boat would "win" or "beat" the other, and the children who were less adventurous participated indirectly by observing the race of vessels. They joined in, commenting and betting.[3] A few steps beyond this point, a group of seven- and eight-year-old girls played potsy and skillfully jumped, first in one box, then in another before they picked up the ring of safety pins, turned about, and returned to the starting place without touching any of the chalked squares.[4] Occasionally, one of the children insisted that the heel or toe of their playmates touched a line. These children didn't seem to compete with each other as much as with themselves. They seemed oblivious to the spray and water activity of the children a few feet away, except when one of the boys, who might have been a brother of one of the girls, moved too far off into the street. He was warned to return to the curb.[5]

The noise on the street was magnified by a motor-driven air compressor, which was used to operate a pneumatic street drill that one bull of a man lifted as if it were made of balsa wood instead of heavy, machined steel. A cluster of children and adults seemed to be fascinated by the way the man lifted the machine and plunged it down into the tarred street. His effortless manner was contrasted by his co-worker, who took turns in operating it. One could see that the weight as well as the violent vibrations of the drill taxed the strength of the smaller, lighter-built, and older man. One child commented to his neighbor, "Look at his arms—he has some muscles!"[6]

Words were exchanged between the men and observing audience. A third man with a pick followed the two who were taking turns with the drill. He joined in the conversation, but seemed to be particularly bothered by his profuse perspiration, which he wiped with a large calico-colored handkerchief. He often adjusted the sweat-soaked handkerchief, which he had tied about his forehead to stop the sweat from running into his eyes. Although he was much older than the two other men, as was apparent by the deep lines in his face, his body was still as pliable as his co-workers'. He seemed to pace himself a little slower, and was more precise in his movements, as if to make sure that no motion would be lost. His pick seemed to find the mark he intended. The manner in which he pried up the earth or rolled the curved back of the pick after the end was wedged in the broken-tarred street was an indication of his skill.[7]

The men tossed words back and forth. Occasionally some of the children imitated the motions of the men who were drilling, picking, and shoveling. One child, a seven-year-old, jumped up and down and screamed at his friends and laughed every time the air was torn asunder by the reverberations of the drill. After each wave of noise, he seemed to relax. When the drilling resumed, his face and body sprung into action and animation.[8]

Not too many feet from this scene, small baby carriages filled with blankets, dolls, and stuffed animals were both parked and in motion just inside the horseshoe-shaped entrance to one of the houses. Mothers and baby-sitters sat and conversed with each other. They sat on beach chairs, their backs facing the cars that were parked. Occasionally one of the mothers called out to one of the children to do one thing or the other. Miniature dishes were arranged on a chalk-made drawing of a table, which two four-year-olds sat around. They served each other, turned to their dolls in the carriage, and included them in the play. Two eight-year-olds had marked off a square in which they made smaller squares inside. One of the boys admonished one of the children for getting in his way, while the other aimed his bottle top, which he used as a checker. He flipped his fingers and sent the object sliding across the smooth-surfaced sidewalk. Each took turns. One of the parents rose from her chair, on which her wire-haired terrier was tied, and walked over the area where the boys were playing checkers. She looked up to one of the windows and called out to an elderly woman who was watching the scene below, "Don't forget to turn the roast off at 2 o'clock." The old lady above nodded impassively.[9]

The scream from a siren grew louder. Everyone turned toward it. The ambulance stopped at the house next to where the construction crew was working. All activity had stopped and now was centered about the doctor and his attendant, who climbed down from the back of the vehicle and disappeared into the house. People milled about the entrance, and the children tried to learn from the adults what had happened and who was hurt.[10] One boy who had just been chased by his friends had his arms about the waist of one of the girls. She sat on the fender of a parked car. The boy grabbed the girl's waist and drew her toward him. The boy attempted to kiss her, only to find himself pushed away, scolded in half-jest for his behavior. Each time the boy bent over toward the girl, she pushed him away, laughed, and chided him. They walked over to where the ambulance was stationed. Instead of circling the ever-enlarging crowd for a view, they walked back, arm in arm, to the car where they had been and resumed the cat and mouse game.[11]

The crowd parted as an elderly man was led up the two steps into the cabin of the ambulance. The people returned to their activities as the siren whined and the ambulance turned out of sight. The wind shifted, the sky was now pitched with dark clouds. Rain began to fall over the hot and muggy street. Moments later, it poured down. Children and people ran for shelter and huddled together inside the entrances of the houses and looked out onto the downpour. Above, one woman frantically pulled in the clothes which she left out to dry on the clothesline that was suspended from her window frame to the railing of the firescape opposite. The rain fell, and slowly washed away the chalk drawings and paper bits, dust, and clods of earth that had settled on the street. It made the air cool and fresh. The street was now empty of people. The fury of the rain held the children in silence.[12]

Case Questions

1. How does the air in your community compare to that in the episode?
2. How would you go about setting up a research project directed toward finding out what people of different ages do?
3. What street games did you play when you were a child?
4. Which of the games depicted in this episode are familiar to you?
5. How would you organize a team of filmmakers to make a film of such a scene?
   a. What scenes would you want included?
6. Do the children identify with the workmen?
   a. What do children learn from such experiences?
7. What do you remember of your own childhood in observing men and women at work?
8. What influence did the work of others have on the value you give to it now?
9. Is there anything about the scene that disturbs you? Explain.
10. Why does an accident draw some peoples' attention?
11. Do these teenagers seem like people you have observed or known?
12. In what way might the street activities in your own environment influence your values, interests, feelings, thoughts, and actions? Explain.

Alex (4) : The Train in the Leaves

He shuffled his feet in quick forward jerks through the dead leaves that had been blown against the railing that separated the park area from the sudden clifflike drop to the railroad tracks below and made the accompanying Cha Cha Cha Cha simulated sound of a train. He chugged his body back and forth along the railing until he stopped, lifted his right arm high over his head as if to signal, then lowered it, at which time he resumed his voyage. Then, he leaned against the barrier facing the tracks below. He stood there, while the distant sound of an oncoming train became more distinct until it was one tearing roar. He stood there unmoving, until the train passed and was heard no more. Once again, he chugged along, but this time his face wore a different expression, one of intense excitement rather than one of fixed preoccupation. His eyes gleamed as he started to roar, "RRRRRR."[1]

Finally, he began to run and turned away from the fence toward his parents. When he saw them, he began to laugh until he crumpled to the ground in front of them. They too laughed, which seemed to increase his laughter until it no longer came easily for him but was punctuated with gasps. They didn't seem to encourage him any further but gazed at him. He rested there, still crumpled and curled, his face red and his eyes teared with the laughter. Not one word had passed between them. They remained there, together. Now the boy spread himself across their laps. After a few moments, he rose, rubbed his eyes with the back of his fingers, put his thumb in his mouth, took it out and said, "I want to eat." The father echoed the same thought and rose to his feet, whereupon he helped his wife to her feet, and the three walked to the large, busy street at the end of the field.[2]

Case Questions

1. What kind of learning exists here?
   a. What subjective dimensions of this description are indicated here?
   b. Make an observation of a child for two minutes and try to capture as much as you can without bringing in hunches, interpretations, hypotheses, or subjective material.
2. What can you say about the relationship between Alex and his parents?
   a. Is there anything about this story that you felt a particular closeness to? Explain.

Toby (5) : The Bomb in the Nursery School

It was to be Toby's first time with the five-year-olds, and I was to meet him and introduce him to the children and the numerous activities available to him. When I saw him walk toward me, I was aware that he favored one side of his body by dragging his left leg after the right. He looked as if he were bucking a strong wind and didn't want the full force of it to hit his body. His eyes darted from the hallway to the room where he now entered. His mother walked slowly by his side as he moved his small body toward me. Then she turned toward the other mothers who were seated on a bench in the hallway.[1]

I was aware that there was something physically wrong with this child. I am not sure whether this awareness set the stage for the kind of responses that ensued, but before I knew it Toby's mother simply said in a low tone, "This is your new teacher and . . . ," but she never completed her thought. Toby interrupted, "See this? I'm going to blow the school up." Balanced in the center of his small, somewhat fleshy palm, he held a cylindrically shaped piece of plasticene a few inches from his face. He then closed his hand over it, and with a drawn expression, repeated, "I'm going to blow the school up." This time he raised his hand to my face.[2] My first reaction was to say nothing, because I didn't know what to say. But, by the time he repeated the phrase, I said, "O.K., let's blow it up together!" And I began to walk to the block area when I heard Toby's mother say, "You know you don't mean that." "I'm going to blow the school up," was Toby's response, apparently unaware of his mother's embarrassment. I tried to make her feel more at ease by telling her, "The children can make believe anything here." Again I noticed how Toby moved; how he had to circumvent different kinds of obstacles such as blocks, toy trucks, and wooden figures. He maneuvered himself carefully. Aside from his tilted and angular walk, most of his movements seemed to be abrupt, contracted, tightly strung together.[3]

I took some small blocks out of the cabinet and asked Toby, "Do you still want to blow the school up?" To which he answered, "Yep." I then said, "O.K., let's do it together." I placed one block on top of the other and turned to him and said, "Come on. Aren't you going to help?" He held his right fist tightly closed over the clay, looked at me directly and said, "I can't. If I let go of the bomb, it'll boom!" I then asked him if he could put it down. He answered, "Yeah, it's sure heavy." "What can we put it in?" I asked, looking toward the truck? "I got an idea," he said, "We'll put it in the truck," and he slowly bent his knees to a squatting position and grunted while he moved his arm in a mechanical fashion to where the truck was. He thrust his arm straight out from his body, then down in a perpendicular until his hand rested over the opening of the truck. Evidently, he was simulating a crane. Before I left the area Toby was busy making "Boom, Pookk," as he shoved his clayfilled fist into the towering then tumbling "school." He repeated this activity for the whole time he was there. Only once did he seem to be aware of anyone else—that was when a boy approached him and asked him if he were a "tat tat gun gun." Toby stopped playing, looked up and said, "No, I'm in the construction business, can't you see?" and he resumed his game. The child turned toward another activity in the room.[4]

Case Questions

1. Is his behavior indicative of most five-year-olds who enter a nursery school for the first time? Explain.
2. What would you have done at this point if you were in charge of the children?
3. How objective is the description of Toby here? Explain.
4. In what way did Toby express his wishes in play?
   a. What do you think might have happened had the teacher reprimanded the child for saying that he wanted to blow the school up?

2

THE FAMILY

Not only the mother but all members of the family shape the personality of the child as he, in turn, reciprocatively influences those about him. The intricate juxtaposition of how feelings, thoughts, values, and actions fit into the scheme of everyday living between family members is too complex a matter to discuss in an introduction. We can only guess at the infinite number of ways that the family has contributed to the image of who we are today. Notwithstanding, the neighborhood, school, community, and society at large play an imposing role in giving different kinds of meaning to the family.

Sometimes the child becomes a victim of family disruption when either death, divorce, illness, or other circumstances deprive him of an integrated home setting. The absence of either parent might make it especially difficult for him to construct a wholesome vision of himself. If, for instance, the father doesn't exist, who then becomes his model, his object of identification? How does he fashion his image of what is expected of him in regard to his psycho-sexual-social role? These are critical questions, too vital and complex to answer here. Nonetheless, some of these matters are dealt with in the articles and episodes that follow.

In R. J. Havighurst's article, the relationship between the health of our children today and the destiny of man are linked together. In the episode, "Middle Class Family," each member's statement helps to develop and qualify the reader's perception of how the individuals relate to one another. Would R. J. Havighurst consider this family a healthy one? It should be stressed here that this middle-class family is by no means indicative of any other one. Each member of it is an individual unlike any other. Perhaps the question that follows then is why I titled these three personal accounts the way I did. If I were to say that they represent a middle-class stereotype, how would you attack my answer and what questions would you raise? Can you relate this article to the next three episodes, which constitute "A Disturbed Family." If so, importance should be given to weighing Pamela's, Richard's, and the uncle's statements against the characteristics of a healthy family. The relationship between Pamela and her brother Richard might be considered in the context of the extract, "Healthy Sibling Rivarly." Special emphasis should be given to examining the dynamic role of each member of the family.

In the episode "Blackout," the relationship between the brothers is a wholesome one; thoughts, feelings, wishes, and interests are accommodated by an empathetic, understanding mother and sympathetic grandfather.

Jim, in the episode that follows, makes an important decision to leave home, but only after much deliberation. His behavior during his adventure cannot be separated from the total picture of how he fits into and contributes to the family picture.

Today's Children and Tomorrow's World

Robert J. Havighurst

Today's children will make tomorrow's world. But we make today's children and we give them today's world to work with. We are responsible for the children; to some extent we are responsible for today's world in which they live.

I propose to consider today's world and its trends and to indicate the nature of the situation in which children will grow and work. Then I shall suggest the kind of person who can best deal with this world-in-the-making and ask how we can produce that kind of person.

An American View of the World

North Americans tend to see the world in optimistic terms. Our country has grown up in a period when the European-North American segment of the world was growing prosperous and powerful. Our present wealth and abundance lead us to take an optimistic view of history. In the nineteenth century we were inclined to believe that the world was getting better in response to some basic law of historical evolution.

This naive optimism has suffered some rude shocks during the twentieth century: two world wars, a disastrous economic depression and the threat of nuclear extermination. These have tempered the American optimism with some realism. Still, we are basically optimistic.

We now believe that the world can be made better if we work at it. We also believe in ourselves as makers of history and see history as a product of human achievement. We are an achievement-oriented people.

We see *our part of the world as an area of abundance with potentialities for a better society*, even though we recognize our waste of wealth on things which do not produce a better society.

We see the world *becoming interdependent*, and we know our future welfare is bound up with that of the rest of the world. We see ourselves as responsible members of a world organization which must work to produce world order.

Finally, we know the *future will be complex*. The solutions of our domestic, international, social, economic and political problems will have to be worked out on terms which have not yet been drawn up. This will require imagination and flexibility on our part.

The outcome of our competition with Russia can only be guessed. It certainly will not be resolved by military means, unless we or they blunder into war or are drawn in by other nations who are about to join the atomic club. This competition will be resolved in terms of politics and economics, technology and ideology. The result is not likely to be what either we or the Russians would call a victory.

Looking at present and probable events, the historian, Robert Heilbroner, warns us that our usual optimism will be strained by disillusionment to come. We will need two other qualities: fortitude and understanding. These will help us see that although this century is not a period of rapid progress and fulfillment of our social ideals, it is not a time of total loss. There is a job to be done. By doing this job we can influence for the better the vast and impersonal process of world-wide evolution.

"Today's Children and Tomorrow's World," by Robert J. Havighurst. From CHILDHOOD EDUCATION, April 1961, Vol. 37, No. 8, pp. 356–360. Reprinted by permission of Robert J. Havighurst and the Association for Childhood Education International, 3615 Wisconsin Avenue, N.W., Washington, D.C.

> . . . For this we need an attitude which accepts the outlook of the historic future without succumbing to false hopes or to an equally false despair; a point of view which sees in the juggernaut of history's forces both the means by which progress painfully made in the past may be trampled underfoot, and the means by which a broader and stronger base for progress in the future may be brought into being.
>
> Such an attitude may retain its kernel of optimism. But more is needed for the display of stoic fortitude than a residual faith in the idea of progress. Above all there is required an understanding of the grand dynamic of history's forces in preparing the way for eventual progress . . . . Only from such a sense of historic understanding can come the strength to pass through the gauntlet with an integrity of mind and spirit.[1]

Certainly there are people who will not see the world in this way. Some will seek to turn back the pages of history and recapture a simpler society. These people, calling themselves "conservatives," like to talk about a need for *positive rebels*. This kind of person, it seems, is one who rebels against all present-day social and educational trends. He seeks to move back to the pre-revolutionary eighteenth century, when a small minority of "gentlemen" had an easy life.

A good many other people will *feel* uncomfortable about today and its probable tomorrow but make no effort to do anything about it.

The world of today will destroy itself if it has too many people who either want to go backward in history or don't want to do anything about history.

Needed—A New American

In addition to fortitude and understanding which we Americans must bring to the world of tomorrow, we need a new set of ethical standards which is less parochial than those which served us—after a fashion—in a world dominated by white Europeans and North Americans. Agnes Meyer has stated this proposition:

> Our central problem at this critical juncture of history is to gain a new idea of man and his relationship to his fellow men. . . . In the era of the atomic bomb, human survival depends on new and higher ethical standards than any heretofore achieved—standards acceptable to all mankind that will lead gradually to renunciation of power in human relations and of war in international relations.[2]

The basic theme of this talk is: *The purpose of a nation depends primarily upon the way its children were brought up a generation earlier. The way to improve the nation for tomorrow is to improve the lives of its children today.*

In every newborn child dwells the destiny of society. This not very profound statement contains a burden and a great opportunity.

The burden is the fact that society must repeat endlessly the education of its young. No infant of today is born with any more knowledge or wisdom than the infant born 2500 years ago. Every generation must start anew. The twenty-one-year-olds of this year were born in 1940. They had no advantage over the children born in 1900. They had to learn with the same pain the same things their parents learned before them.

This tired world's opportunity lies in the fact that each generation starts over again. There is the possibility that the new generation will discover better ways of living. That is why we treat children with such respect. They have potentialities for being better than we. And we, in our relative ignorance of how life should be started and carried on, must do our best to give children a good start on paths we ourselves have not trod.

What should we try to provide for children that will enable them to make a better world tomorrow?

What Kind of People Make a Healthy Society? A healthy society for this latter half of the twentieth century consists of people with qualities that combine to make them a purposeful, peaceful and productive

1 Robert L. Heilbroner, *The Future as History* (New York: Harper & Bros., 1960).

2 Agnes Meyer, *Education for a New Morality* (New York: The Macmillan Co., 1957).

nation with a positive affirmation of the value of human life.

There are nine personal qualities which make a person who can carry his share of responsibility for making tomorrow's world better than today's.

How do people get these qualities? Primarily through their early experience while they are children. The child is father of the man. *The most enduring and most essential qualities of mind and personality are founded in the early years of life.* Some are determined *before* the usual beginning of school life and others are formed *during* school years. The effort wisely spent on giving children a good start in life is a better investment than the same amount of wise effort spent on the individual later in life.

The kind of person who helps to make a good society:

1. *This person's impulses are basically friendly; he sees the world as a good place and people as good.* He is optimistic and he believes that the world will turn out well. This person can trust his own impulses because he knows they will not get him into trouble. He can give his impulses almost free play, without having to be on guard lest he commit some hostile act toward others. He has so little unconscious hostility and so little guilt about himself that he can enjoy being an impulsive person. Other people like him that way.

People disillusioned with the contemporary world have said that we should teach young children to fight, hate, kick and scratch so as to prepare them for this world. But we must resist this doctrine with all our might. We must do just the opposite with our children!

As Erik Erikson tells us so persuasively, this first psychosocial task of the child depends largely on the treatment he gets from his mother in the first few months of life. If she satisfies him when he is hungry, comforts him when he is cold and wet, gives him continual experience of physical care; and if during the following years he continues to receive ample evidence of love and support from his family, he will come to trust in the world as a place which is fundamentally hospitable.

2. *This person is intellectually autonomous and therefore prepared to cope intellectually with the unforeseen and unknown world that lies ahead of him.* What we know about personality development tells us that the seeds of autonomy are sown in the second and third years of life. This is when the child becomes aware of himself as a being separate from his mother and as one who makes decisions, first about his body and later about other activities. If his mental curiosity is allowed to grow by parents and teachers who answer his questions and encourage his questioning mind, he becomes ready to treat the mental disciplines of school as his tools rather than his masters.

3. *He is achievement oriented; he likes to do things well.* This person has a deep, unconscious drive to meet standards of excellence. With so much internal pressure for achievement, he does not need much external pressure. According to work done by Rosen and Winterbottom, the basic drive for achievement results from the child being trained to do things well and independently. This quality is probably established at least by the age of ten. It is more a result of training at home than elsewhere.

4. *This person has strong inner moral control.* His conscience (or superego) has such positive force that he can stand up for what he knows is right against the pressure of the crowd. This quality comes from his experience of love and punishment from his parents. If they are consistent in their rewards and punishments so that they teach the child clearly the difference between right and wrong and if they give him ample affection, he becomes a person of strong moral character.

5. *This person is creative and spontaneous.* His mind entertains new ideas readily. He makes novel connections between things other people have overlooked. He enjoys putting things and ideas together in new ways. This seems to come naturally to the young child—it is a kind of spontaneous movement of the mind toward what it enjoys. We know less about the conditions under which creativity develops and strengthens

itself than we know about the other qualities being considered here. There must be ways of living with children and teaching them which will encourage preservation and development of their early creativity!

6. *This person is rational and foresightful.* This quality is juxtaposed to spontaneity and creativity to remind us that *both* qualities are desirable and compatible. They may *seem* to be in opposition. Rationality means ability to look at facts, draw logical inferences from them and to control one's behavior in light of foreseen consequences. This quality makes moral judgment sounder than it would be if it were simply a set of moral maxims adopted crudely from parents with childish limitations of understanding. This person looks ahead to examine probable outcomes of possible actions and then deliberately chooses what reason tells him is the better course. In a changing world where consequences of individual and national choices cannot always be found in past experiences, this quality of rational foresight separates the wise and good man from the stupid and good man.

7. *This person can tolerate ambiguity.* In a world of uncertainty, with great risks taken by nations as well as by individuals, this person is not driven by a blind fear of the ambiguous into a rigid demand that only one solution of a problem is correct. Instead, this person can stand to live and work in a situation which is open ended with many possibilities for solution and which must be worked out flexibly. This person does not need to have everything so neatly and tidily disposed about him that he will not have to take risks.

This quality is related to the basic sense of trust in the world which has previously been mentioned. One can tolerate an uncertain state of affairs if one is basically sure that both the world and one's own drive-impulses can be trusted. This, too, seems to be largely a product of early childhood experience.

8. *He is altruistic.* He enjoys doing things for the welfare of other people. He has a wide moral horizon which includes people far away in space and far ahead in time. World brotherhood is an immediate necessity and a vital reality for him. His altruism has a considerable element of respect for the ways of other cultures and other peoples.

The basis for altruism is probably formed in a family which has plenty of love and affection and trust for every member. The child of such a family can readily extend his moral horizon to take in friends, age-mates, community members, fellow-citizens and all members of the human race.

9. *This person has a world view that is both scientific and religious in the best sense.* His understanding is comprehensive and accurate with respect to the physical world and the nature of man. In a world in which man is gaining more and more control over the atom, space and the living cell, it is essential for wise men to understand these things.

This is largely the product of education, formal and informal; most of it comes after the person has emerged from young childhood. But here, too, I would venture the hypothesis that the child's ideology is powerfully influenced by his unconscious imitation of the ideology he sees and hears in the lives of his parents and other significant persons.

How Do We Get More of These People? The world of today needs more and more people with these qualities. Only people with these qualities can stand up to the tough reality of this world. They can live and be active and beget children in a time of threatened destruction. They can take part as citizens of the world in the multiple and shifting coalitions of nations that lie ahead during the remainder of this century. They can raise their voices against the prevailing tone of moral lethargy and political ambivalence.

People with these qualities can populate islands of excellence in the sea of mass culture that threatens to drown us all. This sea will recede and permit the spread of excellence if enough people support excellence during the next decade.

We doubt that formal education can

inculcate these qualities, though it can certainly make them more effective. The basic elements of these qualities are learned through the experience of love and punishment, stimulation and example, which young children get in the family. The school extends and supplements the contribution of the home through the models provided by teachers and age-mates and by means of its environment for learning and living.

The secret of getting more of these people in the coming generation is an open one. We can inculcate these qualities best by doing a much better job of rearing young children. Already we *know* enough to do a better job. Our task as educators is to spread this known knowledge about the formation of personality and character in children. *We want to do a far better job of producing more of these people.* This means doing more research on children—young and older children.

Questions and Projects Related to Today's Children and Tomorrow's World

1. Discuss the following quotations and relate them to your own ideas, feelings, values, and actions.
    a. "In every newborn child dwells the destiny of society."
    b. "The child is father of the Man."
2. In what way do you agree with or disagree with the substance of this article?

Barbara (14) : Middle-Class Family

I like what I like. I'm not different than my friends. They do what they want. They don't have more responsibilities than I do. They don't have to make their beds nor do they wash dishes like I do. It isn't doing these things, it is my parents. They always tell me what to do, well, not always, but often enough. Can't stay out late, have to keep my room tidy, I should not wear this, hang up my dress, did I wash my hair, sit and eat with my feet under the table, think of someone else. I can't remember them all but I hear them all the time. Then, when I want to read a book, and I love to read, they tell me that I have to do my homework first, or practice the flute. I like to play but have no time to practice. I don't want to give it up. Yes, I like shoes of one kind, and mother says they are too fancy or not practical. I know I don't always like the same things for too long a time but why shouldn't I be able to choose.[1] Well, I am developing and the boys tease me and I like it but don't like it. I guess I am aware of my body a lot more now than I was before. I look at myself differently. Yes I can stay in front of a mirror but it is important for me to look. My clothes don't fit like they used to. My breasts make it tight so I need new clothes. Going to parties dancing with friends and I want to look pretty. There's nothing wrong in taking time so I'll look nice. My parents don't bother about that but they don't want me to spend so much time over clothes. I really don't, just that I don't have what I want to wear. I have to worry what my friends will wear. I don't want to be different. The grown-ups don't understand these things.[2] They don't know that I love my room just the way it is, without having to pick up this or put my shoes away or hang up my sweater or eat in the kitchen because I'll make crumbs and we'll have bugs. They want me to remember every thing and just the way they like it. What's wrong with playing a game, leaving the checkers around or the books I am using. They both yell at me, say that I have no sense of responsibility, that I'll grow up and think only of myself. If it doesn't bother me then why does it bother them? It is my room.[3] I want pictures on the wall, listen to jazz while I do homework. It doesn't bother me. There are very educational programs. Besides, I like music and why should I turn it off? I can do both at the same time. My father always turns the radio down, says it makes him nervous, that I must be deaf because I have it on so loud. When he turns it down I can't hear it so I turn it up then there's an argument. My mother says that I should be more considerate about these things. When they have friends and it is late do I tell them I can't sleep or that they should lower the radio? I don't.[4]

I love flowers and spring and the smell of grass after it is cut and beautiful things. I think people shouldn't make war and we should learn how to talk with each other. I know that one person is as good as the next and that there is a God and he's good but that we don't know how to behave with each other. I sometimes have dreams that I will die or that my family or friends will die. Not all the time but sometimes. When I grow up, I don't know, but I want to work with people. I can understand them. I can feel what they are feeling. I sometimes wonder what the future will be like when I'm grown-up but mostly I think of today and the tomorrow, not too far. I know what I do today will influence me in what I will do tomorrow.[5]

I think my parents are O.K. but they don't understand me. They are right sometimes. Guess if I were surer of myself I would say I was wrong more often. I feel older than my friends. I wish I were surer of myself.[6]

The boys get along better than the girls. They aren't so picky, but I'm glad I'm a girl but I wish I were a boy sometimes. They don't have to worry about how they dress and what they do. They can curse and fool around with each other. It's different. They are boys and there's a difference. They like to hit each other and kid around;[7] the girls are more careful. I like one boy. He watches me; we talk and tease each other. At parties we dance together and he's not so silly when he's not around the other boys. I feel better when the girls are around although I have had a serious discussion with him. We really talk, not just kid around. He's a little shy sometimes, but he can be the life of the party.[8]

Of course we talk about sex and want to know all about it. We hear from our parents, read, and see films, and just hear about sex. I'm never going to get married until I'm really ready for it. I don't know what kind of man he will be. I don't know what I will be like. I don't think about it but when I read or watch TV I sometimes ask myself who do I know like him or her.[9]

I can spend hours by myself. Guess I can because I'm the only child and have a room to myself and books. Wish I had a sister or brother, not a little one now but an older one I could play with and talk to.[10]

Case Questions

1. What is the relationship between self perception and perception of parents?
2. Do you think she perceives her body as something separate from herself?
3. What are some of the essential complaints of fourteen-year-olds you know?
4. Compare Barbara's attitudes toward her parents to that of another child of the same age?
5. In what way can you identify with what Barbara values?
6. What kind of sense of self does it take for a youngster to admit that he is wrong?
7. If you were a fourteen-year-old, would you want to be a friend of Barbara's?
8. At what age do girls actively start "going out" with boys?
9. How does mass-media influence youngsters' values toward marriage?
10. Does "middle class" suggest different meanings to different people?
    a. What factors in the environment and the individual influence middle-class values?

Mother : Middle-Class Family

Barbara is a very sensitive child. I shouldn't call her a child. She has grown up so quickly. She practically wears my clothes. She has filled out and that makes her self-conscious of herself. She hasn't grown up emotionally the same way. Sometimes she's no older than a ten-year-old or even younger. Other times, she surprises me with how grown up she is. I like the way she is interested in things. I know I am touchy about having a neat house but I guess it is my reaction to just the opposite of what I had when I was a child. My mother never had things in order. I've told Barbara order is necessary, even in a room.[1] Actually she is quite organized in the way she thinks, she has no trouble writing. When I was her age I wasn't as sophisticated. The children nowadays have lost that innocence we had. When I was a child I was naive. I'm still naive, I guess, about life. What can I say? The children have so much around them. I feel we spoiled her but we live in different times. There's the information explosion, if that is what you call it, and radio and TV. The whole world is open to them. They can accept moon landings without blinking an eye or feeling any sense of wonder. I'm not sure whether the children today are any less sensitive than what we were with all the deprivation we went through. Maybe we aren't any wiser than our fathers or grandfathers.[2]

I worry about her, going out late or alone. All I have to do is read about some rape or assault or attack and I'm sure it is going to happen to Barbara or me. Fortunately, we have a car and my husband takes me where I want to go although when I go to work I travel without a car. In the daytime it is different. You hear so many things from this one and that one. Blacks? I used to call them Negroes but I know the fashion is black. They have changed. There is so much violence. Guess the newspapers and TV and all the stories you hear make you think that every black is a potential raper, murderer, or thief. I know it isn't true but I guess times have changed. They are angry. I don't understand it but I know things are getting worse. That doesn't make them worse than whites. We are just as capable of the worst crimes. We make war. There has been a shroud of doubt and controversy in regard to blacks; it has affected me. It's funny, when I hear a real story about a black, about a man or woman or child or what they want and what they don't or how they struggle I don't feel any difference between us. I guess what makes me fear them sometimes is that they have been presented to us so often as objects instead of humans. Humans I can understand.[3] Never had any trouble. Guess I have always put that first.

Yes, I want money, want all the fine things. There's nothing wrong with that. After all, you only live once. I won't steal or be a henchman to become rich but I sometimes wish my husband could earn more and we could have it easier. I would like to be a lady of leisure. I love clothes and fancy things but I can be happy in my home, which I love. I love the way it looks, the walls and being in bed all curled up but I must admit I would like style in my life. I don't want to rough it or have to scrounge. We live much better than many but I like good things. I can walk around in simple clothes and am not afraid of work. I'd like to do less.[4]

I often put away my husband's things and he yells at me that he can't find them. It has happened a few times that I cleared away something, spent hours looking for it—a key, letters, or bill. Well, I am that way. Could be worse. I am a good mother and wife. I try to do an honest responsible job and know I do both in and out of home. I feel at home with rich or poor and can speak with anyone regardless of color or religion when it comes to direct experience. I am not a snob when it comes to friends. We like people who aren't afraid to be free and talk about what they think and have friends who are part of the so-called middle-class establishment and those who have broken with it. I still love to dance. I'm only 35. I think if I had an opportunity to be young all over again I would have danced. I love to dance. We do, with our friends. Barbara feels at home with our friends. We are open in front of her. We don't make special conversation when she's around. Sometimes she has to suffer because I tell her exactly what I think. One thing she knows, I'm not good at keeping things in. If they are there I tell her. Sometimes I'm impossible. I get angry and really explode. A minute or few seconds later I'm full of love. That way the board is clean; there aren't any nasty feelings cluttering our relationship. That's me. Barbara and my husband have to contend with me. May be difficult for them but I really think the way I am is better for all of us. I wish my daughter would be more open sometimes, although she's too open at other times. Why can't she be a sensitive restrained child? I guess the apple doesn't fall far from the tree. She opens up and has a tongue and can say the nastiest things one moment, then come to me and kisses me and says she loves me just as easily.[5]

We argue over hair, how she should wear it, and I know I am wrong but I have my values and I think a child should have some guidance. Just hate when she has to get dressed. She doesn't know what she should wear. When I suggest something else she rejects it. When I tell her to choose for herself she says she is not interested and when I agree with what she is wearing she disagrees. It drives me nuts. Thank goodness not every morning. When she has something special with her girlfriends or at school, she is impossible.[6]

I'm not worried about her schooling. When I was at school I wasn't half as studious as she is. We leave her alone, just want her to be responsible. She spends so much time on details, has to get it just right. My husband and I have wondered why she needs to be a perfectionist. If she had one-tenth the need to keep her room in order, but . . . to get back to school. She learns quickly and the teachers have nothing but praise for her. She is quick but she is also lazy about some subjects. For awhile she had difficulty in math but after a little effort she solved that problem. Then she stopped studying in language arts and we started to receive notes from her teacher but again she studies a few nights and knew as much as the rest. We want her to feel good about what she does, to find a profession she can enjoy to get married eventually and be happy. Guess all parents want that.[7] No ambitions that she should be some outstanding person. That isn't important. She's a girl. We want her to feel beautiful but not use her beauty as if that is all she has to offer. If she is first a person then the rest will follow. She is a beautiful girl. She will have trouble if she uses her charms to get what she wants without being critical. Then she'll have trouble. We have tried to explain this to her but I don't think she understands. She'll have to learn from experience. I was the same way. I didn't listen, did what I wanted, and suffered because of it until I learned better. I would like to save her the heartache but who knows whether I'd be the same woman I am today if it were not for the fact that I had to go through some difficult years in my life. I prefer not to talk about myself.[8]

About my husband, he is a fine man and I respect him but he's from the generation of the naive, if you know what I mean. He still believes people, not that he is a fool, but he is ready to trust people as if they were his brothers. I love him for that but I sometimes become angry with him because part of being grown up is to know when people are fooling you.[9] He's an individual. He's a man of principle and will take a side that is contrary to everyone else and stubbornly defend it out of principle and even though I respect him for it I sometimes wish he'd be less honest and aware of what is human, and do what everyone does. On the other hand he is a fine teacher, and is devoted to his work and students and will spend time with students because he is interested in helping them and because he feels that he can help them and that gives him satisfaction. But he has trouble with his colleagues sometimes because he doesn't play ball with everyone if there is something underhanded. Don't get the wrong impression. He can joke with and enjoy what any man can and that gets me angry because he can also speak with anyone and spend time with them, and I'm more practical. He's not. I'm more down to earth. Sometimes he jokes too much and I don't like it. He also tells me what he thinks. We aren't afraid to be affectionate with each other in front of Barbara and she accepts it. We are both demonstrative and free in loving each other and feel just as young, well, not just as young, as we used to. I'm getting heavy around the middle and I beg my husband not to eat so much bread because it makes me want to eat it too. When he isn't home I barely eat. He has a big appetite and doesn't gain any weight. He's a fine looking man and I love him but wish he'd change. He says that if he were to change to what I wanted him to be he would not be good for either me or for himself. He's stubborn like a donkey with his back legs stuck in the earth. Can't move him when he gets his mind fixed on something. He isn't ambitious as I am. I haven't yet resigned myself to being just a housewife.[10]

Case Questions

1. In what way did your parents' childhood influence them in how they reacted to you?
2. How genuine does this woman sound in what she is saying? Why?
    a. Can you identify with what she is stating here?
3. Is this woman making prejudgments? Is she prejudiced?
    a. In what way can you identify with what she is saying? Why?
4. In what way does Barbara reflect the values of her mother?
5. Do you think parents should express their opinions openly? Explain.
6. Do you think an outspoken mother like this woman is a better model for her daughter than one who is less direct in what she feels and thinks? Why?
7. In what way are the expectations of this woman a reflection of what she values?
8. Is this woman a childish person? Explain.
    a. Is it true that she prefers not to talk about herself?
9. Did she say the same thing about herself?
10. What kind of relationship does she have with her husband? Explain.

Father :
Middle-Class Family

It doesn't pay to argue with either my wife or daughter. They have their own minds. They hear what they want to. I argue all the same. Barbara comes to me with love when she wants something and sometimes, not so often now, when she is happy with herself. I think she needs her friends very badly. If she spends a lot of time with her friends then she's a child, young and full of excitement, and will sing and be silly and affectionate. Must be the frustration of being with herself or with us too much that makes her closed, removed, unspontaneous, not wonderous, sullen. Her response to us is in one word syllables, either yes or no and barely audible. Sometimes wonder whether she hears us and have asked whether we might get her hearing checked.[1]

When she is in a good mood she hears perfectly well, especially if we talk about her. I, too, feel better when she is happy. When I joke with her and she is in one of her sour moods then even the joke falls flat. It might precipitate a crisis or an argument, a short-lived one at that. Sometimes she's completely closed-mouthed-inaccessible. We have tried different techniques. They work sometimes. No sure way. A telephone call from a friend an appointment with one of them and she's immediately revived, full of energy and vivacity. She's fairly independent when it comes to her thinking. I wonder whether this might be because she knows we pretty much say what we feel and think. She has learned from us that we speak our mind.[2]

My wife and I disagree about the small stupid things about everyday life from time to time because I think I am a little bit touchy about how she expresses herself. If I sense tension in her I sometimes take it as an annoyance directed to me. Then whatever it is she says bothers me and I immediately react. There you are—a flare up. It might last two minutes and then disappear. We'll both laugh at each other. She usually is the one who first makes up. I think it is good we are able to be the way we are. Actually I don't want it different between us. She's often right about me and I hate to admit it although I do sometimes.[3]

She's materialistic at times and that bothers me. Don't know how practical she is because she married me. Her concern for our apartment makes our home very special because she has excellent taste but she's mad about order and putting things away. Drives me nuts. I can't find anything after she straightens things up. She says it isn't lost and if I look I'll find money, bills, letters—you name it. Find them between the leaves of books. Was happily surprised one day when I opened a book and found $20 that she didn't remember placing there. Probably laying around, then she stored it away. What can I do. It's my fate to live with this.[4]

About work, I like what I do. Wish I had more time. Find life more interesting now and less time to pursue my interests. Nevertheless, no complaints. Work is work and in my case, as a teacher, I enjoy watching these young people learn. Actually, I learn from them. Once I get to know them they no longer are just students. Their personality, their whole special world is slowly revealed to me in parts. Perhaps that is what happens when people meet each other. In any case I am happy and sad with them, struggle and play with them. Don't have discipline problems. Just find that some kids have troubles and it is my job to find a way of helping them. Most important, I guess, is to find the key, that special way of making contact with them. I am interested in them and what they value. We set up a special atmosphere in class. We become like a family without talking down to anyone. It means I have to be on my toes because if I am unfair to them, they are hurt or bruised and they either attack me or retreat or in general find it difficult to be with me. It's an intricate process, teaching. I don't think you can program a relationship. It has to have that human excitement. Then I have to remember that these kids have their own world of interests, preoccupations, moods, worries, fears, and often what I say to them in class has little to do with their world. May be they are worried about whether the boy or girl opposite them will show interest or concern for them or whether they will be accepted and liked by others. You know how it is. We aren't just machines, hooked in to power and self-propelled. We have our own power units, yet are energized by those about us. I, too, am a victim of my moods, my hopes, and disappointments.[5]

Somedays I don't feel like teaching, feel like being or doing something else or don't want to contend with this student or that one but there's no choice. If the mood persists and it is deep enough it affects how and what I teach the students. They get used to my idiosyncracies as I get used to theirs but that means we have to be flexible enough to cushion each other's differences. There's no way of really telling you what I think about being a teacher. Either you like it and find it a challenge and are not afraid to devote your energy and time to being one or you labor with the ever-increasing burden of finding whatever you do a trial and tribulation, a test of how much strength you have and how soon you'll be able to go home. There's a side of me that doesn't want any part of teaching. That's the side that wants to be a recluse, hidden away. I could easily be a recluse, away from the world, in my own world, I think.[6]

Case Questions

1. Set up a small questionnaire directed to parents, and another one with similar kinds of questions directed to fourteen-year-olds and compare one to the other.
2. Does the father show insight to his dauther's reactions? Explain.
3. How well does he seem to understand his wife? Explain.
4. What constitutes the essential role of a husband in your thinking?
5. What constitutes the essential role of a wife in your estimation?
6. How many teachers do you know who feel the way this man does?
   a. In what way can you agree with what he is saying? Be explicit.
   b. In what way do you feel that this teacher is unrealistic? Why?

Pamela (17) : A Disturbed Family

Pamela Supports Family As a Prostitute

My brother Richard told me that if I didn't give him a three bucks he'd tell my boyfriend that I hustle. When I refused he said he needed it because he was in a jam, because he had "borrowed" someone's bicycle pump and lost it. When I told him it wasn't my business, that he ought to get a job and deliver groceries he said he was 12, only a minor. I told him the world would be a terrible place if all the minors were like him. He said, "Look who's talking. You and your customers, playing the innocent chick with Louie. What do you think he'd say if I told him?" "Just try it and you'll regret it," I said. I was really angry with him. Richard is capable of anything. He's a graft artist. Gets it from all of us. When he stole a bicycle he told my mother he'd tell everyone that he still sleeps in the same bed with her. My mother didn't say anything. I've tried to explain to her how wrong it is for Richard and her to sleep in the same bed but she doesn't listen.[1] Went to a clinic. I was told that the whole family had to register. That's all I need, the police on my back. Tough enough to make a living without having my one place I call home torn apart. I said I would think it over. I'd be on the street corners with tricksters. This way, I am independent and don't have to pay any pimp or landlady a cent. As soon as I get a little more money I'll get my own place and really operate. I have to worry about Richard and my mother, they have no one else to rely upon. Richard is like a pimp, not that he gets me customers, I can get my own, but he always demands money from me and threatens me if I don't pay up.[2] Guess it isn't his trouble. He hasn't had the best home. I had it better. A home without a father isn't much to wish for. My uncle drops by but he's no model for anyone. He's a faggot but keeps it quiet. His place reeks of scent. Behind the woodwork there's fluffy women's drag clothing. He says it belongs to his girl friends. "How come I never saw them," I asked him once. He says it's his business. He likes Richard. He wants to give him a proper education. He'll be lucky if Richard completes school. There's not a week that my mother isn't asked to school. I go for her. He plays hookie, cuts classes, doesn't do homework, and talks back to his teachers.[3] I was never that way. I did what I had to. I actually enjoyed school and could have graduated if my Dad hadn't died and left us penniless. I hated that first job in the button factory. How I envied my girl friends. They were in school, or out playing or studying. It was difficult for me. Now we are worlds apart. They say hello but I know what they are thinking. Like I had some contagious disease. They avoid me. I don't push myself on them. From their point of view I'm a whore. Maybe they're jealous. They see me bringing nice fellows, or men to the house. Maybe they wish they were tricking like me. I'd give anything to be in their shoes, but then, I had the chance. I'd still be in that factory or another one breaking my back long hours for what, just so some boss's son could start oggling me. What would he want? What they all want.[4] At least I get paid well. In a way I am a slave but an independent one. I buy decent clothes and support a family without effort. Even have money put away. Richard has his teeth attended. My mother doesn't have to clean other peoples houses. She's not all there. She lives in a house of royalty. Says my great-grandfather was a count, that we have royal blood. My uncle laughs but says it's true. Where's our villa and the millions? My grandfather lost everything but his horse and wagon. He was a first-class chauffeur. I'd like to have seen him. Trees lining the streets, small houses, fancy dresses.

The maxi's aren't the same. I look much better in a mini or midi. The men like legs—must admit mine are special, not boasting but wherever I go men turn. I can tell. They get that strange look, as if they have candy in their mouth, stripping me and in bed with me. I'm lucky. I can call my song and the men pitch.[5] Nearly got myself in trouble. A cop. A shakedown I thought. He asked too many questions. That's one of the liabilities of the trade. There are others but I am careful. Have a first-class doctor. He keeps telling me that I better get married and settle down before it is too late. Maybe he's right. Louie's a fine fellow. He studies hard. He loves and cares about me. It's different with Lou than with my customers. They want one thing, then off. With Lou there's a relationship, if you know what I mean. He wants me to study something, to get an education. I know what I do is frowned upon but if I could get a decent job then I might give this up. I don't know anything else. He says I should go to night school. That's when I make my money. One or two nights a week he says, then I won't have to care for the sick as he thinks I do. I had to tell him something. Once I asked him about prostitutes how he felt about them and he said he was sorry for them, that they were getting sex without love. Asked what he meant and he said, they were commercial objects, good for one thing. When I hinted that maybe the girls give their men more than just sex, that maybe they need someone to talk to, or to baby or to be their mother. . . if I told you what I have had to do and had to be for some of my customers you'd never believe me. Anyway, I made him think about the subject just a little but I didn't want to press him.[7] He hasn't met my family—that's all I need. Anyway we meet some place in the city and go out and end up at his place. I am different when I'm with him. I'm not pressing him to use his time, which is really mine, to get things over with. We take our time. When he completes his studies we'll get married. Wants me to meet his parents but I'm afraid. I keep putting him off. That would be the end. First his parents, then mine. He would never understand. He's jealous as it is, wants me to play down my looks, to look demure, like some virgin. I can do it but you can imagine how difficult it is. Someone who keeps to herself, doesn't show off what she has. I was like that, shy and didn't want to be in the limelight but what could I do? Wherever I go I'm center. I wore my hair dark and it didn't change anything. Tried light blond and it was worse. Now, just keep it like this, which is something in between. Sometimes I wonder what will happen to me if I don't get married. I can't see myself doing this all my life but what do most people do. They get married, have children and settle down. I'm not ready for that. I want to travel, go places, see things, and be treated first class. I've lived in this dumpy neighborhood too many years. Look at my home and you see rats, nothing green, people, unhappy ones—drugged and scared of today and tomorrow. The young ones don't care what they do. They are just as frightened but they don't know it. No one cares about them. I was one of them. I used to hang out on corners, in hallways, on stoops, by storefronts. The young ones kid and scheme and tease. The older ones think about money, and a way of forgetting this misery—drink, drugs, sex.[7] About drugs I'm afraid. Once you're hooked, that's it. The whole family get caught. Their mothers and fathers sometimes support a habit because they are afraid of the kid going off the deep end and getting mixed up with police. The kids have to if they want to belong. It's their badge to belonging. Who wants to be different? I was and am. I don't have friends. I'm alone. At least I have Lou. What I peddle is the oldest drug, I am told. Why should I try something else. I won't touch a customer who's on it. I am a hooker like they say but I don't harm anyone's health. What I have to offer is special. Why shouldn't they pay for it? I save them lots of money with time, dates, going out to dinner, conversation. Some are married. They still have dinner with their wives. Of course I like a show myself but I only take it when it comes with someone I like.

I get depressed sometimes, something awful. I sometimes feel like a rag and that I'm being used. Not by the men, because that's business and I get paid for it but I use myself. I am good-looking and even smart but it doesn't mean anything to me. I sometimes hate myself, not for what I do but being me.[8] Maybe if I had had a father who didn't die on me things would have been different. I don't remember him. My mother fell apart, I was two at the time when my mother took a border. That's where Richard came from. That makes Richard a bastard. I'm not sorry for myself I never knew it any other way but everyone is sick with something. My brother? I don't know what will happen to him. There's my mother and she's in another world. What she imagines is real to her. Richard at least knows the difference. That's my doing. I call things by their name. My uncle helped us. He was my hero but when I was thirteen or so he started after me one day. I told my mother but she said I was imagining, that he was only being an uncle. I feel sorry for him now. He gets older and watches his looks and knows he's going to be less of an attraction. At least I'm blessed with being a prostitute.[9]

Case Questions

1. What is wrong with a twelve-year-old sleeping with his mother?
2. What meaning do you attribute to money?
3. Why do children play hookie, or cut school?
4. What is Pamela's conception of men?
5. How do the actions of a young woman reflect her experience with her father?
6. Are you judging Pamela in any way? Explain.
7. What is it like for you to walk through or live in an impoverished neighborhood?
8. What generalization can you make about prostitution?
9. In what way did you empathize with Pamela's predicament? Explain.

Richard (12): A Disturbed Family

I never went after her with a pair of scissors. She lies. She just wants to get me in trouble. She says that I have to come here if I want to be well. I'm not sick. I feel fine. I wish she'd stop telling me what to do. She's not my mother. Besides she doesn't need me. She has her friends. That she's going to get married to Lou that's a joke. Who would want her. She's less a sister now. She's too busy with Lou to bother about me.[1] She never wants to play a game like checkers with me. I'm a good player. She loses most of the time. Maybe I'm really good in checkers. Maybe I'll be a checker player when I grow up. A checker player? Never thought of that before. Maybe I can find out what I have to do. I'm pretty strong. Look at my hands. See these callouses. That's from bar work. There's a man at the park whose been training me on the bars. I can do skin the cat, a kip, all kinds of things. Don't see him too often but when I do he shows me. Says I could be an athlete if I wanted to. I like sports but I fight with my friends. They say things about my family. What they say is true but I don't like it. Why can't Pamela be like other girls? My mother never knows how to speak to people. My uncle gives me money.[2] Just things. Have a whole body-building outfit now. Showed my friends. Now they want to come to my house. I don't want anyone coming here. Wish I had a home like other kids. Pamela's O.K. when she's got time for me. Maybe if I could speak to my mother but she doesn't understand. I used to listen to her but now I hear the same stories. She tells me about how we used to be very rich and how big the house was, or when she was a little girl. All kinds of stories. When my father died she became sick. That's what Pamela tells me. Whoever he was he sure fixed up my mother.[3] I sometimes wonder what it would be like to have a father like other boys, a real home like other kids. I know I steal and lie and sometimes even feel bad but why shouldn't I. I want to make lots of money when I grow up. Have a car, clothes, music, fun, films, ball games, and whatever I want. I'd treat my buddies. School? Does it help the kids where I live? I don't know. We don't go anywhere, just hang around.[4] In my home no one listens to me. The only way they listen to me is if I threaten them. I don't threaten them. I was just kidding about the scissors. I wasn't going to do anything. But she gets me angry. She told me that I'll grow up into one of those bums, or scarecrows, as she calls them. I'm too smart, I told her. Then she gives me that jazz about school, and how important it is and if it weren't for the fact that she has to earn money for us she would still be in school. That's not my fault, I tell her. Why should I have to pay for it but she doesn't even listen to me. Maybe yes maybe no but I think she likes doing what she does so why shouldn't I get something out of it? I can't work. Besides, work is for suckers.[5] If I could learn to play checkers then I'd have plenty of money. Watch men in the park play for money. They play for 50 cents or more. Doesn't take me long to play. The men in the park like me because they see I play well. Why shouldn't I play hookie if I can sneak into the ball game, or go fishing, or go to a film? I've learned more about things from films and TV than in those stupid books. There are some stories I like to read. I enjoy the war stories and adventures into outer space.[6] Some day I'm going to have books of what I want to read. I have a few. I can't read at night because my sister and her customers make such a racket. I sometimes imagine what she's doing. One of them slipped me a dollar the other day. That was a surprise. Then my sister found out and started a whole scene, said I had to give it back. This man entered into it. Before you knew it, she was yelling at him to get out. She didn't want his money. He ought to mind his own business. Then she attacked me and said she wanted the money I had taken from him. I said it was mine and she said she wanted it. She said it wasn't for herself. She was against me taking money from strangers.[7] I said she does and she got angry. She said that I better give her the money or else. I laughed and she really got angry and tried to force me to give her the dollar so I saw the scissors and grabbed it. She backed away. She was really scared. You should have seen her face. She did a funny thing. She began to cry but not a little. I had seen her before but this time a lot, shook all over. I told her I wasn't serious about the scissors but she didn't stop. I was worried. I had never seen her that way. I told her I would give her the dollar if she'd stop bawling, she didn't. I went to the kitchen and ate something and when I came back she was all right, decking herself out, like nothing happened.[8] I can't help doing what I do. I take money from her and from my mother because I do.[9] My uncle is always nice to me. We go places together and see films and he doesn't yell at me. When he asks me about school he doesn't tell me that I'll be a good for nothing like my sister does. If I could work with animals I'd like that. Maybe more than checkers because animals are good. They only want to eat and sleep and don't act bad really. If I could work in a zoo that would be fun, lions and tigers. Asked one of the attendants and he said I would have to learn first in school, take courses, even go to college. Imagine me in college. I would teach them all kinds of things. Maybe work in a circus. I could teach them what to do on the trapeze. That's funny. Me teaching a chimp on a trapeze. Well. I mean they'd have to know what to do and when. Don't have to go to college to work in a circus with chimps. Don't think much about working in a circus but read a book about circus life. Always traveling, new places, and the show with all those people. Mine would be one of the main acts.[10]

I guess I like different things. I like bright things, a fancy clothes. My uncle likes the same things. He says I have good taste for clothes and buys me things. My mother doesn't care what I wear but it has to be clean. She goes about smelling my clothes like it were a flower or something and gets excited when they stink. She's got a special sense of smell. She can smell anything for miles. She's always scrubbing and sniffing to see whether she ought to scrub more. Sometimes I think she's happy when she scrubs. We have a washing machine but it never cleans enough for her. Once I dreamt about being dirty, in mud. When I get a car I'll fix it myself and won't worry about getting dirty. Give her a dirty shirt and she's happy, like a dog with a bone. That's what Pamela says.[11]

Case Questions

1. How do brothers and sisters "use" each other?
2. Compare Richard's attitude toward his family to that of a child from a family you intimately know.
3. How does the image of a father influence one's masculinity or femininity?
4. How do values toward one's own sex develop?
5. In what way is Richard's vocabulary and way of thinking an outcome of the kind of experiences he has lived through? Explain.
6. Are these interests age and sex appropriate for a twelve-year-old? How do you know?
7. What role does Pamela assume here?
8. Is Richard's use of language more sophisticated than most children his age? How do you know?
9. What kind of reasoning is Richard using here?
10. What kinds of needs are expressed here and what do they indicate?
11. Can you identify in any way with Richard's predicament? Explain.

Uncle : A Disturbed Family

I'm no judge. Have my own bag of switches. Richard is in a broil but there's nothing I can do. His mother, that's my sister, is ineffective as a mother. We all are in this family. We got the flush when they handed the cards out. Used to pay the rent, supported them all. Was like father and mother to both kids. Now Pamela's the breadwinner. Hardly bread what she earns as a hooker. She's a good kid. Richard, too. They have troubles. Who hasn't. Things better now than before. At least she makes some income and there's this fellow she says she's going to marry. She's a man manipulator, like all women.[1] Has her own schemes for what she wants. Suspicious of me and everyone. Hasn't had it easy. A tough way to make a living. The situation is helpless. We're all bound by responsibilities. If she quits work then what happens. Can't support them like before. My sister is helpless now. Richard is no help. He's too young. He'll shuffle for himself, in any case. There's little hope for my sister. We've tried everything. Went to a doctor once who said she needed psychological help. That was years ago. Could never afford private work. Putters about, cooks, cleans, and putters. I prefer to remain out of the picture.[2] My role is inconsequential, now. Richard turns to me when he wants something. It hurts but I accept it. It's family. Pamela wants nothing to do with me. And my sister? Nothing to say. I'm sorry for all of them but then I'm sorry for me, too. I won't start on my life or what I have gone through or go through. Another world. Just let me know what I can do to help Richard or any of them. I don't think my influence is of much value but I'll help if I can. Can't turn the clock back, or choose our parents, or wipe away experiences. Know I'm philosophizing. I do sometimes when I feel sorry for myself. Guess age has a way of making you look backwards instead of forwards or makes you wonder what will be. They are my family—for good or for bad. I understand what Pamela goes through. It's a terrible way. Richard? With a few breaks he'd be a fine boy without his hangups. But, that's about the way it is.[3]

Case Questions

1. What kind of concept does he have about women?
2. What are your attitudes to homosexuality?
3. What quality of emotionality seems to be expressed in the way he describes the family picture?
    a. Can you identify with the uncle's predicament? How?
    b. Is he disassociated from the needs of his family?

Mr. Knock: The Teacher. A Disturbed Family

Richard is an impossible child. It's a relief when he isn't in class. Once in class his behavior is contagious. There's a gnome in him. He can't sit still. He constantly disturbs his neighbors, shuffles papers, is purposely contrary. I sometimes think he has some kind of nerve disease, the kind that doesn't permit him a moment's peace. I even asked the health office about him and was informed that his health is perfect.[1]

It isn't my job to be watchman over him. I have thirty-five other children. If you know these children, they are difficult. When he isn't upsetting our class routine or the children he is drawing or reading something that has nothing to do with our lesson. I can never predict what he'll do. Suddenly he raises his hand and asks me a question that is completely irrelevant, like if I am teaching history he'll ask me what children liked during the fifteenth century or how do I know whether what they say in one book is more reliable than what is said in another one.[2]

The children claim that he steals things from them but are afraid to report to the principal. He is small but extremely strong. He seems to know all kinds of fighting techniques. In gym he's tops. Children look upon him in awe but they don't always like him because he centers everything about himself. He likes to boast. No-one and nothing is better than what he is. He talks about a father he has but I know from our records that he doesn't have one. I used to feel sorry for the boy and can understand why he wants to be a big shot but enough is enough. I'm a teacher, not a martyr. I find it extremely difficult to contend with him. There's something sick in the child.[3]

About how he learns. Well, he has a good memory. I've noticed that. He's no fool. He understands things when he wants to but he's not interested in learning. He's interested in money, what money can buy. What can you say to a child of 12 who values that? He doesn't listen to me. I can't really punish him because whatever I do doesn't seem to help. Yes, he teases the girls something awful. Never had a kid so brazen. One parent complained. Told her I'd look into it but the principal doesn't want to deal with it because the problem is related to his home and that he doesn't know what to do because Richard's mother is incapable of helping him. The sister is only a grown-up child—although I suspect she's the sole supporter of the family. Difficult situation. Hear there's an uncle but haven't been able to reach him. Like I say, it isn't up to me, I'm a teacher, not a saint with magical powers to change that boy.[4]

Case Questions

1. How objective is the teacher's description of Richard?
    a. Does this influence your understanding of Mr. Knock?
2. Is it irrelevant that Richard asks such a question? Explain.
3. Why do you think Richard claims to have a father?
    a. What would you do if Richard were in your class and you received complaints from other children that he stole?
4. Suppose you are a teacher with a child like Richard in your class, what would you want to know about Richard?
    a. How would you try to help him?
    b. To whom would you turn for help?

Healthy Sibling Rivalry

Everett Ostrovsky

Before we attempt to discuss healthy sibling rivalry it is important to examine briefly the meaning of the family as a unit in regard to its structure, and function. Sibling conflict has to be considered from the point of view of the total personality environment of the family. Although we are not in the position to make any generalizations about the size of families, we can say that the personality of a large family demands a different kind of consideration than a very small one. The number of children, the spacing between them, and their sex, are important aspects of the family structure. Boys without sisters or girls without brothers will have different kinds of experiences than siblings of the opposite sex.

Parents utilize various methods by which they allot responsibilities to their children. Some parents give their offsprings considerable freedom, while others place rigid limits on them and strictly supervise their activities. In a family where the grandparents live in the same house, the complexity of identifications, values, attitudes, and expectations is manifold. Whether this leads to more or to different kinds of sibling conflict is difficult to say without considering the dynamics of the personality of the family. Whether the mother is working or stays home constitutes an important factor in assessing the influence of parental guidance to the children. Are the children home by themselves during the day because both parents are working? Is the economy of the family dependent upon the participation of the youngsters? Do the children contribute to the welfare of their parents?

During the early years especially children need to be in contact with their parents in order to identify with them and acquire values, attitudes and guidelines to what is expected of them. To deprive them of this social inheritance is to give them a less stable structure of standards from which to function. In healthy sibling rivalry the children have an opportunity to test out the value of what they have arbitrarily accepted from their parents. By actually experiencing what they have accepted on face value from them they build-in an evaluative sense of what is meaningful to them.

In a small, informal, closely-knit family there is a give and take between each person in terms of ideas, making decisions and working-out problems. If a mutual sense of trust pervades the atmosphere each member becomes aware of and concerned with the thoughts and feelings of the other. Especially in a very large family the need for organization and leadership is mandatory. Cooperation and conformity are coupled with developing specialized roles and tasks between the older children and the younger ones. The children in such a family tend to be more interdependent. Usually the older children are given the authority to control and to care for the younger ones. These children are generally less possessive and demanding. As a result the children develop close dependency ties to their siblings in addition to the parents. This lessens the strength of the jealousies that might exist between two children in reference to competing for the love of the parents. The allegiances are less singularly focused. Needs can be satisfied by both the parents and the siblings.

The older sibling is generally the one whom the younger one turns to when he needs help, wants direction, or has to explain his feelings. He's the teacher, substitute parent, and the one to whom secrets are confided from time to time. Although the older child may look upon the younger one as a competitor and express jealousy and envy, he might be extremely proud and protective of his sibling. If the older child is still very dependent upon his mother, the intensity and strength of sibling rivalry is increased. However, the above considerations are only partially related to the vast subject of family structure and functioning.

Now, let us turn our attention to the characteristics of healthy sibling rivalry.

The child who has learned the skill of argumentation is using a more mature approach to conflict than the one who still lashes out at the slightest opposition. The rational thinker is capitalizing on a more developed plan of attack than the one who is irrational. Of course, the question might be raised, "What happens when the child has no alternative but to protect himself physically or withdraw?" To answer the question one has to weigh what is considered age-appropriate behavior in the home, neighborhood or milieu. In some family settings, the only authority is strength and physical assertion. A less powerful manner of expressing ones wishes would be inappropriate. In other words the appropriateness of a response is, to a degree, related to the sex, age, personality of the child as well as to the patterns of expected behavior in the home, community and society at large. Children model this behavior according to their perception of what is expected of them from the adults and age-mates they value most and with whom they spend much of their time.

Reality-oriented behavior or behavior that is relevant to the situation is superior to unrealistic action. The retreating, sullen, withdrawing, bitter child who waits for an opportune time to revenge himself upon his sibling is not spontaneously and openly facing his feelings. He is using an indirect, calculating approach to express his hostility. The amount of energy he dissipates in feeling bad, in retreating, in being bitter and sullen could be used more constructively in worthwhile pursuits. The way a child uses his skills, strategies, resources, abilities and knowledge in planning his attacks is pertinent here because it helps us to understand the child's behavioral level of maturity. His ability to mobilize his inner resources in an organized and meaningful manner, and act without capitalizing on the deficiencies of himself and those of his sibling are a measure of his growth and development.

Let us now turn our discussion to the dramatic role of humor in sibling rivalry. The ability of the child to step away from himself, so to speak, and see the absurdity of his actions is a saving grace for him. The humor gives immediate relief to him, removes him from the full impact of the situation. In other words this permits him an opportunity to feel and think about his dilemma without being so personally involved. On one level this might be seen as a means of escape or avoidance; on the other, it objectifies the subjectiveness of the experience. Of course this can be an excruciating time for the other sibling who feels he is the butt of the joke. When the humor is used as a weapon to sting, mock, insult or tease, the initial intent behind the communication is negative.

We have already discussed the use of ridicule, sarcasm and mockery in the chapter that deals with aggression. Here we are concerned with what happens when there is a sudden change of disposition or mood on the part of one child that contagiously infects the other. What makes an explosive situation fall apart into laughter, whimsy, fancy or caprice? It is that quality of experience that transposes the dead-seriousness of differences between children into something that seems funny, amusing or ludicrous. It creates comic relief. The face that screws itself up into a monstrous image might change a potentially extended quarrel into laughter. Both the instigator of the facial contortion and his audience are part of an act; each is dependent upon the other. The more incongruous the character of the act is in regard to the conflict the more effective the humor. A smile on the part of the observer is enough to encourage the performer into making another grotesque, mask-like face. The importance of the resentment or what preceded is eclipsed by the more exciting experience of face-making. Both children might compete with each other. Each stimulates the other's response to laugh. At a certain point the pleasure connected to the laughter perpetuates itself and engulfs them. Or, in another example, one child can imitate his sibling's words, then transform them into nonsense syllables without changing the essential character of the words. He makes a play on words.

Let us illustrate another case in which a conflicting situation is transformed into humor. One child is about to seriously express his discontent and resentment to his brother. Just as he is prepared to lodge his complaint he trips over the rug or knocks over a chair. This predicament is enough to change the whole character of the situation. Or suppose a very young child momentarily becomes tongue-tied because he is overburdened with emotionality and can't find the proper words to express his feelings during an argument with his sibling. Here again, the older child can distract the younger one or redirect his attention away from the area of difficulty to something ludicrous.

Humor is a reality in life for many children. It removes the child from the closeness of the experience; he suddenly sees another perspective. It acts as a relief valve for the tension states related to frustration and conflict. It represents another type of adaptive behavior during conflict and is a dire necessity throughout life. But if humor is used as a substitute for serious confrontation of reality then its purpose is questionable.

Now let us turn our attention to the positive function of conflict. If conflict inhibits action, limits the child's repertory of behavior and experience, creates uncertainty about his own self value as well as his position towards others then it is destructive. The value of it depends upon its function in the child's development. If it paralyzes the emotional forces within him and does not result in an amelioration of the problem which first caused it, then it is detrimental. If, however, it creates effort by the very nature of its tension, it often helps the child to surmount a difficulty, and can be considered an aid in directing behavior into more positive channels.

Conflict as it is expressed through play may be resolved, or tension lessened by the use of compensatory mechanisms which we have seen have their value in permitting the child to enter into an area of experience that he would otherwise have completely avoided. It reduces the danger of direct participation as in role-playing while still allowing for a less difficult manner of dealing with the same form of activity. Such defenses or mechanisms or adaptive behavioral approaches initiate activity; this might eventually lead to the child's emergence from old behavioral patterns and value systems and promote a more direct form of exploration of those areas of experience which he formerly shunned. The value of conflict must be seen against the total spectrum of the momentary and long-term effects it has upon the growth and development of the child involved. To protect the child from it unnecessarily is to deny him the right to learn what it is to face reality.

Each child checks or balances the other in regard to the rivalry; each helps the other to learn the limits and potentials of what he can and cannot do. Compromises develop since both children attempt to get along in a way that is most comfortable and rewarding for them. The way the children arrive at their peaceful settlement is an important issue because one child might be the victor all the time while the other is the loser. If the peace has been settled at the expense of the other child's identity, the value of the solution is questionable. The point between healthy and unhealthy conflict is somewhat a subjective decision which varies from individual to individual and family to family. For each child healthy sibling conflict must be weighed in terms of his total personality, the richness of the resources that have been developed within him and the way these attributes have been utilized.

In healthy sibling conflict, anxiety is not aroused to the degree that it can't be siphoned off constructively. If the conflict contributes to learning new skills that the children can put to use as part of their growth then there is value to the dislocation between them. If the youngsters have to learn to modify their individual drives and develop new means of expressing themselves which are more socially acceptable without giving up their spontaneity, this is purposeful.

When reality becomes too difficult to face directly children use fantasy as one of the means of dealing with their needs. Fantasy can be used constructively in sibling conflict for it externalizes the initial feelings of hostility into acceptable concepts and symbols. We see this in the different forms of play. The dress-up time of young children, shooting each other or acting out particular roles which are acceptable to both parties confirms the value of fantasy in sibling conflict. If the children can accept and accommodate each other's fantasies without using them as a substitute for facing the realities of everyday living, fantasy is constructive. If these fantasies are used as a means of resolving conflicts, enriching the children's relationship with each other, they are desirable.

If conflict contributes to the development of controls that are not so rigid and exacting that they deprive children from taking chances or doing the wrong thing, then it is positively related to growth and development. Conflict that expands the interest of children and broadens their understanding of their respective roles and motivations is instrumental to healthy development. Conflict is purposeful when it doesn't drain the energy of the children but uses it to test limits, to strengthen values, to stimulate thought, to instigate feelings, and to set-up guidelines of behavior. The conflict has to be measured against the specific problems the children are facing at their particular age period. The richness of a child's relationship with his sibling is integrally bound by both harmony and discord.

Questions and Projects Related to Healthy Sibling Rivalry

1. What are some of the factors that should be considered in regard to understanding the personality of a family? Why?
2. How may the conflict between siblings contribute to their growth and development?
3. In what way might parents cause sibling rivalry?
4. How does humor help you in dealing with conflicting situations?
5. Is there such a thing as healthy student rivalry? Explain.

Blackout

Two children, a woman, and an old man sat around the checkered tablecloth, each to his own plate, each to his own piece of light that flickered from the candle stick.[1] The light disrupted the darker corners of the room where two couches were wedged together.[2] One was already set with sheet, pillow, and blanket. It reflected the mechanical repetition of an alternating pink and red neon drug sign that hung just below the lower ledge of the window.[3] The sound of chewing, the cutting of meat, and the swooping of, or more delicate lifting up of a morsel of food was interrupted by the sound of a piano, which was being tuned in the adjoining room . . . tuned in candlelight.[4]

"Can I have more, Mom?" the younger child called out.

"Did you get the chicken at Louie's?" the old man questioned.[3]

"Me, too," the older child requested.

The mother silently got up, and as she picked up the flat plate said, to all of them, "Who's going to finish the parsnips?"

"I ate some already," one said.

"Me, too," the other blurted out between his teeth and stuffed another olive in his mouth.

"She was gone and back with some more parts of chicken and before she had a chance to put the plate down, the arms of the two children reached out.

"Wait until I put the dish down. When are you going to learn manners?"[6]

Each one of the children plucked up a leg and was about to dig his teeth in it when the mother said, "Now suppose grandpa wants a leg—why don't you ask him? How many times have I told you that I don't want you to grab things off the plate?"[7]

The old man just shook his head.

The younger naively asked, "Do Indians eat chicken?"

The brother answered, "No—only people do."[8]

The old man interrupted, "I can't eat anymore," and a weak smile lit his face.

"I'll make you tea as soon as I clean the table."

"You're kidding me, they kill people—but don't eat them," the child continued.[9]

"Sure, they do. They kill them first with an axe, then eat them on a spit," and he laughed, rather hoarsely.

"Don't tease your brother. Indians are people like you and me," the mother informed.[10]

"But," he said, "they eat people," the younger one insisted.

"He was teasing you."

"He's always teasing me!"[11]

"Mom, I'm thirsty. Can I have some coke?"

"No, you're going to have milk," the mother said.

The old man was picking his teeth with a toothpick.

"Who's going to help me with the dishes?" The mother asked.

"I did them last night," the older child blurted out.[12]

"He did not, I did!" The younger one interrupted.

The old man stated slowly, "Joe must speak to the superintendent. We can't live in the dark like this."[13]

"It's fun, Mom. I wish we didn't have lights all the time," the youngest child said.

"It's just like in the old days," the other called out.

"But they didn't have television," the younger seriously stated.[14]

"How many more nights won't there be electricity, Mom?"

"I don't know—but it's impossible to get things done in this dark."

"I wish I knew where I put that other box of candles. I'm going downstairs to the grocers." The mother rose from the table. "Papa—watch the children. I'll be back shortly."

"Can I go with you, Mom?" the older child asked.

"Me, too," responded the other one.

"Alright. But finish eating."

"I'm done."

"Me, too," the other echoed.

"We'll have dessert when we come back," and the mother moved toward the exit of the room.[15]

The three rose and each walked down the narrow corridor toward the door. When they opened it, a glare of yellow light spread over the floor of the darkened passageway.

"We'll be back in a moment," the mother called out and left.[16]

Case Questions

1. Do you think it makes any difference to the way you feel when you eat in candlelight?
2. Do you think some people might become upset when there isn't electricity. Why?
3. Do you know anyone who can't afford to pay his electricity bill? Are there people residing in the United States who lack electricity in their community?
4. What picture comes to your mind when you think of candlelight? Now imagine a piano being tuned, if you can. What image pops into your thoughts?
5. Can you identify with these people at this point? Explain your answer.
6. Is it "typical" of young hungry children to be more impulse oriented? Compare the behavior of an older famished person eating to one who is partially satiated.
7. When do you act as if you were the only one important to the exclusion of the needs of others?
8. What do you think of this answer? How would you answer the younger child's question? Why?
9. Do you associate Indians with eating people? Explain your answer. What do you know about the Indians in our country?
10. Can you accept this statement? Explain your answer.
11. How often do you believe what another person says only to find out later that you were being teased? How does it feel?
12. Do the children you know participate in helping with the household chores?
13. Who is Joe? No direct indication of who he is?
14. What price do we pay for technological progress?
15. Which one of these people seems real to you? Why?
16. What do you imagine happens after this scene?

Jim (8): Leaving Home

No one paid any attention to him. His whole family had gathered in the different rooms and were busy with each other. There was no place for him. What could he do that would make him important to them—make himself important to himself?[1] No, he would leave, and they would not miss him. He would pack up and leave. Then when they looked for him and didn't find him, they would become concerned about him and question themselves. "Why did he go? What did we do?" And then speculate and feel bad, and it would be good for them.[2] After a while they would begin to miss him, and there would be few things that they could do that would not be interrupted by his absence and their desire to find him. They would be sorry that they took him for granted.[3]

Jim went to his bureau and opened his drawer, took out a pair of socks and underwear and a shirt and put them on the bed. Then he opened the closet door to take a sweater. In case it would get cold, he would need a sweater and maybe he ought to take his rubbers, which he hardly ever wore because he hated to wear them.[4] He never liked the way they felt and made him feel clumsy, but since he planned to be away for a long time, it would be important not to get his feet wet and catch a cold. He would have to take care of himself now and would not be able to come home and take his socks off. Besides, his shoes weren't too good, and he didn't want to wear cardboard above the hole in order to keep some of the water from seeping inside his shoe. Yes, he would take them, even if he hated them. He put them on the floor, but then changed his mind and returned them to the closet floor. They would take too much room and he wanted to travel lightly.[5] He would have to keep out of the rain. Now where would he sleep and how? He would have to take pajamas even though he didn't like them. He preferred to sleep in his underwear; it was more comfortable. He placed a pair of pajamas on the bed. They took a lot of room, but he would have to take them. He was going to have to take care of himself now and do things like it was best for him. Where would he sleep? Well, he would find a place. It was just a question of getting a place. He could work. He knew how to deliver packages for a butcher, vegetable man, or grocer. Even worked in a laundry and tailor, so that he was experienced. He would have to find a job. He had to leave now before they caught him packing.[6]

Outside, Jim walked quickly toward the river. He would go down-town, until he couldn't go any further. Even though he didn't have money, he would be able to eat.[7] Besides, he wasn't hungry. He had eaten a good supper, because they ate some of the special food that was prepared for the visitors. Food was always better when there was company. He remembered the chocolate-graham pie that his mother would be serving.[8] She'd look for him then and wonder where he had gone. His father and relatives would all inquire, "Where's Jim?" They would worry. He started to feel bad because he knew they'd worry. He could see their faces. His mother would no longer be able to be a hostess and talk to this one or that one, but would go to his father and say, "What did we do?" or, "Maybe we ought to call the police? Maybe something happened to him?" Everyone would be concerned, and the whole gathering would be spoiled, but it served them right.[9] After all, he waited there between rooms—waited for someone to speak to him, and no one did. No one even knew he existed. They looked past him and laughed about silly things and made all kinds of faces. Why didn't someone come up to him and speak to him, or why didn't his parents come over to him and show some warmth? Instead, they let him stay there, and when he went up to where they were, they didn't pay any attention.[10] He began to feel as if he was going to cry. Maybe they didn't really love him? If they did, they would have gone over to him. He wished his mother had put her arms about him or hugged him just a little, or his father had done the same or something. But they didn't care, although he knew they did when there weren't people about, but that was because he was always doing something they thought was wrong. Well, not always, but often. Always critical of what he did.[11]

He had crossed a large street and was heading toward the darker, narrower streets. The wind was up and chilly, and Jim buttoned his top button about his collar. The streets were busy with people and cars, and no one noticed him in particular.[12] Some people looked at him quickly but kept going on. If they only knew what he was doing now, they wouldn't just walk on. He was a real man now, on his own, and could do everything himself.[13] Still, he would miss his parents. What would he do at night? The lighting in the street was cold, and there was so much blackness everywhere. In the house, it was warm and light and not so much space.[14] Nevertheless, he would have to keep going on. There was no turning back now. He looked up at a clock at a bank. It was after 10 P.M. and time for him to be in bed. He crossed another street and could see the river now. Soon he would walk along it and go downtown where all the boats were. He would get on a ship, stow away, and then the sailors would have to feed him. But then his parents would not know where he was and really start to worry, and his mother would cry, and he would feel so bad. He would feel that he made his mother cry. He loved his mother and didn't want her to cry. Jim could feel the tears come to his eyes.[15] It was lonely walking alone at night. He was tired. His legs were getting heavy, and the package of clothes was beginning to be a burden. Maybe it wasn't such a good idea to take a boat. If he came home late, then they'd still be sorry that they hadn't paid any attention to him. He would turn back now. Besides, he began to feel hungry and remembered that chocolate pie. Maybe he would be given some of that pie and milk. What a wonderful combination. He started to retrace his tracks and feel a rush of energy come back into his body.[16]

When he opened the door, he could still hear the same voices. His mother came over to him, "Where have you been?" and looked at the package he had in his arms. She bent down and put her arms about him and kissed his cheek. He began to cry and said between tears, "I thought you didn't love me." His mother said, "Of course we do. What gave you that foolish idea?" And without waiting for an answer said, "Now let's get to bed, and I'll give you a nice piece of pie and milk. You can have it out here with us or in your room." "I want it in my room. Will you bring it to me, Mom?" She smiled at him and affectionately put her hand over his head and said, "You foolish boy—of course we love you.[17] Now get undressed and prepare for bed." And she left. Jim quickly untied his bundle of clothes. He began to hum as he undressed. Everything was all right now. They loved him.[18]

Case Questions

1. When did you last feel you were neglected by either your parents, teachers, or friends? How did you behave?
2. How do children punish their parents?
3. How successful have you been in evoking guilt in others?
4. Do young children today feel this way about rubbers, boots, or galoshes? If so, why?
5. What meanings do clothes have for children and adults?
6. What sense of achievement do young children receive in working at a job?
7. Can you imagine why Jim thought this?
8. What is it about home you value most?
9. Is revenge the proper word that signifies Jim's motive here? Explain your answer.
10. Is there a certain amount of self-pity in this part of the story? Explain.
11. Is it difficult for you to take criticism from someone you love or value very much?
12. Do you think Jim wanted people to look at him? If so, why?
13. Do you ever feel a false sense of power or feeling of invulnerability? In what kinds of situations and with what kind of people?
14. What is the meaning behind the phrase, "and not so much space"?
15. Is he putting himself in the place of his parents, especially his mother? Why did Jim become so emotional in regard to imagining his mother's reaction?
16. Why did Jim change his course of action and return home?
17. How would you have reacted if you were the parent?
18. Do you think it was better for Jim to have left home and then returned as he did than to have never departed? Explain your answer.

3

SEX AWARENESS

Long before the child is aware of himself as an entity separate from the world, he learns to respond to different kinds of handling, such as how he is held, fed, fondled, talked to, picked up, and a thousand other kinds of experiences to which he first relates through his senses. The lack of stimulation and exposure in his very early life to any one of his senses deprives him of the necessary growth patterns for later integration and maturity. The picture he develops of his body, his body image and the value he gives to it, has much to do with how he will perceive himself as a person and as a member of his sex, and how he will relate to others. That this body is his, with its powers and vulnerabilities, joys and pains, makes it a wonderous thing, but not without a price. Doubt, embarrassment, shame, and guilt, play their respective roles in the course of his development. Perhaps every dimension of the culture, family, and his own individuality shape the way he perceives himself, as an object of affection or as a partner in the giving or taking of love. It is with these thoughts in mind that we introduce this section.

R. Galdston discusses the difference between the self and its relationship to a changing body concept in a world of social-cultural expectations. The internal push or drive that activates the sexual appetite of Matthew in the episode that follows creates an interesting provocative familial situation.

Where, in the episode that follows, do the senses and those special perceptions of Ruth end and the reality of nature begin? What quality of transcendental experience exists in this episode? Is there a relationship between her body and the natural surroundings?

In the next vignette the awakening of Kathy's senses to her body are also not separate from the immediate environment.

In M. Hall's article, impulse disorders, character disorders, and identity conflicts are discussed in light of the adolescent's search for meaning, for clarity, and for maintaining need satisfaction. In the vignette that ensues, Liza reckons with the experience of sensing herself as a merging dimension of the museum only to be reawakened to her new founded femininity. Colin, in the final episode, gives us a close-up of what he questions prior to seeing Betty and how he develops his relationship with her once he meets her. Each one of these young people builds impressions upon impressions through sensing, observing, and using feelings, thoughts, and actions as their guide.

Adolescence and the Function of Self-Consciousness

Richard Galdston

Adolescence is the time for a child to pass into adulthood, a time reserved for the acquisition of physical and psychologic prowess sufficient to resolve his primary dependency upon the childhood configuration of his family as the major source of a sense of security. The adolescent's most compelling task is the establishment of a sense of self-confidence in place of reliance upon parental faith. The quest for self-confidence presses him to pursue a route that the observer of times finds difficult to comprehend, filled as it is with detours, obstacles, dead-ends, and superhighways leading nowhere. Devious and obscure as the route may appear, the ultimate destination remains constant—the attainment of selfconfidence. The key to understanding the many and varied deviations that occur along the adolescent's road is provided in another term so characteristic of the age, *self-consciousness*.

The young child takes himself for granted. His mind and body are objects of sublime indifference to him. He is content to entrust the care of his flesh and spirit to his parents and to remain free to play and master the reality of his immediate world by means of prescribed rote and ritual. His sense of personal worth is derived largely from the reflection of his parents' attentions.

The adolescent becomes acutely conscious of himself, his mind and his body. Even before the thrust of growth that obtains from the biologic burst of puberty, he anticipates the road ahead. The child pays great attention to his peers; but, as adolescence approaches, his vision shifts toward those slightly older. Vicariously he participates in their endeavors and begins to try on for size a variety of postures, mannerisms, and attitudes that ill fit his child's body and frame of mind. The initial discrepancy between the self he is and the self he wants to be commands a self-appraisal that begins in the period just prior to puberty and is greatly intensified by the arrival of the overt changes of pubescence. With these changes, the adolescent begins a through self-assessment and comparison with others. He undertakes a detailed inventory of all his bodily parts in reference to those of his peers and his heroes. His motor skills, intellectual capacities, esthetic talents, and social graces are subjected to agonizing scrutiny. He notes all his psychologic idiosyncracies and adds them to a list that soon grows to be a catalogue of personal attributes along every parameter. It is little wonder that this scrupulous appraisal is accompanied by an air of self-consciousness apparent to all. This consciousness of self is an embarrassment to the cherished image of what he wanted to be and accounts for the characteristic adolescent vulnerability to slight and shame.

The self-assessment is made known to others through the derivatives of the findings. The adolescent girl observes that she has nicer hair than one friend but a less attractive nose than another. The boy announces that he is no good at football but is the class leader in chess. They possess a special vocabulary reserved for grading the results of social and psychologic comparison, currently ranging from "cool" to "ratfink." In the previous generation they varied from "smooth" to "jerk."

Upon completing his self-inventory, the adolescent tabulates the results with painful honesty and derives a profile of what he finds himself to be. He contrasts it with the image of himself that he knew in the family of his childhood. He notes all differences. If the scales of dimension in which the two

"Adolescence and the Function of Self-Consciousness," by Richard Galdston. From MENTAL HYGIENE, Vol. 51, No. 2, pp. 164–168, April 1967. Reprinted by permission of the National Association for Mental Health.

portraits have been drawn are approximately the same, any disparities appear to be of the same order. The adolescent will duly note them and proceed to direct his energies in action toward their correction. Adolescence is a time for discarding unwanted attributes and for building up others in a psychologic "spring house-cleaning."

If the scale of dimension employed in the self-portrait of the child differed significantly from that required in the comparative profile of adolescence, the resulting disparity between the two pictures is enormous. It confronts the adolescent with a big problem: how to think of himself.

Throughout his life man needs to think well of himself. The pursuit of good works and their rewards requires energies not available to those plagued by doubts about their personal worth. The young child leaves the issue of his value to his parents, who provide him with an answer through their conduct toward him. The adult has developed social and vocational competences upon which he can rely to furnish him with a sense of merit. The adolescent can no longer be sustained by the attitudes of his parents, but he has not yet acquired skills sufficient to assure himself of his place in the world. Self-esteem is the issue of adolescence, and its achievement constitutes the major developmental endeavor.

Young people who finish their self-appraisal with results indicating that they can, in fact, become what they thought they were, proceed to do so in a more or less direct fashion. Those who are confronted by major discrepancies between the self they find and the self they knew experience a grievous threat to their self-esteem. The brave and often embarrassing candor with which the threatened adolescent dissects himself and others is equalled only by the florid self-deception with which he attempts to distort the implicit conclusions. The adolescent sees perfectly the major differences between the self he knew and the self he now knows—and he can't stand it. The large, looming self-doubt casts shadows from which he must flee. The particular route of his flight derives from various intra- and inter-personal forces as they impinge upon chance and society. The general direction is prescribed by biologic endowment.

The male has an innate disposition to experience his surroundings through the direct use of his body in motion and contract. Gross motor activity is the primary masculine mode of experience. In childhood daydreams of glory, in youthful games of cowboys or war, in adolescent football, chess, or peddling papers, and in adult employment, the male gains access to the world primarily through the use of his neuromuscular capacities. Even those of passive temperament or sedentary vocation employ the mental representations of gross physical activity: they tackle ideas, push a proposition, force a sale, deliver a sermon, make a deal, or psychoanalyze a patient.

The female has an innate disposition to experience her surroundings through the use of her total person to evoke a response from others. She employs the substance of her being to obtain the reactions of others, which serve to mediate her knowledge of the world. Emotional interaction is the primary feminine mode of experience. In childhood fantasies of Cinderella with her prince, in youthful games of house or school, in adolescent parties, in adult work, courtship, and marriage, the female gains access to the world through her evocative attitude toward others.

Throughout the long years of childhood, the male and female, each through his or her characteristic mode of experience, evolve an image of themselves compounded of parental attitudes and personal fantasies of what they will be when they grow up. "What I will be when I grow up" comprises a cluster of fantasies that are unique and precious to the possessor. To the extent that they are truly personal, they are as claim-stakes on the future. The specific details are subject to change without notice as new fantasies are spun to replace older ones that are set aside.

The function of the promise remains the same—to build the mental framework upon which the adult will be made. Without it the child will need to remain a child. Yet, if he builds too high or too low or without regard for the world of others, the framework will prove unable to withstand the weight of reality placed upon it by the results of his adolescent inventory of self. The adolescent confronted with the inequality of the self he appraises to the self-claim over which he dreamt dominion has but two alternatives: he can deny the results of his own appraisal, or he can jettison the self he knew by forgetting the "what I want to be when I grow up."

Much of the aberrant behavior of youth is an attempt to nullify the findings of self-assessment and thereby to eliminate the disparity between what the adolescent is and what he wanted to be. The adolescent's rebellion is against the truth he discovered about himself.

The techniques adolescents employ to silence doubt are specified by their characteristic modes of experience: action for the male and interaction for the female. The styles with which the techniques are utilized draw heavily upon the principle of childhood play: make-believe. The rule specifies that to act a certain way means that you are that way in fact. The boy who judges himself to be weak and fearful takes to cowboy boots and a beard and becomes tough. The girl who finds her power over boys to be wanting wears eyeshadow and black stocking and thereby becomes a *femme fatale*. The high school genius down on the farm who finds himself in the lower third of his college class carries French novels on the subway and sports Ivy League clothes. Behavior provides instant identity.

Society recognizes this youthful need and generally tolerates the pranks of boys and flirtatiousness of girls. Although the style originates in childhood play, the specific skills are borrowed from adulthood. The combination contains the potential for excess that can be dangerous to the individual adolescent and to the community. The degree of deviation from the norms of behavior is in direct proportion to the disparity between the childhood dream of the self-to-be and the adolescent as he is. The prank that turns into vandalism, the flirtatiousness that becomes promiscuity, the trick that becomes fraud are all eloquent testimony to the desperation with which the actor is driven to shore up his former vision of himself.

The adolescent wields the magic of dress, mannerism, and action in the hope of achieving instant identity, rather than struggle with the slow and uncertain accretion of substance through growth. It always appears easier to change externals than himself. The speed and urgency of adolescent activity point to the intensity with which the young strive to fix a cherished childhood image of themselves in dominance over their contemporary scene. The youth decries his unrealized potential: "I'm 'way behind. Why, when Mozart was my age, he already had been dead for two years." All must be done quickly for fear that it will be too late and the truth will out. Sadly, deeds done in the heat of anxiety often lead to further failure and greater frustration. Nor can the flood to action or interaction be stemmed effectively by others, for its source is a deep biologic urge for fulfillment.

Fat adolescent boys who want to be thin exercise; they seldom diet. Fat adolescent girls diet; they seldom exercise. The boy seals his promise to himself with a picture of a football hero; the girl, with a prom formal hung in the closet or folded up in the refrigerator to dull the pangs of hunger with solace. To prove his virility the boy jousts in mock fights and feats of daring. To show her femininity the girl picks, plucks, preens, and squeezes blackheads.

But if the conclusions derived from self-assessment occasion self-loathing, the adolescent can be driven to desperate extremes. The fat boy exercises to replace himself completely in the muscle madness of physical culture. The girl diets to do away with herself in the self-imposed starvation of anorexia nervosa. Appalled at the sudden recognition that he is nowhere near the man he had hoped to be, the boy abruptly turns from horseplay to murder and stands afterward with no idea why beyond a vague longing for a thrill. Another, to silence an inner voice that mocks the gap between his dream and his reality, invites death to prove his courage, with a gun in Russian roulette or with an automobile in "Chicken." The girl who hates herself for what she feels she is not, picks, and picks open and scratches, and slashes her wrists to exorcise her flesh for failing her dream.

The alternative to such efforts to disprove the adolescent reality through action and interaction is to give up the dream, to forsake "what I want to be when I grow up" and settle for what is here and now. Falling short of his ideal, the adolescent discards it and thereby dissipates the painful inner tension of discrepancy at the cost of motivation. All lies still and quiet within. The missing dream leaves a void, which the adolescent misperceives to be of external origin. He feels himself to be congruent with a world of nothing and attributes his emptiness to his surroundings. He seizes upon philosophies of nihilism to explain his sense of loss. He affects a cynical air and embraces "beat" movements to provide an accounting for his disenchantment. The burden of emptiness weighs heavy, and the world is barren. He seeks relief through sensory stimulation.

Deprived of a dream to defend in action or interaction as the price for appeasing the demands of reality, he is left with nothing to act for. The absence of activity is death. So he must create the illusion of action through the passive exploitation of his senses. Alcohol, marijuana, LSD, and other drugs produce the mental experience of movement and change. They allow the user to believe that he is doing something—getting high, taking a trip, catching kicks—living. The illusion of action endures only as long as the sensation and dies with it, leaving the vacancy of the missing dream. As time passes, the dream passes. The day of adolescence is lost, and with it goes the future as well as the past.

"What I want to be when I grow up" begins at conception in the hopes of parents for their unborn child. It partakes of the fantasies and play of the early years and of the attitudes of parents in their conduct toward their child. It is buffeted by reality in the adolescent crisis of self-confidence. It is molded, shaped, changed, formed, and re-formed by experience throughout all the years of adult life. In old age, though it may bear little obvious resemblance to the original promise, it is still "what I want to be when I grow up."

Questions and Projects Related to Adolescence and the Function of Self-Consciousness

1. What factors influence a person's body image?
2. What role does mass media play in influencing the adolescent's perception of self?
   a. In influencing his perception of others?
   b. In developing values?
   c. In enriching his inner world?
3. In what way is the male adolescent different in disposition than the female?
   a. How would the supporters of "Women's Lib" answer this question?
4. How do adolescents compensate for what they perceive is lacking in them? Give some examples for both sexes.
5. What role does fantasy play in supplementing their needs?
6. Why do youngsters feel the need to turn to drugs, according to the author?
7. In what way did you identify with the article?

Matthew (17): What They Did in the Auditorium

His father slowly lowered himself into the armchair, sighed, curled his upper lip, then winced as he pressed his back against the chair. He crossed his legs, extended his right arm to the armrest, then rubbed his lips. Matthew knew what his father was going to say. He'd be reprimanded, lectured to, and questioned. He also knew what he himself was going to say. He'd say that he was sorry or couldn't help it, or didn't realize what he was doing, that he'd change and be more serious in school. He had packaged all the answers in his head. His father would ask the same questions, "Can I rely upon your word? This is not the first time you have promised. We've gone through this before," or, "I don't know what to do with you. Your grades are just passing. You'll never get into college. What's going to happen to you?", or "We'll send you to vocational school to learn something. You don't know anything. You'll be lucky if you graduate high school. I don't understand, Matt, you're as smart as the next guy. Just apply yourself you'll have a future. I can't afford to send you to college. Who's going to accept you with such grades?" Matthew dreaded the interrogation. The trouble he was in now was far worse than anything he had ever experienced before. He had involved Teresa in a terrible situation. There was a note of despair in his father's words as he began, "O.K. Matt, what's the trouble now? When do I have to speak to the principal, or what didn't you do?" He scratched his ear, pulled at his lip then rested his chin in his palm.[1]

"I don't know," Matthew started, his voice low, his brow drawn down over his eyes. I don't understand why he wants you to speak to him." He knew he was lying, stalling. "He didn't answer when I asked him. I told him that I didn't understand why he wanted you to come to school. My work and attendance are fine. I haven't failed any tests lately. No fights. I didn't bring beer to school." The memory of it brought a smile to his face but he fought it back and gritted his teeth. "Then why should I come?", the father asked suspiciously. "I'll lose work time. I don't mind if it helps, but it hasn't. What happened?" "I don't know, Dad. Like I said, everything is O.K." He could tell that he hadn't convinced his father. "Look Matt, I'm too busy a man to spend time with the principal if there's no reason for me to go. I have the store to attend. Your mother gets too emotional when she goes to school, and I can't send Amy—she's too young."[2]

Matt interjected, "It is important. You have to go. I'll be suspended if you don't." He lowered his eyes and looked down to the floor. He felt the blood rush to his ears and the sweat on his forehead.

"Suspended? For what? You just told me everything was all right. I don't understand. Let's have it straight." There was surprise, anger, and danger in his voice. The emotion in his father's voice unsettled his state. "What does 'suspended' mean? Sounds like you committed some kind of crime."

By this time Matthew had mobilized his strength and was quicker in his words, "I'll be kept out of classes, miss all examinations, report to the principal's office every morning and stay there." "So let him keep you there. What are you going to do then?" There was disgust and sarcasm in his father's voice. "I'll fail all my exams because I won't be able to attend class and have to do the term over. That's all."[3]

"That's all," his father echoed back. "That will sure help you. They'll chuck you out of school." Silence followed, then his father continued, "Go to night school. You told me it can be done. Work in the day. Maybe if you work at some deadening, boring, low-paid job you will learn what it means to have an education and a specialization. All my life I've suffered. I know how to sell vegetables and I'm not too successful at that. You can work for me. You know how to deal with customers. You'll have to awake early to get to the market. You know the routine. As long as there's a paper bag for you to fill, you can work for me. Hard work, long hours, no future except to struggle every day and night for years." The room was filled with despair. He wasn't even angry now. There was bitterness in his words. He was talking about his own life.[4]

There was a knock on the door, and Matthew's mother entered, and said, "You two have an argument again? What is it this time, Matt? School?"

Matthew nodded. His father said, "Have you heard the latest? Mathew is going to be suspended." "Suspended? Over what? What's going to happen to him? My God!" his mother asked emotionally. By this time Amy, who was 10-year-old, walked in and pushed herself against the arm of her father and said, "I want to be suspended, too, like a bridge," and she jumped, her legs apart, her arms spread out, "Like this," and she laughed and the atmosphere in the room lightened.[5]

"All right, Matt," he said. "What's the story? Tell it direct. We'll be with you shortly." and he nodded to Amy and his wife to depart. "I'm still not finished talking to Matt."

"Why can't I stay? What's the secret?" Amy asked. Matthew answered, "No secret. Just want to talk to Dad alone—man to man. We'll be through soon." His mother and Amy left.

Matthew cleared his throat and said, "There's this girl. I like her very much. I was caught kissing her in the back of the auditorium, behind the stage during recess." "You what?" the father asked in disbelief. Matthew repeated, "I was caught kissing this girl in the back of the auditorium." "So, there's no harm in that, Matt. You're old enough to kiss a girl." His sarcasm was more intense now. "There's no crime in kissing a girl. Maybe the principal is a prude." He was really angry now. His voice was louder. "My wise son knows how to handle things. What's wrong with that, Matt? What else happened? No one ever died from a kiss."[6]

"That's not all there was to it," Matthew answered apologetically. "We were both somewhat undressed." "Undressed? Are you crazy?" The incongruity of the situation overwhelmed him. He continued, "Kiss, yes, yes, but undressed in the back of the auditorium? Wow!" He shook his head back and forth. "Are you crazy, son?" "We were caught by the biology teacher, Miss Fisher, the one I had so much trouble with last semester. Remember? I dared to ask her about whether guinea-pigs had orgasms." He had remembered her shock, her embarrassment as her face turned red, then white with vindictiveness. She said, "Mr. Matthew, you are just too clever for your breeches. You're an impudent show-off. If you want an audience you can go to the principal's office!" That was the beginning of a difficult time between them. He barely passed the course.[7] His father interrupted his recollections by saying, "If she's a biology teacher she ought to know something about the sexual appetite of young people." His father tried to reassure himself. "But how stupid can you get." His temper subsided. Matthew answered, "You remember her. That's the old maid with a wig who goes hysterical when the class gets out of order. Once she broke a ruler on the desk in anger, then her wig slipped a bit and the whole class chuckled. We couldn't help it. She looked so absurd, a broken ruler, a face full of grimace, her wig off center. Afterward, we were sorry we laughed because she cried. I guess we didn't realize how miserable and embarrassed she felt. We were on good behavior the rest of the week." He had related the incident to his parents the day it happened. "Well," his father asked, "what did she do after she caught you?" "She took us to the principal's office after she told us that we didn't belong in school but in a delinquent home." His father interrupted again, "Maybe she's right. Then what?" "We sat outside the main office. Heard her tell the principal that we were perverted, a disgrace to the school. The principal told us that we were suspended until our parents came. He didn't say another word. No lecture, but he looked awfully troubled. I don't think he was angry with us." He stopped. His father didn't say anything—just stared at him. Then Matthew continued "I'm sorry, really sorry for all the trouble I'm giving you and now Theresa. I feel worse for her than I do for myself. She's a good kid. She cried after, not because we did what we did but because she was afraid of what her father would say and do. I told her I would tell her father it was all my fault, that it would be easier on her but she said it would make it worse."[8]

"You know what this can do for you," his father's voice was now loud and angry. "You'll be kicked out of school and no one will touch you. My son, the big shot, the hero. Maybe it will teach you a lesson. I can't. Trouble. Trouble. Who needs this?" and he buried his head in his hands.

"I told you I'm sorry. I really like the girl. I wasn't trying to be a big shot. We both did what was natural and we didn't do anything wrong."

"Wrong?" His father laughed a desperate laugh. "Wrong? You don't know what is right. Is it right to get undressed with a girl in school? Wrong? How can you say you are worried about this girl when you didn't have the sense to wait until you were out of school, some private place. You're a selfish spoiled boy. Your biology teacher is right. You need a good lesson."[9]

"Will you come tomorrow?" The question was direct. His father answered, "What should I say to the principal? That my son is a good boy, that he doesn't know what he is doing, that I have tried everything and nothing helps?"

"But this never happened before, Dad. Besides, it wasn't a crime. I didn't do anything bad." He was trying to convince himself. Teresa's reputation was at stake. If the rest of the school ever learned about this she'd become an outcast. As for himself, he'd be marked and in trouble. He remembered how Teresa feared her father. They had only been together for a few minutes when the trouble started. Her father would never allow him to see her again. If he could only speak to her now, find out how she was, try to explain to her father how sorry he was. He wiped the perspiration from his forehead. When his father said, "All right, I'll go. Tomorrow, at nine, what can I do? Whatever you are, you're my son." Then he pushed himself out of the armchair, and said in a lower voice, "This is our business. It will only excite and upset your mother."

"Yeah" he answered, and felt a certain amount of inner turmoil dissolve.[10]

Case Questions

1. What are the prevailing values toward sex in your immediate community?
2. Is his father a stereotype of a middle-class father?
3. How does Mathew appeal to his father?
4. In what way do you try to influence the actions of others by the sufferings you have experienced?
5. Is Amy's remark age-appropriate? Why?
6. What was your first reaction to reading this part?
7. What motives might Matthew have had to ask the question?
8. How would you have approached Matthew if you were his father?
9. How do you weigh the importance of what a person says or does?
10. Why did Matthew feel a certain amount of relief?

Ruth (10): Hilltop Dance

The afternoon air hung suspended with Ruth swaying gently, short swayings, on her back in the hammock. She closed her eyes to see if she could remember the pattern of the moving, slightly swaying leaves and branches that pressed against the sky. She saw it all, the intricate imposed greens, the dark greens against the lighter greens, and the relief of the different partially exposed browns of branches, and the blue, the eclipsed and shuttered blue that opened up from green to blue-framed spaces of sky. As she opened her eyes to check what she had tried to remember, she pivoted her body so that she slid off the hammock and started up the hill toward the thick cluster of trees through which a narrow path rose up to a clearing on top of the hill that overlooked the valley, the house, and a part of the creek, where she swam so often.[1]

Through the pine-scented, spring-footed path she wound her way.[2] The sudden dark of the forest made the hot afternoon air cool in these shadows. She loved to run up the slight grade because the spring of the ground seemed to help her get to the top all the quicker. She could feel the earth through her limbs, the dark smell and cool freshness as part of her.[3] Once she stopped and imagined she was one of the moving shadows in the forest, and she began to hop a few hops, but she found herself getting tired and walked until she reached the knoll on top of the hill.[4] Then she sat down and looked down at the cluster of trees she had just passed through, and the orchard below with the frame house where her family lived. A cloud passed before the sun, and a dark shadow swept the grass-covered hill. She started up and tried to catch the quickly moving sun, but before she had gone a few steps, the sun was once again glaring through the blue sky, leaving few shadows in its wake.[5]

How long she sat there under the sun on top of the hill, she didn't know, but she listened to the sound of the wind as it shifted the blades of grass, as it shuffled the pine trees below her, as it became part of the quiet background for the clearly defined sounds of a distant voice from the valley, an occasional grinding sound of an engine starting as it pulled its load up some steep road, the metallic sound of metal against metal.[6] The clouds were gathering above and the wind was beginning to tug at her legs, skirt, body, and hair. At one point on top of the hill, there was a bald spot, and she watched the dust churn itself into a cloud of whirling, spiraling darkness. She turned each step toward the sound she felt within her, the sound of muscle and wind, sky and earth, dust and cloud, turned slowly effortlessly to the whirlpool within her.[7]

Rain began to fall, first large drops, large and momentarily spaced globules of water. The rain repeated itself with the cold insistency of itself rushing onto itself. She lay there on the ground, her body flattened against the earth, the smell of green saturated with green, and her face and limbs exposed to the falling rain, her body used by the movement and dance, with the wind, sky, and earth, and the sound within her.[8] She lay there, her eyes closed, her mouth partially opened to the water that tasted of coolness and drink. When she arose, her eyes were filled with what had happened to her. She moved slowly, but deliberately, down the hill, her head tilted somewhat up into the slanting rain. Then suddenly, as if the spell had changed, she broke into a run, and her lithe limbs carried her down the hill into the dark and pungent-smelling forest, and out into the field past the hammock and onto the porch. As soon as she saw her mother, she said, "Mother, I'm so happy!"[9]

Case Questions

1. What can a child learn about himself and his surroundings while on a hammock?
   a. What was Ruth aware of?
   b. Compare Ruth's environment to that of the children you know in your neighborhood.
2. What meaning does this description have for you?
3. Is it possible for someone to "feel the earth through her limbs . . ." as it is described here?
4. Where does play end and imagination begin?
   a. Where does reality end and fantasy begin?
5. What sense of belonging does Ruth have?
   a. Compare her experience to that of a child in a slum area, a suburban area.
6. Is Ruth learning anything on top of the hill? Explain.
7. How sensitive is Ruth to nature? Explain.
8. What's the relationship between Ruth's sense of her body and her perception of nature?
9. How many children have the opportunity to experience this?
   a. How would you interpret Ruth's state of mind at the time she descended the hill? Explain.

Kathy (16) : Spring

The morning din of grinding engines, grunting horns, sing-song cries from peddlers. The smell of freshly watered spinach and strawberries, of freshly baked bread from the opened door of a bakery, of honey scents merging with that of oriental spices next to a store where barrels of pickles are sold. The coolness in the shadows and warmth in the shafted sunlight, are mulled in the soot and the dirt. The unrained dust and dirt, scents and noises combine with people who transport their interests to each of the many shops and buildings where what happens is what happened and will happen—all part of the day. The momentary action in a drama of time where few are audience to their own acting.[1]

The morning with the doors and windows opened, coats opened for the first time in months, with some people walking about in light jackets and summer pants. The younger ones thrusting their thighs and chests out, their eyes in and out to that feeling of power, curiosity, body, proudness, comparing, seeking sex and love.[2]

It was morning, and the first smoke from Number 12 building coughed up into the foul air and instead of finding a wind there, it found the night's smog and consumptive restlessness in the atmosphere. The red lights from the neons and cheap barfronts still stained the sky when Kathy woke up and looked out of the window.[3] Twenty minutes later she entered the street. She wore a loose skirt, sweater, and low black leather shoes. Her step was easy and moved off the toe, rolled slightly from side to side as if the weight of her was cushioned for the forward movement yet rested ever so fractionally to enjoy each part of the action.[4] When she entered the park, she stopped to sit and watch. The first leaves were breaking through. Small clusters of green flames, highly developed and intricately worked over etched surfaces reaching to the sunlight. Did the green know green from red, or yellow? This was spring and the air at her throat tugged at her hips and thighs, hands and breasts.[5]

Something in her pierced the heaviness and darkness of the winter months of waiting. She felt the time was for ripening, for testing and for reshaping, for sharing the new strength of the wonder of herself. She ran down a slope and felt the urge to suddenly roll sideways down the decline as she had done many times when she was young. Instead, she stopped and let her weight fall to the ground with her knees under her chin.[6]

Soon the sky was less visible, the greens pivoted their shapes magically to the wind. She lay there looking up, watching the clouds gather and come apart only to be joined by others again. The air chilled, the birds started to cover the darkening sky in fast swoops. Suddenly rain began to fall. First large drops fell, then a continuous downpour of smaller ones followed. She lay there under the full wet sky, her body opened to the rain, feeling the cold penetrate over her face, arms and legs, then through her sweater and skirt. The cold fell continuous, gently pressed against her as she gave herself to the rain and earth, as she gave her senses to that first beginning, penetrating spring.[7]

Case Questions

1. List and classify all the sensory experiences indicated in this paragraph.
   a. Which of the ones mentioned above are you familiar with?
2. How many teachers are aware of spring as it is described here?
   a. Are you still in touch with what is described here?
   b. How would you change the description here?
3. In what way does the pollution in your environment affect your perception?
4. Describe someone walking.
5. Is there any part of this description that is superfluous? Explain.
   a. When did you last describe an experience in which you mentioned different colors?
6. Is there a relationship between the surrounding environment and the way she senses her body? Explain.
7. Would you add another part to this episode? Why?
   a. How would you change it.
   b. What do you still want to know about Kathy?

Understanding Adolescent Sex Behavior

Marian D. Hall

One of the challenging, tormenting aspects of our decade is the fact that we are all too often aware that we are living through a time of revolution—social, racial, sexual—but that we cannot define it. We are *in* it but not *of* it; and we feel peripheral, out of communication with something we know is going on just outside our office door. We have sense enough to distrust our self-report surveys and to question routine interview information. We identify the retrospective fallacies of comparisons with a past generation. We fail, frequently, to attempt an overview, to synthesize research data, interview material, and day-to-day observations into a frame of reference that can be subjected to critical examination. The purpose of this paper is to attempt such an overview of contemporary adolescent sexual behavior.

When we look at referrals and adolescent self-report data, three patterns of sexual behavior seem to emerge, similar in their present symptomatology but significantly different in their history and predictive implications. Any of the three patterns can, and does, result in personality dysfunction, pregnancies out of wedlock, unwanted children, abortion, precipitate marriage, psychologic consequences of long-lasting importance, and social impact. The similarity, however, is limited to these phenotypic signs. In intrapsychic genesis and implications for current coping ability and future ego-integration the three types of sexual behavior are markedly different. Two of the patterns of behavior, the impulse disorders and the need-determined identification conflicts, are those we have always had with us (at least since mankind "invented" adolescence!). The third type of behavior, characterized by a conscious and concerned effort to redefine premarital relationships between the sexes, appears and is given new expression in this generation.[1-3]

Impulse Disorders and Character Disorders

The most overt and active of adolescent behavior problems are the character disorders. Redl and Wineman[4] have described the defective inner controls and Johnston and Szurek,[5] the superego lacunae that are characteristic of adolescents with character disorders. Frequently coming from an environment in which promiscuity and family instability are the prevailing pattern, these youngsters have internalized the model they have seen and have made partial identification with a long series of transient adults whose lives have touched theirs superficially. For them, sex is only another fast ride, and the partner is as insignificant as the seatmate on a plane ride; the kicks are in the moment of takeoff, and the danger is estimated only after the crack-up. This kind of adolescent sexual behavior (which is by no means limited to high-school students) is part and parcel of the general impulsivity, paucity of ego controls, and shallowness of feeling characteristic of the whole array of character disorders. The aim of such behavior is to ward off closeness, with its dangerous memories from a repressed past, and to foreclose the possibility of a durable relationship, which is equally threatening because it lays claims on the future.

Identity Confusion

The second group of adolescents who present signs of dyscontrols and disjunction in the

"Understanding Adolescent Sex Behavior," by Marian D. Hall. From MENTAL HYGIENE, Vol. 50, No. 3, pp. 371–373, July 1966. Reprinted by permission of the National Association for Mental Health.

area of sexual behavior is the group that rushes *into* intimacy rather than away from it. These youngsters have arrived at physiologic adolescence with many of the early pregenital developmental tasks poorly resolved. Many of them, particularly the girls, are seeking tenderness and caretaking unknown in their own lives. They are actively in search of closeness and continuity. These girls may be seen to run toward pregnancy in order to fill nurturing needs that were never fulfilled for them by their own mothers. Frequently they are driven, by long exposure to their own hostile mothers and by anger against fathers who have not rescued them, to turn to the first postpubertal love-object, no matter how inappropriate. The feelings of isolation and alienation are then both lessened and increased. Instead of being alone, the person is now one of two in the capsule; and the two are, in a real sense, encapsulated from the outside world.

This first sexual conquest is more a conquest of self than of the other. Traditionally linked with initiation rites, it brings, in our culture as in primitive cultures, many accolades of coming of age. The pressure on both boys and girls to join the initiate, to avoid the humiliation of being alone among the children while the others drive off in pairs, is more intense than we realize—or remember. There are also internal pressures—flight from homosexual fears, from incest fantasies, from threats to the security of the parental marriage and home. All of these are forces that drive the adolescent toward sexual behavior along a path of development that is universal and essential to the maturing of the individual but that is, nevertheless, ringed around with hazards and roadblocks, some that are culturally imposed and some that are intrinsic to the human conflict between impulse gratification and ego integration.

The New Search

Both of the above patterns of behavior are old and familiar stories. They are part of a picture of evolving sexual mores. The third pattern, one we have more difficulty defining because we are not always allowed in the "high councils" of its proponents, is a more revolutionary one. It differs from the second primarily in that it is a *conscious* mode of behavior. In the privacy of the in-groups there is long and painful searching into their own needs and feelings. There is a new openness in conversation between boys and girls. There is questioning of old shibboleths. Conscious and searching, this new approach to youthful sexual expression is as closely tied to a thought-out morality as is the traditional and church-based morality of an earlier generation, and it involves as genuine a commitment; but it is more individualized and more personally and verbally communicated. The young people of college age and, following our "seepage" system of cultural exchange, also of high-school age, are seriously rethinking and making decisions about love and sex and marriage. And they are acting upon their decisions; they are not just "falling" into them—to use the tell-tale expression of an older generation. They haven't bought the package deal that love, sex, and marriage are identical and inseparable. This conscious re-evaluation brings with it strengths as well as dangers. Its dangers are well known. Its strengths are too frequently underestimated: straight and self-aware thinking, clear communication between the sexes, a challenge to outworn sexual restrictions, an open, risk-taking attitude, and the substitution of responsibility and fidelity for prohibition and chastity as the desiderata of intimate relationships between the sexes.

* * *

If the varieties of adolescent behavior patterns are to be understood, it will be increasingly important to look beneath the surface phenomena. The three types of sexual experimentation mentioned here are infrequently discriminated, either in research tallies or in counselors' judgments. The extent of the divergence among the three patterns and the significance of the differences for the individual and for society are not made clearer if the traditional nosology is applied. In fact, the limitations of such labels as "psychopathic" or "schizoid" personality are nowhere more sharply apparent. Application of basic, unitary measures such as, for example, Erikson's[6] qualities of ego identity or Menninger's[7] orders of personality dysfunction is more helpful in assessing the extent of the divergence. If the wide range of behavior that is presently disguised behind a mask of similarity is to be understood and dealt with, it will demand more than collecting, counting, and classifying information under old labels.

References

1. Freedman, M. B.: *Merrill-Palmer Quarterly,* **11**:33, 1965.
2. Glassberg, B. Y.: *Journal of Marriage and the Family,* **27**:190, 1965.
3. Walters, P. A., Jr.: *American Journal of Orthopsychiatry,* **35**:670, 1965.
4. Redl, F., and Wineman, D.: *Children Who Hate.* Glencoe, Ill., Free Press, 1951.
5. Johnson, A. M., and Szurek, S. A.: *Psychoanalytic Quarterly,* **21**: 323, 1952.
6. Erikson, E. H.: *Journal of the American Psychoanalytic Association,* **4**:56, 1956.
7. Menninger, K.: *The Vital Balance.* New York, Viking Press, 1963.

Questions and Projects Related to Understanding Adolescent Sex Behavior

1. How do adolescents develop ego restraints?
2. What are some healthy and unhealthy reasons an adolescent will turn to sexual intercourse?
3. Why might an adolescent be driven to developing a close relationship with the opposite sex?
4. Make a list of the adolescents you know who are clear about what is expected of them in regard to sexual relations.
5. a. How do your values compare to them?
   b. What are some of the problems of these youngsters?
6. What is meant by individual commitment?

Liza (Adolescent) : Street Scene Then Museum

She looked down at her breasts, felt the movement of her hips and strength of her legs as they cushioned her steps. She swayed and shifted her shoulders as she moved the supple weight of her body.[1] She felt she was an animal, a lioness in the forest, naked and free, unhindered, sensing all the time that written in her flesh were unknown secrets.[2] She walked through the streets, over the mica-squared sidewalk. She felt her new awareness—like a new season suddenly ripened after a time of anticipation.

She entered the museum. The cold marble floor and wood-paneled walls, which were sectioned off with colored paintings, gave her the impression that she was walking among the pictured images of the dead. These were their painted preoccupations, and the shapes shifted sludgedly on the canvasses, from form to form, color to color, and depth to depth.[3] At first, the space slowly stirred, the waves, the heavy leaden-painted waves, the stagnant waves, shifted the horizon. Then, the body of her body responded to the dreams and preoccupations of the painters. She was an integral part of the paintings.[4]

She walked out of the exhibit room into a partially enclosed stone-arched garden, and listened to the sound of running water as it fell from a spout into a stone trough. The pungent smell of plants and the sight of straining and wandering vines growing on and over the walls sharpened her senses of her body.[5] She wanted to sit and quietly contemplate the atmosphere, but as she lowered herself to the hard stone seat, she felt that her legs resisted the slow descent. She looked down at her breasts, then pressed her arms against her abdomen. Suddenly the sound of water was partially eclipsed by the recorded music of a flute and voices of young women. She felt the menstrual pain. She pressed her wrists against her abdomen.[6] She did this with each wave of pain. Her lips were dry, and she moistened them. She sat there feeling the pain mount, rise from an unpain to a slow incline. She braced herself by tightening all her muscles, then relaxed as the pain declined and melted away.[7]

The flutes filled the archways and shuttled the silence with unfrayed harmonies and blended in with the converging and diverging voices. All the air was transfixed with the currents of sounds, each one woven into the next. She ran her fingers through her hair and over her face as the pain began to mount. She went to the water fountain, drank, looked up and saw a young man a few feet away. He held her in his eyes, openly and unashamed, and she looked down. She felt her body naked and exposed, and she stepped back and tried to avoid his concentrated and penetrating presence, but she felt that his eyes lingered on her.[8] She returned to the bench, sat down carefully, then quickly glanced at the young man. He hadn't moved. He continued to confront her—quietly and openly. Finally he walked over to where she sat and sat next to her.[9] Neither one spoke until the music was over. Both sat there, aware of each other, aware of the music and each other, the water and vines and music, the paintings, and wooden-paneled, square-filled, colored walls. Both were aware of the animal and the sense of the hunter and the hunted. Both wanted to be captured. But both were afraid.[10]

Case Questions

1. What does it mean for a young person Liza's age to sense her body the way she does?
2. Can you identify with Liza's state of being?
3. Is there any relationship between the way Liza perceives the paintings and the way she feels about herself? Try to explain.
4. Is it possible for a person to project himself into a painting, or music or other external stimuli? Try to illustrate how this works for you.
5. In what way does your sensory equipment sharpen your awareness of your body?
6. Is there anything uncommon about this kind of description? Do you think Liza was embarrassed because she had menstrual pain?
7. Can you imagine what Liza is experiencing? Is it possible to identify with someone's feelings without really experiencing what they are going through?
8. Why do you think she felt her body was naked and exposed?
9. How aware was Liza of this young man?
10. Why do you think that both were "aware of the animal and the sense of the hunter and the hunted"? What do these words imply? Why do you think they wanted to be captured and why were they afraid?

Colin (16): The Date

They teased him, said he was going to make love to Betty, that she was well stacked. They playfully slapped his back, made gestures to suggest what he would do when he was alone with her. He was sorry he told them, because she was different. They didn't understand; instead, they twisted his words.[1] He knew they chided him because they were envious of him, jealous that he was taking Betty out. Even though he sometimes felt anger creeping in his blood, he tried to remember that they were his friends, that they were testing out their own imagination as he had done so many times. Also, he thought, they were proud of him, proud that he was brave enough to date her alone.[2]

After a while the youngsters switched to their own fictitious sex-involved exploits. They tried to outdo each other.[3] Colin began to ask himself whether he had been wise to ask Betty for a date. What will they do, talk about?

The sudden uneasiness he felt had nothing to do with the unconditional indulgence of his friends' imagination.[4] Maybe he could call it off. Then he'd have to answer to his gang. This way he enjoyed the honor and attention the situation bestowed on him. To cop out would castigate him.[5] Besides, he liked the girl. Really, that was the most important thing. He was slightly annoyed with himself for being dependent on his friends' approval at the expense of making public to them what was his personal concern. Still, he couldn't help sharing his anticipated date with them because he didn't know his own feelings. He intended to discuss the matter with Chet in order to clarify his own feelings, but he didn't. Maybe he told them because he wanted to brag. Well, why not? After all, she was all the things they said she was, except he didn't want to think of her that way.[6]

* * *

Meeting her mother at her home wasn't as bad as he had anticipated. It took the edge off his fear of being alone with her. Now, at least he could tell her what a nice lady she was. The bus ride was difficult. He tried to think of something to say to Betty but couldn't. He watched two people talk to each other and wondered what it was they had to share. He wondered whether she thought he was stupid and was sorry she had agreed to go with him.[7] She seemed preoccupied. When they reached the beach, and he saw the sea, he felt more in touch with himself.[8] The smell of brine, the scattering of white caps, the awareness of her presence combined to create a mysterious unity between them, he felt. He wanted to embrace her or even touch her but was afraid to—she might withdraw or reject him. The wind caught at her hair and touched his face. The silence he first experienced with her on the bus was transformed into a type of contract of sensing between them.[9] There was a certain undefined heightened excitement in it. Her eyes and face, the smoothness of her movements were signs of it. He felt it in himself. It made him swagger more, made him catch her arm in his hand as they walked, made him take her hand gently then more strongly as they walked closer to the water.[10] Then they began to run. They both were laughing. She stopped suddenly and lay down, her back against the sand, the curve of her blouse accentuated with each deep breath. He lay beside her and began to laugh. He closed his eyes; the sun created swirls of pools, of gold and blue under his lids.[11] "That was fun, wasn't it?" she said. He agreed and the silence returned. He felt the pressure of her shoulder against his. His whole attention was centered on the pressure. He wondered whether he ought to shift it and whether she was aware of the contact.[12]

He had first noticed her that first day in class. That was the beginning. At night her image preoccupied him. He imagined her without clothes and it excited him, her nakedness under him, between her thighs, her breasts. His groin ached until he masturbated. When he returned to school and saw her he felt that he had misused her and felt the guilt. With such thoughts he had trouble looking at her directly.[13]

Now it was different. She was beside him in the sun and he no longer feared to be with her although he still was uneasy in the silence, aware of how it separated them.[14]

Suddenly she sat up and said, "Let's walk barefooted and wade," and she flipped her shoes off. They ran to the water, kicked up sand, laughed at the wind and surf. Should he take her in his arms?" he asked himself? He fought the sudden impulse back. Suppose she misunderstood his intentions, and believed that his primary concern was a physical one.[15]

They found a cove and sat there hand in hand. Desire and wonder quickened within him but he still fought the urge. They had drawn pictures in the sand, compared opinions about and experiences with teachers they liked and disliked, and watched each other uneasily. He felt she sensed his struggle. Maybe he ought to tell her how much he wanted her, to hold and kiss her, to share with her. His desire was transformed to a sadness and pain.[16] "What's the matter?" she asked, her voice low and gentle. "Did I do something wrong?" "I'...;" but the words didn't follow. He couldn't tell her what he felt. "No, everything's fine," he blurted out. "Are you sure? Maybe I said something or insulted you?" "No", and he hesitated before he added. "I just feel different about you." "Like what?" she asked, as if she half guessed what he meant by the word "different." "Well, I don't know," he said slowly, weighing his words more carefully. "I don't know how to put it in words." "I think I know what you mean," she said, her face flushed. And, in a softer voice added, "I feel different, too."[17]

Their eyes met and he no longer was thinking. He reached out to her. How long they held each other he didn't know.

The sea gulls swooped and dived, hunted up their prey in the dark blue waters, lingered in suspended flight, cawed a sharp reedlike cry. How the water rushed to engulf the rocks and sand then returned to itself again, not the same but different.[18]

Case Questions

1. Why are Colin's friends teasing him?
   a. Is their behavior age-appropriate according to your understanding of teenagers?
2. How logical is Colin's reasoning? Explain.
   a. Is their any validity to saying "even though he felt anger in his blood"? Does one feel anger in one's blood? Explain.
3. Why do you think these youngsters tried to outdo each other?
4. Is it true that what he felt here had nothing to do with what his friends said? How do you know?
5. How dependent is Colin on what his friends think? Why?
6. What might have been Colin's motive for telling his friends?
7. Did this ever happen to you?
8. Why do you think Colin felt more in touch with himself? What does this mean?
9. What caused Colin to feel this?
   a. Has this happened to you? Explain.
10. Why do you think Colin swaggered more?
11. Is their anything alien to you in regard to this description. Why?
12. Is it possible that one's whole attention is centered about one's shoulder?
    a. Has this happened to you? Explain.
13. Have you ever considered the fact that a teenager might feel guilty because he has masturbated? When? Why?
    a. Why does Colin feel guilty about masturbating?
    b. How many sixteen-year-olds might feel the same way?
14. Why is Colin concerned about what Betty thinks?
15. Try to explain why his desire was transformed into pain.
    a. Has this happened to you? Explain.
16. In what way is Betty sensitive to Colin's behavior?
17. How can you explain what Betty experienced when she flushed?
18. Does this last paragraph add or detract from the meaning of this story? Explain.
    a. What do you think happens after this?

4

SCHOOL AND ITS HORIZONS

Although the physical structure of the school generally has its boundaries embedded in concrete and steel, the individual in the learning process has no limits. He brings his private world of wishes, fears, preoccupations, failures and successes all packaged within him to class. The influence of his home and community are inextricably part of him and affect how he relates to the teachers, pupils, and learning process.

The horizons of the classroom inescapably touch on all dimensions of existence. The laboratory of ideas in school is not separate from the human marketplace—the home, the community, and the world at large.

E. P. Torrance underscores the importance of trespassing the limits of an idea by first exploring it spontaneously. Gabriella's adventurous preoccupation with the man mopping, her interest in dancing, overstep the immediate realm of the class lesson. Is Torrance's creative approach to investigating phenomena particularly different from the kinds of inner seeking Gabriella utilizes? Both deal with different aspects of relating to the environment. Are the personal ruminations of Gabriella more important than the history lesson? Notwithstanding, the inability of the student to attend to classwork is an important matter not to be underestimated. We cannot indulge our fantasy without paying a price for it.

In the next vignette we see the antithesis of what Torrance suggests. Mac blunders into a conversation with a girl friend instead of studying for an examination. Instead of broadening his scope of understanding at the time he constricts his ideas to aggravating explanations. Nonetheless, one may question whether the lesson he learns will not permit him to approach a similar situation differently. The thin line between the mundane and the creative experience is sometimes difficult to define.

L. S. Kubie underlines the importance of developing a curriculum in which the unconscious and conscious dimensions of the student's personality are given an opportunity for expression. Little would one imagine that Julia, who apparently wriggles in her seat in anticipation of the bell, is sensitive to the images reflected on the glass and recalls an incident with a fruit peddler. How many teachers are aware of the richness of the child's private dwellings, meanderings, flashes, and insights?

According to G. W. Allport the teachers we most value have a personal meaning to us. He also discusses how the adolescent's search for identity often necessitates crises.

In both Diana's and Gwen's statements we are given a glimpse of their inner world, part of which constitutes their desire to excell in their studies. The central motivating force behind their endeavor to succeed is an imposing father. Once again, we are faced with the school and the horizons that encroach upon it. The converse is also true—what happens in school assuredly affects the outer environment.

Conditions for *Creative* Learning

E. Paul Torrance

Fundamentally, man prefers to learn creatively—by exploring, manipulating, questioning, experimenting, risking, testing and modifying ideas. Learning creatively is the natural way of learning; yet we have almost always insisted that people learn by authority. We have maintained that it is more efficient and economical. Some research, however, suggests quite strongly that many things can be learned more effectively and economically if they are learned creatively rather than by authority. It also appears that some individuals have a strong preference for learning creatively, learn a great deal if permitted to use their creative thinking abilities, and make little progress when we insist that they learn by authority. Such ideas open exciting possibilities for better ways of individualizing instruction and for educating some individuals who do not respond favorably to present educational programs.

How Is Creative Learning Different?

Burkhart[1] has differentiated creative learning and learning by authority by use of the terms "spontaneous and deliberate ways of learning." On several occasions I have differentiated these two ways of learning by likening creative learning to the cat's preferred way of learning and learning by authority to the dog's preferred way of learning.

Creative learning takes place in the process of sensing problems or gaps in information, making guesses or hypotheses about these deficiencies, testing these guesses, revising and re-testing them, and communicating the results. Strong human needs are involved in each stage of this process. If we sense something is missing or untrue, tension is aroused. We are uncomfortable and want to do something to relieve the tension. This makes us want to ask questions, make guesses or otherwise inquire. Uncertain as to whether our guesses are correct, we are uncomfortable. Thus we are driven to test our guesses, correct our errors and modify our hypotheses. Once we find out something, we want to tell somebody about it. This is why it is so natural for man to learn creatively.

We learn by authority when we are told what we should learn and accept something as true because some authority says that it is. The authority may be a teacher, a parent, a textbook, a newspaper or a reference book. Frequently it is majority opinion, the consensus of the peer group. In our democratic culture, some teachers emphasize so strongly the importance of voting and the rightness of the majority that children seek to determine the truth by voting. For example, one group of children decided to determine the sex of their baby rabbits by voting. Less conforming and more creative children, however, rebel at this authoritarian approach to determining the truth. The mother of one highly creative boy recently wrote me as follows:

> My second boy has a rigid, peer-oriented person for a teacher, and she never encourages her class to deviate from the accepted, standard way of doing things .... What the *group* thinks is important to her, and they vote on everything. My son says he hates to vote and will be glad when he grows up and won't have to vote. What an attitude to develop in second-graders!

1 R. C. Burkhart, *Spontaneous and Deliberate Ways of Learning* (International Textbook Co., 1962).

From the foregoing differentiation, we might infer that learning by authority brings into play such abilities as perception, memory, logical reasoning and the like—the abilities most frequently assessed by traditional intelligence tests. In contrast, creative learning brings into play such abilities as evaluation (especially the ability to sense problems and missing elements), divergent production (fluency, flexibility, originality and elaboration) and redefinition (seeing something in a way different from the usual, established or intended way, use, etc.).

The well-known studies of Getzels and Jackson[2] and those of the author[3] indicate that the creative thinking abilities can indeed be important in educational achievement. These abilities are far less useful, however, in classes and in schools where teachers insist that children learn almost entirely by authority.

What Can Teachers Do?

At an early age some children appear to develop a preference for learning by authority. The human needs which make creative learning a natural process, however, appear to be sufficiently universal to make this way of learning a powerful one for all children. (There will, of course, still be many things which must be learned by authority.) What, then, can teachers do to provide the conditions in which the creative thinking abilities have a predominant role?

One of the most obvious ways of creating conditions for creative learning is to provide a curriculum with many opportunities for creative achievement. This can be done in many ways. It can be done by making assignments which call for original work, self-initiated learning, experimentation and the like. It can be done daily by the kinds of questions teachers ask in class and by the kinds of problems used for discussion. One study showed that ninety per cent of the questions asked by teachers of junior high school social studies courses called only for recall. Few questions called for any kind of thinking.

Reward Creative Achievements. Educational research has repeately indicated that people tend to learn along whatever lines they find rewarding. If we want children to think creatively, we must reward creative behavior. We reward children through the kinds of personal characteristics we encourage or discourage and by the way we treat curiosity needs. *We need to be respectful of the unusual questions children ask.* Nothing is more rewarding to the curious child than to find the answer to his questions. *We need to be respectful of the unusual ideas of children.* Children who learn creatively will see many relationships that their teachers miss. *We need to show children that their ideas have value.* This is done by listening to their ideas, considering them, testing them, communicating them to others, and giving them credit for their ideas. *We need to provide opportunities and give credit for self-initiated learning.* Overly detailed supervision, too much reliance upon prescribed curricula, failure to appraise learning resulting from the child's own initiative, and attempts to "cover" too much material with no opportunity for thinking seriously interfere with such efforts. *We also need to provide chances for children to learn and discover without threats of immediate evaluation.* Constant evaluation, especially during practice, makes children afraid to learn creatively.

Provide for Continuity of Creative Development. For years students of creative development have observed that fourth-graders become greatly concerned about conformity to peer pressures and give up many of their creative pursuits; that the beginning junior highs show a new kind of concern for conformity and their thinking

2 J. W. Getzels and P. W. Jackson, *Creativity and Intelligence* (New York: John Wiley & Sons., 1962).

3 E. P. Torrance, *Guiding Creative Talent* (Englewood Cliffs, N. J.: Prentice-Hall, 1962).

becomes more obvious, commonplace and safe. Through the use of creative thinking tests, we have documented these discontinuities in the development of creative thinking abilities, especially those which occur at about the fourth and seventh grades. On the basis of comparative studies in cultures outside the United States, we have concluded that these discontinuities in creative development are man-made and due primarily to discontinuities in our culture and in our educational program.[4]

For healthy creative development, the creative imagination must be energized and guided from birth. If it is stifled early, as in Western Samoa and in some of the subcultures of India, it will become imitative, if it survives at all. It is true that a vigorous creative imagination can survive early stifling; but if it learns only to act vigorously without direction, it is likely to become dangerous.

Establish Creative Relationships with Children. All efforts to establish conditions for creative learning may fail unless teachers are able to establish creative relationships with children. I like to call the kind of relationship I have in mind a "creative relationship," because it takes place in much the same way as does creative thinking. The creative relationship requires a willingness to permit one thing to lead to another, to embark with the child on an unknown pathway. It is also like the creative thinking process in that the teacher may work hard to establish this kind of relationship and fervently want it and still fail. Then suddenly it happens. The teacher has to be ready to accept it when it does happen, just as the inventor or the scientific discoverer has to do when great discoveries occur.

4 E. P. Torrance, "Cultural Discontinuities and the Development of Originality of Thinking," *Exceptional Children,* 1962, **29,** 2–13.

Questions and Projects Related to Conditions for Creative Learning

1. How would you distinguish between creative learning and learning by authority?
   a. Can you illustrate the difference?
2. When you were a child in elementary school, were you given the opportunity to use a creative learning approach?
3. What kinds of things do you think children ought to learn by authority? Why?
4. What kinds of experiences can the teacher offer his children in order to provide the curriculum with many opportunities for creative achievement?
5. List what you do in a conversation with someone that helps the other person to genuinely ask himself a question and seek out an answer?
6. What importance does Torrance give to establishing a creative relationship between teacher and child?

Gabriella (17): Kings and Mops

She imagined kings and queens in royal splendor, in gold and purple robes, amongst aged castle walls, arched stained-glass windows that cut the sun into a thousand chunks of light. She sat there, at her desk, her thoughts far removed from the teacher's lesson on the history of the American Revolution. She ruminated further, that there was a villain hero, dark and swarthy, the protector of the poor. With dagger at the King's throat who commanded the whole regal entourage to submit to his wish or else . . . "My people free or your blood." Within eyesight stood a princess, who secretly loved this scoundrel and usurper of the sovereign. She blushed modestly before his eyes when . . . . But Mrs. Fletcher, the history teacher, interrupted the serial adventure and asked Gabriella to list the causes of the Industrial Revolution. Gabriella stated that she didn't know.[1] The teacher scowled in annoyance but turned the question to someone else. Gabriella had a passing image of cotton plants, machines, people working at piecework, small glimpses of films she had seen in class, but the pictures vanished as she looked toward the hall and saw Mr. Gordon, the porter. He was mopping the floor, now drawing the thick splayed strands of the mop from the wringer of a bucket. Then with wide pendulum strokes he mopped the floor. At this point the teacher called on her again, "Gabriella, do you agree or disagree with Patricia's statement?" Evidently, the teacher was aware that she was not paying attention. Gabriella was startled and upset with the sudden interruption. She was in the wrong; she should have been listening. She anticipated a reprimand. She condemned herself at the moment that she said, "I'm sorry, Mrs. Fletcher, I was thinking of something else."[2] She felt the blood rush to her face and the muscles of her neck tighten as all the students scrutinized her.

"I know," the teacher answered sarcastically. "I want you to stay after class. Your attention is always somewhere else." By this time the youngsters in the class started to whisper. Gabriella wished she were invisible.

"Your reports are good," the teacher continued, "but you are impossible in class." Gabriella shuddered. She tried to think of something to say but she couldn't. The feeling of embarrassment was growing. She pinned her eyes on her desk and remembered how she felt after she had borrowed her mother's perfume, spilled it accidentally, cleaned it the best she could, but was aware that she had done the forbidden thing. That was when she was a small girl. Here again, she felt she had done the wrong thing and fought the feelings that made her feel it was the forbidden thing. After all, she had just been watching Mr. Gordon. The teacher had resumed the lesson again while Gabriella was drawn to the dancelike movements of Mr. Gordon as he rhythmically coordinated arms, shoulders, waist, and legs with every stroke of the mop. None of his gestures or movements were extraneous. The dance teacher had told the class that the more the action is related to the meaning of the dance the closer it is to art. Now she understood it. She'd try to simulate the mopping scene at home. She'd start her performance from the dark corner of the stage, then slowly work herself to the spotlighted center, while shifting chairs, emptying buckets, straightening books on shelves. All this in dance pantomime with no props. Then with a real bucket and mop she'd start the second scene. She'd be earthbound and dance to a trancelike beat with her mop. . . .[3]

"Gabriella, Gabriella." The young man next to her nudged her arm and said, "Teacher wants you." Mrs. Fletcher stood with her head erect, a large Delaney book in her hand. "Yes, Gabriella, you evidently didn't hear me. Now take this note to Mr. Trow, the principal." Gabriella rose, gathered her books and sweater from her desk, took the note from the teacher, and left the room. A few seconds later the bell rang, the first session of the day was over and there was a ten minute break before the next class.[4]

Case Questions

1. Is there anything wrong with daydreaming? Explain.
2. Suppose you were a teacher and Gabriella was in your class and answered the way she did, what would you do?
3. How sensitive is Gabriella to the problem of black and white?
   a. Is Gabriella learning anything constructive by imagining?
4. In what way did you imagine yourself in this episode?

Mac (17):
How to Study

He put the sports page down, thumbed through a magazine, chewed peanuts to the beat of radio jazz while he eyed his history book from the side. A half an hour for each chapter and fifteen minutes for his notes would give him time enough. No hurry. He punched and puffed up his pillow, crossed his legs and closed his eyes to the soft sound of blues.[1] As the image of Cheryl merged with the music he extended his arm to the telephone, dialed. "Hello Cheryl .... I haven't started yet ... just listening to music ... thinking of you .... I know it won't help me pass the exam ... pleasure first and business later .... ha ha .... It won't help the grasshoppers survive in the winter, ha, ha .... I know talking to you won't help me survive the exam tomorrow .... I'm not talking in riddles, wanted a distraction from my work so I called you .... Yes, that's why I told you about the grasshoppers .... I don't know what grasshoppers do in the winter, guess they jump around and have a hell of a good time in the summer and don't worry about the winter .... I don't really know maybe they have a tough time during the cold weather .... How do I know? Well, I don't really know but I said what I said just like that. If you read the story about the grasshopper and the ant you'd have appreciated what I said .... No, I'm not angry. Why should I, I didn't call you up to discuss grasshoppers .... Hello .... Well, I have to get back to work. See you."[2]

When he placed the phone on the stand he felt his hair curl, his blood boil, and the sweat under his arms exude. He had nearly exploded while talking to her. Why had he called her? To speak about grasshoppers? Why had he been so stupid to put himself on the defensive because he wanted to be clever? She was a straight-laced dud who took everything literally. She didn't know a joke from a hole in the wall.

He jumped up and stormed into the kitchen, poured one glass of milk after another down his gullet, stuffed his mouth with graham crackers until he left nothing but crumbs in the box, then loosened his belt, belched, and slowly walked back to his room.[3] When he tried to read the history lesson the words on the page started to swim under his heavy lids, the weight of the book made it impossible for him to hold. Now the words were under water, merging with the shadows of oblivion, now thicker and darker. Then he entered the dark and peaceful waters of sleep.[4]

Case Questions

1. How typical is Mac's behavior in regard to his approach to studying? Explain.
2. Could you imagine what Cheryl was saying to Mac?
3. Why do you think Mac ate and drank the way he did?
4. Has this ever happened to you? Explain.
   a. In what way does Mac represent a credible person?
   b. Is there anything about him that disturbs you? Explain.
   c. Make up an additional part to this episode.

Bellamy (16) : The Examination

Bert slipped the answers to test question number one under his desk, and between the backrest and the seat of Bellamy who surreptiously took the three by five card from behind him and placed it just under his thigh. Mrs. Stewart, the math teacher, who was correcting the students' homework, looked up just at the moment Bert tilted his body to one side, his right hand no longer on the desk. Bert, who had already passed the card to Bellamy in front of him, saw Mrs. Stewart look at him. Bert scratched his leg and smiled wanly to the teacher. He hoped that Bellamy was skillful enough not to throw suspicion on both of them. Bellamy, however, never looked up from his paper, kept his left hand shielded over his forehead, as if in deep concentration.[1] Mrs. Stewart noticed the shifting movements of Bellamy's right hand but didn't respond to either his or Bert's actions. She returned to the work on her desk. Meanwhile, Bert completed the second answer to the exam and quickly in miniscule numbers copied what he had written on another card. Then, with the same deftness, he repeated the performance by slipping the answers to his friend in front of him. Bellamy continued his ponderous efforts to solve the problems of the exam by concentrating on the pressure he felt against his buttocks. Automatically, without shifting a muscle on his face, he quickly grasped the second card and placed it just under his thigh so that when he looked down he saw it. This time, however, the answers were on the other side of the card, so he flipped it over. Now, however the example was upside down, too difficult to copy from, especially since the handwriting was even smaller than before since the math answer was a more complicated one. It was at this moment that Mrs. Stewart rose from her seat and walked directly to Bellamy's desk with the intention of asking him why she had not received his homework.[2] Bellamy looked up and twisted his face in fear that she would see the card. When she noticed his frantic expression she stopped midway in her tracks and suspected something was amiss. She signaled him to come to her. Bellamy was petrified. As he shakily walked toward her, Bert, who had sized up the situation, saw the card on the seat. He had to snatch it. He shoved the test page off the desk. As he leaned over to pick it up with one hand, he reached over with the other and grabbed the card. By this time Bellamy and the teacher were in front of the room. "What's the matter, Bellamy?" Her voice was gentle, not threatening or accusative. "She doesn't know," he thought. He was safe, and he felt the blood return to his legs and stomach. "Nothing, Teacher, just a difficult exam. I'm nervous." He felt his heart pound strongly and wondered whether she could read his mind. He looked down to his feet, then to her plain sensible-heeled shoes.[3]

"Bring your paper to me," she said with an austere manner. She was no longer the gentle Mrs. Stewart. She was his hangman and he was the victim. There was no way out now. She knew. His thoughts raced quickly through his brain. When he tried to talk the words were unclear. "I'm sick," he mumbled. "I'm very sick, Mrs. Stewart," he slurred his words. With the word "sick" he felt that he had found a solution. Now he grabbed into the idea of being sick and played it with his whole being. "My stomach," he winced, doubling over, his hand pressed against his abdomen. "I want to go to the nurse," he blurted in a half-whisper, half-hoarse voice.[4] By this time the whole class was alerted to the disturbance and situation in the class. The youngsters were whispering to each other, asking one another what had happened. Bert, who was watching everything, had trouble in restraining the broadening grin on his face. Mrs. Stewart suddenly realized that she was no longer in control of the class and said, "Everyone quiet. This is a test. I expect you to behave accordingly." Then, almost in the same breath, she motioned Bellamy out of the class and said in a loud whisper, "Go to the Nurse's office and ask her to send me word of your condition." As he straightened his back and set himself toward the doorway she detected a slight smirk on his face to which she immediately reacted. "On second thought, I want you to wait outside the door until I come to you." Again, the tide had changed and Bellamy sensed danger in her voice and in his predicament. This time, however, the faded smile brightened despite his pretended words. "But Mrs. Stewart, I'm sick, my stomach hurts."[5] "Of course it does. I think you're too sick to go by yourself. I'm going to call the assistant principal here." This she said with a slight tongue in cheek expression that only destroyed the defenses Bellamy had created for the situation. "No, not the assistant principal. I can go myself." This time he was pleading to her. "In fact, I feel better. Maybe I can sit in class and I'll be all right," and he started toward the classroom to his desk. "O.K., sit down. If you're sick don't take the test. I'll have a special makeup for you after school." He was saved, he wasn't going to be punished for cheating. Even if she knew, she was giving him another chance. It was a pity that he couldn't take this one. He couldn't possibly pass the makeup without cheating. "Can I get credit for what I did, Teacher?" Since there were only four questions to the exam he wanted credit for the one he did. "All right, if you can explain how you obtained your answer." She knew. He was trapped. She knew. Why else would she make the request? "Maybe you're right, Miss Stewart. I'll take a whole makeup this afternoon, if I'm well enough. Can I go back to my seat?" He planned to leave school during the lunch break and not return. Maybe, he could get help and study in the afternoon and evening for a makeup tomorrow. "Yes, Bellamy," and she turned her back to him as she returned to her desk. The students were once again occupied with their calculations. Bert was relieved that Bellamy had not been caught and that the episode had ended the way it did. Bellamy planned to ask Bert to help him learn algebra. Miss Stewart opened the bottom window, then sighed as she scribbled something on one of the pages of homework.[6]

Case Questions

1. Compare this approach to cheating to one you heard about.
2. If you were a teacher, what would you do if you caught Bellamy cheating?
3. What actions would you take if you were caught cheating?
   a. Is there anything wrong with cheating if you don't get caught?
4. How important is role playing here?
   a. What does Bellamy have to know about Mrs. Stewart in order to successfully play the innocent student?
5. When did you last put on an act in order to bluff a teacher?
   a. Did you feel guilty after you did it? Explain.
6. Can you identify with Bellamy's predicament?
   a. Why do children cheat?

The Psychiatrist Considers Curriculum Development

Lawrence S. Kubie

Some day education must take on the responsibility of helping to prevent the distortion of human development which we call the neurotic process. The goal is quite clear to me, but the methods must still be developed. The goal is to attempt to prevent or minimize the dichotomy between conscious and unconscious psychological processes—a dichotomy which occurs in every infant and child, and which determines the role that unconscious forces will play throughout life. This is an intricate topic. To make it entirely clear would require a discussion of what we mean by the contrast between normal and neurotic; what we mean by the contrast between conscious and unconscious; and why it is that man's capacity to think in symbols can at the same time make possible his highest development and his neuroses. In other words, we must face the fact that the universality of neuroses in human life is the price we pay for our highest capacities. Education has not yet attacked the problem of how to develop these highest capacities of Homo sapiens, while at the same time preventing their neurotic distortion. This, then, is my objective, and I shall discuss curriculum only in relation to this, because to me it seems the most important goal of education. In short, I have placed education on the front firing line of preventive psychiatry.

Consequently, I have to acknowledge that when confronted with a symposium on curricular change, my immediate reaction is to ask, How important is curriculum anyhow? My bias in the matter is that curricular changes and curricular concepts are of importance in the education of the head, but almost meaningless in the education of the heart.

This led me to look up the meaning of curriculum. To my surprise I discovered that curriculum is derived from the word *curricle,* which means a light, two-wheeled open carriage drawn by two horses abreast. Then all became clear to me. We are the light, two-wheeled carriages, and the two horses abreast are obviously the head and the heart. This gives me a wonderful out. I will turn the head over to educators and give my attention in good conscience to the heart.

In any ultimate analysis human advance always depends on the development of new techniques. Sometimes it happens that scientific foresight can pose questions and advance theories of such a nature that as soon as an appropriate technique is developed its use is understood. At other times, new techniques appear before their full significance is appreciated. They may even remain unused for a long time, or be misused, until scientific thought catches up to them. It seems to me that in education we need both a new (or at least a more inclusive) definition of the goals of education and new techniques for reaching those goals. In this discussion all that I can hope to do is to present a conception of these goals from the psychiatrist's viewpoint. The psychiatrist cannot pretend to know how those goals can be reached. He knows something about therapy—that is, about the techniques by which individuals who have been diverted from the path of normal development can be brought back to healthier ways. However, the techniques of therapy and those of education, although they are related in many important ways and have much to learn from each other, can never be identical. As a psychiatrist, I want to emphasize this, lest it be thought that the members of my profession are blind to these differences.

As a psychiatrist, I do not believe that we

"A Psychiatrist Considers Curriculum Development," by Lawrence S. Kubie, Vol. 50, pp. 241–246, 1949.

know the answers to the questions that should be asked; neither do I believe that educators today have the answers. I have in mind a specific point. I think that what we need to add to the goal of education is something that can be called emotional maturation, but as far as I have been able to observe, this cannot be imparted by the same methods as those that are used for intellectual maturation.

By emotional maturation, I mean essentially self-knowledge in depths, and the harmonious coordination and integration of conscious and unconscious levels of the personality. It is this self-knowledge, a self-knowledge which penetrates below the level of conscious awareness, which integrates all levels in the make-up of the human being who is the forgotten man of our educational system.

Perhaps it is inaccurate to use the word "forgotten," since it implies that he has once been known, and this is not true. Indeed only in recent years has it been possible to sense the full significance of the dichotomy of the human spirit which occurs during the development of every human infant and child, the dichotomy between conscious and unconscious levels of psychological organization. It is rather the little man whose existence was not even known, the little man who will ultimately become the lord of human culture if we do not destroy ourselves in the meantime.

At this point a brief resume of a few steps in the recent history of educational philosophy is desirable to place this goal in true historical perspective. The first step might be called the emancipation from the idea that, like medicine, education must "taste bad" in order to do us any good. This was a step toward unseating the great god discipline from his tyrannical throne. It was a step toward breaking down the curious, fantastic, and unrealistic distinction that mankind has made between work and play. The second step brought emancipation from a second fetish, the fetish of the "trained mind"; that is, the idea that when the mind is used on one subject it acquires an almost mystical capacity to deal easily with another. These two advances recognized first that discipline is often a euphemistic way of referring to the destructive influence of coercion; and second, that the trained mind in actuality turns out to be a trained heart. Without these two steps the third step which we are now facing would be impossible.

It should be remembered, however, that these two advances also brought with them their inevitable temporary fallacies. All new ideas must be misapplied many times before we learn to apply them correctly; and it was inevitable that this should happen in the educational field.

In the first place, these two developments, together with the early and rather naive interest in unconscious psychological processes, led to a confusion to which I have already alluded, namely the confusion between therapy and education. This is a matter of great importance; but it is not relevant to the main theme of this discussion.

Secondly, these two developments led to an increasing dependence upon the child's conscious interests as the compass and guide to lead him through successive steps in his education. Unfortunately, this is an erratic and undependable compass, because a child's conscious interests are symbolic representations of his unconscious yearnings and hopes, his fears and angers and regrets, all interacting in his mind in a complex pattern. Indeed, all through life our interests are more dreamlike than we are willing to believe. It will be difficult for many of you to believe me when I say this, or to apprehend its full significance. It is only after one has had an opportunity to study the conscious and unconscious levels in the developing personalities of many human beings that one gradually comes to understand the strange way in which a child's interests, whether at work or at play, serve as a masquerade for intricate buried emotional problems with which he may be struggling. I can give some illustrations of what I mean, but they may seem hand-picked and exceptional and scarcely credible, and they cannot possibly carry the conviction that I should like them to convey. They may, however, serve to make my meaning clear.

Yet it is important to keep in mind that a child's apparent interests are often misleading representations of his internal problems. This fact has a great deal to do with the capacity of the child to sustain his interests and to enjoy success, as well as to profit by the lessons of failure. We know that this is true in the adult world. We know that men pursue careers successfully only to end up in depressions, when the career turns out to be a faithless jade, a miserable substitute for unconscious goals. This has been realized in the adult world for many years, but it has not been recognized that it is equally true at the level of the child's interests. Nevertheless every educator knows how ephemeral these interests can be, and how easy it is for a child to double back on his tracks and turn against those very activities which for a time seemed to absorb him.

Let me give you a few examples.

A brilliant young girl in early adolescence developed a passionate interest in Greek sculpture, costumes, culture, political organization, and literature. Suddenly the interest all evaporated. She stopped all studying, and after being a leader in her class dropped to the bottom. On investigation it gradually came to light that what had captured this youngster's interest in Greek civilization was the fact that the men and women seemed to dress alike, which meant to her that they *were* alike; that this was a world in which the difference between herself and her brother, a difference against which she was rebelling, did not exist. This strange, mysterious, unreal world was what Greece meant to her. A chance remark from her teacher suddenly exploded this fantasy, and plunged the girl into reality and into a depression in which she felt enraged, cheated, and resentful. It was this disillusionment which initiated her sit-down strike.

A little boy of seven became in essence a cartographer. Not only did he take great joy in the most painstaking and meticulous execution of maps, but he also memorized timetables of train services all over the world. He became the class spokesman in all matters that had to do with things geographical. Geography led to history, history to politics, politics to the law. There, unfortunately, he tumbled into an illness which had many serious schizophrenic features. It was not an irremediable illness, however, and in the course of time and as the result of long searching treatment, the meaning of his early interests came to light. He had lost his mother in a foreign land when he was four. Then shortly before he was seven he was taken on a trip, and during his absence his nurse, on a visit to her home in Scotland, died there. In each instance death had been described to him as "going away," and the youngster's heart and soul had become entirely absorbed in an unconscious fantasy of finding again these two whom he had loved and lost. I have seen the same kind of response more than once as a reaction to the early death of a parent who was far away at the time.

Another lad at an early age became a radio expert in a modern school. He built radios galore, but he never played them. His almost obsessive preoccupation with electricity carried him through school and college and into graduate training in mathematical and nuclear physics. Then the break came when he found that his mathematical processes were touching off violent erotic excitement, often culminating in orgasm as he worked. Illness brought him to treatment. Treatment led us back to the earliest sources of his illness, which were identical with the original roots of his interest in radio. This started with a panic at the sound of a telephone bell, panic which related to many highly charged early problems the nature of which I had better not discuss at this time, beyond saying that the radio meant keeping in touch with his absent father to protect himself against certain fears which were generated by his mother's overstimulation of his erotic fantasies and needs.

Let me give one other illustration. A gay, eager, and extremely intelligent youngster, always the leader in her class, went through a long series of special interests: American Indians, Vikings, writing, painting, the modern dance, piano, economics, and several others. (Bear in mind that they began with Indians and the Vikings.) She wrote stories about little Indian and Viking boys. She painted their pictures. She dressed up to look like them. She acted their roles in little plays. She danced them. It turned out that in all of these "interests" she was acting out in infinite variety her fantasies of being made over in her older brother's image. In the end, however, since every activity left her unaltered; since everything that she attempted failed to work this magical change, it is not strange that in spite of her exceptionally high endowments she should run through such a long series of changing and inconstant interests.

These striking examples are by no means unusual. In less dramatic fashion similar forces shape the interests of every child. Furthermore, the child who develops the ability to use words at an early age is the one whose apparent interests are most symbolic. The precociously verbal child always uses words which he does not understand in a real sense. The fantasy content of speech always is greater than we realize, and the earlier verbal facility develops, the greater is the role of fantasy in the use of words. Sometimes this makes me wish that in some magical way adults and children would not share the same language; because when a child uses adult speech, he fills this bottle with wine of his own imagining, a wine which the adult cannot recognize.

If this is true, then we must ask ourselves how much difference does the curricular appeal to interest make? How much difference does what we study make? What function does interest serve? To me it seems that a child's interests are important primarily as a clue to his underlying emotional conflicts and make-up; and that his capacity to pursue his apparent interests in a sustained way spontaneously and without external pressure is a quantitative measure of the relative roles of conscious and unconscious forces in the organization of his personality and his activities. With this in mind, the curriculum becomes a kind of divining rod, a diagnostic test instrument to tell us something about the child. This may be more important than its pedagogical value in formal education.

I believe that the next problem which education must solve is how to lessen the dichotomy to which I have already referred, the dichotomy between conscious and unconscious levels in human personality.

In focusing on curricular problems, the Conference of Leaders in Curriculum Development implies that the nature of the subject matter studied, its organization and arrangement, and the method of presentation are matters of primary importance. My emphasis is the other way around. It is that the eagerness and aptitude, the duration of interests, the level of interest which is maintained, the attitude of activity or of receptivity—all of these are expressions of multiple and complex forces lying deep within the student's personality, forces which play themselves out on the curriculum. In my experience curricular innovations may cause at most a brief flurry of initial interest, which lasts only as long as the new subject matter carries with it a promise of some kind of secret magic, but no curricular change ever causes lasting differences in a student, or makes half the difference that a change of teachers can work. This in itself is significant because it places the emphasis where it really belongs, namely, on the fact that in his relationship to the process of acquiring knowledge a child (and for that matter an adult too) expresses directly or indirectly the quality of his relationship to other human beings.

All of this depends then upon the incessant, unstable equilibrium that exists in all of us between conscious and unconscious forces. Education as we now conceive it plays a direct role in the conscious area only. The goal of *psychotherapy* is always to expand the area of conscious control in human personality and to shrink the empire of unconscious control. The goal of *education,* as I hope it will some day be understood, will be to use every technique which it can muster to prevent, correct, and limit this fatal and universal dichotomy in human development.

I should like to see this begin in the kindergarten. There is where I feel sure that we could apply to infants and children the techniques of education which during the war frequently were used with troops, under the name of group therapy. Instead of bringing up infants and children under a system of taboos which make it impossible for them to talk among themselves or to adults about their hates and fears, their jealousies, their bitterness against the adult world, their bodily shames and envies and lusts, all of this could be lived out, acted out, and talked out in groups from the nursery years on. This would be a process of socialization for the savage human infant and child which would tend to block and to counteract those forces which exist in everyone and which make us repress into unconsciousness the most vital emotional problems of our development.

I have sometimes called this the Fifth Freedom, the child's right to *know* his own feelings and thoughts and impulses—not to act them out blindly, but to be consciously aware of them. This to me is where education and preventive psychiatry merge. And this is where new techniques, which have nothing to do with curricular developments, are sorely needed.

Questions and Projects Related to How the Psychiatrist Considers Curriculum Development

1. Under what circumstances is the emotional maturation of an individual student considered an important aspect of the learning process?
   a. Who is the forgotten man of our educational system?
2. Is it true that education, like medicine, must "taste bad" in order to do us any good?
   a. Does a "trained mind" create a "trained heart"? Explain.
3. In what way are the apparent interests of children often misleading representations of their internal problems, according to Kubie?
4. In what way is the curriculum a kind of "divining rod, a diagnostic test-instrument to tell us something about the child"?
5. What does Kubie mean that "in his relationship to the process of acquiring Knowledge a child (and for that matter an adult too) expresses directly or indirectly the quality of his relationship to other beings"?
   a. Indicate some examples.
6. What does Kubie propose as a "Fifth Freedom"?
   a. Does this have meaning to you? Explain.

Julia (II):
Afternoon in School (Friday)

Julia watched the hands of the clock move. There were still a few minutes before recess. The other children were also aware of the time and were anxious to leave the room. The children wriggled their backs against the seats, shifted their buttocks from one cheek to the other, slid and tapped their feet, crossed and uncrossed their legs, chewed their fingers, pulled at their fingers and pressed them against their ears, picked their noses, scratched their scalps, rubbed their eyes and eyebrows, traced an invisible line or pattern on the desk, or drummed their fingers lightly.[1]

Julia looked out of the window at her side and watched how the sunlight was reflected on the windowpanes, how each pane reflected a part of the city and the sun, captured it, captured the pool of light with the reflected pieces of roofs, other buildings, clotheslines, and refracted angular glares of light.[2] There were no trees, no swaying branches of buds or blue waters, only concrete, tar, wood frames, and glass. There were wrecked parked cars, push-wagons piled high with crates of fruit, apples in round containers, grapes in rectangular boxes, yellow pears individually exposed in rows with purple paper cushioning each one.[3] The owner was a long-faced, heavy-coated, eager-eyed man who made conversation with all who came by and talked to the children the same way he talked to the adults.[4] Julia remembered how he told her that the sun was good for warming up his bones. She didn't know how or what to answer him, so she just looked at him. She also didn't understand him—how the sun could reach the bones? There were skin and muscles, nerves, and many things covering them, so how could the bones be warmed by the sun?[5] The pears he gave to her were delicious. What she like best of all was the way the cool juices flooded her mouth when she bit into the skin and penetrated part of the fruit. She always had to breathe in carefully not to lose some of the juices, or the fluid would run over her chin, down to her blouse. This happened often when the fruit was ripe, and she took large hungry bites.[6]

The bell suddenly rang and all the children simultaneously rose before the last vibrations of the bell had disappeared. There was the rustle of books, shuffling of feet, and voices that mingled with voices in the corridor between the classrooms. Julia and her girl friends hugged the side of the staircase wall, while the boys leaped down two and three steps at a time, down to the level-landing and disappeared.[7]

Julia turned to Miriam, who was a small, narrow-faced girl with large brown eyes and smooth black hair that hid her eyes and covered the upper part of her cheeks, and asked her whether she wanted to go to her house and babysit with her. Miriam agreed and decided to meet her after she went home and helped her mother. Miriam then asked Carla if she could also come. Carla was a tall, large-boned girl with a small purple-colored scar on her cheek. The scar resulted from being hit by a rock in a rock fight. She said she couldn't because she had to help her father in the laundromat. She invited both Miriam and Julia to visit her, because they could have fun in Joe's candy store, which was next door.

The girls parted—each in a different direction, each to her responsibility. Julia arranged her books in front of her—against her chest—as she called out to her friends, "See you later."[8]

Case Questions

1. Make a list of the kinds of thing children do a few minutes before school is out.
    a. Compare this list to what college students do.
2. Are children more sensitive to this type of vision of the city than adults?
3. What neighborhood comes to mind?
4. What is meant by "talked to children the same way he talked to the adults"?
5. Do children really ask themselves questions like these? How do you know?
6. Do children actually think about these things?
    a. How do you know?
7. How typical is the behavior of the children here?
8. Are these children from suburbia?
    a. How do you know?

Crisis in Normal Personality Development

Gordon W. Alport

There is one trick every teacher knows: When trapped in a state of ignorance throw the question back to the class. Without suspecting the teacher's predicament, bright students will often rescue him.

This is the strategy I employed to learn something about crises in normal personality development. I passed along the assignment to my class of 100 captive undergraduates, and they obligingly provided me, through their own autobiographical writing, with the insights that I articulate now. Parenthetically, let me say that in my opinion no teacher or counselor has the right to require intimate autobiographical documents from students. Yet when given a completely free choice, the large majority will choose to write in the autobiographical vein. For the few who would find the experience too threatening, it should not be prescribed.

Influence of Teachers

First I shall report a minor investigation related to our main topic. I asked the hundred students, mostly sophomores and juniors, four questions with the results reported here. My first question was "Approximately how many different teachers at school and college have you had up to the present stage of your education?" The 100 respondents mentioned a total of 4,632 teachers. The three remaining queries were concerned with varying degrees of influence exercised by the teachers on the development of these students. With the percentages indicated as having played formative roles in student lives, the questions and their answers were as follows:

How many teachers had a very strong or powerful influence on your intellectual or personal development? (8.5 per cent)

How many others would you say had a reasonably strong, well-remembered influence? (14.8 per cent)

How many do you remember only vaguely, or who seem to have had no substantial influence on your development? (76.7 per cent)

We are immediately struck by the fact that more than three-quarters of the teachers are remembered only vaguely and are credited with no appreciable influence, whether intellectual or personal. As teachers, we all know the shock of discovering how little impact we have had. A former student of mine brightened my day by remarking, "Years ago I took a course with you, but all I can remember about it is that the textbook had a blue cover." He grinned pleasantly while I shuddered inwardly.

Only about eight per cent of teachers are reported as having a very strong influence, and about 15 per cent are credited with a less strong but well-remembered influence. Another way of stating this finding is to say that the average teacher (assuming all teachers are equally effective) "gets through" to less than a quarter of the class, and exerts a really strong influence on not more than one student in ten.

Varieties of Influence

Asked to tell when and in what way they were influenced the students give us three facts of special interest. First, about half of all their examples deal with experiences of intellectual awakening. For example,

She encouraged me to read poetry and drama beyond the class assignment.

"Crisis in Normal Personality Development," by Gordon W. Alport, Vol. 66, No. 3, pp. 235–241, December 1964.

In chemistry the instructor asked us why bubbles appeared overnight in a water glass. When we said we had never wondered about that, he told us that everyone must question even the most common and seemingly trivial things.

And about half of the examples deal with personal development:

She made me see that others did not judge me as harshly as I was judging myself.

He had so much warmth and humanity that I wanted to be like him.

She seemed tough and disagreeable, but was so kind and helpful to me that I realized I must think twice before passing judgment on anyone.

A second insight, based on the large array of illustrative incidents, reveals the remarkably *casual* nature of the influence. In hardly any case could the teacher or counselor have known that what he was saying at a given moment would make a lasting impression upon the growing mind and character of the student. Elsewhere (1) I have argued that in teaching values and attitudes it is not the deliberately adopted curriculum that is effective; it is rather the *obiter dicta,* the parenthetical remark, the "little true things," and above all the example of the teacher that count. And what holds for teachers no doubt holds for the counselor, too.

Finally, and most relevant to my topic, is the finding that in elementary school there are few remembered influences of special strength. Apparently development is gradual at this time, and the teacher does not often bring a sudden and traumatic experience of "dawn" to the pupil. Only 12 per cent report any strong or even appreciable teacher influence in elementary school. Fully 88 per cent of the reports date the occurrences in high school (58 per cent) or in college (30 per cent, with the college years still incomplete).

So it is in middle and late adolescence where the role of the teacher is most vivid to the student. It is in this period, according to Erikson (4), that the identity crisis is in the ascendance. The young person seems to be moving from past childhood into present adulthood in a jerky manner. Development is not continuous like a hill; rather, it is episodic like a flight of stairs. It is this episodic or crisis character of development that brings both challenge and opportunity to the guidance officer.

Nature of Crisis

What precisely is a "crisis"? It is a situation of emotional and mental stress requiring significant alterations of outlook within a short period of time. These alterations of outlook frequently involve changes in the structure of personality. The resulting changes may be progressive in the life or they may be regressive. By definition, a person in crisis cannot stand still; that is to say, he cannot redact his present traumatic experience into familiar and routine categories or employ simple habitual modes of adjustment. He must either separate himself further from childhood and move toward adulthood, or else move backward to earlier levels of adjustment which may mean becoming disorganized, dropping out of school, escaping from the field, developing hostilities and defenses, and in general becoming a thorn in the flesh of the teacher, the parent, the counselor, the dean, and occasionally of the police. Sometimes, following a crisis, the adolescent will become stabilized anew after four or five weeks of severe disorganization; but in many cases the trauma retards development for a year or more, and may even leave a life-long scar.

Turning now to my data, drawn from college undergraduates, we ask first about the phenomenology of crisis. What does it "feel" like to the student? Common is a sense of numbness and apathy. Upon entering college, the youth finds fewer strict role-prescriptions than at home. He is no longer tied to his domestic filial role, to the highly structured routine of high school, to his siblings, to his church connections, to his teen-age sub-cultures. He has left his possessions behind—his stamp collection, his television, his girl friends, his boy friends. All his familiar roles are in suspension. As one student writes,

The complete freedom of college is itself a crisis. For the first time I live in close contact with people who are not members of my family. They don't even resemble people I have known before. They have different opinions, different origins, and different emotions. I feel numbed by it all.

Interestingly enough, this sense of hollowness does not necessarily have its maximum effect during the freshman year. The excitement of new scenes and especially frequent correspondence with and visits back to the home town keep the silver cord intact. The student feels that he should prove to his parents, teachers, friends, that he can master the college environment and thus please them and win their approval as he has done in the past. The impending crisis has not yet overwhelmed him (or her—for what I am saying is as true for college girls as for boys).

It is the sophomore year that seems (from my data) to be the year of crisis *par excellence*. Suddenly it becomes no longer tolerable to live one's life for the edification of people "back home." The time has come for the child of the past to be separated once and for all from the adult of the present. Here are typical phenomenological statements of this stage of the crisis:

I feel I have been dragged into something against my will.

I feel like a rat in a maze.

I want to be a law unto myself, but cannot.

It seems suddenly that the decisions I make must be valid for the rest of my life.

To shake off parental norms and values seems to me the most important thing I must do.

The life of the past and the life of the future seem suddenly to be at cross purposes. There is often an intolerable feeling of suspended animation. Recrystalization is not yet possible. The youth is waiting still to make a choice of careers, a suitable marriage, and to find an integrative philosophy of life which his diverse college courses are too discordant to supply.

Apathy and Anxiety

It is small wonder that apathy and a paralysis of will often occur. But apathy is only a mask for anxiety. The whole framework of life is disturbed. Whereas the majority of students contrive gradually to build a new framework in spite of, or perhaps because of, the goals of anxiety, yet a large minority cannot cope with the situation unaided.

From my data, I would estimate that three-quarters are able to take the progressive road in creating their new frame of existence. About one-quarter cannot immediately do so. Proof of this point is that the dropout rate during undergraduate years is surprisingly high—over 20 per cent at Harvard, about three-quarters of the cases representing voluntary withdrawals (3). The dropouts present a special problem of guidance. Blaine and McArthur (3) write,

The drop-outs as a group ultimately do quite well if properly handled. We attempt to establish a relationship, however brief or tenuous, with these students, not so much to prevent their leaving school, but rather in the hope of giving them some insight into the determinants of their difficulties so that their dropping out can be ultimately converted into a meaningful constructive experience instead of mere failure."

After a year or two of constructive work elsewhere, the majority of voluntary dropouts return to college and graduate. But they could not have met their crisis by remaining in the environment that was the context of their conflict.

The regressive road is surprisingly common. Among eventual dropouts, but also among other students, we find such self-destroying behavior as quitting classes, a compulsion to do trivial things, playing bridge until 4 A.M., drinking bouts, feelings of unreality, fugues, and general debauchery. The candid documents received startle me a bit by the extent of plain juvenile delinquency among my innocent-appearing students:

One student finding himself unable to handle his conflicts over choice of career and over friction with his roommate, indulged in plagiarism on a term paper in such a way that he would be caught and forcibly separated from college. In this case a wise instructor, catching him in the transgression, turned the occasion into constructive counseling, forgave the deed, and put the lad onto the progressive rather than regressive road.

Here I venture a theoretical digression. The problem, as I see it, is one of interiorizing motivation. To put it in a student's words: "I am fed up with having everybody else cheer me on. I want to work to please myself rather than others, but I don't know how to do it." This plaintive statement points to a serious dilemma in our educational process. In school, the child is rewarded and punished by good grades and bad grades. Even in college, As and Bs are pats on the back, Ds and Fs are punishments. To gain love, the student must read books and toe the academic line. Finally, he obtains his degree (which is a symbol of academic love) and is freed from this external form of motivation. What then happens?

We know that a shockingly high percentage of college graduates rarely or never read another book after receiving their bachelor's degree. Why should they? Their love now comes from their employer, their wife, their children, not from the approval of parents and teachers. For them, intellectual curiosity never became a motive in its own right. External rewards are appropriate props in early childhood. But we educators, being limited by current inadequate theories of learning, do not know how to help the student free himself from the props of reward and develop a functionally autonomous zeal for learning. With our slavish dependence on reinforcement theory, I think it surprising that we arouse as much internal motivation as we do. In any event, we cannot be proud of the many educational cripples who after graduation, lacking the routine incentive of college, sink into intellectual apathy.

Crisis Areas

The counselor or teacher, of course, cannot wait for better theories of learning. He is confronted here and now with crises in the concrete. Four areas of conflict, judging from my data, are especially common.

Intellectual Crises. First, there are students whose problem is one of intellectual malplacement. Among my cases, a large number report that in primary and secondary school they were too bright for their class. The penalty is one of boredom lasting down into college work, which they still do not find challenging enough for their abilities. At the same time, double promotions in elementary and high school are not a solution. To be placed with older children often creates social difficulties far more serious than boredom. In fact, the evil consequences reported from double promotion are so numerous that we should challenge this particular solution of the bright child's dilemma.

The opposite type of intellectual crisis is also common. It is the deep disturbance that often results in college from intensified competition. It is statistically impossible for most students to maintain the same relative superiority in college that they enjoyed in high school. While this fact does not trouble the majority, it is a critical experience for those who depend on scholarship aid or who frame their self-image almost entirely in terms of scholarly pre-eminence. They are suffering a severe narcissistic wound.

Specific Inferiorities. A second area of crisis is the old, familiar "inferiority complex." Besides the sense of intellectual inferiority just described, we encounter deep disturbance due to physical handicaps or to plain physical appearance, with resulting shyness, loneliness, and misery. To be poor at athletics creates a crisis for males, probably more acute in high school than in college. To be a member of a minority group likewise creates an inevitable crisis somewhere along the line. Here again I suspect the major adjustments and defenses are prepared before the college age. Occasionally, the inferiority concerns guilt due to moral lapses. One student is still haunted by her dishonesty which enabled her to pass a certain course three years ago. She has felt miserable ever since about this critical experience and badly needs a means of expiation.

In this connection we may speak of religious crises. While they are uncommon in my sample, Havens (6) estimates that at any given time 12 per cent of college students have a critical concern, and sometimes acute crises, due to their religious conflicts. I suspect the concern is even more widespread, but since it pertains to one's whole ground of being, it is seldom configurated as a specific crisis at a given moment of time.

Another area, seldom mentioned but surely important, is the ideological crisis of modern society as a whole. Youth is inevitably worried, as are adults, by our uncertain future. Elsewhere I have discussed the withdrawal of American youth from their social and political context (5). Both the earlier and present data show an almost exclusive concern among American youth with their own lives. Compared with autobiographic of youth in other cultures, the American documents are far more self-centered, more privatistic. They are too baffled to articulate their distress, and so take refuge in their private concerns.

Sex and Family

Sex Conflicts. Needless to say, our candid discussions of crises frequently, in fact usually, report acute sex conflicts. Extremely common are breakups in boy-girl relationships which are usually taken as a disaster only slightly less fatal than the end of the world. Such breakups are so recently experienced that college students do not realize that they will, in spite of their present feelings, eventually make a good recovery.

We should face the fact that at least in the early years of college life crises in the sexual sphere are for the most part frankly genital in their reference. The biological drive is so powerful that the youth is concerned with it almost by itself. Its integration into mature love, into marriage, into career plans, into an embracing philosophy of life, exceeds his present capacity. He is likely to think that genitality by itself is maturity. Sexual gratification is frankly the aim, often with devastating consequences. At this stage of development, the students have much to say about sex and little to say about mature love.

Family Conflicts. I have left until last the most pervasive area of conflict and crisis. I am referring, of course, to the situation that exists between every adolescent and his parents. It is not enough to say that adolescent rebellion against the parents is the rule. Of course it is; but my documents show that the whole history of the relationships from the time of earliest memories is important. Almost any irregularity in normal family life is felt bitterly and may trouble a student even into adulthood. A mother who is neglectful or self-centered, or perhaps over-possessive and neurotic, leaves traumatic traces in the child's life. A father who is ineffectual and weak, or cruel, or absent (if only for wartime service) leaves the child with a lasting feeling of protest.

One document of unusual maturity notes that many college students seem to need their parents as scapegoats. They find it comfortable to blame parents for their own shortcomings. Perceiving that their parents are not all-powerful, all-wise, and all-perfect, they can say, "Well, no wonder I am having a hard time growing up; they didn't raise me right." Thus, an adolescent, having no genuine ground for complaint, may yet soak himself in self-pity, not being mature enough to relate his restricted image of his parents to the totality of human nature—not yet ready to appreciate the fact that his parents, considering human limitations, may have done a good job. Even if the job was not especially good, the adolescent seems not yet able to appreciate his parents' good intentions as an important value in their own right. From talking with many parents, I hazard the hypothesis that normally it is not until the age of 23 that a child encounters his parents on a mature, adult-to-adult basis.

This brief account of crises emanating from the parent-child relationship leads me to a final point. My students were required to discuss their crises from the point of view of personality theory. They were free to employ any of the theories they were studying in my course. Most of them took Freud. (I may add that the reason was not because Freud was their instructor's favorite author.)

The Conditions of Theory

Now my observation is this: Their Freudian interpretations seemed to fit well if and when the family situation in early life was disturbed. When the father was absent or ineffectual, when the mother was notably aggressive, when there was deliberate sex stimulation within the family—in such cases, it seems that the Oedipal formula provides a good fit, together with all its theoretical accoutrements of identification, superego conflict, defense mechanisms, castration threats, and all the rest.

When, on the other hand, the family life is reasonably normal and secure, a Freudian conceptualization seems forced and artificial. If we say, by way of rough estimate, that 60 per cent of the students try a Freudian conceptualization of their own cases, about 10 per cent turn out to be wholly convincing and theoretically appropriate. The remaining 50 per cent appear to be somehow contrived and badly strained.

I am wondering whether the same ratio might be applicable to cases that come to counselors. If a counselor or a therapist approaches every client or patient with the preconceived belief that his life must fit a Freudian frame of conceptualization, he may win in a minority of the cases, but lose in the majority.

Even where a Freudian approach is clearly justified, exclusive adherence to it may distract the counselor from many significant developments within the life—for example, from the present functional significance of religious and aesthetic values, from the competence and interests that extend beyond the neurotic core, from the client's conscious plans for the future, and from his "will to meaning" and extential concern with life as a whole.

Every person concerned with guidance, or for that matter with teaching, needs as background some general theory of the nature of human personality (2). Our tendency, I fear, is to draw our theories from the realm of illness and deviance. It is somehow tempting to apply psychiatric rubrics to all personalities, for psychiatric rubrics are vivid, incisive, dramatic, and easy. Our conceptual banners bear such sloganized concepts as Oedipal complex, character disorder, identity diffusion, schizoid, acting out, and maybe an array of dimensions drawn from the Minnesota Multiphasic Personality Inventory. All such concepts, of course, have their proper place. But personality theory for guidance and teaching needs also to be woven of less lurid fabrics.

Youth, whatever neurotic threads may lie in his nature, is busy with his realistic perceptions, with his gradual learning and quiet coping, with the slow extension of selfhood, with non-critical failures and successes, with developing a generic conscience and a personal style of life. Even in the throes of crisis, he seeks in undramatic ways to consolidate his gains and continue on the path of becoming. A theory of personality adequate to undergird the art of guidance will keep such nondramatic facts in mind. Crises in normal personality development are important, but so too is the slow growth of each youth's unique style of life.

References

1. Allport, G. W. Values and our youth. *Teach. Coll. Rec.*, 1961, **63,** 211–219.
2. Allport, G. W. Psychological models for guidance. *Harvard educ. Rev.*, 1962, **32,** 373–381.
3. Blaine, G. B., & McArthur, C. C. *Emotional problems of the student.* New York: Appleton-Century-Crofts, 1961.
4. Erikson, E. *Childhood and society.* New York: Norton, 1950.
5. Gillespie, J. M., & Allport, G. W. *Youth's outlook on the future.* New York: Doubleday, 1955.
6. Havens, J. A study of religious conflict in college students. *J. sci. Stud. Relig.*, 1963, **3,** 52–69.

Questions and Projects Related to Crisis in Normal Personality Development

1. Do you think a high school teacher should give his pupils an opportunity to work on an autobiography?
   a. What factors do you think should be kept in mind?
2. What do you remember most about the teachers you valued the most when you were in elementary and high school?
3. What is your first reaction to a crisis situation? Give an example.
4. What do you think ought to be done to help a student who continually cuts class, sleeps poorly or very little, drinks heavily, has feelings of unreality, and lives a life of general debauchery?
5. Do students study or attend a course because they are obliged to?
   a. What can a teacher do to motivate his students?
6. In what way are your readings related to your values?
7. What should be done to help the slow learner?
8. How constructive is competition? Explain in detail.
9. What kinds of racial and religious crises exist in your school?
   a. What has been done about them?
10. How dramatically involved are the young people you know with political issues? What are they doing?
11. What kinds of constructive experiences in school can be offered to young people who need sex education?
12. What conflicts exist between adolescents and their families?
13. When are parents used as scapegoats? Explain.
    a. Have you used your parents as scapegoats? Why?
14. What have you learned about yourself in reference to this article?

Diana (17): Two Sisters

. . . a fine community, lots of trees. We just had another section of the church completed. I teach Sunday school. Love it, although the children sometimes are slow in learning. Have little patience with the lazy ones.[1] The minister wants to send me to a special church camp this summer. He's a friend of my father's so I'll probably go. He is very young. I sometimes feel awful when he doesn't pay attention to me. I don't think he knows that I like him. I'm a perfect fool when I have to talk to him. He says that I shouldn't worry about not being able to pass all my classes with the highest marks, but I think he's wrong. I have to. My father and I have battles; well, not battles, but he attacks me if I get anything less than 100 or A in any of my grades. He throws up the fact that he completed M.I.T.—had to struggle and work after school. He didn't fool about in high school like the way he thinks I do. My mother either listens or says that I should listen to my father.[2]

I am good in mathematics and play a mean game of tennis, but don't really know what I will do when I go to college. My father thinks I should major in mathematics. My sister Gwen is 24 and already has her Master's and is working in an important job as a computer programmer. She's a genius, I think, and my father says I ought to be serious like her.[3] She studied hard. I think she is unhappy, lonely, if you know what I mean. No real friends. My father knows math and everything attached to his work as an engineer and he never lets us forget it. When I was a child he tried to teach me to play and fight like a boy and for a long time I was a complete tomboy. Could beat up the strongest kid, swim faster, run, and play ball with the boys. I was a complete terror, if you know what I mean. Now, well it's different.[4] I am scared of boys my age and must admit that I prefer to be with my girl friends. Maybe there is something wrong with me. We have our socials and dancing but that's all. Gwen is active in the church and in her community. No boy friends . . . don't think she ever had.[5]

We don't really fight, just squabbles, little ones. Guess she's too much like me or what I don't really want to be and that makes it difficult. I'm annoyed with myself often. Well, I can't do things well enough, feel perfectly stupid. Know I am a good student but really when I compare myself to my sister or to what my father says I ought to be doing then I am stupid. He's right, most of the time I ought to work harder.[6] We, my father and I, don't always argue. He plays the organ at home and I sing. I sing for the church choir and often am the lead singer. At home, he plays the organ and I sing. It really is fun. He's a different man when he plays music.[7] I love to sing but not performances. I can't stand audiences. You don't know what I go through; I could die before every performance. Even in school, I am in the music club, and a leader. I like the group. We have fun. I don't care for jazz.[8]

At night I sometimes dream but don't remember them.[9] Wake up in a sweat and then have trouble getting back to sleep. I love nature and can spend hours and days in the surrounding woods. I am a bit of a recluse. I like people, of course, but I feel most at home in the country. Don't give me the city with all its noise and people. We go in for shows, or for some celebration, but I'm happy when we return to our community.[10]

Case Questions

1. In what way does Diana qualify her love for teaching Sunday school?
2. Compare the minister's attitude to achievement to that of Diana's father.
3. What can you say about achievement-oriented parents?
4. Does Diana understand why she was a tomboy? Explain.
5. Do you think there is anything "wrong" with Diana? Explain.
6. What seems to have been the center of Diana's concern until now?
   a. What evidence do you have to support this thesis?
   b. Is there anything about your personal environment that seems to emphasize the same values? Explain.
7. What can you say about Diana's relationship with her father?
   a. What do you know about her mother?
8. Why do you think Diana dislikes jazz?
9. Why do people forget their dreams?
10. Is Diana a person you would like to meet? Why?
    a. What don't you know about her?

Gwen (24) : Two Sisters

I am taking courses at the University. The company is sending me. They think I have a fine future with them. They are pleasant enough. Many of the people at work are my age or older. They keep to themselves, joke with each other at coffee breaks. There are a few intrigues between them but none affect me. I haven't been lucky with men. I don't know why. I don't seem to attract anyone. I joined the church socials, but nothing ever happens.[1] Maybe I'm too old. It doesn't really bother me because I'm so busy with work and studying at the University and weekends I'm home with the family.[2] We do things together. My father plays the organ, my sister sings, and I play the recorder. My mother makes delicious cookies and cakes that I can't resist. Look at how much weight I ought to lose.[3] My mother and I are close now. When I left for my job she changed. She used to be critical of me all the time. I couldn't wait to leave home. My father was proud of me, said I was a good student. Must be difficult for Diana sometimes because I think my father makes me her model. There's nothing I can do. There's less tension between Diana and me now because I'm not home; she is the center. I was when I was home. I must say I enjoy being made a fuss over when I come home. My father used to tease me in front of my friends. He acted like a big adolescent. My mother used to become angry with him, but he has changed. Diana gets more attention now although I must admit I received more love and affection from him than she does.[4]

I think he wished he had a son. My sister and I have talked about it and wonder whether he tried to make us into tomboys because he wanted boys.[5] I was a tomboy until I began to develop and that was late unfortunately. Never wore dresses except when I had to. Saw Diana go through the same things.[6] You know, I think I always thought of my father as a kind of hero. He's an imposing man, fine looking. I think he knows it. My mother does, too.[7]

Case Questions

1. What is Gwen's primary concern here?
2. Is Gwen really not bothered, as she states here? Explain.
3. How critical is she about the way she looks?
4. How close is Gwen to her father? Explain.
5. What might have caused the tension between Diana and Gwen?
6. What can you say about Gwen's former concept of her body?
7. What is Gwen's central problem? Why?
   a. In what way have you learned something about Diana from this report by Gwen?
   b. In what way have you learned something about Gwen from the report by Diana?

5

THINKING AND CREATIVITY

The boundaries of thought seem to be unlimited. Man's constant search for meaning, self-realization, and exploration of his own internal or external environment is a testimonial to this thesis. The sciences, arts, and humanities are in a constant flux. Every shifting of the existing pattern of thinking creates a new constellation of approaches for experimentation and reevaluation. New perspectives create new awareness and raise a multitude of questions.

The vibrant beginnings of man start at birth, perhaps even before, in his effort to master and control his destiny and fulfill himself. The machinery of his brain undergoes constant metamorphosis as internal and external forces converge on it. For what purpose, to what end, with what emphasis, we might ask? The answer is everybody's baby.

Novelty is one of the elements of a creative thinking, according to J. P. Guilford. Which approach to problem solving is most appropriate for your use? Is there anything creative in Judith's thinking? What needs affect Maureen as she thinks about the empty lot? How tangible is the reality of what Joe experiences as he gazes into the sun? Is he using what J. P. Guilford would call divergent or productive thinking? These are just a few questions that you might consider as you read the article and stories that follow?

Keeping in mind D. Elkind's examination of Piaget's Conservation concept, you might want to give special consideration to whether your own experiences concerning reality are in constant flux. What quality of logic do you use in order to maintain a constancy, stability, and order in your thinking? Does Betty, in the article that follows, portray in her behavior what D. Elkind states in his article? "A child, in the presence of his parents will undertake adventures he would never contemplate in their absence?" How permanent is Betty's concept of the moon?

In reading E. B. Titchener's article you might ask yourself about the role of images and senses in your own daily life. David, in the episode that follows, nearly experiences death. What might have precipitated the dream? What is the connection between the dream and his physical state? In the episode of Leon, how would you account for the images he experienced before asleep? Is there anything bizarre about Nicholas's thinking, or can you identify with what he is experiencing? How immediate are his images? Can they be separated from the dental work he is receiving? Where does the organic dimension end and the psychical one begin? What role do senses play in the world of dreams? The answers can only be guessed at. In the episode of Claudia, the problem of separating the dream from reality is evident. How organic and how psychical are her images?

Creative Thinking and Problem Solving

J. P. Guilford

Creativity is a magic word. It catches immediate attention. Inevitably it appears in the context of the subject of productive thinking. The term is a kind of "catch-all" label, too loosely employed; only when we break it down into its several manageable implications are we able to do much—creatively—about it.

We gain some degree of clarity by discriminating among several things appearing under the label. We can define "creative potential" as a collection of abilities and traits that contribute toward successful creative thinking. Creative thinking is distinguished by the presence of something novel; novel, that is, to the thinking individual. The degree of creativity shown is directly proportional to the degree of novelty.

Another common use of creativity means creative production. We can make two further distinctions. Output might be in the form of tangible products, such as a poem, a scientific theory, a machine, or a musical composition. Some suggest that the product be socially useful. This adds the requirement of value judgments, something that is outside the scope of basic science, but is significant in the spheres of technologies dealing with human affairs.

To the psychologist, there can be creative thinking even when there is no tangible product. There are always some products of thought and it does not matter whether or not they are expressed. They can still be detected in a number of ways. The approach must be largely indirect and inferential, which is not to suggest that we cannot make observations, for we can. If we cannot get a look inside the organism's psychological functioning, it must be remembered that the physicist is no better able to look inside the atom.

For nearly 40 years we have accepted a general description of a complete act of creative production in terms of four familiar stages: preparation, incubation, illumination, and verification. The breakdown has been a matter of convenience in dividing up the total chain of events for the purposes of closer examination and discussion.

After studying over 700 productive inventors, Rossman in 1931 suggested seven stages: observation of a need or difficulty, analysis of the need, survey of all available information, formulation of all objective solutions, the birth of a new invention—the idea proper, and experimentation to test out the idea.

The most striking thing about the two lists is their resemblance to a number of sets of hypothetical descriptive stages proposed for the rough description of problem solving, from that of John Dewey in 1933 down to the present. Dewey recognized five stages: recognition of a problem, analysis of the problem, suggestion of possible solutions, testing of the consequences, and judgment of the selected solution.

Changes in behavior—the novel aspect of the individual's behavior—that come about through efforts to cope with problems, and that endure for any appreciable length of time, are in the category of learning. Thus we have logical connections between creative production, problem solving, and learning. I think it safe to say that all problem solving is creative, but it is not clear that all creative thinking is problem solving.

Productive thinking plays some role, even in the process of gaining understanding or cognition. A cognitive ability is an ability to know, to recognize, or to discover a kind of information, where the kind of information is specified by its kind of content and its kind

"Creative Thinking and Problem Solving," by J. P. Guilford, **LX,** pp. 9–10, January 1964.

of product. The use of the term "discoverer" in this connection should be restricted to instances of prompt or immediate discovery.

Where cognition is not immediately forthcoming, some productive operations, in the form of divergent or convergent thinking, or both, may be required. Realizing that one needs a better understanding of something is, in itself, a recognized problem.

Motivating influences are behind all problem solving, as they are behind all behavior. Sometimes the problem seems to arise entirely from within the motivating condition of the individual, the state of his needs, and his drives. An artist's product expresses both his conflict and the solution of this problem. Other problems arise by virtue of the interaction of the individual with his environment.

If we accept the belief that drives include the thrill of surmounting difficulties and gaining competence, we can welcome the belief that children can be motivated by needs other than hunger, thirst, pain, and sex; that they can learn to know and to value the sweet taste of intellectual achievement.

We can agree with Einstein that imagination is more important than knowledge, but we are forced to maintain that information is essential. The information that we can use is offered to us by the immediate environment, is sought after by us in the immediate environment, or is recalled or retrieved from our memory storage.

At this point, association principles become inadequate if we think only in terms of the principle of contiguity. Novel thinking means that the retrieved information is to be used in a new form or in new connections—and this means transfer learning. Information recalled for use in a new form is a phenomenon of transfer. A thing learned in certain connections is torn out of the context in which it was learned, for use in some new context.

Educators' attitudes toward the phenomenon of transfer have gone through many swings—from the extremes of "formal discipline" to belief in specific learnings only. Gestalt psychology brought us back from the latter extreme, but has failed to exert much influence.

The most interesting, and sometimes the most spectacular, phase of problem solving is that during which possible solutions are generated. The flashes of genius that occur during this phase catch the popular eye. The vast majority of generated ideas are insights of such insignificant note that they hardly justify the label of "illumination."

Facility of information retrieval depends in part on certain abilities to produce information fluently. These three abilities differ in terms of the product category in which the items of information belong; units, related correlates, or systems. Three kinds of flexibility factors help to keep the search from becoming too limited in scope and to transform the nature of a product or to redefine it for new uses. Elaboration abilities help to make additions and to achieve completions.

At all stages of problem solving, evaluative abilities contribute to the selection of the best information and the rejection of unsuitable information. The initial step of sensing a problem is itself an act of evaluation, as is the final step of accepting the finished product. At any step of the way, evaluation provides guiding influences, although there are times when judgment should be relaxed for the sake of idea production in large quantity.

The most obvious aspects of creative thinking appear to depend on the ability to do divergent-productive thinking and to effect transfer of information. Fluency, flexibility, elaboration, and redefinitions are factors playing significant roles in creative thinking and in the larger context of problem solving.

An understanding of the factors and processes in this significant aspect of learning is essential if educators are to succeed in their work, particularly with our more academically talented students.

Questions and Projects Related to Creative Thinking and Problem Solving

1. Illustrate the following four stages related to a complete act of production.
    a. Preparation.
    b. Incubation.
    c. Illumination.
    d. Verification.
2. Now illustrate J. Dewey's five stages and compare his theory with the one above.
    a. Recognition of a problem.
    b. Analysis of a problem.
    c. Suggestion of a possible solution.
    d. Testing of the consequences.
    e. Judgment of the selected solutions.
3. How might the teacher help children to use divergent productive operations rather than convergent thinking in dealing with a problem?
4. In what way do you use fluency, flexibility, elaboration, and redefinitions as creative operations in problem solving?

Judith (8): Sick

The heat didn't move except when a fly stirred it with his zigging and zagging . . . with its abrupt-lined flights and suspended intermissions. It was hot and the air was coated with sweat. Judith had been asleep and had just opened her eyes. Her mother was pressing in the other room. She could tell by the sound of the iron on the cloth, the way her mother turned the iron pointed up on its heel.[1] It was that metallic sound and the rustle of dry material, the spray from the nozzle of the bulblike container that she heard.[2] The fly was making geometrically shaped lines in the sunlight, positioning itself like the pieces on a chessboard. Judith watched it criss-cross through the dust-filled sunlight.[3] She wondered whether the dust in the sunlight fell or rose; there seemed to be golden specks that were always there. The phone rang. She heard her mother walk across the floor to the little table next to the couch, pick up the phone, and speak. "Hello . . . . Oh, yes . . . . I would love to . . . not at all . . . if you can . . . no, not now . . . yes . . . Judith's better . . . her teacher called . . . that's nice of you . . . my husband will go tonight . . . no, not tomorrow . . . . The other children are at a neighbor's. Isn't it terrible? . . . ? heard it over the radio . . . twenty-eight killed? . . . nothing—just ironing . . . she's asleep . . . I'd say about seven o'clock, after supper . . . thank you . . . goodbye . . . ."[4]

Case Questions

1. Make a list of household noises that you can recognize without seeing.
    a. Compare this list to your neighbor's. What did you forget?
2. Try touching different textures and listen to how they sound. Describe what you hear.
3. What do flies in the sunlight remind you of?
4. Can you imagine what the other person is saying? Fill in the gaps.
    a. Does this episode evoke an experience of your own? If so, describe it.

Maureen (11): Sparkling Stars

The dull backs of the pots were still dull after she rubbed them with steel wool and the red soap. She rubbed the black off, the black and red combined, and rinsed away the soap and grit. The machine-lathed concentric circles converged onto each other at every point of the surface of the pot. A radial spread of finely etched lines started from the very center point of the pot.[1]

"Aren't you finished washing those dishes?" her mother called out. She had returned from the bedroom where she had put the baby to bed.

"No, mom." She closed the faucets and reached up to the towels, which were hanging on a metal rack on the side of the dish cabinet. She looked out at the night through the window over the sink. A slight breeze tugged at the rust-colored curtains.[2]

"I'll dry them," the mother said. And she reached over for a towel. "Joseph was so tired, he had trouble falling asleep. He gets so cranky when he can't fall asleep."[3]

"Mom?"

"What is it?"

"Can I go to see Vivienne? It's early."

"All right, but make sure you're back by 8:30. Go now. That will give you more time."

"Yeah, that's a good idea. I'll leave now." And she skipped to her room and grabbed a small pad of paper and pencil and called out to her mother as she closed the door behind her, "I'll be back by[4] 8:30, mom."

It was a cool night, cool in comparison to the other nights. There was a slight wind that tugged at her skirt and legs as she walked. The night seemed dark against the lights from the houses and lamp posts. At one point she stopped and looked up. It was before she crossed the length of the lot. There wasn't any house there or lamp post, nothing but bare ground with the reflections of the lights from the building grazing gently on the broken ground. She felt the urge to go to the center of the lot. She had always been afraid of walking past the lot at night. She remembered that a house had burned down before she was born. She was told that a whole family had lived in a wooden-framed house, that they were away visiting an aunt in another city when the house went up in flames. No one ever found out how the fire started. When the family returned to find a charred shell of what once was a house, they salvaged what they could, and that was the last anyone ever saw of the family. Some people said that the fire was started by an arsonist; others, a witch. She really didn't know what an arsonist was, but she knew it was someone who was no good.[5]

She walked across the lot to the center. Nothing happened. She felt that she was defying her fear. She enjoyed the power over what for a long time was a definite feeling that something would happen to her if she would tread on that barren land. Nothing had ever grown on that land. The earth was still, charred except for a few weeds.[6]

When she was in the center, she looked straight up and saw stars. She closed her eyes and could still see the sparkle. She breathed a deep breath, and opened her eyes again. They were still there, those trembling, fixed lights. They seemed fastened on to a giant web of darkness. When she closed her eyes again, she reached up as if to brace herself by holding the stars. She caught herself as she lost her balance for a moment. When she looked across the lot to the sidewalk that led from and to her house, she felt reassured. The space was so small, so easily accessible, so small against the vastness that she had reached out at. She skipped back to the sidewalk and hurried a few more steps to Vivienne's house and disappeared through the doorway.[7]

Case Questions

1. Do you think children are sensitive to details that we often overlook?
   a. What purpose might it serve Maureen to be aware of the details mentioned in the first paragraph?
2. What can you say about Maureen's sense of responsibility?
   a. Is there anything superfluous here?
3. What is Maureen learning about Joseph?
4. What type of relationship exists between mother and child? Explain.
   a. What don't you know about their relationship that you feel might be important?
5. What meaning might this story have for Maureen?
   a. Do you think children should be told about catastrophies? Why?
6. How much magical thinking is present here?
   a. Do fears and superstitions still control your actions?
7. Have you ever experienced what Maureen did? When?

Joe (12): Gaze into the Sun

It was only after he closed his eyes and directly turned his face to the sun that he saw the red blotches explode into the white light of his eyes.[1] He felt he was high above the world looking down through the limitless atmosphere, through the slow swelling and contracting rings of darker blue clouds. "What was it like sitting high over the universe watching below?" He sat there, his back against a rock, his legs tucked under him, his head tilted toward the sun with the sea below him.[2] He watched the shifting circles of blue on blue-white and imagined that he was high over the earth looking down, suspended in space like a space ship. He tried not to feel the ground under him.[3]

The wind came and went. The sun warmed his face. It was no longer hot. He watched the blue swirlings merge with each other. He was careful not to open his eyes for fear that he would break the sensory spell.[4] "There's nothing here, nothing but space and the fullness of the emptiness. How long will this experience last before something definite moves across my eyes?"[5] No shadow crossed his closed vision, only the darker light blue against the lighter light blue.[6] He held his hand in front of his face and tried to cast a shadow across his eyes, but nothing changed. He saw nothing but a vague image of light on light, color on color, moving in and out of itself. He saw without seeing what he knew was there but he tried to shut that out in order to see only the swirlings. He could see without seeing, know without knowing what was there in the merging of the lights.[7]

The world of experience was too much with him. He could not shut it out and he didn't want to. He felt a certain exhilaration when he finally opened his eyes.[8]

Case Questions

1. Is this a common experience for you when you close your eyes while facing the sun?
2. Can you picture yourself experiencing something similar to this?
3. Is it possible to shut out other sensory experiences and concentrate on the light that penetrates through the closed lids, the wind on your face? Explain.
4. The "sensory spell"—does that mean anything to you? Describe different sensory spells.
5. Does this sound like the language of a twelve-year-old? Why?
6. When are you particularly sensitive to different sensory experiences?
7. Try to explain what is meant here.
8. Try to imagine why he felt what he did when he opened his eyes.

Piaget's Conservation Concept

David Elkind

Always changing, always the same is a French expression which nicely captures the spirit of Piaget's notion of conservation. The child, to an even greater extent than the adult, is daily confronted with change. As he grows and as his world expands beyond the home to school and community, the child repeatedly encounters new experiences and new challenges to his intellectual innocence. He is, moreover, himself a growing being so that he is progressively viewing the world from new heights and with increased sensitivity and acuity.

Change and Constancies

The ability and zest for coping with change rests, however, upon a foundation of stability. The faded, tattered blankets and dolls so cherished by children are but one manifestation of the need for constancy or conservation amidst a world in transition. And, more generally, it is the secure person who can most tolerate change while the insecure person shrinks back from new experience. Personal security in turn is based upon the assurance that something—and for the child this something is parental love and acceptance—will remain constant. A child in the presence of his parents will undertake adventures he would never contemplate in their absence.

Distinguish Between How Things Look and How They Are

What holds true on the level of personality holds equally true in the intellectual realm. The child's intellectual curiosity, his eagerness for new concepts and knowledge, is directly proportional to his awareness of constancies in the physical world. To discover such constancies the child must, however, learn to distinguish between reality and appearance, between how things look and how they really are. This is necessary because the child is confronted at every turn with apparent alterations which mask an underlying permanence. Such masks prevail on both the physical and social planes of reality. Whether the child is looking at a spoon that appears bent in water or is listening to a hostess pleading for him to stay when she really wishes him to go, he must distinguish between how things look and how they really are if he is to effectively adapt to his world.

How the child comes to distinguish between appearance and reality, the permanence within apparent change, is the issue which Piaget has attacked in his studies of conservation. In these studies he has explored the child's progressive solutions to problems, such as the numerical equivalence of six pennies in a pile and six pennies in a row, and the quantitative equivalence of substances in different forms, such as a ball and a sausage of clay. On the basis of these and a host of other researches, Piaget has evolved a general theory of intellectual growth. The essence of the theory can be simply stated: the child discovers conservation—permanence across apparent change—with the aid of reason. It is by reasoning about his experience that the child is able to overcome illusions and discover how things really are.

Growth of Intelligence

The simplicity of this conclusion should not

"Always Changing, Always the Same (Symposium—Piaget's Conservation Concept)," by David Elkind. From CHILDHOOD EDUCATION, January 1968, Vol. 44, No. 5. pp. 292–294. Reprinted by permission of David Elkind and the Association for Childhood Education International, 3615 Wisconsin Avenue, N.W. Washington, D.C.

detract from its significance or from its radical opposition to prevalent views about the growth of intelligence. Piaget is arguing that knowledge about reality is not attributable entirely to experience (the action of things upon us) but also to reason (our mental actions upon things). The permanence behind apparent change is therefore not thrust upon us from without, like the wail of a siren or the flash of lightning, but rather arises from within by the force of our own logic. Said differently, the reality behind appearance is never perceived by our senses; on the contrary, it is *conceived* by our intelligence.

Implications

The implications of this view for education are far reaching. It is probably fair to say that the teaching of concepts is at the very heart of the educational enterprise. But education has most often focused upon the static aspect of concepts and has ignored their dynamic features. It is easy, for example, to teach a child that a Winesap, Pippin and Golden Delicious are all "apples." But when is an apple no longer an apple? Across what transformations does it remain an apple and as a result of what transformations is it no longer a member of that class? Is it still an apple when peeled and quartered, when painted blue, or when made into applesauce? Such dynamic questions may seem trivial but are often of much more consequence to the child than is the static labeling of objects into one class or another. Yet the dynamic features of concepts are for the most part bypassed in the classroom. This is understandable. *The static features of concepts can be pointed to, while the dynamic features can only be reasoned about.*

Discover Constancies

We can help the child deal with the transformational character of his world both by providing the relevant forms of activity—allowing him to perform transformations of various kinds—and by engaging him with questions about states and transformations. By directing the child's actions and thought towards the transformations which alter things or leave them invariant, we can help the child discover the constancies amidst his onrushing world. It is the child, however, who must discover conservations; we at best serve as guides who make the discoveries more possible. By abetting the child's discovery of conservations, we help him establish the intellectual security which is the necessary starting point for seeking out fresh encounters with the environment. The more the child becomes aware of the truth inherent in the saying, "always changing, always the same," the more he will look upon new experience as a challenge to his intelligence rather than a threat to his existence.

Questions and Projects Related to Piaget's Conservation Concept

1. What does change and constancy imply to parents? Relationship to their children?
2. How do you distinguish between appearance and reality in regard to:
   a. People you meet in class.
   b. Things you buy.
   c. Your own physical appearance.
3. How do you help children to develop their reasoning powers?
4. What are the implications of Piaget's view to education?

Betty (5) : Her Mother and the Moon

Although the moon was blocked out by a dark cloud, the rest of the sky was spaciously lit by its rays.

"Where's the moon, Mommy?"

"Behind the clouds," her mother answered.

"Why did it go there?" Betty asked. "Is it looking for its Mommy?"[1]

"Does the moon have a Mommy?" her mother questioned.

"Maybe the moon gets up at night because it has a stomachache."[2]

"Like you had last night?" her mother added.

"Yes," the child answered.

The cloud had shifted and no longer shrouded the moon.

"Look, Mommy."

"Yes, the clouds went away," her mother stated.

"Does the moon have friends?"[3]

"What kind of friends?" her mother inquired.

"Owls have owls. I have friends. Why can't the moon play with other moons?"[4] In the next breath she changed the subject: "Tommy pulled my apron off. I pulled his. I painted first. I made popcorn all by myself."[5]

"Was it good?"

"Delicious. Umm, I wish I had some now. Mommy, I'm hungry."

"O.K., milk and crackers and then to bed," and Betty and her mother moved from the window and went to the kitchen.[6]

Case Questions

1. What assumptions might you raise about Betty's question?
2. Is Betty's way of thinking personally detached from the moon? Explain.
3. Is Betty's question a logical one from her point of view? Explain.
4. In what way is Betty using her own experiences as a frame of reference in answering her mother's question?
5. How different is the quality of thinking here compared to what it was during the discussion of the moon?
6. How did Betty make the transition from the moon to saying that she was hungry?
    a. In what way do you react to the inanimate environment as if it were alive? Give specific examples of how you do this.

Organic Images

E. B. Titchener

I wish, in this note, to enter a plea for a more systematic study than has yet been made of the images of organic sensations and their complexes. It seems to have been taken pretty much for granted that the human mind is capable of images of *all* sensations.[1] Sully says outright that "revival under the form of an image holds good of all classes of percepts or sense-impressions."[2] Ladd, whom I understand to deny the specificity of organic sensations other than the kinaesthetic,[3] appears to agree.[4] James does not raise the question. He begins his chapter on Imagination with the words: "Sensations, once experienced, modify the nervous organism, so that copies of them arise again in the mind after the original outward stimulus is gone," and his discussion does not take us farther into the body than the voluntary muscles.[5] In writing on emotion, however, he uses the phrase "either the vivid feeling of the manifestations, or the idea of them" : a phrase that seems to point towards an imaging or ideation in kind of the bodily "expression" of emotion.[6] Lay asserts that "we have mental imagery from all the senses; that is, some of us are conscious of it"; and his list of types includes images of pain, organic and emotive images.[7] Stetson remarks that "perhaps in early child life, all sense presentations are remembered equally well," but that later on attention is predominantly directed upon visual memory. "There is no doubt," he goes on, "that attention to a single sense tends to develop memory images of that sort."[8] The presumption that all sensations *can* be imaged appears to run through the general questionaries, from Galton down.

I have lately been led to take a somewhat different view of the scope of mental imagery. My present belief, acquired inductively, may most easily be put in teleological form, as follows. I think that we have free images in the higher sense departments, where such images are needed. We must have images of sight and hearing, if conversation and the various other forms of intercourse are to go on.[9] The stimuli act "from a distance," and are at any given time present only in small part. Images are therefore essential, as filling out the gaps in actual stimulation. Contrariwise, images are not needed at the lower end of the scale, for the organic sensations *sensu stricto*. We have our own bodies always with us; and the organic sensations will, consequently, be renewed or revived or reestablished when necessity arises; there is no biological sanction for the existence of images of these sensations. One might, therefore, expect to find a great variety of free imagery, say, in vision; and no free imagery at all, say, for hunger and thirst. Between these extremes, one would expect to find all sorts of intermediate stages. There may be sensations whose images can be evoked separately and voluntarily, like the images of visual sensations; there may be others whose images appear separately, but only involuntarily.

1 I write this note in some haste, and without an adequate review of the literature. This sentence may, therefore, be exaggerated; but it conveys my impression.

2 "Human Mind," II., 1892, 281.

3 "Psychology, Descriptive and Explanatory," 1894, 118 f.

4 *Ibid.*, 234 f., 244.

5 "Principles," II., 1890, 44.

6 *Ibid.*, 458.

7 *Psych. Rev. Mon. Suppl.*, VII., 1898, 4.

8 *Psych. Rev.*, III., 1896, 409 f.

9 Even here, it is not safe to generalize too hastily. "Nobody except the born blind and deaf," says Lay (*op. cit.*, 4), "would deny the existence of visual and auditory mental imagery." French, however, declares that he has "never been able to discover any distinct and separate auditory images" (*Psych. Rev.*, IX., 1902, 51). The point is not important for my present argument.

"Organic Images," by E. B. Titchener. Published in the *Journal of Philosophy*, Vol. I, No. 2, pp. 36–40, January 21, 1904. Reprinted by permission.

There may be sensations or sense complexes which occur, voluntarily or involuntarily, not in separation but merely in total situations. Thus the choking or strangling which is characteristic of certain forms of anger might be incapable of separate recall in kind, but might be imaged along with the other sense components of the emotion when anger is recalled as a total experience. It seems to me to be important that these distinctions, and others like them, should be borne in mind, in the study of imagery; in other words, that the study should be systematized. It seems to me, too, to be extremely important that the image should be differentiated from the renewal or reestablishment or reinstatement of a sensation. Certain writers upon the subject—not all!—actually take the renewal or revival of peripheral sensations as evidence of the existence of imagery in the particular sense department. They take, *e.g.*, the "lip feeling" of the word "bubble" as evidence of motor imagery. But the lip feeling is, of course, a present sensation; not the image of a sensation. The lip feeling and the image of the lip feeling are as different as the sight of a red square and the image of a red square. They can be introspectively distinguished; they belong to different mental categories. If the lip feeling occurs as such, the chances are that the image of it does not occur.

I have not doubt, in my own case, of the existence of visual and auditory images,—free images, capable of separate voluntary arousal. I have no doubt, from the reports of others, of the existence of free kinaesthetic images, verbal or other. From my own introspection, I find it extremely difficult to say whether I have these images or not. I can very easily reestablish, in present sense experience, a kinaesthetic complex; the least cue of present "muscular sensation" brings up the whole. But I doubt whether I have free kinaesthetic images; whether there is not a faint but real renewal of the sensations in all my kinesthetic "memory." In the sphere of cutaneous sensations, I can imagine pressures, and, I think, warmths; I do not think that I image colds. Taste images, if I have them at all, are extremely rare. Smell images seem to occur only sporadically and involuntarily. I notice with smells, however, something of what I have just mentioned with regard to kinaesthetic complexes. The least hint of a real smell may be amplified and changed by attention into almost anything I like. I can smell out, from the scent of a good cigar, a large number of flower perfumes: I seem to myself really to imagine these perfumes. If, on the other hand, I try without any olfactory cue to recall the smell of violets, I get to the verge of the smell image, tingle with the expectation of it; but I do not attain it. The organic sensations proper I can readily reestablish, and almost as readily inhibit. When, however, I try to secure their images, I am almost invariably balked. Pain, though I have had a large and varied experience of it, I cannot image. If I think of stubbing my toe, I get either a picture of the event or a real sympathetic shrinking and quivering, that makes me move my toe uneasily. If I think of the pain of a particular tooth, some toothpain that I know very well, I have either a verbal description or an actual thrill in the tooth: I can find no pain-image. Neither, so far as my present introspection goes, have I any image of yawning, hunger, thirst, lust, tickling, nausea, dizziness, choking, stuffiness, "sinking of the stomach," and a number of other complexes that I am familiar with but have no name for. These things come to me either in surrogate images or as actual experiences.

It is notoriously unsafe, in this field, to generalize from one's own experience. And I am aware that there are marked individual differences as regards the lower forms of sensory images. I have found persons, trained in introspection, who assured me that they had, on occasion, flashing cold images, lust images, dizziness images. On the other hand, I have never found a competent observer who affirmed the existence of images of hunger and thirst. I believe, too, that organic images are always rather the exception than the rule; and I believe that no single mind has any large variety of them. There is a great discrepancy between my introspections and those of other trained observers (Lay, *e.g.*, finds only 1.1 per cent of organic imagery in his own case), on the one hand, and the mass-results of questionnaire, on the other. Thus, of 116 Vassar students examined by French, 80 (or 69 per cent) "report that they can call up organic sensations in general, though many of them are unable to recall some of those suggested. Several note that they cannot recall any image of organic sensation unless at the time they are inclined to have that sensation."[10] A statement of this kind is, I take it, practically worthless. The second sentence shows some power of introspection; but the "several" students have evidently confused the renewal or reestablishment of an organic sensation with the appearance of its image. We have no warrant whatever for supposing that the remainder had advanced even thus far in introspection. It may quite well be the case that one and all of them have confused the weak or partial reinstatement of a certain sensation or sense complex with the occurrence of an organic image. The question asked is a question of very considerable introspective difficulty, and cannot be settled by so rough a method. I regard this and similar statements in the literature as distinctly misleading; and it is largely for this reason that I venture to plead for more refined and systematic work. I should like to know precisely what organic sensations can be imaged; whether those that can be imaged are recalled alone or only in total contexts; whether they can be recalled at will, or occur only "of themselves," involuntarily; whether and to what extent their images enter into the ordinary texture of consciousness in minds of a certain constitution; whether we all have the *Anlage* for organic imagery, and can evoke it by practice and attention; and so on. To problems of this kind the questionary method, as ordinarily applied, is not adequate.

10 *Psych. Rev.*, IX., 46, 54.

Questions and Projects Related to Organic Images

1. Despite the fact that Titchner wrote this article in 1904 is there any meaning you can attribute to the following quotes?
   a. "Images are therefore essential, as filling out the actual stimulation."
   b. "The sight of a red square and the image of a red square."
2. In the sphere of cutaneous sensations what meaning can you attribute to the following words? Experiences?
   a. Imagining pressures.
   b. Thinking—warmth.
   c. Thinking—cold.
3. Indicate in what way, if any, you experience the following images. Explain.
   a. Taste image.
   b. Smell image.
   c. Pain image.
   d. Yawning.
   e. Hunger.
   f. Thirst.
   g. Tickling.
   h. Nausea.
   i. Dizziness.
   j. Choking.
   k. Stuffiness.
4. Why is it dangerous to generalize from your own experiences in attempting to make a definitive statement concerning images?
5. How would you go about developing a research project related to "organic images"?

David (10) : Grandmother's Death

He knew that his grandmother would die because his mother and father were called away during the evening. He never saw his mother look so stony faced. She was holding herself from showing what was going on inside of her. She told him that she'd be home late. His father simply said that they were going to the hospital because grandmother was worse. He didn't say anything. He could tell that words weren't supposed to be said—that everyone was within himself, especially his mother, who kept herself together by not saying anything. She usually explained things to him, but she didn't this time.[1] No, she was afraid. He knew that grandmother was going to die. It would come to death. He really didn't understand. How would she be . . . he had never seen a dead person.[2]

His father shaved and put on a white shirt. They both said goodnight, that he shouldn't forget to check the gas and listen to what his aunt said, prepare his books for school. They said this mechanically, as if they didn't hear their own words. Before they left him, they kissed him good-bye.[3]

He was now alone. He had never seen his grandmother at the hospital. Did she breathe with difficulty, heavily like he saw dying people in the films, or did she lie quietly, with a peaceful expression on her face?[4] Once he had died. He could still remember the last part of the dream. . . .[5] He was in a rowboat by himself, rowing. The sky was dark with quick-moving clouds, the winds were thrusting the waves about. He had difficulty maneuvering the oars when a sudden wave rolled under the boat and toppled him. He remembered going down into the deep. He held his breath. The pressure of the still air in his chest began to mount until he felt that his chest was about to explode or collapse. His temples throbbed, first lightly, then strongly. The pressure in his chest and head increased quickly. The pain progressively became worse. All during this bodily experience of finding it more and more difficult to maintain himself with the mounting pressure in his chest and head, he knew he was descending the depths of the water into a darker and darker clime. Finally, after this combination of pain and growing darkness, he remembered the explosion of all his senses.[6] The end all of all awareness. The moment that followed, however fractional it might have been, was oblivion—peace, but not peace in terms of awareness.[7] He had died or slipped into that fractional state before he awoke.[8] When he awoke, he was in a cold sweat. It took a long time before his breathing was normal and his body warm. He'd never forget that dream.

When David opened the door, he was greeted by his aunt who said, "I'm cold. Let's make something hot," and walked in the kitchen still wearing her coat and gloves.[9]

Case Questions

1. Should a ten-year-old be told that a close member of his family is seriously sick and that there is a possibility that he will die? At what age should a child be told the facts of death?
2. In what way do the feelings of parents affect the child in regard to the matter of a death in the family?
3. Imagine a situation in which the adults present are so preoccupied with a matter of great concern that they have difficulty relating to or being involved with a child. Does it happen to you that you are absorbed with someone or something and mechanically react to people or situations without really knowing it?
4. Do you ask yourself or your friends about death? What are some of the explanations you have heard?
5. Do you sometimes dream about things that seem even more real than the actual everyday world? Can you remember a dream in which you experienced something close to death?
6. Can you identify with the description of the dream?
7. What does "oblivion-peace" suggest to you? Do you think there can be peace without awareness? What does awareness mean to you?
8. Is death here a fractional state of awareness or an actual death? Are you sure of the meaning of the sentence? Explain.
9. Is there a change of feeling in this vignette when the aunt enters the scene of the apartment? Explain.

Leon (12): Night Restlessness

Another rain and streets cleaned over—a few people scurrying over the walks, others picking their way from lamp-post to lamp-light and back into the dark again. It was the hour when the city slept, when the cats wandered from under one car to the next, when a scavenger examined and reexamined the contents in a garbage can. The hour when a dark silhouette of a house was broken by a rectangle of light and a child's shrill cry stirred the silence.[1]

The night's silence disturbed by a voice, a car, a siren, or a rattling hinged gate or shutter. For Leon, it was a time of not being able to sleep, of listening to what was on the outside, the muffled and distinct sounds, of listening to what was on the inside, fleeting thoughts, pictures that seemed to be tossed about by currents of other impressions. Words . . . pictures . . . wanderings and the awareness of not being able to sleep and knowing that tomorrow was another day.[2]

The stomach cramp didn't subside when he held his hands over the area. He tried to find some relief by lying on his stomach but it didn't help. He wondered how people managed to sleep on their stomachs. He wished he could move his bowels. Maybe that would help him, but he didn't feel any pressure in his intestines. No, it was something he ate. The pain was a dull one, not intense enough to disturb his parents . . . not bad enough, but unpleasant enough to keep him awake.[3]

He rose, went into the kitchen, and was about to drink some water, when his mother entered. Her eyes were somewhat puffy. She shielded her eyes from the light.

"What's the trouble?"

"My stomach hurts."

"How much?"

"Just pains a bit, don't know what it is."

She put her palm on his forehead, then on the back of his neck.

"You're hot. Go to bed. I'll take your temperature, and make you something hot."

She opened the faucet and filled a kettle. Leon had 102 when his mother gave him two aspirins and a large glass of hot lemonade. The lemon was inside the glass, the bits of lemon were sweet. The glass was too hot to handle at first. His mother closed the window and kissed him good night. He knew that the lemonade would be delicious when he woke up. He sipped the drink—it was still hot, but it didn't burn his throat.[4]

He felt the weariness come over him . . . the heat of his body was intense. He was uncomfortably hot, but he knew that he had to keep the blankets on. He covered himself up to his neck, but turned up the blanket to allow the cool air to enter, then pulled the end up to his chin. He reached out and closed the light. It was better in the dark. The dark was filled with swarms of black dots. He tried to figure out the path they took, but they converged onto each other whatever way he looked. After a while, the black behind the dots was less black.[5] They came, they disappeared, into the larger blackness. It was probably due to the after image of the light. His eyes were not yet used to the darkness. His eyes were heavy now. He was slipping over a smooth surface, caught in some slow tide, on top of a large wave . . . over a smooth surface. First there was the largeness and smoothness and the vision and the actual physical sensation of it.[6] Then there was a contraction of the wave. All this happened automatically. He was careful not to budge or think about anything . . . for fear he'd upset the whole pattern of the internal image. It was at such times that he completely concentrated on the experience, that he knew if he disturbed the self-perpetuating process, he would have difficulty sleeping.[7] He was slipping into sleep now because the space was smaller, less visible, neither up nor down, nor sideways . . . just there . . . there . . . there . . . .[8]

Case Questions

1. What part of the city is being depicted here?
   a. How would the same rain and hour look in a plush suburban community?
2. Describe a child trying to fall asleep.
3. Is Leon aware of others even though he doesn't feel well? Explain.
4. How "typical" is Leon's mother's behavior toward Leon?
   a. What drinks do you remember you drank at night when you were sick?
5. Is this an actual image or what he is imagining?
6. Have you ever experienced this? Explain.
7. Describe a similar experience of your own.
8. What do children of different ages think about before they go to sleep? How do you know?
   a. How would you go about setting up a research design in order to investigate this phenomenon?

Nicholas (14) : At the Dentist

He looked up at the dentist, who adjusted the rims of his glasses closer to his eyes. They had dislodged themselves from his ears after Nicholas had yelled some inarticulate sound. What had happened was that the drill had slipped from the side wall of the tooth and hit the nerve directly. There was nothing he could say, but he could yell. The pain was sharp and went quick and direct all through him, especially through his head. Smooth, a velvet pain, black and complete.[1] The expression on the dentist dentist's face changed from a fixed concentrated look to one of slight relief each time he turned away from his patient to take an instrument.

He was about to drill again. Nicholas knew the dentist didn't like it when he yelled. Maybe it was safer if he didn't complain. He didn't want to wince or show any signs of discomfort, but that last one was awful. Suppose he really likes to hurt. Maybe he really doesn't care when he says, "Sorry," as he did before. Maybe he says that because he wants to give the patient the impression that it isn't intentional. Look at him now. He's gritting his teeth again as if he's trying to vault a fence after a short spurt of running. Why should he use all his effort? Here it comes. I'm not going to think of . . . the droning, buzzing, and drawing pain that . . . "AyeeOWWWW." The bastard . . . he's trying to kill me.[2] Zzzz. Didn't I see him smile just a bit? He's enjoying this. Stop hurting me. "Aye oogh urth." He didn't understand. How can I speak with all this junk—pads and stuff—in my mouth? That hook is starting to hurt my tongue. I wish he'd move it or take some of the weight off it.[3] Now he's starting to fix another drill bit in the vice . . . it looks smaller. Maybe I should have taken some of those shots . . . that cane stuff, but I hate it the way he puts it in the gum. For hours later I feel like I have hot potatoes in my mouth and my gum hurts. This is better . . . .

Here he goes again. I'll think of . . . let's see . . . taking a subway ride. Now all the people are entering. There's a girl wearing[4] . . . the droning, droning, drilling, shaking, ayeahh, now he's putting water on it. It wasn't as bad as before . . . . He's starting again . . . he's getting closer. I'll try to relax and go with it when it hurts . . . think it's enjoyable like . . . ayeahh . . . . Now he's blowing that hot air into it . . . ayeahh . . . . I wonder what he thinks when he sees me here . . . whether he knows that I hate him.[5] He's mean . . . just like those kids that purposely enjoy killing animals. Wonder what he'd be if he were an Indian? A witch doctor? He'd give people all kinds of initiations. He'd be one of the worst because . . . now he's starting on another tooth. When I hold the armrests right, it helps because I can yell by digging my nails into the leather-covered armrests. It helps. For some reason I continue to hold the armrest with all my strength, even after he stops drilling. I still feel that thing digging away at me. I wonder whether he really sees the nerve. It's supposed to be small. It feels big—as big as my head when it blooms into pain.[6]

He doesn't have much chance to speak to anyone. He just drills. His nurse isn't here today. When she holds my bottom, I don't feel the drilling. Wonder whether she knows that I like it. She's much older than I. She's about 19 or so. She doesn't smell like that medicine in my mouth. She wears a special perfume, like flowers.[7] Now he's rolling the silver between his fingers. What's this? He's taking some of the padding out of my mouth. What's that . . . yes . . . it's that metal ring that he tightens about my tooth. I guess it's necessary, but it hurt last time . . . so the filling doesn't go off the side. The tightening . . . my gums, I can feel it cut into my gum. It hurts, but it doesn't compare to drilling . . . at least when the pain is there and constant you get used to it. It doesn't come right away. I wonder whether my nerves get pain-tired after a while, or, I do. Less resistance to pain. I'm sweating here, feel the back of the chair stuck to my shirt.[8] He's rolling the stuff together . . . he'll press it into my tooth . . . sounds like someone walking on snow, the kind that packs . . . feels like it sounds.[9] Now he's running that tool over it and smoothing it out. He's tired . . . maybe he gets bored with filling teeth all the time and having people look up at him as if he's a murderer. I suppose he's important to have around. Ayee aye . . . that ring . . . the clumsy bastard . . . it hurts . . . the bastard! I don't trust him.[10]

"We have to clean your teeth next week." I know what that means—another session of his drilling as he searches under the gums for that tar stuff.

"Yes, Doctor. When should I come next week?" He's busy with his books . . . everything is so neat . . . with all those different colored charts and negatives and small writing and all of it filed away. What would he do if he tried to figure out what I write in my notebook when . . . ?"

"Next week, the same day and time."

I hate that train trip—it kills the whole afternoon.

"Thank you, Doctor—I'll see you next week. Right?"[12]

"Yes," the dentist answered and looked up from what he was writing.

He's annoyed with me because I talk too much. I feel like telling him what I think of him but he knows he has the upper hand.

"O.K., Doctor. Good-bye and thank you!"

Why did I thank him? I didn't have to do that, I was thanking him for what, for hurting me or working on my teeth. He gets paid for it. Maybe I thanked him because I'm glad he didn't make it worse for me.

"You're welcome, Nicholas."

That was nice of him to call me Nicholas! It makes me feel like I'm a person instead of a card or a numbered patient. He's not so bad . . . I guess he's all right. I'd better leave now before I spoil everything . . . and Nicholas left the dentist's office.[13]

Case Questions

1. Can you identify with Nicholas's predicament?
   a. Is the image of "smooth, a velvet pain, black and complete" an appropriate one for what Nicholas is experiencing?
2. Have you ever wondered whether a dentist finds pleasure in hurting his patients? When?
   a. What is it like for you when you go to a dentist?
3. How well can you think with something weighed down on your tongue, or with your tongue touching the roof of your mouth?
   a. Find out how well children can add a series of numbers while they hold their tongues?
4. Why do you think Nicholas is thinking of a girl on a subway?
5. Why are his feelings so intense?
6. Have you ever dug your nails into anything as a means of lessening pain? Explain.
   a. Why did the pain feel as big as his head?
7. What can you tell about Nicholas's interest in the opposite sex?
8. Why does our attention shift from one thing to another?
9. Is the image of walking on snow appropriate here? Explain.
10. Does cursing serve any function here? Explain.
11. Is Nicholas sensitive to the dentist's reactions? Why?
12. Is Nicholas polite to the doctor? Why?
13. Why do you think Nicholas felt more like a person just because the dentist called him by his name?
    a. What will happen when Nicholas returns to the dentist?

Claudia (16) : The Dream

It was morning and the thick dew that hung over the grasses neither rose nor descended. Claudia had the impression that there wasn't any sky, only a thick cloud of translucent material drawn down over the green earth.[1] It was morning, and her sleep had been disturbed by dreams intermittently throughout its course. At one point she dreamt that she was a ship at sea sailing against a furious wind.[2] She was rocked, pitched, and buffeted by wave and gale.[3] She had no center—no hold. She was a three-dimensional amoebic mass in constant shift.[4]

When she awoke, she was drenched with perspiration.[5] It was as if one of the waves had caught and enveloped her in its passage. She lay there exhausted without fully remembering the dream recalling only its skeletal framework.[6] She was the wrecked hull of a ship, moored to its own desecration, partially sea sogged and sand logged.[7] After a while, sleep fell over her, and she returned to the darkness of another dream that spun its web within her.[8] She was going down a long passage. Water dripped drop by drop, in repetition and in predictable beats just behind her, like footsteps following her.[9] When she stopped, the beat continued at the same tempo.[10] When she ran, the pace didn't change. She was cold and called out but didn't hear her voice until after she stopped calling.[11] She jumped and found herself pinned to the ground. She suddenly rose from, then fell to the ground. She clapped her hands but didn't hear any sounds until a moment after she stopped.[12] Still the water fell. Each time a drop touched the ground, she heard its reverberation. She cupped her hand out to catch the water, but the water fell through her palms onto the ground.[13] Then as she listened more carefully to the beat, it was saying something to her.[14] It was one word, always one word, but the sound was too feeble for her to really know what it was.

Then the beat stopped, and there were no more drops. She was no longer in a tunnel but all was black. She woke up and found the room just as black as her dream. She wasn't sure whether she had entered into another dream.[15] Perhaps this was just a continuation of the same one. She reached out behind her where she knew there was a lamp and when she touched it, pressed the switch. There was no light. This was the dream. She had to get out of it.[16] She rose from the bed and touched and examined the furniture that she knew was in her room. Maybe the electric cord of the lamp was disconnected, or the filament of the bulb blown out? She had a plan. She'd call out. She heard her voice. She dug her fingernails into her palms and felt the pain. She still didn't know whether she was still in a dream. She walked out of the room and into the bathroom and switched the light on. She saw herself in the mirror. She rinsed herself with cold water and felt the water temperature cold. There wasn't any real way of really knowing. She returned to bed and reawoke. She looked out of the window and saw the dew hanging over the grasses, only partially lifted, suspended like a net between two poles hung after a catch.[17]

Case Questions

1. What is meant by this description?
2. Do you think it is possible to dream that you are an object other than a person?
3. Who makes the ship and the furious wind?
4. What do you think it is like to be a "three-dimensional amoebic mass in constant shift"?
5. Does this happen to you? Any explanations?
6. Describe a personal experience in which you remember "only its skeletal framework."
7. How could you say this in other words?
8. Is this the usual way of expressing what happens when someone goes to sleep and dreams? Translate this passage to your own words.
9. What mood does this suggest? A happy one, a fearful one, or what?
10. What's different about this than what usually happens in wakeful reality?
11. What would happen to you if you were awake and this happened?
12. How important is it to be able to predict the effects of our everyday activities?
13. Can you imagine this occurring when someone is under the influence of a drug?
14. What do we attribute to sounds when we are frightened?
15. Has this happened to you? How do you think you would feel if this did?
16. Did you ever awake and feel that the dream you experienced was more real than the wakeful state?
17. Is Claudia awake or still in a dream?

6

BECOMING AND BEING

Are all things ever-changing, in constant flux, in the process of becoming, transposing structures into new equations with new sets of functions, demands, and horizons? Does every step in the process of becoming change the state of being, shift our kaleidoscopic perception, create a new constellation of the universe of our place and meaning in it? Is there a central core, a unified system of self? What is it like to say and feel and know that I am, I, me, in time or in timelessness, with you, or, a part of whatever it is that moves me?

Becoming, sensitivity, and meaning are all part of being and not being, of feeling whole or disjointed, in contact or alienated. In the process of becoming, there are contradictions, conflicts, fears, joys, and insights, to mention a few of the characteristics of experience. It is during these crises, and/or settled states that the personality undergoes growth and development. Old ways are given up sometimes, no longer functional, while new approaches to adapting to ourselves and the world are learned.

Perhaps what is real or imagined to us is symbolically related to the history of our personal life and to the evolution of all people who have shaped and given meaning to us. If this is so, then nothing is fixed, static or without a host of symbolic meanings. Part of ourselves is invested in whatever has significance however minute it might be. Imagine the potential of being if the whole world is a part of us as we, in turn, are an aspect of it. Is it not then that we sense the inner depth of ourselves, that our wishes are involved in the struggle of being?

In the article by K. E. Meyers, "Becoming: For Child and Teacher," the self as an emerging dimension of the human experience is discussed in reference to its educational implications. In the episode "Morning in the Country," Sheila's sensitivity to her own needs and pleasures alerts us to the vital role of her senses, perceptions, and youth.

In the following vignette, "Camp," Nina experiences homesickness. How do her needs affect her perception of the immediate environment? What aspect of herself is in search of feeling more complete, and how does it influence her awareness of time, place, and situation? A fluctuating awareness of self, wishes, surroundings, and imaginings are likewise depicted in the next incident, "At Home Alone." Here Phyllis ruminates about the immediate and remote concerns typical of a youngster her age.

Ashley Montagu's global dynamic view of sensitivity reaffirms what we have seen is so important in trying to understand the process of becoming and being. When Barbara empathetically communicates with the elderly man at the bar we are given an insight into how two people can add to the awareness and being of each other. In a similar manner, Joan, in the incident that follows, "The Man on the Radiator," responds to the man with understanding and compassion, despite her age.

The impact of meaning, according to the Louis Raths article, is embedded in the human condition; all aspects of life impinge on the individual. The teacher or parent needs to guide the child's search for meaning with love and respect. Through the use of magical thinking Steven, in the episode, "Fears in the House," manages to control certain dangers in the corridor and closet. The thin line between reality and fantasy is seen in the way he reacts to his immediate world. In a different vein, "The Witch in the Country," illustrates how a group of children collectively reinforce mystery and impending danger with pleasure.

Becoming: For Child and Teacher

Kent E. Myers

From the beginning the human organism is striving for individuality. The development of self is intrinsic, and in the early months of life the baby is self-centered and perceives the world through senses governed mainly by basic organic needs. All of us, however, at an early age develop a concept of ourselves as a person. Although this perception of one's self as a person may have certain stable factors, it is in continuous development.

Interaction with Environment and Own Values

Teachers should be aware that within us all there is a power to do, to build, and in doing and building to become. This becoming is ongoing. Not an end product which has no change, becoming is a process of interaction of the individual not only with the environment but with his own—essentially private—motivations and values.

The self is not initially there at birth, but develops from an individual's relations to his environment in the process of social experience and activity. The configuration of the self-image is therefore rooted in this social interaction which continues throughout life. (8)

As the child and the teacher have new experiences, the self draws on those experiences. Each new involvement with the environment may mean not only assimilating but giving up something of one's self, an adjustment involving some alteration of the self-image. "One is to some degree remade as one incorporates the new and leaves something of one-self behind as one moves on." (9)

Self-realization is not an easy task. Each person strives to become the image of an ideal established by his own value system. As most of us would like to be better than we are, the ideal we establish as the self we want to become is usually not the same as the self we perceive ourselves to be. The greater the difference between the perceived self and the ideal self, the more dissatisfied we are presumed to be. (7)

Understanding Self

Understanding of self is the most crucial of all understandings. Teachers and leaders who must interpret the actions of other persons and the physical environment must have some understanding of self. There is really no way of accurately measuring or testing the real self. We can compare what a child says he is with what those who observe him say he is and make some generalizations about what appear to be real self-characteristics. The self-image is significantly valuable only to the individual. His attempts at determining what he is in a *real* world are significant to others only when they interact with him. (4, 7)

"Self-Actualizing"

The process of becoming for a child or teacher who does have a self-image based on what he is rather than on what he should be has been described in a report by Maslow. He termed these persons "self-actualizing."

"Becoming: For Child and Teacher, An Ever-Changing Self-Image," by Kent E. Myers. From CHILDHOOD EDUCATION, September, 1964, Vol. 41, No 1, pp. 35–38. Reprinted by permission of Kent E. Myers and the Association for Childhood Education International, 3615 Wisconsin Avenue, N.W., Washington, D.C.

Self-actualizing persons who were studied show the following characteristics:

More efficient perception of reality and more comfortable relations with it
Acceptance of self, others and nature
Spontaneity
Problem-centering (on problems outside themselves)
The need for privacy
Autonomy, independence of culture and environment
The "Mystic Experience" (feeling of greatness yet helplessness)
Gemeinschaftsgefuhl (word invented by Adler (1) to describe the variety of feelings one has toward mankind)
Interpersonal relations
Democratic character structure
Means and ends (strong ethical convictions and values)
Philosophical, unhostile sense of humor
Creativeness (6)

Outer SHOW or Inner KNOW? Which?

The self-image of the child or of the teacher is often clouded by expectations forced on him by other factors in society and the physical environment. The perception of a self-image can be shaped by parental or peer attitudes which place value on outer *show* rather than inner *know*. Perception by an individual of his self-image can be warped by unrealistic stimuli; then he sees himself as others want him to be, not as he is.

Teachers must be open to a complete self-evaluation, for they must see themselves through children's eyes to evaluate the "self" the children see. Children's evaluation is often an eye-opener for teachers who perceive themselves only through their own senses. Teachers and children who have not achieved a self-image based on realistic perception of self can change that perception. The critical examination of self is a difficult task, as self-acceptance must be achieved. The facade which has served as a self-image must be stripped away so that interaction with reality can take place. Teachers and other leaders who provide patient and sympathetic help are opening the doors of understanding for children; principals and superintendents who help are giving teachers a new base for the processes of teaching.

Once some self-acceptance has been achieved, an opportunity for self-realization is assured. As the child or teacher looks closely at what he really values, he must discover that he can trust himself and may even begin to evaluate his internal stress in the light of his new self-knowledge. A form of consistency replaces inconsistency of self-image. Consistency does *not* mean an unchanging self-image; it means consistency in evaluating experiences and values and making changes consistent with that which is perceived as best for the individual. Teacher or leader achieving consistency of this kind gives active stability to the classroom.

Flexible Self-Assurance

Flexible self-assurance is part of this becoming. The replacement of fears and anxieties by self-assurance which can accept good times and bad and yet remain intact gives one knowledge that the self-image can shift if the occasion demands and incorporate the shift into the changing perception of what it means to become. Teachers who have this flexible self-assurance, which allows them to change to meet the new and ever-changing classroom challenges, can help children achieve self-assurance. This is achieved not only through the model of their own actions but by their ability to counsel children to make choices which will enhance the self-image of the child. In this case, self-assurance breeds self-assurance.

Carl Rogers deals with many of the factors discussed above and also adds the intriguing thought that the becoming of an individual must include his "willingness to be a process." This indicates that "self" development of child and teacher is not a fixed entity but an ever-changing process. (10)

The Self and Learning. Learning is the result of what the self perceives, accepts, reviews, synthesizes, interprets and uses from the great bulk of perceptual inputs before it at every waking moment. The self-image is modified by learning and especially so when that learning enhances the position of the organism, but even more often the inputs of information are modified to fit and maintain the self-image that has already been attained by the individual. Teachers should be aware that learning which modifies the self-image requires vigorous introspection by children and should help them toward new self-evaluation in these moments of stress.

Maintaining and Enhancing Self

The self-image is considered by some researchers to be primarily unchanging, and the learning which enhances the self is the only learning which actually takes place. This theory would contend that little modification or change of the self-image is possible. Snygg and Combs report that "the phenomenal self has the feeling of complete reality to the individual. Whatever he is, whatever he does, the maintenance and enhancement of this self is the prime objective of his existence." (11)

The self has alertness and vigilance. If the child has developed a self-image which is healthy, the perceptual inputs are used or rejected in such a way that learning enhances or modifies the self-image and little conflict is created. If the self-image is not healthy, the inputs which modify the self-image are resisted and change in the self-image can take place only through rigorous struggle. (5)

Learning is integrated with the self-image. Learning is most useful when it is appropriate to that image. The teacher of children who learns to observe his own self-behavior has taken a forward step in the process of self-realization.

Summary. Becoming is not an easy process, but it is an exhilarating one. Each teacher and child should be willing to accept change and strive for openness to new and varied experiences. The process must be ever ongoing with the thrust for growth in each organism being self-directed to add new dimensions to the self-image.

The act of becoming produces a sensitivity to others and the environment and embraces a continuous flow of experiences which result from interaction of self with all other forces. The responsibility for becoming lies mainly within the individual. Others may give direction and inspiration or serve as a sounding board for an individual's self-evaluation, but the final concept of self-image is intrinsic. *Teachers, parents, leaders of all kinds must have a perception of their own self-image before they can become helpful to others who want to achieve self-understanding.*

Even though an individual may receive guidance and encouragement from others in his quest for self-image, the process of becoming is full and vital only when the great responsibility of being a unique individual is accepted by one's self, a self that is ever changing and developing, even though some relative continuity is maintained.

Educators and leaders of youth must not forget that *becoming continues throughout the life-span.* Teachers should form patterns of continuous self-evaluation which will allow them more realistically to meet the ever-changing child-teacher interactions of the class-room.

Bibliography

1. Adler, Alfred. *Social Interest.* New York: C. P. Putnam's Sons, 1939.
2. Engel, Mary. "The Stability of Self-Concept in Adolescence," *Journal of Abnormal Psychology,* Vol. 58 (1959), p. 211.
3. Festinger, L. *Theory of Cognitive Dissonance.* Evanston, Ill.: Row, Peterson & Co., 1957.
4. Henderson, Richard L. "Creativity for What?" *Educational Leadership* (October 1956), p. 45.
5. Jersild, Arthur T. *In Search of Self.* New York: Teachers College, Columbia University Press, 1952.
6. Maslow, A. H. "Self-Actualizing People: A Study of Psychological Health," *The Self,* ed. C. E. Moustakas. New York: Harper & Bros., 1956.
7. McCandless, Boyd R. *Children and Adolescents*

Behavior and Development. New York: Holt, Rinehart & Winston, 1961.

8. Mead, George H. *Mind, Self and Society.* Chicago: University of Chicago Press, 1934.
9. Murphy, Gardner. *Human Potentialities.* New York: Basic Books, Inc., 1958.
10. Rogers, Carl R. "What It Means To Become a Person," *The Self,* ed. C. E. Moustakas. New York: Harper & Bros., 1956.
11. Snygg, Donald and Arthur W. Combs. *Individual Behavior.* New York: Harper & Bros., 1949.

Questions and Projects Related to Becoming

1. Whom do you understand better than yourself? Why?
2. In what situation are you more concerned with "outer show"? Do you know why? Explain.
3. How much of yourself do you present to the following people or in the following circumstances?
   a. Your best friend.
   b. The person you like least.
   c. Your fellow students.
   d. When you are unsure of yourself.
   e. When you are very sure of yourself.
   f. When you are tired.
   g. With children.
   h. A member of your family.
   i. A business acquaintance.
   j. A dog or cat.
   k. When you write about something you are not familiar with.
   l. When you love.

Sheila (8) :
Morning in the Country

She didn't want to move in the morning because the warmth from the sheets would disappear, then she'd never find the complete warmth again.[1] It was morning, and she smelled the open freshness of the country air as she lay there, waiting for her mother to call her downstairs again.[2] She lay there, but she began to feel the growing pressure to urinate. She heard the smell of brown cakes below.[3] She took a deep breath, threw off the blankets, and jumped to where her clothes were draped over a chair. She slipped off her heavy nightdress and in seconds was dressed. What she disliked most of all was the cold water in the shiny, white pitcher. She poured a bit into the basin, and in less time than it took her to jump to the chair, she brushed her teeth, dried her face and hands, and was on her way to the toilet.[4]

"Sheila," her mother called, "Breakfast." But Sheila didn't have to hurry anymore. She was at the bottom of the staircase. She had descended the stairs without touching any of them. Her mother told her that one day she would fall and hurt herself "the way you go down those stairs."[5]

Case Questions

1. Have you ever experienced this?
2. What do city children smell when they awake?
3. Is it possible to hear the "smell of brown cakes"? Explain.
4. How thorough a washing did she give herself?
   a. What role do rituals play here?
5. Do some children descend steps without touching them? Explain.

Nina (7) : Camp

Neither the silence nor the sound was stirred by the settling darkness. It was twilight, and all the children knew that it was time to sleep. It was that time of the day and night when the strength and weakness of oneself is fused into the privacy of one's feelings, which are not to be shared with anyone except in that realm of imagination where wonder and yearning combine, where the sea of many happenings tosses up pieces of the past. It was that moment, before the chill of the night meets the last rays of the sun, when green is no longer green but a light silhouette, where the eyes of oneself are turned inward to the recorded, moving, shifting pictures of the past, the mood of many times rooted to feelings.[1]

When the sun descended into the darkening trees that faced Nina's room, she knew then that this was the hour when she wanted her mother most. First there would be the putting away of the dirty clothes and preparation for the next morning's dressup. Then there was going into bed. The slight cold of the evening chilled the sheets. Then there was the waiting, waiting quietly—alone—in the large room where other children did not speak. Then out of the settling darkness a bugle sounded the clean brass pacing of taps.[2]

The green and yellow fields were in the musk of night now—in the chilled aftermath of twilight—wrapped in sheets of mist—ready for sleep. All the children knew that this was the hour when sharing was with oneself, in the private world of imagining and wanting. It was the hour when the day's activities are recounted and stored away, when the time to do things is swept away—when the shop is closed.[3] It was that time when all that was, is suddenly eclipsed except for that wanting—that imperceptible magical yearning that starts slowly from a dot then looms into a blot and blots all feelings with hunger. She was lonely and wanted her mother.[4] It came upon her, this feeling, like the chill with the deepening shadows.[5] First there would be the waiting and listening to the crickets as well as the movement of leaves in the wind. Then, like a wave that suddenly came upon her, engulfed her, there would be the first sound of taps.[6]

How the movement forward and backward, up and down, riled her longing to be held—to be loved. One vast sea of wanting caught in its own drownings—she felt her fragileness exposed to the shoreless waters of herself. Home was nowhere here, nor there in that sound, as it moved to its own ending. The ending of the taps and the stark silence—the silence and the sleep.[7]

Case Questions

1. In what way can you relate to this first paragraph?
    a. What would you add or void? Why?
2. What is stated here in regard to mother separation?
    a. Can you imagine any experience of yours that is similar to this one? Describe it.
3. Ask a number of young children to tell you what they think of before they go to sleep the day before school, before their birthday, before an examination, or when they feel alone.
4. Does the image here help you understand what Suzanne is going through?
    a. What other images, if any, would you use?
5. Why is Nina in need of her mother?
6. What does taps mean to a child?
7. Do the images help to create mood? Explain.
    a. What is meant by, "she felt her fragileness exposed to the shoreless waters of herself"?

Phyllis (13) : At Home Alone

There was nothing to do and no one to do it with. She was alone in the house, and no one would be home for some hours. Outside the wind raced from building to building and blew at everything in its way. The soup greens smelled good and fogged the kitchen window, and miniature bubbles hung from the ceiling just above the pot of cooking food. She wasn't hungry, although she felt like eating. She opened the refrigerator and looked inside. There was some applesauce . . . no, she wouldn't eat anymore . . . she had eaten a few slices of bread with butter and applesauce.[1] She went to the window and looked out and could see very little until she drew a few strokes across the pane with her fingers and left a few strokes of clearer yet wetvisioned aperture.[2] There was only the outside. The courtyard was empty. The cats were probably curled up against the wall of the boiler room where they could benefit by the heat. The smell of garbage was sometimes overpowering but she guessed the cats didn't mind as long as they had the heat. After all, the cold was unpleasant.[3] What would she do if she were a cat and had to forage for her own food and . . . just then she noticed a cat walking stealthfully along the wall, hugging his own skin in a most contracted way. He jumped onto the top of the fence that separated the one yard from the next and disappeared behind it. Where do they go . . . maybe they have a route just like deer.[4] She had heard that deer follow a more or less predictable path. She would think about that if she could and ask her teacher, maybe she knew. Now it was so barren down there with bits of wood and an empty garbage can with a rattling loose cover. It seemed to lift every time the wind rose. She wondered whether it annoyed people at night.[5] She heard the trucks and cars below and sometimes voices, but they were mostly inarticulate when it was cold because the wind tore the words apart and spread the pronunciation. She would ask her teacher about that. Did the wind really break up words? She knew that she had trouble hearing her friends speak to her when there was a strong wind and lots of open space. How did the people in the cold and windy lands hear each other? Did the people in the Arctic have trouble hearing each other?[6]

She heard a buzz that sounded as if it came from her door, but it was the neighbors'. They must hear everything because the walls are so thin. Once she remembered that her father had asked her mother what time it was, and she heard the woman next door say, "9:10." They all had learned to talk quietly at first, but later, they didn't care who listened to what they said to each other. It was only when the neighbors had a party and they started to drink that the words were heavy and loud and ugly. She knew they were ugly words and sounded as if they came out of a mouth that didn't really mean to say those things. It was funny how after one night of cursing each other, they greeted her with all the dignity and politeness she could hope for the following morning. She wondered whether they knew that she and her parents knew about them . . . about the drinking and ugly words.[7]

Phyllis entered the living room. As she reached out toward her homework notebook, she noticed the mailbox keys. She was reminded of another neighbor, poor lady. She had asked her mother about her. Why the old lady who lived by herself in that corner room always came out to check her mail even on Sundays or late at night when she knew that the mail was only delivered in the mornings everyday but not on Sunday. Her mother had said she didn't know, but imagined that the old lady was lonely and didn't have anyone to talk to so that for her to greet someone was human social contact. What did the woman think of at night, alone . . . ?[8] Sometimes she wondered about death, about her parents, Jimmy, and people. Sometimes she wondered what it would be like if she died . . . would everyone be sad, and what would they say about her.[9] She knew that her mother and father would cry and that they would be anxious about where she was, what she was doing, whether she was all right or hungry or was wearing the warm socks or tucked in or ready for tomorrow's school, or had brushed her teeth. If she were dead, they would not need to worry about her. What would they do without her?[10] They'd be very sad. She began to feel sorry for them. She'd be very careful . . . would watch the cars, the matches when she lit the stove . . . she'd be careful.[11] How could she when . . . tomorrow she had to speak to Francis and ask her about Jimmy. She liked Jim . . . the way he walked and his eyes. He was cute and not as sure as some of the other boys. She liked that about him. He wasn't sure, but was proud so he kept away so that he would not let anyone know that he wasn't sure. He wanted to help her do the homework, but didn't insist when Stuart came by and asked her if she understood. Why didn't she tell him that Jim was helping her? Maybe that's why he left her. He really didn't feel she wanted Stuart to help her. Jim felt bad . . . felt she turned on him or couldn't stand up to him. He was hurt, he didn't say anything—just went away. It was foolish. She knew she did something wrong because she really didn't listen to Stuart when he spoke to her. Actually, she didn't need help. She knew that the boys offered to help her because she was wearing a sweater and the boys liked the way her breasts stood out.[12] Jim was shy and liked her for what she was, because she understood him. She knew when he was sad or happy, when he liked her but was afraid to let her know. She also knew when he joined the boys, was part of their group, and he was the leader most of the time. She wished he'd feel surer of himself, with her. Sometimes he clowned and was funny, but she knew that he didn't want to show her his real feelings.[13]

She remembered how he showed her how to draw modern-print letters for a poster. He was careful not to rush her. She felt awkward because he watched her so carefully. She didn't know how to look back at him. Sometimes he stuttered . . . like the time they were discussing the poor people, how they live. He seemed sure of what he was saying about how he felt. How many brothers and sisters did he have? Is that why he didn't have well-fitting clothes? Perhaps they were hand-me-downs.[14]

Here's the reading . . . now where did I stop . . . no . . . I read that, but I don't remember too well . . . what's this . . . "In the beginning, there were only . . . ." That's it . . . gee, I'm thirsty . . . I'll get a drink and then start . . . wish I could go to a film . . . don't like the violent ones . . . would like those romantic historical ones. He's dueling on the side of the ship for the girl who's kidnapped below in one of the cabins with her father and mother tied together in another side of the cabin. The villain has a long black mustache, dark brows, and is always unshaven. He's different. The hero jumps from one side of the ship to the other and at one point grabs one of the hanging ropes from the sails and swings like Tarzan from one side of the ship to the other. He knocks the villain and a whole crew off their feet. Then he quickly bolts down the steps to the cabin . . . meanwhile the scrambled crew unscrambles itself. They pursue the hero who is now lowering a boat from one side of the lower decks. The hero kisses the heroine. Did they really kiss each other? They did it so well . . . held each other so long. Wasn't it uncomfortable to have someone's face next to you for a long time?[15] She wouldn't like it.[16] She knew that the older boys and girls did it like that in the park at twilight. She saw the young man and woman clasped in each other's arms with their faces buried in each other. They had no space between them. Weren't they embarrassed? Perhaps they loved each other and would have sex together? Joe and Mary don't love each other . . . they always argue. Do they have sex together? They fight all the time. She looks so unhappy. So does he. They don't know how to look at each other . . . maybe they aren't in love and can't really speak or feel good together. She wished they'd smile toward each other.[17] She liked them both.

Mary smiles, but it isn't real. She smiles yet she doesn't, like she wants to cry . . . like she's listening to something else inside of her. She felt the same way, didn't want to tell anyone. At such times she couldn't really listen to anyone or when she did, she heard the person through what she felt sad about . . . like the time she didn't take the girl's candy and was blamed for it. The teacher was angry with her. How hurt she was, insulted. She couldn't talk. She wanted to cry but was too proud to. She couldn't wait until it was time to leave class. She went to the bathroom and cried in one of the stalls. Frances came by, made her feel better, said the teacher was nasty but really didn't think she took it. Besides, the teacher knew that she'd never steal. Later they found the candy on top of the boy's closet. The teacher was glad that the candy was found but didn't say she was mistaken and wrong and accused anyone.[18]

The water was good and cold, but milk was better with graham crackers . . . then she'll read . . . MMM . . . that was good . . . she remembered when she was sick and ate the graham crackers with hot milk . . . she never liked boiled milk, but the milk-soaked graham crackers . . . were delicious! She never minded being sick when she could have food.[19]

That night of thunder and lightning. It rained. The sky sparked. The room lit up with a blue-white light. Everything was clear as daylight even after the lightning disappeared. She remembered everything in the room . . . the dresser, the glasses, and the clothes . . . . Everything just as before. The experience was like a picture . . . a snapshot, black and white, mostly . . . . How that one lightning flash struck the aerial wire—how the spark leaped across the window and into the room. For one long moment, she saw a flame—a white-blue flame shoot across the windowsill. That was strange. She wondered what would have happened to her if she had her hand there. Was it true that they could discharge the electricity from a lightning-filled man by plunging a special needle into him? It would hurt unless he's dead to begin with.[20] She sipped some more milk. It was awful the way she drank a whole container of milk, nearly ate a whole box of crackers. . . . Mother thought she'd get fat if she ate like that. Didn't want to be fat like Betty. Betty ran away from anyone else who was fat. Perhaps she was afraid to be reminded of her weight. Everyone would think that she was fat like the other one. They'd become doubly aware of her size.[21] Anyway, Betty sang beautifully. Why did she make fun of Jim and the other boys just because she was so smart? She knew that the boys become angry with her, tease her. She was miserable even though she fought back with words and laughed because she wanted to be liked like us. The boys came over to us and teased us differently.[22] Mrs. Franklin is so heavy. She looks like a duck waddling. She's happy with her husband. I wouldn't want to be heavy like that . . . but maybe it's all right . . . no more crackers . . . well, I'm not hungry now. . . . There's that sound again . . . like a ship . . . the sea and the waters . . . the gulls circling and circling over the boat house. Even saw the hand move, but there wasn't any sound from the clock . . . couldn't hear with the waters . . . the waters washing back and forth over the sands and the sandpipers like woodchucks making lightning strokes with their beaks into the sand. What was it they ate . . . and that sound, that lonely sound at night like some sick beast, but they said it wasn't sick. The cow was giving birth and was moaning. But, out there . . . sometimes I feel like those horns that call for what they want . . . out there in the dark all alone. . . . Maybe she moans inside of her for someone or everything and feels bad because she's alone.[23] I remember how we made faces in the sand. I was too shy to get undressed under the covers because the boys were nearby, and I didn't want them to see my special parts because they would giggle and besides I would be embarrassed because it isn't right . . . that's funny . . . we did it anyway and we laughed . . . . I'm glad I did it because my bottom gets itchy after awhile when I don't take my bathing suit off.[24]

I felt so alone when I was walking by the sea and watching those birds and came upon that dead fish on the sands. . . . It must have been washed up by one of the waves . . . the flies were on it, it was ugly, and I knew if I looked at it, I wouldn't be able to get rid of the picture. It would always be there . . . I know those things . . . I always do and yet I had to look at it and I can see it now with the flies and everything, but it doesn't bother me now, but it did that night when I was trying to sleep.[25] I'm tired . . . I'll rest a few minutes before reading . . . besides, I'll feel better, and I have time and . . . now that's better . . . I'll close my eyes and watch the pictures . . . there're flowers, green and yellow flowers, and my hair is long, and I know how I look by the water. My mother is making a bias on the dress . . . I'll wear one like that but different . . . not with the neck like that . . . I'll be a little larger and fuller about the chest. When I walk, they'll move a little like my teacher's.[26] I want to read and talk and go to dances. He'll be kind like Uncle Bob. He knows how to make us feel at home. Lots of food for us . . . especially the tongue and potato salad and those olives . . . the others are too salty . . . my lids . . . BzzzBzzz . . . that must be Mom . . . I'd better get up and answer and get back to studying . . . . "Coming . . . ."

Case Questions

1. Why do you think Phyllis ate even though she was not hungry?
2. How is Phyllis expressing her thoughts here? Explain.
3. What can you say about Phyllis's feelings toward cats?
4. Do children identify with the needs of animals? Explain.
5. In what way is Phyllis aware of the needs of others?
6. Is Phyllis aware of cause and effect relationships? Explain.
7. Can neighbor's influence children's perception of themselves?
   a. What do you think Phyllis learned about her neighborhood?
8. How aware is Phyllis of others? Explain.
9. What quality of self-awareness and social awareness exists here?
10. What might Phyllis learn by asking herself these questions?
11. Do we govern our own actions according to our perception of what others expect of us? Explain. Who are the others? Does it matter?
12. How does body image influence the sex-role behavior of thirteen- and fourteen-year-olds?
    a. What is sex-role behavior?
13. In what way is Phyllis critical of her friends?
14. Is there a great difference between the likes and dislikes of thirteen-year-olds and adults?
    a. List similarities and differences.
15. What role does fantasy serve in developing thinking approaches?
16. What can you say about Phyllis's attitude toward sex?
17. What values are involved here? Explain.
18. Does this paragraph evoke any associations? If so, which ones?
19. What questions do children ask themselves during the day?
    a. Did "lightning" have a special meaning for you as a child?
20. What significance does Betty have for Phyllis?
21. What does Phyllis seem to understand about the way boys threat Betty?
22. In what way do the environmental sounds influence Phyllis's thinking?
23. What kind of concept does Phyllis have of her body? Explain.
24. How does time influence Phyllis's thinking?
25. Is it natural for Phyllis to be aware of the body changes?
26. Compare Phyllis to another child the same age.
    a. What did you identify with in this episode?

The Need for Sensitivity

Ashley Montagu

All reality is relationship, and all relationships are enlarged and enriched in proportion to the sensitivity with which they are lived. Indeed, to be sensitive is to be alive; and the more sensitive one is to the world in which one lives, every aspect of it, the more alive one is. Excess of sensitivity is, of course, to be avoided, as is excess in anything. Excess of sensitivity is a pathological state and does not arise from the education of one's sensibilities but from other causes which have nothing whatever to do with the healthy nourishment of those sensibilities. It is, rather, from their inadequate nourishment that the pathologies of sensitivity are likely to arise.

All education should be directed toward the refinement of the individual's sensibilities in relation not alone to his fellow men everywhere but to all things whatsoever. Human beings are the most extraordinary of instruments that can be tuned to respond to the greatest variety of wave lengths of any instrument ever devised. Just as beauty is produced on a fine musical instrument by a sensitive performer, human beings can learn to receive and to respond to all those things that cannot be spoken as well as to all those things that can.

No one who has failed to have his sensibilities realized to the optimum can be said to have been fulfilled as a human being. Indeed, those who have not been so fulfilled are the only truly tragically disinherited of the world. All of us, to some extent, suffer from this disinheritance; and that failure has affected our selves, our relationships and the world. The world is in the state it is because of our massive failure not of nerve but of sensitivity to the needs of other human beings and, not least, to our own needs.

Who shall awaken humanity to the need for sensitivity, for the strange necessity of beauty, for vulnerability, for the recognition of the sensitive precariousness of human life? Who?

It is the teachers in our schools, the unacknowledged leaders of the world.

Questions and Projects Related to the Need for Sensitivity

1. How do you want the following people to react to you?
    a. An adult whom you value greatly.
    b. An acquaintance.
    c. Your favorite teacher.
    d. A fellow student.
    e. A member of your family.
    f. Someone you love.
2. In what kinds of situations are you most sensitive to the criticisms of others?
3. When do you consider yourself insensitive?

Barbara (6) : At the Boat House

The owner of the boat house, Fred, told me that it was an eight-to-ten mile wind that would bring the dark clouds from the north down our way.[1] An elderly man whose skin shined as if it had been rubbed by pumice raised his bony and protruding veined hands to the clouds in the distant horizon and, in what seemed like a voice of doom, said, "Rain."[2] The little girl whose mother was pushing the pinball machine with short, light jerks, in order to guide the ball from one coil of wire to another, lowered her head, and coyly smiled.[3] She lowered her head but opened her dark brown eyes a little more.

The old man's face changed instantaneously when he caught sight of Barbara. What was a deeply cast look changed into an eager expression of warmth and one big wink.[4] Barbara pushed up against her mother's backside. This seemed to add to the pressure her mother was applying to the frame of the machine, "Look out, Barbara. Damn it! Now look what you did."[5] Apparently the machine was jolted too much, and the score was no longer registering. The abruptness and harshness of her mother's words seemed to erase the coy smile that was directed to the old man and replaced it with large, watery eyes that began to spill tears. Her accompanying sobs were stopped by her mother's kisses. Although her face was streaked with tears, her small mouth and large eyes were once again filled with warmth and curiosity.[6]

The old man seemed to have painfully observed the whole event and went through the various changes of the child's moods. He, too, was now smiling and apparently relieved. This was also evidenced in the gentle way he picked up his glass of beer in contrast to the way he had gripped it while the child was crying.[7] Her mother was now playing a new game. The sudden rising of the large woolly dog from under the table brought Barbara to his side.[8] A moment later her mother called out, "Barbara, it's time for Daddy to be back. Let's go to the pier."[9]

Both the mother and child stood together in silence on the broken walk that led to the tar-stained wooden pier. The darkening, grey sky gave the distant horizon an unreal, undefined look. Some of the light from the sky seemed to penetrate the massive, overcast ceiling. The shore, some of the waves, old wooden docks, and houses seemed to be painted in bone-white light.[10] Barbara looked above her and seemed to be watching the anchor lines that were suspended between long poles that were deeply set into the muddy bottom under the docks.

Each time the boat rocked, pitched, lurched, and pulled at the line, Barbara looked up at the squeaking pulley.[11] Evidently she had located the source of the sound. She began to survey the different pulleys and lines with her eyes gazing first at one, then, another.

"I hear birds, Mommy, but I don't see any."[12]

"Well, there are birds, but I can't hear them," the mother answered, "because the waves make too much noise."

"Mommy, I hear them."

Then suddenly her mother discovered what her daughter had been listening to and bent over and kissed the top of her daughter's head.[13]

Case Questions

1. There's a social problem here, not as it is presented but as it exists in some communities: the extent to which the black community shares in the ownership of boat houses. Who owns the local boat houses in your region? Can you or a group of students devise a method of developing an investigation of this issue? How would you organize a research committee in regard to this matter.
2. Can you visualize the elderly man? Write a description of the skin texture of an aged person. Compare his skin to that of a younger person (an adolescent girl or boy, a baby)?
3. Have you ever observed a woman playing a pinball machine? Try to describe what you felt when you first imagined her playing this game. Were you shocked? Explain. Can you imagine the reason why Barbara lowered her eyes?
4. Can you identify with the old man? Why do you think his expression changed? Write a description of someone who encounters someone else. What words are used in a book of your choosing in which descriptive dimensions of change of mood are indicated? Try sitting opposite your neighbor and try to find one word that captures his facial expression.
5. Is this the kind of language expression you would expect of the typical mother you have observed in your community?
6. Describe an incident in which a child is admonished by his mother. Consider the situation and people connected to the incident. Did you find yourself taking sides with the adult or with the child? Why?
7. To what degree do you think the man was influenced by Barbara and her mother? Explain.
8. The dog is an unexpected addition to this episode. Do you think he fits into it without being properly introduced? Why?
9. Does Barbara's mother come through to you as a real person? Can you imagine such a person? What don't you know about her that you feel might be important. Is she your idea of a feminine woman? Who is this father? Create his character. Describe in one paragraph your conception of a friend's father.
10. Does the description of the sky evoke a mood within you? Is the language used in this part too flowery for you? Describe the sky over a factory, an apartment house, a grassy plain, or over water. What about winter, spring, summer, or fall sky? How does the sky seem when you are happy, sad, or anxious? Try to find a description of the sky in a novel, a local newspaper, magazine, or a book of poetry. What meaning does the sky hold for a thirsty man in a desert, in contrast to someone in a flooded area during a storm? Explain.
11. What do you know about the movement of waves, their pitch, height, weight, or other characteristics? Is the movement of a boat in water determined by its weight, volume, or the amount of water it displaces, among other characteristics? Where can you obtain information concerning these questions?

12. What made the pulley squeak? Why did Barbara interpret the sound as birds? Can you relate an experience in which you had difficulty coordinating what you saw with what you heard?
13. Do you think it would have been wise for Barbara's mother to tell her daughter the truth about the source of the bird sounds?

Joan (9): The Man on the Radiator

The old man grunted some words. His head hung down as he sat on the low metal-covered radiator. He held his arms with his hands—huddled. He mumbled, then looked up at the children.[1] They ran back and forth from one side of the hall to the other. They were playing ball with a crumpled-up piece of paper. One of the occupants of the house opened his door and yelled out to the children, "This isn't a playground. I'm trying to sleep. Play outside." The children disappeared.[2] The old man continued to mumble. He looked up before him when the man called out, then let his head return to the position it had been.

Joan stood in front of the entrance of the house. She was waiting for her friend. She felt chilled and entered the building. The old man was huddled over his lap. She stood quietly behind the door. She looked at the man who had started to mumble to himself. He turned his head to Joan, then looked away in front of him. The lines on his face were uneven. His eyes were close together. His lips were thick. He smiled at Joan and said, "It's cold." Joan smiled back and answered, "Yes, it's cold." He repeated, "It's too cold to be outside." His mouth hung a bit twisted and open.[3]

"Yes, it's cold. It's cold outside," she answered. She liked the man. She liked his eyes. They were simple eyes—more like those of an animal. Once she had seen a man in the street. He had been leaning against the wall of a building, when she had passed by. He was drunk. She could tell by the way he swayed. The weight of his body tilted precariously back and forth against the wall. When he smiled, he seemed to change his whole expression from one of utter disgust and futility and confusion to a spark of recognition. She wondered why his whole facial expression had changed. Why he had suddenly looked out of himself and into himself and had found something that warmed him?[4] This man, too—this man who sat on the radiator, who smiled at her, had the same kind of expression. She knew that she meant something special to him. She hadn't done anything. She really hadn't said anything, yet he was there—his face alive, his eyes kind. She wanted to hug him, tell him that she liked him, that he was good and that he should go home.[5] She wondered if he lived in a house with other people and whether anyone took care of him. Whether he had someone to take care of, whether someone loved him.[6] She didn't know what to say to him. She just liked him. He didn't say anything. He looked away, stared for a few moments ahead of him, then looked up and smiled, but then looked away. Finally, he said, "Maybe it'll be warmer tomorrow." He seemed happy now. He looked directly at her and waited for her to say something. When she didn't answer right away, his face changed to a kind of fearful expression, but then Joan said simply, "I hope so. I like it when it's warm."[7] A door slammed from the floor above and quick, light steps sounded down the staircase. "Oh, there you are. Come on, let's go." Before Joan left, she smiled a big smile to the man and said, Good-bye, mister."[8]

Case Questions

1. What's your first impression of this man according to the description thus far?
2. Do you have neighbors who react in a similar manner? Explain.
3. What is your impression of the man?
4. Can you answer Joan's question? Express her liking for this man.
5. How many people do you know would like to hear this from you?
6. Do you ever think these things when you see someone in the street? If not, what do you feel and think?
7. In what way was Joan satisfying her own needs?
8. Can you explain the quality of communication that existed between Joan and the man?

How Children Build Meanings

Louis Raths

The world starts its work of impressing meanings upon us as soon as we are born. The first and probably the most persistent meanings come to us in these early years. We are participants in situations which involve love and hate and indifference; intense activity and quiet; excitement and monotony; laughter and grief; accomplishment and failure; pride and guilt; poise and anxiety; and a thousand-and-one others.

These meanings are not thrust upon us without our involvement. Very early we must venture to think or to guess the character of a situation and as we act we find our judgment confirmed, rejected, or neglected. It is through this continuing testing of our opinions that we build meanings.

We learn thus to listen for the feelings that are behind the words. We find cues relating to rewards or deprivations for us, and these cues help us to identify the meaning of each new situation. We use past experience to find new meanings in the present but it is in the "here and now" that they are tested.

Our own actions in a situation are steppingstones to meaning. If we act aggressively and it leads to success for us, we more readily recognize the cue for the expression of aggression. And so with other kinds of responses, we learn through the consequences of our doing, and slowly and steadily we build our meanings and make them a part of the world in which we live.

The learning of new meanings is probably best achieved where this learning is a shared experience—if others, near and dear to us, are also concerned. Out of this sharing we can assert or deny; exchange opinions or be quiet; we can test ourselves in shared action, and this is probably mankind's greatest good.

We build meanings also in spontaneous and imaginative play and in reverie. As children we try out hundreds of the ideas suggested to us by things and fantasy, by songs and dreams, and by people in our environment. We need freedom to dream, to imagine, and to try; through the use of that freedom we venture to build meanings.

Sometimes the meanings which we have built become stumbling blocks. Usually these meanings are rigid: the "never, never change" kind. Probably the context in which we acquire meanings has the greatest influence upon flexibility or rigidity. If the reward or deprivation was for us very intense, if those whom we love and respect were rigid or flexible, our own meaning will be considerably influenced.

As we grow older we become involved with more social institutions all of which have their patterns of action. These institutions tend to impose requirements upon us and they reward and penalize our conduct. Through our participation we learn the cues for action; we watch others, we imitate, and we experience the consequences of our behavior. In this context the school begins to have certain larger meanings for us; so does the church, industry, government, communications, and the others.

And as we learn to read, new areas of experience are opened to us and to the extent that we can identify cues, generate opinions of our own, try them out, or share them in a "testing" manner with others, we continue the task of building meanings. As with reading, so with the arts and music and play and work. We need almost boundless opportunities for exploring the world and as the range increases, and opportunity to share increases, we more richly and more securely build meanings.

"How Children Build Meanings," by Louis Raths. From CHILDHOOD EDUCATION, December 1954, Vol. 31, No. 4, pp. 159–160. Reprinted by permission of Louis Raths and the Association for Childhood Education International.

Inevitably it happens that some of our meanings conflict with each other. Our attempts to resolve these differences are the central character of child development. We *develop* as we integrate the meanings we have experienced. We do this through puzzling over the conflict; through reflecting upon it. We try sometimes to choose one or the other. On other occasions we see a middle ground or a synthesis. On still other occasions we go forward, confused and uncertain. We build meanings as we tackle the never-ending job of reducing these conflicts born of our own experience.

If *our* meanings are so greatly influenced by those whom we love, cherish, and respect, and who hold us dear, it probably follows that if we as a group have very different home-and-experience backgrounds, that our meanings also will differ significantly. How these differences are handled by the adults around us and by our peers are also strong determinants of meaning. If *our* meanings gained from *our* experiences are frowned upon—are devalued—it constitutes a rejection of *our* life, and that is intolerable to every one of us so treated.

There are two major reasons for the pride in and defense of our own experience. Meanings tend to persist and to have a large share in guiding our lives. Meanings which we hold uniquely identify us as individuals. We are what we believe; at least we act so, and hence we want respect for what life has meant to us and our development.

In the second place, we have come to learn that there is no single "right" meaning for everybody. Just as we respect the meanings of others and share in testing them, so do we expect an initial acceptance and further testing of the meanings which we bring to a situation. If those around us have genuine respect for us, they will not want to remake us into images of themselves. They will respect what is unique in our own living and so will encourage us to share with them the aim of being ourselves. Under these circumstances we, too, can contribute to a world which expects so much from us and yet seems to have so little time to listen or to share.

Questions and Projects Related to How Children Build Meanings

1. How do we first start to build meanings, according to Raths?
2. How do you determine meaning in regard to the following aspects of your life:
    a. Cues related to rewards.
    b. Cues related to deprivations.
    c. By what's behind words.
    d. Here and now.
    e. Your own actions.
    f. Sharing with others.
    g. Spontaneous and imaginative play.
    h. Reverie.
    i. Dreams.
3. How might the context in which we acquire meaning influence flexibility or rigidity?
4. What does Raths mean in the quote, "We develop as we integrate the meanings we have experienced. We do this through puzzling over the conflict; through reflecting upon it."?
5. How does the meaning we attribute to people we cherish, love, and respect influence our receptivity to what they say?
6. Discuss the following quote in regard to how it relates to you: "We are what we believe."

Steven (6): Fears in the House

It was at that certain hour when no one was home, and the street noises were especially clear. The creaking of the floor creaked in that special way. I was afraid to go through the long corridor from my room, to my bedroom, to the toilet. I heard my own steps, and sometimes I was sure that there were steps behind me. I knew this was ridiculous, but I found it difficult to breathe, and my heart pounded strongly, and I felt as if my neck was especially difficult to maneuver.[1]

When I went to the toilet . . . I remembered that I would have to return to my room and go through the experience again. It was winter and the wind whined and shook the windowpanes in any kind of disorderly beat, in some unpredictable tempo, which made me look quickly toward this or that window.[2] The whole house creaked and seemed to be straining under some heavy weight. When I opened the hall closet to get my jacket, I was sure that there was someone behind the hanging overcoats and suits and dresses of my parents, and that a person was there waiting, quietly—that he was holding his breath.[3] I knew that I had to get what I had to as quickly as possible in order that he could resume his breathing without fear of being discovered. I had to be concerned about him, or he'd reveal himself to me, and I feared that encounter.[4]

I remembered that I even whistled or made a little noise just before I opened the closet, so that he wasn't caught unprepared, had time to inhale a large breath.[5] I tried to imagine how he stood there in the dark, his back against the wall and corner, the hanging clothes about him. One sunny day I entered my closet and made the discovery that it wasn't easy to stand there in the dark. I didn't fully close the door, because I didn't want to be locked in.[6] Once I really was frightened. I ranted and cried until my parents came. They looked in the closet.[7] They teased me, said that I was foolish, that I wasn't a baby, and that there were no such things as people or monsters that would hide in closets. I didn't care what they said, I knew he was there. Before they left the room, they opened the door and slowly shifted the clothes on the rack. They were trying to show me that no one was hiding. When I was no longer afraid to be alone, I told my parents. They smiled, kissed me and left.

But, I developed another fear. I wondered whether my heart would stop.[2] I heard it under my pillow. Sometimes it beat loudly but when the pounding was less pronounced, I wondered why. Although I knew I was healthy, I started to imagine what would happen if it stopped. Would I be dead? Who would cry? How my parents would miss me.[9] I became sorry for myself. I imagined that I was lowered into the ground the way I had seen my grandmother lowered into a large pit. I wondered how it would be to be there—all enclosed and not moving.[10] I became petrified with the idea and carefully listened to my heart. When I didn't hear it, I felt my pulse. Was I dying? Would I be dead? I cried out. When my mother entered the room, I immediately felt better.[11]

Case Questions

1. Describe an experience in which you were afraid of being in the house.
2. What do you think Steven was really experiencing? Try to describe the experience as fully as possible.
3. What would you do if you were a six-year-old faced with this situation?
4. How does Steven control the actions of the "person" he feared?
5. How much of our own understanding of ourselves do we transfer to a "phantom" figure?
6. Why didn't he choose a dark, gloomy day?
7. What would you have said if you were the parent?
8. Do you think this fear is a typical one of a child at this age?
9. How do you think a child would feel if no one would miss him?
10. Do you think young children really consider these problems? When? Why?
11. Again the parent is there to reassure Steven that all is well. Why do you think the parent is associated with security here?

Marsha (8) : The Witch in the Country

The small wooden creakings in the adjoining room parched the silence in the same way that newly starched pillowcases sounded under her ear when she shifted her head, in the same way that the sea gasped in short intervals, as if she intermittently placed a shell against her ear and heard the distant thunder of the waves inside.[1] Every sound was sharply defined; the creaking in the darkness, the sound of movement in the bed, the rustle of sheets, the breathing and sighing, the cough, and the intermission that followed while she waited for another car to pass through the streets.[2] And when it rained, the repetition of its falling fell into silence as she entered the thoughts of her private world or heard the oncoming rush and spray of cars that rolled under her window.[3]

Rain fell on the windowpanes, combined with the thrashing wind in the trees, and instilled fear into Marsha—for she knew the rain and the wind disturbed the witch. Won't the witch be wet and cold and want the shelter and the warmth of a house?[4] If she didn't have a place of her own, if she were too heavy to live in a tree, would she force herself on her? Maybe if she locked the window, the witch couldn't enter, but she might become angry and break her way in.[5] Perhaps it was better to leave the window the way it was. Watch the opening of the window in case she entered? She'd scream if she saw her. Her mother and father would come, switch the light on, hold her.[6] Maybe if she closed her eyes, the witch would stand and wait quietly in the room until the rain stopped and then leave. Would it be wise to leave an empty chair for her so that she could sit and wait? Otherwise, she might decide to rest on her bed. She knew the witch, heard her in the forest, heard her when she went with her teacher and classmates over the narrow path through the cemetery, which was just outside the village and before the forest.[7]

When they were in the cemetery, the children broke away from each other, played tag, scampered from headstone to headstone, and played hide and seek, but as they entered the thickly treed entrance to the forest, they tightly held each other's hands—two by two—closely knit, and clung together. Each pushed and huddled behind the other, because it was there, where the light could not penetrate, that the witch lurked. And it was important not to breathe too many breaths or talk, because the witch didn't like noise or words. They whistled, however, because she was afraid of whistling. They had to be especially careful not to trip on or break a fallen twig or branch.[8] This was difficult because they weren't always sure whether the shadows were shadows or wood. The teacher never told them whether she ever saw a witch or not, but she, too, quietly moved down the path with them. Sometimes they laughed when one of the children stopped and pointed to an area where the witch was supposed to be hiding.[9]

When they finally reached the clearing on top of one of the sloping hills, they exploded with laughter and told each other stories of what they had seen.[10] We sang until the sky turned red and the trees were black against the sky. We knew that we had to return quickly because the witch took victims for her lair when the sun went down.[11] The way back, over the dampsmelling leaves, sharpened their appetites. They talked about how hungry they were and how good it would be for them to be home. Then, just before they left the forest, they passed a heavily darkened area. Once again they cautiously watched their feet and whistled until their ears felt the pressure of the sharp piercing sounded air. Although all the children said they saw the witch, I never did, except in my dreams, and it was always too late for me to whistle. She was there before me, until my father and mother entered my room and frightened her away.[12]

Case Questions

1. Are these images related to each other? What other examples could you add?
2. When do the night sounds become most distinct to you?
3. Describe what it is for you to listen to the rain at night—when you are happy, and when you are sad.
4. Do young children really think this? When did you stop making up stories about make-believe figures that you felt were real?
5. Is the child learning how to logically imagine different aspects of a situation, to weigh the pros and cons of her considerations?
6. How is Marsha trying to quell her fears?
7. Can you imagine yourself afraid of a witch in the same setting? What would you do?
8. How did the children control the actions of the witch? What else might have they done?
9. What kind of laugh do you think it might have been?
10. How do you explain the sudden outburst of emotionality?
11. Can you sense any degree of beauty and earthiness for the children in this situation?
12. What did you like or dislike about this episode? What stands out most vividly to you? Why?

7

THE DISADVANTAGED

Perhaps the most impoverished people are the ones who feel haunted by a sense of failure. They sometimes perceive themselves as inadequate, inconsequential, inferior, no longer capable of respecting themselves. These are the most disadvantaged of the disadvantaged. Their children incorporate their parents' fractured, defensive images. Insecurity, disruption, disorganization, and unpredictability, embue the home atmosphere. If the community is compounded by these families there is little space for the child to draw his sustenance for healthy growth. To whom can he turn for support, reassurance, guidance when in need? In addition to this, the child sees the people he loves hurt, bitter, and resentful. What does this do to the child's conception of himself, to what he might be able to aspire to? Even the one-parent family can survive and contribute the essential ingredients for a healthy development if the parent in charge has a good sense of himself. Imagine being dependent on someone who feels he is not in command of his destiny, a victim of the forces around him? Of course, this state of affairs is not limited to any economic, racial, or religious class. Unfortunately, however, the ghetto breeds more misery. If the child's home and neighborhood environment is trodden with dispair, disappointment, alienation, resentment, and pity, not to mention violence which generally results from compounded frustrations, then what meaning does he invest in school? How is he shaped by the community values and actions? What are the survival techniques he learns and utilizes? How insulated from the brutal realities is he? These are some of the questions that are considered in this section.

Dr. Coles deals with the issue of violence in the ghetto where contempt toward authority figures is often the established expression of the young generation. On the other hand, he emphasizes how the courageous parent contributes constructively in enriching the growth and development of her children despite the negative forces that exist in the slums. Within the confines of the human configuration of a neighborhood one is struck by how the adolescents play in the episode "Steel-Wool Flares." Nearly all the elements of existence are there to be observed, open and unabashed by the presence of others.

In Stella Chess's article we are asked to be more cautious about intervening indiscriminately into setting up projects or making changes in the disadvantaged areas. Only after problems are identified and diagnosed is intervention warranted. What happens to Jay, in the episode that follows, might happen to any child from any neighborhood. The code of ethics, quality of concern for one another, can be weighed in terms of values. In the episode with Lois, we see an older sister watching over a younger brother who is exploring the contents of a garbage can. The motive to experiment, to seek out that which whets the appetite of curiosity, and his sensitivity to the surrounding environment is underscored in this episode.

In M. Deutsch's article, he carefully examines the existing research related to our subject and among other things highlights the problem of the lack of communication between the teacher and child. The educational implications to this will become apparent to the reader. Although the adolescents in the next episode, "Adolescent Contemporaries: Street Scene," speak differently than those from other communities, their group coherence and rules of conduct essentially serve the same purpose of permitting each member an opportunity to belong to a group, to enhance his position and status, to share his everyday wishes as well as to develop a sense of self. Are these particular teenagers emotionally impoverished?

Violence in Ghetto Children

Robert Coles

When I worked as a child psychiatrist in a children's hospital, I spent most of my time with middle class children whose parents very often seemed earnest and sensitive; certainly they were worried about their children, at times excessively so. The boys and girls, for their part, were usually quiet and controlled. They were suffering from "school phobias" or the various fears and anxieties that have been described by a generation of psychiatrists. If they were disobedient and loud, usually it was a specific form of disobedience I saw, a very particular noisiness I heard, all connected to something they dreaded or dared not to look at. In a sense, then, the unruliness I noticed only confirmed my impression of a general restraint (emotional tidiness, I suppose it could be called) that middle class children by the time they are 2- or 3-year-old are likely to have acquired, never to lose.

Yes, there are the usual signs of aggressive tendencies in the "latency years" (the years preceding puberty when sexual urges are quiescent)—the bold and even nasty games, the play that seems involuntarily brutish—until a long look reveals how curiously formal, even restrained, the unruliness of these children actually is. Despite all the "drives" one hears psychologists and psychiatrists talk about—the surges of desire, spite, and hate that continuously press upon the child's mind and in dreams or daytime fantasies gain control of it—the fact remains that by the time middle class American children first reach school, at age 5 or 6, they are remarkably in control of themselves. As a result, when the violence in such children erupts in a psychiatrist's office during a session of drawing or in the midst of a game played by the psychiatrist and the child, it is almost a caricature of violence—violence so safe, so exaggerated, so camouflaged, and so quarantined that the very word seems inappropriate.

We in psychiatry are often accused of seeing only the drab and morbid side of human nature. If it would be any comfort to people, I suppose we could easily make partial amends for that morbid bias by letting it be known how overwhelmingly law-abiding man is: if he is vindictive, he is likely to be so toward himself. Psychiatrists spend most of their time helping people take a look at violence removed enough from their own recognition to be, in effect, somebody else's property. If in time the patient, whether child or adult, owns up to what he secretly or temporarily senses, he will be in greater, not less, control of himself. Thus, I remember treating a 10-year-old boy who drew wild and vicious scenes, filled with fire and death or at least an injury or two. When I wanted to know about what was going on, he let me know the score rather quickly by pointing to the people in his pictures and saying, "I don't know, you'd have to ask them."

A Different "Ball Game"

Not everyone in America is brought up to disown violence so consistently that its very presence in his own drawings can be adroitly (that is, innocently) denied. In the past few years, as I have worked with children in both southern rural slums and northern "ghettos," I have come to appreciate how useless it is to think of, or judge, the growth and development of the children of the depressed poor in the same way I ordinarily view the development of middle class children. It is, as one boy in a Boston ghetto recently reminded me, "a different ball game when you're out in left field, instead of in there pitching."

"Violence in Ghetto Children," by Robert Coles, from CHILDREN, **14** (3), pp. 101–104, May-June 1967.

If we consider what a child of the slums goes through, from birth on, and if we keep a special eye on what in his experience may make him "violent" even at the age of 7 or 8, we may well gain, rather than lose, respect for the upbringing he receives. In fact, I have seen how much childbearing means to poor women: it is the one thing *they* can do, and do creatively. It is the one chance they have to show both themselves and others that there is hope in this world, as well as the next.

By pointing this out, I am not arguing against keeping families to a sensible size, nor overlooking the impulsive, dreary background that is also commonly associated with pregnancies among the poor, whether in or out of wedlock. I am simply saying to others what a mother once felt she had to let me know:

They all tell us to cut down on the kids, cut down on the kids, because you can't keep up with them as it is, and even a few is too much if you're on welfare for life, the way we has to be, like it or not. I tries to cut down, and I want to, but it's not so easy. You have to watch your step all the time, and we can't afford the pills they have for others. Anyway, it's the one time in my life I really feel like I'm *somebody,* like I'm doing something. People come around and expect me to feel ashamed of myself, like I've done something wrong, and I'm adding to crime on the streets—that's all you hear these days, *our* crime, not anyone else's—but instead, I feel proud of myself, like I can at least make a baby, and maybe he'll have it better than us, who knows, though I doubt it.

If we want to help this woman keep her family small, I hope we also want to give her what she needs to feel like the somebody she still desires to be.

I know this woman's children, and already I have seen them readying themselves for what their mother herself calls "the goddam street." Each one of those children has been held and breast fed in ways I think some middle class mothers might have cause to envy. The flat is cold and rat infested, but there is real and continuing warmth between that mother and her babies. "Symbiotic" some of my colleagues—who have a name for everything—might call the relationship of that mother and her children; it is also a bond that unites the fearful and hungry against the inevitable day when the home has to yield to the outside.

Preparation for the Street

Slum children do not go unprepared when that time comes, contrary to the assumptions of some social critics who can only see the life of the poor as aimless, neglected, and always "deprived." Chances are these children receive specific and brutal instruction about the "realities" of life at the age of 2, 3, or 4 so that when they emerge from the home the police, the hoods, the addicts, the drunks are already familiar, and what happens in the schools or on playgrounds is not disappointing but expected. The mother I have already quoted has also testified to the morality and lawfulness she tries to inspire in her children:

I don't know how to do it. I don't know how to keep my kids from getting stained and ruined by everything outside. I keep them close to me, and sometimes I feel like everything will be O.K., because they know how much I want for it to be, and they'll go make it be, the way I thought I could. But after a while they want to go out. You know how a kid is when he's 3 or 4, he wants to *move,* no matter where, so long as he keeps going. And where can he move in here? So I let them go, and I stop and say a prayer every morning, and ask for them to be saved, but I have to say it, I'm not expecting my prayers to be answered, not around here, I know.
And when the kids come back upstairs, I give them a look, if I have the time, to see what's on their face, and what they've learned that'll make a mess of everything I try to teach. And I can tell—I can tell from day to day what's getting into them. You know what it is? It's the Devil and he tells them to give up, because there's no other choice, not around here there isn't.

She is a churchgoing woman, as are many of her neighbors. I have found that she knows her Bible better than I or my neighbors, and in fact she doubtless puts more store in prophetic, messianic Christianity than most Americans do. When her children start walking and talking, she starts teaching them rules and fears—enough of both to satisfy anyone who is worried about the decline of "morality" in America. At least in that home, and others like it I have visited, children are not allowed free reign. Instead they are told to obey, and they are swiftly slapped or punched if they falter.

Over the years I have learned how loyal slum families can be to America's ethic of "rugged individualism." Children are taught through the ubiquitous television to seek after all the products of our proud technology: the cars that can speed faster than any law allows; the records and clothes whose worth can only be seasonal; the bright and shiny places to frequent; the showy, gadget-filled places that not only shelter people but also make statements about their power, influence, and bank accounts. At 5- and 6-year-old, ghetto children in today's America share through television a world quite similar to the one known by their wealthy age-mates. I find it almost unnerving when I see drawings from a child not yet old enough to attend school that show the appetites and yearnings our advertisers are able to arouse. Precisely what do such children do with such wishes and fantasies, besides spell them out on paper for someone like me?

In School

When a child of 6 or 7 from the ghetto meets up with the politics of the street or the schoolyard, he brings along both the sensual and the fearfully moral experience he has had at home. Slum children live at close quarters to their parents and their brothers or sisters. They are often allowed to be very much on their own, very free and active, yet they are also punished with a vengeance when distracted or forlorn parents suddenly find an issue forced, a confrontation inevitable. They face an ironic mixture of indulgence and fierce curtailment.

Such children come to school prepared to be active, vigorous, perhaps much more outgoing on an average than middle class children. But they are quick to lose patience, sulk, feel wrong and wronged and cheated by a world they have already learned to be impossible, uncertain, and contradictory. Here are the words of an elementary-school teacher who has worked in a northern ghetto for 3 years and still feels able to talk about the experience with hope as well as bitter irony:

They're hard to take these kids, because they're not what you think when you first come, but they're not what you'd like for them to be either. (I don't mean what I *used* to like for them to be, but what I want for them now.) They're fast and clever, and full of life. That was the hardest thing for me to realize—that a boy or girl in the ghetto isn't a hopeless case, or someone who is already a delinquent when he comes into the first grade. The misconceptions we have in the suburbs are fantastic, really, as I think back—and remember what I used to think myself.

I expected to find children who had given up, and were on the way to fail, or to take dope, or something like that. Instead it was in a lot of ways a breath of fresh air, talking with them and teaching them. They were friendlier, and they got along better with one another. I didn't have to spend half the year trying to encourage the children to be less competitive with one another. We don't call middle class children "culturally deprived," but sometimes I wonder. They're so nervous and worried about everything they say—what it will mean, or what it will cost them, or how it will be interpreted. That's what they've learned at home, and that's why a lot of them are tense kids, and, even worse, stale kids, with frowns on their faces at ages 6 or 7.

Not a lot of the kids I teach now. They're lively and active, so active I don't know how to keep up with them. They're not active learners, at least learners of the knowledge I'm trying to sell them, but they're active and they learn a lot about the world, about one another. In fact, one of the big adjustments I've had to make is realizing that these kids learn a lot from one another. They are smart about things my kids will never understand. They just don't think school is worth a damn. To them it's part of a big outside world that has a grip on them, and won't let them get any place, no matter how hard they try. So what's the use, they ask themselves; and the answer is that there isn't any use—so they go right on marking time in class until they can get out.

We teachers then figure they're stupid, or they're hopelessly tough and "delinquent," or their homes are so bad they'll always be "antisocial" or "incorrigible." I've found that when they're playing and don't know I'm looking they are different kids—spontaneous, shrewd, very smart, and perceptive. Then we go back into the classroom, and it's as though a dense fog has settled in on all of us. They give me a dazed look, or a stubborn, uncooperative one, and they just don't do anything, unless forced to—by being pushed and shoved and made to fear the authority they know I have.

We have compared notes many times, this teacher and I. One child we both know is a boy of 8 who does very poor work in school. He is a belligerent child, a troublemaker. I see him in his home because his brother is going to a predominantly white suburban school, one of the very few children in the neighborhood who does. Their mother, living on public assistance with six children and no husband, has her hands full. She finds her "difficult child" smarter than her "model" one, the boy I watch riding a bus that takes him away from the ghetto.

The teacher and I agree, the "difficult boy" is a smart boy, but an impatient, agile, and provocative boy. He is headed for trouble, but as I talk with him I find *myself* in trouble. I have asked him to draw pictures—of himself, of his school, of his home, of anything he wishes. I get from him devastating portrayals: schools that look like jails; teachers whose faces show scorn or drowsiness; streets and homes that are as awful to see on paper as they are in real life; "outsiders" whose power and mercenary hostility are all too obvious; and, everywhere, the police, looking for trouble, creating trouble, checking up, hauling people to court, calling them names, getting ready to hurt them, assault them, jail them, and beat them up—even if they are children.

Once I asked the boy whether he *really* thought the police would hurt someone of his age. He said: "To the cops, everyone around here is a little bad boy, no matter how old he is or how many grandchildren he has around."

At moments like that my psychiatric, categorical mind finds itself stunned and for a change ready to grant that boy and others like him freedom from the various diagnostic, explanatory, or predictive schemes people like me learn so well and find to be (in our world) so useful.

An Impossible Situation

I often find welfare workers as well as the police present in the pictures ghetto children draw. They stand near the police like dogs, caricatures of themselves, with huge piercing eyes, ears that seem as twisted as they are oversize, and mouths either noticeably absent or present as thin lines enclosing prominent and decidedly pointed and ragged teeth. To ghetto children, as to their parents, the welfare worker is the policeman's handmaiden, and together they come, as one child put it, "to keep us in line, or send us away."

I have listened to public welfare workers and their "clients" talk, and I recognize the impossible situation they both face, the worker often as insulted as the family he visits by the rules and regulations they must contend with—and find a way around. I often compare the relationship between the workers and their clients with one that develops in psychotherapy as for a while powerful forces pull both doctor and patient backward in time toward those early years when parents check up on children, trying to keep them on the right side of a "line" that constantly puzzles the child and perhaps also the parent more than she or he realizes.

One welfare worker recently summarized the situation for me:

They behave like evasive kids, always trying to avoid getting caught, for this or that. And me, I'm like a child myself, only an older one—always trying to take care of my poor brothers and sisters, but also trying to get them in trouble or find them in trouble, so I can squeal on them.

No wonder I encounter anger, frustration, and violence in ghetto children. Everywhere things go wrong: the lights don't work; the stairs are treacherous; rats constantly appear, and they are not timid; uniformed men patrol the streets, certain that trouble will appear; teachers work in schools they are ashamed to call their own, at work they judge hopeless, under a bureaucratic system that stifles them, that is, if they are still alive; jobs are few, and "welfare" is the essence of the economy.

Yet—and I am writing this article chiefly to say so—the ghetto does not kill its young children. That perhaps comes later, at age 12 or 14, when idleness becomes a way of life, when jobs are nowhere to be had. For a while, during the first decade of their existence, ghetto children huddle together, learn about the world they have inherited, and go on to explore it, master its facts, accept its fate, and burn from day-to-day their inner energy and life, able for a while to ignore the alien outside world.

I find in these children a vitality, an exuberance, that reminds me often of the fatally ill I once treated on hospital wards: for a long time they appear flushed with life, even beautiful, only to die. I remember hearing from a distinguished physician who supervised a few of us who were interns: "They're fighting the battle of tuberculosis, and they're going to lose, but not without a brilliant flash of energy. It's a shame we can't intervene, right at the critical moment, and help them win."

He, of course, had the faith that some day medicine would intervene—with one or another saving treatment. Ghetto people have no such confidence, and I am afraid that I, at least today, share their outlook.

Questions and Projects Related to Violence in Ghetto Children

1. How do you camouflage your feelings of violence?
   a. In what kinds of circumstances have you felt a sense of violence?
   b. What role does your imagination play in dealing with these feelings?
2. What does Coles mean by a "different ball game"?
   a. Does anyone ever play the same "ball game"?
3. Is Coles glorifying mothers from slum areas? Explain.
4. What do children from slums learn that helps them to adapt and survive in their environment?
   a. Is it fact or opinion? What's your criteria?
5. What did the teacher mean when she said, "I've found that when they're playing and don't know I'm looking they are different kids—spontaneous, shrewd, very smart and perceptive. Then we go back into the classroom, and it is as though a dense fog has settled in on all of us."
6. Does Coles really see the situation as an impossible one? Explain.

Steel-Wool Flares

Just a few feet from where a cluster of boys were winding broken wire clothes hangers around steel-wool pads, two young men in their early twenties were singing and strumming their guitars in harmony with each other.[1] The boys were now prepared to dip the pads into a jar of gasoline that one of the group had siphoned from a tank of a car.[2] They then struck a match to the gas-soaked pads, which flared like torches. Like some ancient rite they held the flames in a circle. Children of all ages, as well as the adults, backed away as the boys began to swing the wire-held steel pads of fire above their heads. Streams of sparks, smoke, and glowing bits of wire trailed the flaming pads.[3] The young men had stopped playing their guitars; the voices in the streets were muted by the brilliant spectacle. Eyes and faces reflected the red-white light. The people were silhouetted as they leaned over their windowsills. Something ominous stilled the air. It was as if the people were waiting for something to happen. The night was ripped and cut with circles and scribbles of fire. Some adult voices punctuated the wild cries of the performing children. There were warnings from parents to their youngsters to keep away from the flames and falling streams of sparks.[4] As the flares burned themselves out into embers and chars new ones were lit. The guitar playing began again. High and low pitched voices of children cut through the junglelike calls of the torch swingers. Some of the girls resumed jumping rope in time to the sing-song cadence of words. The fire swinging was now part of the familiar variety of the street activity.[5] The people left their window views and retreated to their rooms. The young teenagers pushed and shoved and resumed their teasing games. All, was almost as it had been, except for the twirling steel pads of flames. Although radio and TV voices blasted the air it didn't deter the old and the young from sharing secrets with each other; they sat crowded and huddled in two's and three's on the steps of the stoops of their homes.[6] The air had a peculiar burnt charred odor but this, too, was assimilated into the environment.

Suddenly one of the boys stopped in his tracks, pressed his palm against his eye, and began to scream: "My eye! It's burning, I can't see! Help me!" In seconds his friends dropped their torches, and crowded around him, while one of the onlooking adults pushed himself between them and examined the boy's eye. "Your eye is all right but you burned your lid, I think. You better put something on it right away."[7] The boys led their wounded contemporary into one of the nearby tenements. A few minutes later, they were winding broken wire hangers around new steel pads, soaking them in gasoline, and igniting them. The music continued; the noises and sounds of the night combined with the smell of burnt metal, gasoline, and smoke. In time, though, the children had exhausted their supplies of steel wool. The game had come to an end.[8] The boys were now in pursuit of three girls who had their hair in curlers. These girls, however, knew how to keep their adversaries some distance from them. They used a banter of words that matched the railery of their pursuers. One boy, however, seemed somewhat separate from the group. He didn't join the others in the teasing.[9]

Minutes later the boys and girls were seen walking toward the corner candy store, into which they disappeared.[10]

Case Questions

1. Can you identify a neighborhood that reminds you of this description?
2. Is this a current type of activity of children you have known?
3. What kinds of rules can you imagine these children establish amongst themselves?
4. What do the younger children learn?
5. Compare a summer evening's activity in your own community to what is occurring here.
6. Do the people in your community sit and share their "secrets" together as these people do?
   a. With whom do the older members of the community talk in your community?
7. Is this typical of what adults in your community do when a child is hurt? Explain.
8. How important is variety for these children?
9. What do boys and girls learn together during these teasing experiences?
   a. How important is it for an adolescent girl to be teased by boys? Explain.
10. How would you list and classify the different kinds of activities of both the children and grown-ups in this episode?
    a. What quality of value would you give each one of these activities?
    b. What would you want to change in this particular environment? Why?

Disadvantages of "The Disadvantaged Child"

Stella Chess

It is time for the psychiatric community to take a closer look at "the disadvantaged child." This concept may have outlived its usefulness. During the past decade it served a positive function in focusing attention on the potentially noxious effects of environmental deprivation on the psychological and educational development of children. But the term "disadvantaged child" has come to be applied as an all-purpose label blurring the issues it was intended to sharpen.

To avoid being misunderstood, let me emphasize my high regard for the many excellent studies that have been reported in this subject in recent years. These studies have reflected a vital awareness that the conditions of life in economically blighted areas generate special problems for the children who live in them. Professional workers in the fields of mental health and education have become increasingly concerned about fulfilling their responsibilities to these children.

But our efforts will be hampered if we fail to guard against certain pitfalls. One of these is the tendency to recommend interventions before determining the exact nature of the problem. In order to change the course of events constructively for children brought up in slums, ghettos, and other poverty-burdened areas, we must be clear about the meaning of "disadvantaged."

The trouble is that the term is so often used in a global way. When we speak of "the disadvantaged child" we tend to assume a homogeneous group embracing all lower-class youngsters. This lack of differentiation produces not a diagnostic tool but a stereotype. To be sure, there is a sense in which all children in the lower socioeconomic group are indeed handicapped. The penalties of poverty are not illusory. Among lower-class families the incidence of malnutrition, prematurity, and brain damage is higher than among economically privileged families. Nevertheless, it would be a mistake to neglect the wide range of variations within the impoverished group even in respect to such matters as diet.

Outside of economic categories, we are on uncertain ground. We have as yet little information about the psychological impact of poverty on different children. There is not a uniform "mark of oppression." As Robert Coles has vividly shown in *Children of Crisis*, the so-called disadvantaged youngster may show strengths that are beclouded by the stereotype. It is well known that some children raised under conditions that are presumed to produce cognitive deficiencies, motivational impairment, and defective self-images do achieve success in academic functioning and cope in a competent fashion with the challenges in their lives.

The children in the "disadvantaged" group represent many different cultural backgrounds. They exhibit a host of medical, neurological, perceptual, intellectual, and psychological characteristics that vary widely. It is therefore essential that in gathering descriptive behavioral data we distinguish between capacities that reflect neurological deficit from those that reflect class identity; we must separate perceptual ability from attentional habits that are culturally determined; we need to identify the difference between intellectual capacity and verbal patterns characteristic of a group.

The stereotype, no matter how benevolently intended, ignores the rich diversity of individuals within a group. And psychiatric measures, when they are needed, cannot be usefully planned if they are directed toward a stereotype. To assess any individual child it is essential to know *both* the group charac-

"Disadvantages of 'The Disadvantaged Child'," by Stella Chess. From the *American Journal of Orthopsychiatry*, Vol. 39, No. 1, pp. 4–6, January, 1969.

teristics and the variations within the group.

Unfortunately, however, there is a lack of systematic criteria for categorizing group behavioral norms for children brought up in specific socioeconomic and cultural settings. In psychiatry, the uncritical application of white middle-class norms to lower-class children of Negro, Puerto Rican, and other cultural backgrounds has often resulted in significant errors of diagnosis and therapy. In the field of education, it is clearly important for the teacher to distinguish those behavioral deviations that represent functional adaptive responses to the disadvantaged child's life experiences from those which represent idiosyncratic maladaptive patterns of psychopathology.

Thus, there is an urgent need for a body of studies that will concretely examine the behavioral characteristics of lower-class children. Such studies must take a number of considerations into account:

1. Marked differences in family structure, parental practices and attitudes, and ethnic background may exert significantly different influences on psychological development.

2. Behavioral functioning may be influenced by levels of general health, neurological intactness, and perceptual and intellectual functioning.

3. Individual differences in temperamental characteristics and behavioral style may influence the child's social development.

4. The typical behavior exhibited by a lower-class child may vary significantly with the nature of the environmental situation or demand. For example, the child may behave one way in the familiar intragroup situation and quite differently in an alien, threatening environment.

5. Patterns of emotional expressiveness, language usage, and style of social functioning may be different in various cultural groups.

One cannot overemphasize the importance of cultural evaluation in psychiatric diagnosis and treatment. Some 15 years ago I noted that "an evaluation of the healthy or morbid psychological aspects of an individual can be made only in terms of what is appropriate and effective functioning within the specific cultural milieu."* This is as true today as it was in 1953.

Today, however, it has become more imperative than ever to challenge the tendency of a dominant group to impose its preferred style on other groups. Some persons of good will make the mistake of refusing to accept the fact of differences, as if all differences must be categorized as higher or lower on a scale of absolute worthiness. Nevertheless, there are differences in children's behavior originating in genetic endowment, temperamental qualities, cultural background, socioeconomic status, and individual experience.

For proper carrying out of psychiatric responsibility it is necessary to be familiar with these differences, not only among groups but also among individuals within groups. Failure to take such differences into account leads to unwise and ineffective interventions. Because the concept of "the disadvantaged child" masks a wide range of attributes and levels of functioning, its value is to be questioned.

* S. Chess, K. B. Clark, and A. Thomas. "The Importance of Cultural Evaluation in Psychiatric Diagnosis and Treatment," *Psychiatric Quarterly*, January 1953.

Questions and Projects Related to the Disadvantages of the Disadvantaged Child

1. Why is it important to be clear about the meaning of "disadvantaged"?
2. Are all children from lower-class environmental settings victims of cognitive deficiencies, motivational impairment, and defective self-images?
3. Define the difference between the following terms:
   a. Neurological deficit versus class identity.
   b. Perceptual ability versus attention habits.
   c. Intellectual capacity and verbal pattern characteristic to a group.
   d. Group characteristics.
   e. Variations within the group.
4. Make a study of any one of the behavioral characteristics of lower-class children listed by Chess.

Jay (9): Car Cushion and Cut Head

The smell of gasoline mixed with oil still emanated from the wrecked body of a car that stood next to a gas station. Jay pulled one of the backseats while his friends dragged the front ones next to it. Then they pulled the seats to the small garbage-filled lot and placed them together. Then each boy ran from a point about thirty feet away—over rocks, cardboard boxes, empty cans, and jumped feet first into the seats that catapulted them high above the ground. Within minutes children from the neighborhood lined themselves one behind the other behind the starting point and took their turns in running, jumping, and being launched into the air.[1] One child, a smaller boy who wore a black handkerchief about the back of his head leaped head first, somersaulted, and landed on his feet.[2] The game proceeded until the gas attendant stormed out of the station and bellowed in a menacing voice, "Put those seats back, you little bastards." Within seconds the children took flight, their heels in the wind. They streaked into the alley that led to the next street that ran parallel to the park, which they entered. They yelled, laughed, punched, and taunted each other playfully.[3] One child discovered a couple locked in each other's arms and his friends whistled, joked, and hugged one another in mock imitation. Another quietly watched the pair, then turned his head as if to avoid seeing them.[4] Next the children climbed on the swings and began to pump themselves back and forth, higher and higher. One of the boys called out to Jay defiantly, "I bet you can't do this," as he lifted his feet off the seat of the swing by holding the chains then lowered himself down to the seat. Jay tried to do the same thing but descended too quickly, his backside missed the seat. He released his grip on the suspended chains and catapulated forward with all his weight. The seat of the swing grazed the back of his head. Jay rolled on the ground, his head in his hands. "My head," his face contorted, "My head," and tears welled up.

"Get the park man," one child shouted while another took to his heels.

Jay continued to squirm in pain, his cries now mixed with tears. Dirty handkerchiefs were extracted from the pockets of the boys and placed on Jay's bloodstained hair. One boy dipped his kerchief into the drinking fountain and gently pressed the wet wad over the scraped area. "That burns," Jay complained between gritted teeth. Another of the group proclaimed, "It's nothing, just a bump and a little cut. You should have seen what happened to my brother. His head was a bloody mess before the doctor cleaned him up. Did he get hell from my old man." Jay was on his feet now, his head bent over the water fountain. Jay's face was no longer twisted in pain. The paths where his tears had fallen were dry and stained.[5]

Moments later the children started to toss an empty can back and forth. "Let's play touch football," one boy suggested. The teams began to charge each other when the park attendant entered the scene and inquired about Jay, who was seated on the bench. After medicine was applied to the abrasion, Jay ran to his friends, who were now in deep conflict over a contested foul play. The teams pushed and cursed each other without entering into actual battle. Moments passed before the game was resumed.[6]

Case Questions

1. If you saw one of your children doing this what would you do?
   a. What kind of playground environment do these children have?
   b. How ingenious are these children?
   c. Do you think the children of other community settings might be interested in this game?
2. What kinds of rules do these children abide by?
3. Do you think they were upset by the word "bastard"?
   a. Do you think these children should be punished for having taken the car seats out of the car? Why?
4. Why do you think the children behaved the way they did?
5. How important is it for children to prove their prowess to each other as the children here do?
   a. What do these children do to make a friend in trouble feel better?
6. What memories does this episode evoke? Describe it. What quality of mood does it have? Is there any nostalgia attached to it?

Lois (10) : The Pickles

Lois called sharply to her younger brother who was five, "Put it back. Remember what Mama told us," but Jack continued to explore the garbage can contents. He had already extracted a red plastic truck with three wheels and an old clock. He was bent over in search for more. At one point he looked as if he would fall into the can, his small sneakered feet barely touching the ground. Lois had run to her small sister, Amy, who was toddling after a small grey kitten next to a truck loading and unloading platform, where men were rolling barrels of pickles onto two wooden tracks that extended from the platform to the back end of the truck. Amy was already close to the truck when one of the men called out to the other.[1]

"Hey, Mike, give the kid a pickle."

Mike had been in the enclosed part of the truck, leaned over the side and said, "Hi!" then looked toward the other man and said, "She's about the same age as Roy. He's nearly two."[2]

Lois, who by this time was next to her baby sister, said, "Come on, Amy. Come with me." But Amy's only response to her sister's pulling was a "Meow."

"Hey, kids . . . you want a pickle?"

And without waiting for an answer, one of the men disappeared into the truck. A large-bellied man with a small twisted mustache and a pair of thick glasses entered the scene from the side doorway of a large refrigerator storeroom and called out.

"Mike, I got a rush order for you."[3]

Lois was slowly pulling Amy away, when Mike, who had returned from the inside of the truck's cabin, held two gleaming dill pickles out to the children. Jack had just entered the area with his plastic truck held against his chest when Mike turned to the large man and said, "O.K., right away."

Jack called out, "Me, too!"

Lois said to Mike, "My mother said I shouldn't eat before supper."

"Take them anyway—for later," the man uttered.[4]

And Lois reached up to the pickles, while Jack watched how the other man rolled another barrel toward the truck. Mike caught it, turned it right side up, and pushed it into the cabin. Jack reached out and grabbed one of the pickles from his sister.

"Am I hungry." He was prepared to bite into the pickle when Lois said warningly "No."

She had her nose close to her pickle and said, "Mmmm, smell it. Doesn't it smell good?" Jack agreed. Amy called out, "Me!" her arms outstretched toward the pickles.

"No, you can't have it," said her sister.

Then Amy began to stamp her feet, screwed up the features of her face, and cried.[5]

"Not now, later," Lois insisted.[6]

By this time Amy had developed enough momentum to utter a small, steady low cry, which, like a siren, slid up in pitch and in intensity. Jack, who was holding a pickle in one hand and the broken clock in the other, said, "Amy, look what I have," and he held the clock out to his small sister, who immediately stopped crying, pushed herself eagerly toward the clock and showed a smile under the tears that had fallen to her lips.[7]

Case Questions

1. What responsibilities did you have when you were a child?
   a. What might children learn when they have to care for a younger child?
2. Make a list of behavioral characteristics of five-year-olds while observing them in a nursery school.
3. How important is the behavior of strangers in influencing a child's perception of adults?
4. What might have motivated the man to have suggested that the child take the pickle?
5. How else might have the child responded?
   a. Do these children know how to check their impulses?
6. Are children severe or lenient when placed in the position of authority over others, according to your observations.
   a. What factors might make them one way or the other?
7. What kind of psychology is Jack using with his sister? Explain.

Some Psychosocial Aspects of Learning in the Disadvantaged

Martin Deutsch

It has long been known that some general relationship exists between the conditions of social, cultural, and economic deprivation and cognitive deficit. The environment having the highest rate of disease, crime, and social disorganization also has the highest rate of school retardation. Deficiencies in linguistic skills and reading are particularly striking. School dropout and failure, apart from what they represent in lost potential to the individual and his community, mean that, as adults, those who have failed or dropped out will be confined to the least skilled and least desirable jobs and will have almost no opportunity for upward social mobility.

A large body of empirical literature supports the assumption that certain environmental conditions may retard psychological processes, including intellectual development. This conclusion is borne out in research on both animals and human beings (12, 13). One of the most comprehensive reviews of the effects of environmental impoverishment on intellectual development, by Clarke and Clarke (7), presents data collected on adolescents and young adults who have experienced severe deprivation as a result of cruelty, neglect, or parental separation. Bruner (5) writes that "exposure to normally enriched environments makes the development of (cognitive) strategies possible by providing intervening opportunities for trial and error . . . that there is a impairment under a deprived regimen seems . . . to be fairly evident." Although he does not refer specifically to the environment of the lower-class child, Bruner's remarks seem especially relevant here. The obvious implication is that disadvantaged children, who have a meager environmental basis for developing cognitive skills, are often unprepared to cope with the formal intellectual and learning demands of school.

Facilitating Growth

Nevertheless, a fostering environment for such children can facilitate intellectual development. Bruner (6), for example, suggests that certain environmental conditions increase the likelihood of learning cognitive strategies. And Clarke and Clarke (7) report striking increases in IQ in a deprived group during a six-year program aimed at reversing deprivation effects. That improved environmental conditions may have a positive impact on the intellectual development of children is also supported by the studies of the Iowa group (16, 17). Informal observation shows that, even in the most economically depressed areas, where school retardation rates are highest, some children manifest considerable school success and academic proficiency. If we assume a causal relationship between environmental conditions and cognitive development, then variation in such development could partially reflect variations within the environment. We can assume that no so-called under-privileged area is homogeneous: There are, indeed, considerable variations in the home environments of children from such areas—variations ranging from large fatherless families supported by public assistance to small intact families with inadequate but regular income.

Moreover, learning contexts are as heterogeneous as environmental backgrounds. Although the two contexts are not actually disparate, early socialization, mediated through home and neighborhood environments and mass media, requires responses different from those necessary for school learning and

"Some Psychosocial Aspects of Learning in the Disadvantaged," by Martin Deutsch, Vol. 67, No. 4, pp. 260–265, January, 1966.

subject mastery. The formal learning processes carry well-defined criteria of failure and success not mediated through such behavioral indices as group leadership, influence, and the like, whereas the informal learning environment has no explicitly stated criteria or marking systems. In the latter, success may be more highly related to leadership, and failure to rejection or subordination by the group.

Psychological Contexts

Even as his learning context changes when the child enters school, so does his psychological context for achievement. At this point the amount of continuity between the home environment and that of school can strongly influence the child's responses to the learning and achievement context of school. The discontinuity between the lower-class child's background and the school impairs his successful responses in the new situation.

The middle-class child is more likely to have been continuously prodded intellectually by his parents and rewarded for correct answers, whereas, in the main, the lower-class child's parents have seldom subjected him to the pressure of a formal adult-child learning situation. The middle-class child is likely to have experienced, in the behavior of adults in his environment, the essential ingredients implicit in the role of teacher. For the lower-class child, relating to the teacher and school officials requires a new kind of behavior, for which he has not necessarily been prepared.

School curricula and learning techniques usually imply an assumption that the child has had prior experience in the complex learning area, where there are logical assumptions as to appropriate behavior and where success is rewarded and failure is disapproved. The teacher, trained in our not-so-modern teacher-education institutions, assumes—probably consciously as well as unconsciously—that the school child is a quasi-passive recipient of knowledge, and that he clearly understands the teacher's educative and remedial functions. In this, the teacher is as likely to be as confused about the child's expectations as the child is confused about the school's expectations.

Lacking sufficient sociological sophistication, school authorities understandably tend to expect from children a level of comprehension and motivation that can only be built through positive experiences in the learning situation. Children who are used to a great deal of motor activity and who have certain environmentally determined deficiencies in learning to learn, often respond with an inappropriate academic orientation. Teachers meet this situation in several ways, most of which cause serious problems for the socially marginal child. Some teachers establish low expectations, anticipate failure, and, true to the Mertonian self-fulfilling prophecy, find an increasing rate of failure.

Projection and Blame

Another reaction seems to be, "They can't learn; they don't care; their parents are not concerned." This projective device serves to relieve the professional of responsibility, since it does contain a grain of truth: Often older siblings and neighbors of the lower-class child have experienced so much failure and so much class and cultural arrogance as to generate a great apathy out of which none of them expects positive consequences from the school experience. This very apathy is sometimes reflected in the attitudes of the educational apparatus toward the lower-class community.

Still other teachers say, "It is all the environment-impoverishment, economic insecurity, segregation, second-class citizenship, historical chains. Of course, none of these things is the child's fault, but neither are they the school's fault." This approach has greater validity, invoking as it does social circumstances obviously crucial to the developing organism. Yet such a view often leads to negation not only of the essential responsibility of the school but also of the actual and potential strengths of the children. Most important, it induces an elaborate rationale for the further alienation of teachers from their primary function, teaching. The essential element, which is both professionally and psychologically threatening, is simply that, for the child inadequately equipped to handle what the school has to offer, it is up to the school to develop compensatory strategies through a program of stimulation appropriate to his capabilities. Essentially, the disadvantaged child is still further disadvantaged when the school, as the primary socializing and teaching agent, refuses to accept its own failure whenever any such child fails. For the school to assume its full responsibility requires constant self-criticism and self-evaluation; these have not been characteristic of educational systems, despite noteworthy exceptions.

To put it more bluntly, when teacher-training institutions and educational systems foster an atmosphere of critical evaluation of their procedures and establish high criteria for professional training and development, teachers will maintain a psychological connection with their children that today is often severed, especially when the teacher, with neither a theoretical nor a working model, must bridge social-class discontinuities. Were more of today's children succeeding in learning to read at grade level, we would be forced to reconstruct our theory considerably. They are not, and the total atmosphere in the majority of our urban schools having large groups of disadvantaged youngsters becomes less and less conducive not merely to the learning process but also to the positive child-teacher relationship that establishes motivation and gives rise to high standards of achievement.

Reflections of Failure

Responsibility for this unfavorable learning situation is not the school's alone. It lies in a combination of social circumstances, historical apathy, economic exploitation, and a society that does not put its money where its explicit values are. Even so, the school most directly reflects society's failure: It is the one institution that has the opportunity directly to affect the situation.

In this total atmosphere, what are some of the additional handicaps that the disadvantaged child brings into school? If we expect the school to organize so as to meet the child on his own developmental level, then we must know a good deal about the specific intellectual sequelae likely to be associated more with economic impoverishment than with affluence. Further, we need simple and adequate ways of measuring the actual development of each child's abilities, because they are the foundation for the skills the school is to teach him. Such specific information will enable the teacher to teach him more adequately and to present him with the most appropriate stimuli. Moreover, the child's probable success will increase when the material presented is truly consistent with his developmental level, since engendering a sense of competence, in White's (19) terms, can sustain motivation, thereby facilitating learning.

The self-image is vital to learning. School experiences can either reinforce invidious self-concepts acquired from the environment, or help to develop—or even induce—a negative self-concept. Conversely, they can effect positive self-feelings by providing for concrete achievements and opportunities to function with competence, although initially these experiences must be in the most limited and restricted areas. The evidence leads us to the inescapable conclusion that, by the time they enter school, many disadvantaged children have developed negative self-images, which the school does little to mitigate.

Another significant element, usually ignored, probably helps shape the perception of himself that the child develops in school, namely, the use of time. Generally, time is inefficiently used, there is minimal individualized attention, and the child often spends much time in unproductive rote activities, while the teacher focuses her attention on remedial subgroups or the omnipresent paper work. Given the high pupil-teacher ratio, the critical need is for autoinstructional devices or preprogramed curriculum elements to which the child can turn. This is part of a situation where responsibility cannot be placed on the teacher, and the frequent use of this down-trodden professional as a scapegoat reflects chiefly only her position as the psychologically operative instrument in the education of the child.

In a sense, after passing through the whole of society's educational echelons, the buck stops with her (but not in her pocket). Nevertheless, this understanding does not improve the situation. Too often, the child is seriously understimulated, even with the best of teachers, and there is little over-all curriculum planning for the needs of disadvantaged children. Most important, society has furnished neither funds nor the educational leadership and training necessary for the new supplementary technologies that would enormously increase the effective use of time. These would, in turn, help the child develop a sense of purpose and belonging in the school context.

Decreasing Alienation

Autoinstructional and programed devices and methods might also give the child a sense of greater mastery over the unfamiliar school environment: They could reduce his passivity by giving him greater control over the timing of stimuli, thus minimizing cultural differences in time orientation. Further, in the self-corrective feedback of programed materials, the teacher's role of giving reward and disapproval would be shared; for a child unaccustomed to these as means of motivation for intellectual performance, it might help decrease his alienation from the school. If these hypotheses are valid, then the new educational techniques could socially facilitate the learning process.

The extent of the disadvantaged child's alienation as a crucial factor in handicapping his school performance and achievement has been emphasized. Much of this is structural, and much of the psychosocial problem lies in the interaction between the child and the school. However, cognitive variables which have been socially influenced or determined also contribute to the whole process of increasing the mutual alienation of the school and the child. Among these, one of the major difficulties is the often nonfunctional language system he brings to school. My colleagues and I have discussed this at length elsewhere (8, 9, 10, 11, 15).

Language and Learning

I would like to point out here that social-class determination of linguistic styles and habits is an effective deterrent to communication and understanding between child and teacher. To illustrate, the child is unaccustomed to both attending to, and being the object of, what are for him long, orderly, focused verbal sequences. Yet this is the primary scholastic teaching and discipline method. Further, because the disadvantaged child is less familiar with the syntactical regularities and normative frequencies of the language, he has difficulty in ordering its sequences and in both deriving meaning from, and putting it into, context. This is all the more disadvantageous for the lower-class child because he has a short attention span for the verbal material to which he is exposed in school. Consequently, he is likely to miss a great deal, even when he is trying to listen. For such a child it is extremely important to feel some mastery in handling at least receptive language. This is made more difficult by what Bernstein, the English sociologist (1, 2, 3, 4), has described as the different dialects spoken by lower- and middle-class people.

This discussion keeps returning to the need for helping the educator to develop a comprehensive consciousness of the psychological as well as the learning difficulties of the disadvantaged child; the real potential for change; the specifics involved in training children, for example, to ask questions, or to become aware of syntactical regularities, or to use autoinstructional materials; and the imperative need to maintain as high as possible the level of stimulation and relevancy in the classroom. Here the research and insights of the behavioral sciences should be able to contribute significantly, provided the educational albatross takes a few "risks" to accommodate social change.

References

1. Bernstein, B. Language and social class. *Brit. J. Social.*, 1960, **11,** 271–276.
2. Bernstein, B. Social structure, language and learning. *Educ. Res.*, Vol. III, June 1961.
3. Bernstein, B. Linguistic codes, hesitation phenomena and intelligence. *Lang. and Speech*, 1962, **5,** (1).
4. Bernstein, B. Social class, linguistic codes and grammatical elements. *Lang. and Speech*, 1962, **5,** (4).
5. Bruner, J. S. *The process of education.* Cambridge: Harvard Univer. Pr., 1960.
6. Bruner, J. S. The course of cognitive growth. *Amer. Psychol.*, 1964, **19,** 1–15.
7. Clarke, A. D. B., & Clarke, A. M. Recovery from the effects of deprivation. *Acta Psychol.*, 1959, **16,** 137–144.
8. Deutsch, M. Facilitating development in the pre-school child: social and psychological perspectives. *Merrill-Palmer Quart.*, 1964, **10,** 3, 249–263.
9. Deutsch, M. Training programs as preparation for social change. Paper read at Amer. Orthopsychiat. Assn., Chicago, March, 1964.
10. Deutsch, M. The role of social class in language development and cognition. *Amer. J. Orthopsychiat.*, 1965, **1,** 78–88.
11. Deutsch, M., Maliver, Alma, Brown, B. and Cherry, Estelle. Communication of information in the elementary school classroom. Washington, D.C.: Cooperative Research Project No. 908 of the Office of Education, US Department of Health, Education and Welfare, 1964.
12. Hebb, D. O. *The organization of behavior.* New York: Wiley, 1949.
13. Hunt, J. McV. *Intelligence and experience.* New York: Ronald, 1961.
14. Hunt, J. McV. The psychological basis for using pre-school enrichment as an antidote for cultural deprivation. *Merrill-Palmer Quart.*, 1964, **10,** 3, 209–243.
15. John, Vera P. The intellectual development of slum children: Some preliminary findings. *Amer. J. Orthopsychiat.*, 1963, **5,** 813–822.
16. Skeels, H. M., Updegraff, Ruth, Wellman, Beth L., and Williams, A. M. A study of environmental stimulation: An orphanage preschool project. *Univer. Iowa Stud. Child Welf.*, 1938, 15, no. 4.
17. Skodak, Marie, and Skeels, H. M. A final follow-up study of one hundred adopted children. *J. genet. Psychol.*, 1949, **75,** 85–125.
18. Wellman, Beth L. Iowa studies on the effects of schooling. *Yearb. Nat. Soc. Stud. Educ.*, 1940, **39,** 377–399.
19. White, R. W. Motivation reconsidered: The concept of competence. *Psychol. Rev.*, 1959, **66,** 297–333.

Questions and Projects Related to Some Aspects of Learning in the Disadvantaged

1. What are some of the cognitive skills that disadvantaged children lack?
2. What are some of the informal environmental experiences that these children lack?
3. What is meant by "the discontinuity between the lower-class child's background and the school impairs his successful response in the new situation"?
4. Discuss the following quote: "Children who are used to a great deal of motor activity and who have certain environmentally determined deficiencies in learning to learn, often respond with an inappropriate academic orientation."
5. In what way do teachers become alienated from their primary function—teaching?
    a. What does Deutsch propose in order to combat this state of affairs?
6. What is the relationship between the child's self-image and his motivation to learn?
    a. What role does the school play in developing a positive or negative self-image?
7. How does the child's use of time help him to shape his perception of self?
8. Why does Deutsch suggest autoinstructional and programmed learning devices and methods as a means of helping the child develop mastery and control over the unfamiliar school environment?
9. In what way does the social class determination of linguistic styles and habits effectively deter communication and understanding between child and teacher?

Adolescent Contemporaries : Street Scene

Some of the younger children of about nine were milling about the candy store with the young adolescents who were gesticulating, laughing, and pounding each other's arms.[1] Between each upsurge of action, an intermission existed. Sometimes the boys and girls barely moved or exchanged words. They stared out into the street to watch other youngsters move by, or they watched the cars that passed. Occasionally one of the group of adolescents fired a word out to the other group. For a moment the others responded with a scurrying of words and emotions. Then the silence intervened.[2]

"She's a bitch. She gave us homework over the weekend again," one boy said to his companion.[3]

"Yeah, a real bitch. Hey, you know that stacked babe, Marla?"

One of the girls nearby, whose hair was in curlers under a kerchief, answered, "She's in my typing class. A nice kid. She's got a brother who's in the Army. Showed us his picture."

The first boy answered, "I never spoke to her. She's quiet. Keeps to herself."[4]

One of the other girls answered, "Maybe she's shy. I'm quiet, too." To this the boys laughed and jostled each other, one beating the other on the arm and saying, "Did you hear that? That's a good one. You're quiet? That's funny," and a kind of a forced laugh left his lips.[5]

The silence returned, and another car passed down the street and stopped at the light. One of the boys said, "That's a cool job. Costs two berries."

One of the girls interrupted and said, "You guys talk big, like millionaires with your money talk."

The first boy answered her. "Hey, honey, you've got berries, too." To this remark, they all burst out into laughter. The girl to whom the words were directed laughed as well.[6]

One of the boys whispered something to Frances. Frances opened her eyes and mouth wide and then closed them to small slits, and with baited breath and very controlled words, said, "That's dirty, Frank. You better be careful or I'll slap your face."[7]

The boys as well as Frances' friend laughed.

Frank said, "I didn't say anything. I only said that that Caddy was a nice job—that it cost two berries." They all began to laugh again.[8]

The owner of the candy store came out with a broom and yelled out to the boys, "Who's going to sweep up this mess? Look at all those peanut shells and candy wrappers." And he began to sweep the contents and swing his broom in the direction of the young people.

"Hey, Joe," Frank asked, "Where's Pete? What's he doing?"

Joe answered, "He's working—delivering. He can't stay around the streets like you. And he turned toward Frank's friend, "George, I thought you were going to help him. They need two boys."

George answered, "I can't. I have to work for my father at five. He wants me to sand some furniture down."[9]

Frances' friend asked him, "Boy, does that place smell of paint! My eyes tear."

George answered, "Stupid, that's not paint. That's varnish remover and shellac."[10]

One girl joined in, "Well, that's the same thing. Isn't it?"

The owner of the store had collected a pile of empty peanut shells, candy and gum wrappers and said, "One of you boys go to the back and get me a shovel for this trash." George and Frank jumped and disappeared into the store. In a moment they had returned with the pan. They watched the old man work. Then one of the boys said.

"Hey, Pop, when's Pete coming home?"

Joe answered, "For supper."[11]

Frank asked, "Can I go over to his house?

No one will be home in my house."

Joe answered with a warm smile, "Sure. Sure. Go over to the house. My wife will fix food for you, too."

Frank responded simply with his head down, "Thanks."

Frances asked him, "Where's your kid brother? Who's going to take care of him?

Frank answered, "He's going with my uncle for the weekend."

"Why don't you go, too?" she innocently asked.

George interrupted and said, "Hey, how about a game of handball?"

Frank's eyes lit up, "Sure." And as they moved toward the end of the street, Frank called back to Frances, "Why don't you watch us?"

Frances answered, "I have to go and baby-sit." And she smiled at him and waved, "See you later."

Frank didn't answer but suddenly started to run between two parked cars, while George chased him first around one car then another. By the time they reached each other at the corner, they were on the sidewelk again. They turned and disappeared.[12]

Case Questions

1. Why do boys pound each other's arms?
2. Describe the behavior of a group of adolescents in different situations without recording any of their verbalization.
3. Do adolescents need to criticize their teachers? Why?
4. Is this youngster telling you anything about what he values by what he says?
5. Do you think it helps these teenagers to kid each other while they discuss girls? Explain.
6. In what way are certain words used as a means to impress others?
7. Is the girl putting on an act? How do you know?
8. Is there any value to this play on words? Explain.
9. Do you perceive these youngsters differently now that you are informed that they work after school? Why?
10. How does language serve the purpose of permitting adolescents an opportunity to express anger?
    a. How is it illustrated throughout this episode?
11. How does Joe feel toward these younger people? Explain.
12. What kind of relationship do the boys and girls have?
    a. What aspects of the episode have a personal meaning to you?

8

CONFRONTATION AND AGGRESSION

When a person acts out what he believes in or wants while confronting opposition or conflict he gives credence to what he values. To recognize and act on one's convictions is a necessary part of being a healthy individual, of feeling whole, instead of alienated from oneself. In this section we have combined confrontation and aggression under the same heading because in different degrees, the articles and episodes depict both these themes.

In regard to aggression, the subject is vast but we will introduce it by stating that whenever there is too much frustration or threat to what a person values, wants, or wishes, there is a likelihood that he might attack that which threatens him in a direct or indirect manner or turn the hostility toward himself. At times he might disguise the aggression by utilizing fantasy, subterfuge, or work it out in substituted ways. A whole array of ego controls and defenses are brought to bear in such situations.

For our purposes, aggression is a symptom, to be understood only after the causes are sought. The factors that precipitate aggression are many. They might spring from the person himself, home, community, or teaching environment. These issues are given consideration in the episodes and articles that follow.

M. Schwebel, in "Confrontation or Cop-Out," attacks some of the criticisms that have been directed against the current wave of student demonstrations and defends the right of the student, layman, and professional to take issue where critical human problems are unresolved. The problem of being is dealt with when Andy, in the episode that follows, clarifies to himself what he has to do despite the impending dangers involved. In a broader context, but no less human, Bud is faced with a less determined concept of how he has to assert himself, but, as it turns out, experiences a more violent type of confrontation. The similarities and differences between these two episodes are open to examination.

In a down-to-earth manner, F. Redl discusses some of the causes, effects, and practical ways of dealing with aggression in the classroom. Tom, in the next incident, brings to bear his knowledge of group threat and behaves accordingly. In a more elaborate manner, Paul, in "Gangs and Football," tells us how he and his contemporaries play out their energies and conflicts in a constructive manner. In "the Three Hookie Players" the aggression exhibited takes on both a destructive and constructive meaning for the children involved. Lou, in the ensuing incident, "Sunday, Jobless Father," is suddenly faced with the consequences of his temper and the reactions of his family. The significance of his actions in reference to his family creates a human drama.

Confrontation or Cop-Out?

Milton Schwebel

Not so long ago there was a time when social protests were safely muffled and practitioners, professors, and scientists enjoyed the comfortable and undisturbed life. Conflicts there were, some of them professional, like the comparative merits of competing personality theories or therapeutic practices. And not infrequently some were social conflicts, but even these we could contend with comfortably in the solitude of our office or, with more heat and excitement, at our meetings by means of a theoretical analysis of the problem or a resolution calling for the government to change its behavior.

Now many have been wrenched from this state of relative detachment and, willingly or not, have been confronted with social conflicts in daily professional life. There is no longer time to wait for an annual or even a monthly meeting; resolutions don't help nor do analyses, even the most profound, that are not immediately convertible to operational decisions. The dean, principal, or agency director must decide *now* on the posture to take in response to demands submitted by spokesmen who may at this moment be awaiting his decision. Those in positions of authority or influence are compelled to make decisions that are unavoidably controversial.

For all who lead and have influence (which means all professionals), it is profitable to examine the kinds of responses that are likely to exacerbate rather than resolve conflict, to frustrate rather than midwife change, to stimulate rage and violence rather than trust and responsibility. Each such response is a flight from confrontation, an avoidance of the necessary dialogue, or, in a word, a copout.

Laymen (or students) are not competent to make decisions about professional (or academic) matters.

One can find evidence that seems to back this up, like the controversy and violence connected with the Ocean Hill-Brownsville experimental school district in New York. But searching analysis generally reveals that the failure in such cases is not of the community's making but due to ill-considered planning on the part of ambivalent top-level leaders. After years of neglect, the poor planning almost suggests that failure was built-in.

Personal experience with a student advisory committee and with student participation in a combined faculty-student senate has shown me that the student perspective adds a necessary dimension and contributes to the wisdom of the group's intelligence. Experience with a community group, consisting of some adults who had not gone beyond eighth grade, was even more of a liberal education. Community representatives came forth with a plan not essentially different from and as good as any that professors or school people would have created, but what is more, it was their creation and it was they who were to profit from it.

The greatest obstacles to effective working together are in the pride and stereotypes of the professionals; once these are dealt with, students and laymen are seen to need experience, encouragement, and a warm welcome to enable them to make contributions that are unique—unique because their perspectives are different.

The demands of social protestors should not be taken at face value because their motivations are unconscious.

This response too has at least some grains of truth because every organization and every mob attracts some whose personal motivations, conscious or otherwise, are quite independent of and sometimes antagonistic to the group's. To indict a group's behavior because allegedly it is innervated

"Confrontation or Cop-Out?," by Milton Schwebel. From the *American Journal of Orthopsychiatry*, Vol. 39, No. 3, pp. 378–382, April 1969.

by unconscious drive is to lead to absurdities.

Lewis Feuer, a sociologist, writes that student movements though altruistic are "pulled toward extreme and amoral means because the driving energy comes from unconscious sources."[1] Writing about the Berkeley movement in particular he refers to the moral surrender of the elder generation and the dethronement of the superego: "A psychological parricide had taken place on a massive social scale; the fathers were in debacle, defeat, de-authorized, floundering; the fathers confessed that their values were wrong, but only under the physical compulsion of the sons. Freud once described the guilt which followed a primal parricide. Here the parricide was psychological, and compounded by the elders' own abdication."[2]

The consequences of Berkeley according to Feuer? Drugs, public sexuality the lowering of the country's public ethics, the election of Governor Reagan. Associated, yes, but only simplistic thinking could lead to the conclusion that any of these, even the election, was a "consequence" unrelated to issues that were rending the nation.

In the same issue of *Change in Higher Education* in which Feuer gave his views, Henry Mayer said that the hostile reaction to student actions is elicited not by the form they take, for these are quite acceptable if these actions follow a football victory (e.g. disruption of traffic), but by the ends that are sought. Some of the very people who condemned student action at Berkeley and Columbia applauded it in Czechoslovakia. Most Americans, Mayer said, are not yet prepared to commit themselves to the stands that the students have taken. Hence the hostility, student activists, he says, are not the troublemakers. "They are responding as outraged human beings to all the brutalizing and irrational conditions that disfigure and trouble this country and diminish the quality of our common human life."[4]

The use of the unconscious as an explanatory principle in social-historical movements could lead to the following absurdities: The French Revolution with all its good aims deteriorated to violence because the childhood experiences of Robespierre *et al.* created a reservoir of repressed sadistic impulses which suddenly erupted with orgiastic fury. Our forefathers accepted the enslavement of blacks and wrote it into the Constitution as a displacement of anger and humiliation at being subjected to control by the *mother* country.

The attribution of the unconscious to those arguing for change only beclouds the issues and is more likely to lead to frustration, outrage, and violence.

The issue is not whether the students are unconsciously driven to parricide but rather whether Mayer's estimate of their goals is valid or not. If they are, student behavior is easily explained by a careful reading of history—American or any other—which shows that social gains are initiated, if not largely won, by pressure and power not by gentle petition.

The scholar, scientist, and professional must maintain his detachment from secular demands if he is to protect his integrity.

This response to social conflict, a sophisticated rationalization for escape, is not easily dismissed, because the objectivity required in our work does necessitate a certain degree of detachment whether we are engaged in laboratory or field research, in diagnosis or treatment, in social service or residential care. This old problem has anguished many a physical scientist, especially since the second World War.

The philosopher Northrop Frye has made this analysis: "The scholarly virtue of detachment, we said, is a moral virtue and not merely an intellectual one: what is intellectual about it is its context. It turns into the vice of indifference as soon as its context becomes social instead of intellectual. . . . Detachment becomes indifference when the scholar ceases to think of himself as participating in the life of society, and of his scholarship as possessing a social context."[3]

The uses made of all scholarship and all science, including behavioral science, are social and are a matter of concern. There is no escaping the moral implications of a professional group's decision as to the allocation of its resources. What it studies and whom it serves are social concerns, a fact that is apparent when glaring and monstrous examples are used, as in the study of the comparative merit of different types of human skin for the manufacture of lamp shades. Such a study involving multiple variables calls for sophisticated design. The moral problem is more subtle but no less real when questions arise about the use of short-supplied researchers or practitioners to increase industrial profit rather than serve the needs of the slum dweller.

Just as vocal groups are now challenging the hoary practices of the schools and universities, and exerting grassroots power to influence foreign policy, they are likely in the coming decade to do this in connection with all professional services. So at least is the prediction of three social scientists[6] in their study of social problems of the future who contend that authenticity will be the hallmark of professionalism in the coming decade.

Social and behavioral scientists are equipped to study social problems but not to introduce action programs for their resolution. They should stay in their studies and laboratories, emerge for purposes of observation and data-gathering, and return to the campus.

Charges like these have been made against those social scientists in the foundations and universities who have given leadership in the formulation of structures for school decentralization. In his recent book, *Maximum Feasible Misunderstanding,* Daniel P. Moynihan, now President Nixon's adviser, makes the most systematic attack on social scientists and social work leaders for the gross errors (implied in the book's title) in their community action theory. Social scientists, in effect he says, should stick to their own affairs and stay out of action programs. Their involvement, he writes, led to the intensification of social conflict and hence to the backlash and the Wallace movement of this past election year. Instead of community action, what was necessary was "... a fixed full-employment program, a measure of income maintenance. ..."[5] Adam Wolinsky reviewing Moynihan's book points out what Moynihan surely knows: that the community action program costs far less than a massive public works program whose cost neither the Kennedy nor Johnson administration was willing to support.[8]

If social scientists are to be faulted, it is not for involvement but for their support of patently inadequate programs that were doomed to fail to win "the war on poverty." Toy guns don't win wars.

A recent Harvard faculty report entitled "The University and the City" questions the frequency with which the intellectual knowledge of the disciplines is relevant to the judgments vital to the direction of public policy. "Even the best social scientists rarely answer, expertly, a question put to them by a public official; typically they tell the public official that he is asking the wrong question."[7] But if a question is wrong, then is not posing the right question an important contribution to social action?

The solution for professionals and behavioral scientists is not withdrawal from broad social policy-making, even though withdrawal can be safer because attacks on established power or ways of life always elicit counterattacks; the solution is in more forthright positions, especially if we really are honest in our concern about primary prevention.

There is one major occupational hazard that obstructs even the best-intentioned in this endeavor—an excess of "scientism." In our best tradition we seek evidence, carefully sifted objective evidence, from reliable and valid sources as a basis for testing hypotheses. Data of that type on many of the important questions about people-involvement, school decentralization, the prevention of alienation in all its many forms, are simply not available, but that is no reason for timid responses. History itself suggests some of the answers, and these are supplemented by theories and some hard data in the social and behavioral sciences. Now that we have "rediscovered" that even in this affluent society there is hunger and starvation, it does not require a controlled experiment to permit us to assert without violating the canons of science that the correction of poverty will have a salutary effect on mental health and intelligence, nor need we be hesitant to predict on the basis of historical precedents that this "war on starvation" will be opposed as vigorously as the food-stamp program and the war on poverty.

One way to characterize the stage of development of a profession is by the extent to which it seeks to anticipate the future. As stated earlier, some social scientists predict that laymen will be involved in establishing policy and evaluating services in the coming years. Even those professionals who respond unwillingly to change ought to make a virtue of necessity and bring to bear in our developing professions the acumen of those who have been recipients of services and probably will be participants in shaping the services in the not too distant future. Chances are, only then is our society likely to begin winning these "good" wars— victories which are indistinguishable from primary prevention.

References

1. Feuer, L. 1969. New York Times, February 14.
2. Feuer, L. 1969. Berkeley and beyond. Change in Higher Education, **1**:51–53.
3. Frye, N. 1967. The knowledge of good and evil. *In* The Morality of Scholarship, Max Black, (ed.) Cornell Univ. Press Ithaca: 9–10.
4. Mayer, H. 1969. No peace in our time. Change in Higher Education, **1**:22–25.
5. Moynihan, D. 1969. Maximum Feasible Misunderstanding. Macmillan-The Free Press, New York.
6. Roby, P., S. M. Miller, and M. Rein. 1968. Social problems of the future. Mimeo.
7. Un-Fair Harvard?: Faculty report surveys university-city relations. 1969. Science, **163**: 658–660.
8. Walinsky, A. 1969. Review of Daniel P. Moynihan's Maximum Feasible Misunderstanding. New York Times Book Review, February 2.

Questions and Projects Related to Confrontation or Cop-Out

1. At what point should laymen or students make decisions about professional or academic matters?
2. If you were a professor would you want your students to have some say about whether you were rehired for another year or given tenure?
3. At what point should the University make demands on the students in order to maintain their authority?
4. At what point should the students make demands on the faculty in order to maintain their authority?
5. Should the scholar and scientist be primarily concerned with scholarship and science or should they be involved in issues which deal with their own personal-social values?
6. Defend or attack the following statement: Social and behavioral problems of students should be the business of the faculty.

Bud (17): The Demonstration

"No," his father said emphatically, "Wear a button, sign a petition if you wish, but don't go. You're too young to get mixed up in a political rally and demonstration, they'll be thousands of people. One less won't matter. Besides, the last one was a bloody mess with fights, cops and arrests. Call one of your friends. Go to a show. Here's money," and he reached into his pocket for his wallet.[1]

"But my friends are going. I am old enough. Next year I'll be eligible for the draft. War isn't our business, killing civilians, poisoning crops. I'm going," he said with conviction.[2]

"Don't start your politicking with me. Save it for the street corners. I suppose the communist fascistic warmongers in Russia and China are a better substitute. How would you like your life controlled, where you work, what you read censored by a Gestapo-type of authority where appeal is impossible?"[3]

Bud interrupted, "I'm late. Have to go," and he grabbed his button-covered denim jacket and said good-bye.

The young and middle aged spilled out of the buses, taxi's, and underground with their slogans against murder, for love today and not tomorrow. Some were conservatively dressed. Others wore minis, maxis, bell-bottom pants, and different-colored beads. They conversed, teased, jeered, preached, and pushed. Their voices rose above the traffic noises as others chanted in unison, or called out separately their plea to end the war.[4]

Bud walked with his friends, and took an account of how the police grouped together in two's and three's along the rim of the mass gathering, how they fingered their clubs uneasily, adjusted and readjusted the position of their helmets and holsters while they vigilantly watched the swelling throng of people grow louder and larger.[5]

A lieutenant and captain stood amidst their subordinates, not far from a number of police-filled vans. Nearby fireman were seated on or milling about the fire-engine wagon.

Bud pushed himself closer to the speakers' stand. His friends had brought posters that they had tacked to on long pine wooden sticks. "Come On, Sing Out, Stop the War, Peace, Not War, Love, Not Hate, Peace, Not War, Love, Not Hate." Bud found himself repeating the words mechanically at first. People around him joined in; his voice was lost in their collective monologue. Then, the contagious effect of the group spirit moved him, imbued his voice with emotions. The power of incantation from his lips and throat spread throughout his limbs.[7] Voices and bodies pressed against him. He no longer was alone. He had joined the ranks in communion with his fellow humans. He was part of a great human movement. Despite the feeling of being an emergent part of the total population, feeling the impact of sharing, he was conscious of his own separateness as an onlooker, an observer of himself and the others about him.[7] This was a demonstration; its strangeness was less strange now. He was saying what he believed with less hesitancy, with a deeper sense of himself. Still, he wasn't sure about how critical he was. He realized how little he knew about war. Nonetheless, he was definitely against killing or making war as a method of working out conflict; he was opposed to violence in principle although he felt it in himself. Not too seldom, in disagreement, the muscles of his arms and shoulders tensed. He was aware that behind his apparent settled state lurked a beast. Perhaps a beast lay waiting to battle in every man a few layers beneath the coat of civilization, a beast who dressed himself in every fashion, used ugly uncommunicable words as well as precise delicate ones.[8] It was sometimes difficult to know what was right. He remembered his social science teacher saying that critical thinking was subject to the logic of belief that was handed down from generation to generation, packaged and ready to be assimilated in the bloostream.[9]

The loudspeaker from the platform blasted the same words the people were now changing. "Peace, Not War, Love, Not Hate." A spokesman from the stage raised his hands high and signalled for silence. The silence was still filled with the voices of the people. But then, a scuffle started—men were fist-fighting at the side platform construction. The spokesman who had looked toward the disturbance immediately, shouted out "Let's sing, 'We shall overcome, We shall overcome'. . . ." But the disorder spread like a brush fire.[10] There were growing numbers of people besieging each other. The police were now alerted, the men spilled out of their vans and spread side by side, their clubs raised against their chests, their gas masks ready for use. A loudspeaker from one of the police cars blasted, "Clear the square!" The singing had stopped. Fighting, pushing, yelling from all corners erupted. Sticks, clubs, fists, and feet thrashed and flew. Bud's first response to this was that he was in a trap, a human one in which reason now played a subordinate role to violence and panic.[11] What originally drew his concern at the beginning of the dislocation was quickly transformed into a survival sense.[12] What had been a peaceful demonstration against war had turned into a physical confrontation where the actual issues were being dealt with in battle. The warmongers and antiwar demonstrators were at each others throats. The issue of Vietnam had descended the least common denominator; both sides were victims of each other. The logic of confrontation was meaningful only to the extent that it symbolized belief. Yet here the feeling and thought were self-survival. The people had not yet established a collective sense of their own identity. The feeling of being a part of a larger entity had not yet taken root for him.[13] This was his first encounter. Bud pushed, tried to make headway out of the jungle of feet and bodies about him. Whistles and sirens stuttered with cries, moans, curses, and commands rose into a din of pandemonium, as the words "tear gas" were uttered. A new surge of movement gripped the crowd. It was no longer a face to face battle with anger and fear selecting its victims. Now both sides had a common enemy—gas. Bud's first wish was to flee, to escape the suffocating sting of gas that blinded and gagged him. He struggled through arms and bodies that lashed at him indiscriminately. He was bound by a stampede of bodies with flailing arms and kicking feet with no exit. All access was blocked. It was no longer a matter of fighting or fleeing. The very air was a weapon. The fumes came in wafted clouds. Suddenly he felt a sharp surge of movement. The impass was broken, firemen were now using a powerful jet of water that streamed forth at the people. Bud slipped, fell, but regained his feet. The momentum of the multitude pushed him along. The tightness in his chest, the rawness of his throat and eyes didn't hinder him. All his energy was channeled in his legs. He was unbound now and ran with all his strength headlong, away from the fury, from the convulsive tumult. He was aware that at any moment he might become a victim of violence.[14]

"The bastards. Look at them," he heard to the side of him. The police were mobilized into squads of three's as they closed in on some of the demonstrators, who despite the tear gas and attack, stood their ground, posters in hand, voices raised. Clubs and blows fell while these weaponless adversaries tried to escape from their assailants. Some of the demonstrators were dragged like dummy figures to a waiting police van. Sirens whined with new recruitments of firemen.[15]

Bud and his friends had managed to stay together. None of them were physically hurt.

As they walked away from the area of the square they spoke little; it was still too soon for them to decipher their feelings about what they had experienced.[16]

Case Questions

1. What seems to be the father's point of view?
    a. What are his motives?
2. What is Bud's position here?
    a. Does he contradict himself in any way? Explain.
3. What kind of logic is the father appealing to?
4. Can you identify with any part of this description? Explain.
5. What associations are evoked by this description?
    a. Can you tell anything about the point of view that is being presented by the way the police are described? Explain.
6. Try to explain how Bud became more emotionally involved in the demonstration?
    a. What characteristics of a group activity have contagious effect?
    b. Compare your findings to that of your neighbor's.
7. What does Bud mean that he was no longer alone?
    a. Why did Bud no longer feel alone?
    b. How did the people about him influence his feelings in this part of the story?
8. How do you feel about what Bud thinks here? Explain.
    a. How strong are your convictions about war and peace?
    b. What have you done to support these convictions?
9. Try to put what the social science teacher said in your own words.
10. Why do you think the spokesman started to sing when the scuffle started?
    a. What else might he have done? Why?
11. What do you think you would have felt in a similar situation?
12. What is meant here by "survival sense"?
13. Is it true that both sides were victims of each other?
    a. How do we know about both sides of the issue here?
    b. Is it true that the issue of Vietnam had descended to the least common denominator?
    c. Does this statement suggest that the significance of the demonstration is any less important?
14. What aspects of the description here are meaningful to you?
    a. How do you think you would have reacted in a similar situation?
15. What can you identify with in this scene?
16. In what way do you think Bud might have changed after such an experience? Why?
    a. Does belief about what you do affect your behavior? Explain your answer in regard to the subject of demonstration.

Andy (10) : Fight

His lip was partially numb. He swung his fists and thrashed his arms out as he started to feel the tears come. Again he felt a blow on his face, only this time he felt the blow on his cheek and his head hurt. He lunged forward with both hands out before him and grabbed the other boy's throat. He went down over his opponent.[1] Andy started to swing blindly until someone pulled him up and away. His hands and face and clothes were full of blood. The other boy's nose was bleeding, one eye was partially closed. It was a policeman who had separated them. The tears were still streaming out of his eyes. In spite of the tears, the anger, the pain, and the frightening exposure to his blood, he felt some kind of joy. He had fought without any hesitation at one point. It was what he had to do. Fight! He was no better or worse off than his opponent.[2]

"Who started this?" the policeman rasped out.

Neither one of the boys answered. They were wiping their lips and nose. Andy found an old handkerchief to wipe the blood from his lips.

"Al right, you kids, you'd better go home, wash up, and stop this fighting. Look at you. Now go ahead." They both detected a gentleness behind the gruff voice.[3]

Andy tried to remember how the fight had started. He remembered that he had been called a name he didn't like, and had been laughed at in front of other boys. He had been called a "sissy" in the lunch-room in school because he carried a briefcase. It was the first time he had carried it. The boy called out, "Sissy. Look how he has to carry his books." He laughed, then all the boys who were with him laughed and teased him with the same name.[4] He didn't know what to say or do, nor quite how he felt about what had happened at the time the whole event occurred, but it started to bother him a few moments later. He started to feel bad because he hadn't said anything. He tried to imagine what he should have done. Maybe he should have gone right up to the boy and said, "Is that so?" and put his briefcase down and rushed the boy. He knew that it wouldn't have been a good idea because all the other boys would have ganged up on him. Then he should have sneered and cursed at them, maybe one or two words. But then they might have recanted with the same word and laughed or teased him more.[5]

At night he couldn't forget the situation, how intimidated he had felt. He became angry with himself for not saying or doing something to them. Even if he had started a fight and the other boys had joined in against him, he would have felt better. Besides, what's a bloody nose or swollen lip when it's the principle that counts. No one was going to call him a sissy. The boys would have respected him if. . . . Now, wherever he'd go, they'd call out, "Hey, Sissy, where's the briefcase?" He decided that if he saw the kid, he'd tell him just what he thought of him. What would he say? "Hey, you! You called me a sissy, didn't you?" The boy would see that he was angry and try to laugh the situation away. Andy knew that if he allowed the boy to get away from him without punishing him, he'd tell his buddies, and they'd gang up on him with the same taunting and teasing. No, Andy decided, he'd have to get into a fight and establish himself. It took some time before he slept.[6]

The next day Andy waited in front of the school after class. He didn't bring his briefcase. For some reason, he didn't see the boy in school. He waited outside the entrance. When he saw him walking down the few steps from the exit of the school building, he followed him as he swung away from his classmates and turned down a street. They were alone now. This was his chance. He felt a great amount of tension in his body. He didn't know what to say when he stood in front of his opponent, his fists clenched, his eyes and lips fixed. Without saying a word. The other boy swung his fist against Andy's face. He felt his lip against his teeth. That was the beginning. . . .[7]

Now that he was on his way home, he felt relieved. He knew that he had done what he had to do. It would be alright now. He would carry his briefcase wherever and whenever he wanted to. None of the boys would dare say anything. As he approached the street on which he lived, he began to review the battle in his thoughts. He no longer was angry with the boy. Instead, he looked forward to seeing him again. He didn't know why, but he felt a kinship toward him.[8]

Case Questions

1. Have you ever been in an actual fistfight and felt the overpowering urge to pursue your adversary despite the danger of being hurt? Explain.
    a. What aspects of description do you feel should be omitted here? Why?
2. Did Andy feel joy? Why?
3. Does the policeman come through as a person or as an object? Why?
4. Can you imagine anything else that Andy might have been called that could have upset him? Explain.
    a. Why did the word "sissy" upset him, do you think?
    b. Were you ever called anything that infuriated you? Explain.
    c. Do you know anyone from an ethnic, racial, or religious group who was called a derogatory name? What was his reaction?
5. Describe Andy's state of mind.
6. Why was it important for Andy to gain respect from these boys?
7. Name a decision you made that demanded a certain amount of sacrifice on your part.
8. Why did Andy feel a liking for the boy whom he had fought?
    a. In what way might a disagreement or conflict bring two people closer together?

Aggression in the Classroom

Fritz Redl

There's plenty of minor aggression in the classroom that nobody objects to. The real problem is the aggression that prevents good teaching and good classroom life. This aggression comes primarily from three areas.

First, it is an input from the home or from the community. A teenager gets hopping mad at his old man, but he doesn't dare let off steam until he gets to school. Now, the teacher didn't produce the aggression, but it's there and he's got to handle it.

Second, is the discharge from within. Some youngster sits there daydreaming, and all of a sudden during a wild fantasy, he thinks of something that upsets him and he conks his neighbors on the head. None of them have done anything to him, and the teacher hasn't either. Something just burst out from within. (If youngsters are seriously disturbed, most of the aggression comes from way within, and neither they nor anyone else knows why.)

Third, the aggression is engendered right there is the classroom. It may be triggered either by what the teacher does that's right but that doesn't happen to fit the kid, or by God knows what—the kid's reaction to the group or to other kids, or to something that maybe the teacher wouldn't have done if he had stopped to think. But anyway, it's reactive to something in the environment at the moment.

Now, if I were a classroom teacher, I would like to know how much of which of those three packages is exploding before me, because it makes a difference in terms of long-range planning. It also makes some difference in terms of what to do at the moment. Most of the time we are not sure, but different sources of aggression smell different when we are confronted with them. Experienced teachers develop an uncanny skill at sensing "This is something the kid brought with him. I've got to help him recover from it before he acts it out." The outsider, though, wouldn't know.

Some aggression does not affect us directly because certain youngsters may be model pupils in the classroom, but then after school they may go out and rape or murder someone. So a youngster may be full of sick aggression without being a classroom problem.

On the other hand, there may be a great kid sitting over there who's bored stiff. He likes you a lot, but he gets mad at the fact that you bore him stiff. Finally, he's just had it, and he runs out and slams the door. A normal youngster like that whose aggression is classroom-produced is our problem. Too often, an article on aggression in the classroom concentrates on a few examples of youngsters who should have been in a mental hospital for the last 10 years anyway and ignores all the other kids who bother us.

The term *aggression* is so overused now, you've got to watch out for it. Don't ever let anybody trap you into discussing aggression without first asking him: "Listen, brother, which aggression are you talking about? What actually happened?" Because aggression has a wide range—all the way from reacting to boredom to wrestling at the wrong time in the wrong place with another pupil.

Discharge of surplus energy or of displaced needs from the home or neighborhood; loss of control in the face of seductive equipment like a slingshot or a knife or whatnot; personal battles with adults, other kids, the group, or the teacher—all these fall under the heading of aggression.

The way Joe or Jane expresses aggression, while not the end of what we're looking for, certainly should be the starting point. Unless

"Agression in the Classroom," by Fritz Redl. From *Today's Education*, Vol. 58, No. 6, pp. 30–32, September, 1969. Reprinted by permission of the National Association.

you know what lies behind their behavior, you will have trouble knowing how to handle it. Sometimes you may understand perfectly well how come. So the question then is what do you do to help him, which is a separate matter from knowing what was cooking to begin with.

I want to give special warning here not to make aggression synonymous with violence. The two are not the same, although they are obviously related. There is a theme in violence that we can legitimately call aggression. On the other hand, not all violence comes from aggressive drives. The behavior is aggressive, but the basis may be quite different. Let me give a few-illustrations of violence that does not spring from aggression.

Panic coping. A kid may get scared stiff, so scared that he doesn't know what to do anymore. So he does something violent; he tears something apart. The fact that the behavior is violent is important. But this child is not hyperaggressive; he is frightened and desperate.

The need to be heard. A frequent source of violence is the feeling that nobody listens. The child finally concludes that the only way to get someone to listen is to be violent enough. So when other avenues are blocked off, violence is a substitute for verbal and nonverbal communication.

The desire to display guts. If a kid is supposed to be tough, how can he show it? Who is going to believe it? "I'd better not let them know I'm scared. So I've got to find ways to show I'm brave." In order to do this in a peaceful life, he's got to create problems.

Demonstrating loyalty to the group code. This source of violence is not originally meant to be aggression for aggression's sake. ("If the rest of my gang thinks school is no good, I'd better show that I'm with them. So I put a thumbtack in the teacher's chair. I don't hate the teacher; too bad it's her rear that gets stung. But I'm a regular guy and I'm going to prove it.")

Risk taking—to study survival skills. For instance, how can a boy know if he can run fast enough to outrun the cop, unless he swipes something first? Or else picks a rat out of an ash can, swirls it by the tail, throws it in somebody's first-story window, and then hops over the garage roof fast before they can catch him? A kid has to know how good he is in handling a dangerous assignment.

The stink and the dust produced in the decay of group psychology. If a group suddenly gets anxious or panicky or wild or disorganized or elated or mad at each other, you get a lot of behavior that involves violence but that did not start as aggression. Although Joe and Jane may be doing something, they're not doing it as Joe and Jane but as members of a group.

Last on my list of violence that does not start with aggression but is secondary to it is, of course, *an invasion of societal turmoil from the outside.* Someone or something in the community ties a package of emotional TNT to the back of a kid and it blows up in the classroom. The kid responsible wasn't originally aggressive; he carries the whole load of community or neighborhood or subgroup aggression. As his teacher, you're just an innocent bystander. What he does has nothing to do with the way you taught him or whether you bawled him out or flunked him.

In short, there is some relationship between violence and aggression, but not a simple one. For teachers it's very important to begin to sense the difference between Joe's being loaded with personal anger at what you just did and the explosion that results when his TNT package goes off at a given time. They are different problems.

Now let me give a few abbreviated hints of what to do about various kinds of child behavior—hints that are not fancy enough to be written up much in books.

First, you sometimes need to get kids off the hook. The aggressive behavior is beginning but without having really been planned, and if you get pupils off the hook *now,* they don't have to continue. Another way of putting it is that you sometimes need to cut a contagion chain without making a big deal out of it. And in most cases knowing how to do this is very important in dealing with a normally well-behaved child as well as with a wild one.

Take Joe, for example. He's sitting over

there shaking imaginary dice, and at the moment you're too bothered. You catch his eye and he stops, but only momentarily. After a while everybody else gets interested. You want to cut that contagion chain now, because if you wait another five minutes, you'll have a mass problem on your hands.

If you interfere too early, everyone thinks you're a fusspot, a dope, or chicken, and you only aggravate things. If you don't interfere at the right time, you'll have trouble. Getting Joe off the hook at the right moment will stop his behavior without a big scene, and the rest of the group will not be too heavily afflicted. This skill of cutting contagion chains without making too much of a mess is, I think, one of the most important for anybody who deals with groups.

A second important technique for the practical handling of aggression in the classroom is signal interference. Signal interference in time saves nine. Very often teachers underestimate the possibility of stopping minor forms of misbehavior quite casually before the kid gets too carried away by it. They don't take the behavior seriously, because it isn't bothersome enough. So they wait until it does get bothersome enough, and by that time the situation is tense, the kid is already off his noodle, and anything they do now will have an explosive effect.

The big problem is that most teachers lack a good inventory of preaggression signals for their pupils. In some youngsters, the signals are easy to spot. Others apparently go aggressive all of a sudden from nowhere. That's because the teacher's radar doesn't pick up their signals. But if the teacher works at it, after a while he begins to get the messages from all around the room. One kid, for example, gets glassy-eyed and sits there quietly in a certain rigid position. If the teacher goes over and taps him on the shoulder, he'll go up like a rocket. Two minutes ago, if the teacher had gone around and said, "Come on, let's start working," that would have been fine.

A good many teachers—particularly those who are new to the classroom—do not know enough about the physiological and gestural signals that indicate the work-up to aggressive behavior. Everybody with experience understands them, but conveying this understanding to the other guy is hard. Apparently we don't think it's important because we don't have any fancy lingo for it, but if I were a beginning teacher, that's the kind of information I would like to have.

If you send me a kid with an unknown aggression work-up potential, I'd like to get to know that kid and figure out what he looks like before he goes off the handle. After that, I can tell at a glance that this is the moment to go over to him.

In observing classrooms and watching teachers with disturbed youngsters, I am constantly amazed at the terrific skill people with experience develop, and they can't ever explain it. What's more, they don't even mention it. They think it isn't worth discussing.

Let me describe one incident I observed:

A kid is sitting stiffly at his desk, obviously determined that he "ain't gonna do *nothing*." The teacher walks over to him, pats him on the shoulder, and says: "Now, how about it? You don't feel so good, huh?" And he doesn't say anything. What does she do then? She says: "OK, I'll come back in a while. Maybe by then you'll be feeling better." That's all. She doesn't push him. ("Why don't you. . . ? What's the matter with you? What kind of family do you come from, anyway?")

She uses her judgment, and sooner or later he's over the hump. His face clears up; his posture is relaxed. Then she comes over and puts the pencil in his hand and he starts working.

Now, number three: Watch out for the choreography of the dare. In our present society we all have an insatiable, unquenchable thirst for tribal rituals. We still perform tribal dances. Take this scene:

We have what looks like a relatively normal classroom at the moment. Here is Joe back there, who wishes I'd leave him alone. But he knows I'm a nice guy, that I've got to make a living, after all. And I'm pretty harmless, though a little crazy, maybe.

Still, somehow, the noise gets too loud, and I finally say: "Listen, you, you'd better stop that now." Then maybe things get worse, and maybe by this time I'm angry, too. So I say: "All right, now, if you can't be quiet here, why don't you go out and cool off?"

Let's assume I'm relatively lucky in my diagnosis, and the youngster gets up and moves to the door, but on the way he mumbles something under his breath. If I ask him what he said, he probably feels he has to lie—so I make a liar out of him. Or if he is decently honest, I have to send him to the principal.

The foregoing is one way the scene can be played. But it also can be played differently. If Joe is sensitive of his prestige in the group, and I happen to have adults looking over my shoulder, then both of us become involved in a tribal dance. He has to say, "Make me," and I have to say, "All right. I'll make you." So either I try to bounce him or I call the principal or whatnot. Then for three weeks, lots of procedures go on—all nonsensical and having nothing to do with the original issue. Joe's become a discipline case, almost.

What I've described here is a personal interaction, a limit-setting process of a very simple nature, really. Most of the time it works like a charm, but in the second instance it became a tribal dance. If I were a principal assigning teachers to study halls or other large groups, I would like to know how vulnerable they are to the tribal dance routine, because in a dare situation the pressure is terrific. If you send me a kid who is tough, I don't mind. But I would like to know how involved this kid is in a tribal dance.

You see, some kids who are plenty tough don't fall for that kind of nonsense. In fact, some of my best delinquents would never be so stupid as that. If I really challenged them, they would think: "All right, so let the guy have his little victory for a change. So what! So I go out. I'm tough enough. Nobody will think I gave in." If, however, the youngster isn't really tough enough, but has to pretend he is, then he has to do the tribal dance in order to impress the others with his plumage, or whatever.

This is a big danger. And many a teacher could avoid many a large discipline problem if he were able to recognize the first drum beats of a tribal dance. Very often we push relatively tough kids who mean well into tribal dances because we are unaware of the position they are in. At other times, we do not interfere when we should because we are too afraid we'll provoke a tribal dance when actually we wouldn't.

So the tribal dance is a whole phenomenon—separate from the usual problem of discipline—that is a rather deep psychological problem.

Number four: Watch out for the subsurface effect. Whatever I do also has a side effect, and it is not always visible right now. If we are aware of what else happens besides the immediate effect of what we do, we won't simply say, "Because I blamed him for being noisy or because I praised him for being quiet, everything is hunky-dory right now."

So it's important to look with one eye to the possible nonvisible side effect. I can do something about it afterwards, but only if I'm on the lookout for it. Like that boy we've been talking about. Let's say he leaves the room and doesn't start the tribal dance. In that case, I'll want to make sure we have a brief get-together afterwards to tell him that I appreciate his doing what I asked and that I'll defend his reputation with the rest of the kids. I'll say that there are no hard feelings; it was just that I couldn't let him get so loud in class. That's all; nothing more.

If you have to live with aggression, at least try not to breed it. We breed it, of course, by exposing even otherwise normal boys and girls to experiences, to space arrangements, to life situations that invariably produce inner frustration.

For instance, if I bore a youngster, I expose him to frustration. Or, if I have to delay giving help that is needed—say, a boy over there is stuck in the middle of a long division problem, and I can't get to him for a while because I have to be over here with the others. Sooner or later he's had it, and he gets mad.

Or I may breed aggression if I intervene with too little sympathy. If a youngster is doing something interesting, something he likes, do I say, "Get going this minute. Do you want to be late again?" when I could just as well say, "Look, I'm sorry to have to break that up, but you know we've got to get out now."

One final point: Don't forget that from time to time, your own aggression will start showing. As you probably are aware, your hostile feelings and how you deal with them make a story no less complex and touchy than the one just presented. That you anger may be righteous and justified is not the only issue. You must ask yourself some questions: How does my anger make me behave in the classroom? Which (if any) of the behaviors it produces in me seem helpful in reducing youngsters' aggressive feelings, and which ones just make matters worse? Figuring this out requires clear thinking and real objectivity, but it is worth the effort. Your professional obligation is to handle your own aggression in such a way that the individual pupil or the class can manage the spillover effect.

Questions and Projects Related to Aggression in the Classroom

1. In what way might the home environment of a child affect aggression at school
2. What is meant by "the aggression comes from way within"?
3. What kind of conditions or situations in the classroom might precipitate aggression in children?
4. What kinds of violence have you experienced?
5. What are some of the effective methods you know of getting children "off the hook"?
6. What kinds of class situations might precipitate aggressive feelings in high school people?
7. Describe a child in a situation who is challenged to show his "tribal plummage."
8. In what way do your own aggressive feelings affect the way you listen to what is said to you?
9. In what way do your own aggressive feelings affect the way others react to you?
10. When do you feel justified in expressing your anger?

Tom (13): The Gang Threat

Tom walked down the street and noticed that as the boys on the corner looked his way, the configuration of the group changed as if a magnet had been placed under it. They seemed prepared for action, although there was no apparent change in their behavior except the sudden silence among them.[1] Tom slackened his pace, but wondered whether it might be more desirable to walk at the same speed he had assumed before he noticed the group. One child, medium-sized compared to the others, stood challengingly, feet apart, hands in pockets, by the curb. This meant that in order for Tom to pass through the area, he would have to walk between the boy at the curb and the others who were grouped in front of the building.[2]

Tom became aware of his shorter breath and faster heartbeat. He sensed the muscles in his arms and legs tighten. His usual relaxed gait was stiff and self-conscious. He felt that he was being transported by a moving floor. Each step was less weighed.[3] He knew he was afraid. He wanted to run, but he was afraid that if he turned the children would pursue him, so he kept on moving to the fear-looming area. He walked straight toward them. As he came within steps from where they were, he found himself walking as if he were on a tightrope walk, all his concentration on a fixed line—the passage between the boys.[4] The rigidity of his body was flexed in every muscle. He could sense the nearness of the first two boys as he approached them. He found that he adjusted his step and maneuvered his body position ever so little, in order to pass without touching anyone. The tension in him mounted when he passed the group and couldn't see what was happening behind him. He felt the muscles around his neck tighten. He was afraid one of the children would jump him, break the stalemate.[5] He was only a few steps beyond them when he heard one of the boys call out,

"Hey, you're in my class. You're Tom!"

And as Tom turned about toward the boy who called out to him, he felt a deeper breath of air enter his body. A sudden wave of relief swept over him.[6]

Case Questions

1. What factors determine how children arrange the space between themselves?
2. What do you think Tom felt at this point in the story? How do you know?
3. Why was each step less weighed? Can you imagine a similar situation in which you felt somewhat weightless?
4. Does the "tightrope walk" add to your understanding of the situation? Why?
5. What tactics do children learn from each other in conflict situations?
6. What do you think Tom felt after one of the boys called to him?
    a. What happens next?

Paul (16): Gangs and Football

Sure I was scared of fighting, because I didn't know whether I'd get hurt. I hated the whole idea of the violence. It didn't have any predictability.[1] I sometimes became so angry I wanted to fight, but I didn't like it.[2] I knew I could fight if I wanted to, that I could fight well if it were for fun, but I didn't want to for real. I felt sorry if I hurt someone, so I tried to get out of fights.[3] Sometimes there'd be a gang that ganged up on you, and then it was a good fight because you had a reason, and there wasn't a choice. You had to fight because there wasn't anything to do but fight to survive.[4] They'd last a few minutes and it was a free-for-all, if there were two gangs. If you were alone with a gang against you, there wasn't anything to do but hope for the best. The smallest boy intimidated you. He called you dirty names, was a wise guy. There wasn't anything you could do but hope for the best if one of the boys from the other gang cut a few hairs off your head with a knife that he waved over your head.[5] Imagine twenty lined up behind you, smiling and enjoying the "game." You're the game and the gang is playing it. You could try to make a mad for it. If you had time the thing to do was to get your buddies out of the houses, join forces by a united front, and wait together on one side of the street before the other group came up the street. They backed off sometimes if they saw they were outnumbered, or they'd chance the battle. It was sort of a game. If we recognized a schoolmate, there was a nod or a greeting, a temporary break of tension, but that was rare.[6]

To watch the boys on either side was to watch them prance and flex their arms and chests. They would swagger and sometimes make believe that they had reinforcements in the alley.[7] If anyone had any ideas of using force, they'd have to contend with many numbers. This deception worked. When we saw them from far away, one of us would disappear and invariably return with a few bats, gloves, and balls—sometimes sticks for stickball. Of course, these were potential weapons. I don't, however, remember using anything but our fists. Even our feet weren't used in fighting—that was being dirty. There was our honor among the worst of us.[8]

When we played football on the sandlot, bruised our knees and faces, tore our pants and jackets, we sometimes played against the same fellows who were our enemies outside of play. They played dirty. I guess they thought we also did. They didn't do anything out of the ordinary, because we could do the same thing, but when there was unnecessary roughness, they were responsible.[9] We fought hard and when we lost, it was a tragedy and when we won, it was a victory. There wasn't any inbetween. We fought to win. There were fine catches or passes or tackling or running or skilled maneuverings. Some of us used to work out the plays while in school and try them out on the field.[10] There was usually a fight that exploded out of what one member felt was an injustice to him.[11] In short order, sometimes without a word, there would be a fight. It ended quickly, when we were torn apart. Some of the same kids we fought against became good friends.[12] We had to depend on each other for the game, or there wasn't any. The game was the thing, which permitted us to test ourselves out both as individuals and groups. We thought in terms of "we" although there was always someone or two who always wanted to carry the ball and do the spectacular. They usually did and were very much valued, since they were the scoremakers. Sometimes I wondered whether they needed us more than we needed them. But that was football—with bloody knees and noses and sprained ankles and sometimes a black eye, but always fun, even when it hurt.[13] We played until it was dark, when it was really cold. We played with all kinds of shirts and sometimes two pairs of pants. We didn't own any fancy equipment. We made shoulder guards out of cardboard rags, which we sewed into a sweater or sweatshirt. We padded our knees with cloth and kept the pads from falling off by tying our pants with large rubberbands that we made out of cut inner-tube strips.[14] It worked, kept us from really getting hurt. If there was one helmet among us, we took turns using it.[15] That was a luxury. It meant you could put your head down and charge the group with your arm straight out. Of course, a broken field runner didn't need a helmet, if he was good.

Where did we get the energy to play for hours and never get tired, running back and forth, falling hundreds of times, only once in a while really getting hurt?[16]

Case Questions

1. What do you think Paul meant by this?
2. Can you talk about fighting in the abstract or do you have to consider the situation, people in which the stress occurs?
3. There is no mention so far that he was afraid of being hurt. Is this a factor to consider here?
4. Describe an experience in your neighborhood in which you had to fight.
5. Here again there is no mention of fear on Paul's part. How do you think you would feel and what would you do if you were alone facing the threat of a gang?
6. Do other animals maintain power over geographical locations—or fight for possession for certain land rights?
7. What part of this description is real to you? What would you add to it to make it more vivid?
8. Do children keep to these rules in your neighborhood? Are children concerned with fair play?
9. "An eye for an eye" exists here. What qualities of allegiance are maintained in a competitive activity?
10. If you were a teacher and you discovered a youngster working out plays for football in class, what would you do?
11. How important is it for children to stick to the rules in a game? When do children try to break the rules?
12. What do you think happens to children to make them friends if they battle with each other?
13. Do the children in your community play like this?
14. How would you apply the quotation "Necessity is the mother of invention" here?
15. How important is it for children to learn how to share?
16. How would you answer this question?

Three Hookie Players

There was no light on the street. The sudden darkness was matched by the sudden disappearance of the three children who had partaken in the smashing of the lamp post globe and bulb.[2] Two of the boys had goaded the third to break the lamp by calling him "chicken," daring him to throw the empty coke bottle at the lamps. The taunting continued while the victim challenged his friends to do the same forbidden act. The culprit was a small boy, slight in construction, narrow headed. He gave the appearance of being out of proportion because of his long arms, which seemed to hang helplessly at his sides. He pleaded his cohorts to "lay off."[3]

They taunted him with the word "chicken" until he dared himself to do it. He grabbed the bottle, pivoted his weight to one side, and pitched his arm overhead. The impact disintegrated the bottle, globe, and bulb. The expression on the boy's face was fixed and impassive, as if the violence of the act had nothing to do with him.[4] The lines about his eyes seemed to be emphasized by the intense light that emanated from his eyes. With the crash of glass, swift sounds of steps followed. The children quickly disappeared.[5]

All was quiet except for the occasional steps of a passerby or the muffled sound of grumbling or cursing from some dark corner of the buildings, as one person kicked at the pieces of glass. After awhile, the three boys returned to the street.[6] Their dark elongated shadows gave them a gaunt identity. All three were silhouetted against the light from the corner. All three kicked a can. The hour was slightly after midnight. All was silent except for the rolling and rattling of empty beer cans, which jolted the night. When the three reached the broken-glass area, the small one with the long arms waved to the other two and said, "I'll see you tomorrow at the pier. Don't forget to bring some hooks." Before he entered the house opposite the broken glass, the others called out, "Yea," and skipped down the street—one foot on the sidewalk, the other on the curb. Even when they turned the corner and were seen no more, their voices could still be heard in the restless silence of the night.[7]

Case Questions

1. Did you ever play hookie? What were the circumstances?
2. Does the episode suggest any particular neighborhood to you? Why?
3. Is the description of this child a positive, neutral, or negative one? Why?
4. Is there justification in making this inference? Why?
5. Did you do anything forbidden when you were a child?
6. What don't you know about these children?
7. What assumptions can you make about the values of these children? What is your criteria?
   a. Write a short addition to this episode and compare it to your classmates.

Sunday—Jobless Father

As Lou rammed his fist through the cabinet door and cursed at the same moment, the two children ran over to the mother and began to cry.[1] "The bastards. The bastards. The miserable bastards."[2] And he held his tensely clenched fist, which was now covered with blood, in front of the cracked cupboard door. The children sobbed and lowered their heads against their mother's skirt, while she held her arms protectively over their heads.[3]

Suddenly the tempestuous air was stilled except for the intense concentration of what had occurred and the sobbing of the children, which quickly subsided.[4] He lowered his arms, looked at his fist, and uttered, "I'm sorry. I'm a fool," and he rigidly moved to the sink and rinsed his hand and bound the kitchen towel around it. Then without looking at the children or his wife, went to the bathroom and closed the door behind him.[5] Michael said, "Mom," fearfully. To this his mother responded, "You know your father when he gets angry." Then Michael asked, "But why did he hit the wall and say those things?" "He is angry because he lost his job," his mother answered. "Can't he get another one?" By this time George, the older brother called out, "Why do you ask so many questions? Daddy'll hear and get angry again."[6] The bathroom door opened and as Lou walked out, he said, "I'm sorry." The words were directed to his wife, Debby, who went over to him and said, "Let me see your fist. You big idiot![7] You know you can get another job, and we aren't in the poorhouse yet." The two children went over to see his fist, and George said, "I can make and sell shoe boxes. I was only kidding about wanting a pair of skates."[8] Michael turned to his father and asked, "Did you say you were going to buy George skates? I want them, too."[9] The father, who by now was sheepishly smiling, said, "I have to fix that door." As he went into the kitchen, followed by both his children, his wife opened the closet and said, "Someone has to help me set the table. It's time to eat."[10] She sat down and pressed her fingers against her temples, then covered her face with her hands. Carla, who had been taking a nap, now began to coo, but in seconds started to cry. The mother slowly got up from the chair and walked toward the bedroom.[11]

Case Questions

1. What happens to children when they see a parent lose control of themselves and show violence?
2. What purpose does cursing serve the father in this story?
3. Can you identify with the children, or put yourself in their place? How old do you think these children are? How do you know?
4. How would you explain a tense family situation in which the air seems stilled?
5. How can you explain this sudden change about in this man's feelings? (First he cursed and now he is sorry.)
6. Can you say anything about the children's understanding of their father? What is George really trying to tell his brother?
7. Do you think Debby really means that her husband is an idiot? Explain.
8. Can you identify with George's concern for his father's feelings? How?
9. Is it typical of a younger child to want the same thing that his older sibling has? How would you explain the fact that Michael doesn't seem to understand the reason why his father is upset?
10. Is the mother being unfair to the children in requesting them to help her set the table? Do you think it appropriate for children to help around the house? What are the arguments for and against helping a parent?
11. Do you think Debby is the type of person who can take difficult times in her stride without falling apart emotionally? Explain.

9

PREJUDICE

The growth and development of every child, regardless of his ethnic, racial, and religious affiliations, adhere in principle to the same internal and external bio-psycho-social influences. Notwithstanding the uniquness of his constitutional endowment, family, peer group, school environment, and community, he grows up and takes his place among his fellow men. For the black child the problem of growing up is sometimes marred by the fact that the color of his skin takes on a personal—social—cultural mark of defect, degeneration, inferiority, contempt, and mistrust instead of a biological aspect of the external covering of his body. This color stigma affects the way he perceives himself as a member of his family and as an included or excluded member of the community. The price of not belonging to the esteemed economical and educational white group often places him in debilitating settings, deprives him of cultural opportunities, or in general, perpetuates a vicious cycle; he sees himself at the bottom of the ladder in regard to status, achievement, and value. This is not the case for all blacks. There are concerted efforts of both black and white citizens to change this state of affairs. The fight for human rights for all people is more than a slogan for those individuals and groups who are acting out what they believe is their justified claim to existence. New images of black identity are shaped despite the cultural lag, opposition, and apathy. With these thoughts in mind we turn to E. S. Newton's article, which underlines the importance of using selective literary media as a means of compensating for the lack of real object relationships. It is his contention that through the use of literature the child will learn to perceive himself as a more valued, worthy person.

In the episode, "The Question of Skin Color," we are witness to what happens when Mary is confronted with the valued image of her friend and the devalued image of herself.

Cyril, in the next episode, "The Question of Being," gives us a thumbnail sketch of what she has lived through and how she feels about being black.

Both vignettes are by no means an illustration of what is indicative of all people who are black; on the contrary, they are simply singular perceptions of two individuals. Whether the themes of this section suggest generalizations about other minority groups subject to victimization and prejudice is a question to be determined by the reader himself.

Bibliotherapy in the Development of Minority Group Self Concept

Eunice S. Newton

Within the past few years special projects and services have proliferated which are designed to increase the academic attainment of students who progress ineffectively in conventional American educational programs. Despite differences in the materials and activities of these innovative programs, and in spite of the fact that the target populations range from pre-school to the college years, almost without exception their proponents subscribe to belief in the vital role that a positive concept of self plays in the development of a fully-functioning personality.[1] A positive concept of self, it is argued, is essential to the learner's personal, social, and intellectual growth and development. Bibliotherapy is frequently utilized in these compensatory programs as one of the vehicles through which personal and ethnic identification may be effected as a means of enhancing concepts of self.

An examination of the educational activities of some of the current programs for inadequately-functioning students will reveal that while bibliotherapy is presented as a standard feature to be utilized in the development of self-concept, rarely if ever is there given the rationale of its use or specific suggestions for practical classroom application of bibliotherapeutic procedures. In this paper, therefore, an attempt will be made to 1. review significant psychological theory relevant to the development of self-concept through identification, 2. present a rationale for the use of bibliotherapy in this process, and 3. suggest some possible bibliotherapeutic procedures to be utilized specifically by teachers of so-called minority groups—Negro, Puerto Rican, Appalachian White American Indian, Mexican and, most recently, Cuban.

Theories on the Acquisition of Self Concept

The composite portrait of the child who does not benefit from conventional educational programs has been drawn within recent years with increasing accuracy by Clark, Goldberg, Davis, Deutsch, and others.[2] The relevant literature attests to the fact that the so-called minority-group child learns of his assigned inferior status at an early age and, as a result, experiences deep feelings of humiliation and rejection. Consequently, even prior to his ability to verbalize his feelings, the minority-group child may become confused about his personal worth because of the lack of social support for positive self-esteem. Under certain conditions usually found in depressed areas in our country today—physical and economic deterioration, family transiency and instability—the child may develop conflicts with regard to his feelings about himself and about the group with which he is identified. The end product of these conflicts, doubts, and confusions frequently is self-hatred, a defeatist attitude, and a lowering of personal ambition.

Personality theorists[3] emphasize that from early childhood the individual's concept of

1 Edmund W. Gordon and Doxey A. Wilkerson, *Compensatory Education for the Disadvantaged, Programs and Practices: Pre-School Through College* (New York: College Entrance Examination Board, 1966).

2 A. Harry Passow (ed.), *Education in Depressed Areas* (New York: Bureau of Publications, T. C. Columbia University, 1963).

3 "Psychological Aspects of Education in Depressed Areas", *Part II, Education in Depressed Areas* (New York: Bureau of Publications, T. C. Columbia University, 1963); and William C. Kvaraceus, *et al., Negro Self-concept: Implications for School and Citizenship* (New York: McGraw-Hill Book Company, Inc., 1965).

"Bibliotherapy in the Development of Minority Group Self Concept," by Eunice S. Newton. From the *Journal of Negro Education,* Vol. 38, No. 3, pp. 257–265, Summer 1969.

self is an important factor in guiding both his immediate behavior and the later development of his personality. The child acts consistently in terms of the kind of person he believes himself to be—bright or stupid, attractive or unattractive, capable or inadequate in meeting the challenges of life. The concept of self is thus his personality viewed from within, and into it are integrated the sum total of the child's experiences.

The development of a concept of self appears to evolve through a sequence of experiences similar in nature to those in the development of attitudes—emotional interaction of the learner with an adult or peer model. The learning of attitudes and the development of concept of self, therefore, may be explained by the same general process which we believe functions in other types of learning. It is generally accepted today that the learner confronts a situation, identifies goals, makes a provisional try, and finds his expectations confirmed or denied. In his choice of beliefs (whether about himself or others), he is guided to certain provisional tries, beliefs, by the example of other people—that is, the learner imitates certain models. He "tries-on" roles successively and adopts those with which he feels "comfortable"—roles which meet his needs and already developed attitudes.

The child's first identification is normally with his parents (or parent substitutes) within the immediate family circle. The parents are termed the "primary identifying figures" and the child's initial interaction is believed to establish with them his basic style in subsequent coping behavior with others. Whether the child's personality will be basically *adient, abient,* or *ambient* may be a result of his early emotional interaction with his primary identifying figures.[4]

Adults outside of the home may be identifying figures, too. Teachers, recreation leaders, and close relatives with whom the child frequently intermingles, as well as his intimate and constant playmates all may be categorized as "secondary identifying figures." In a hierarchy of prepotency, these secondary identifying figures influence the development of the child's concept of self almost as much as the primary figures. In fact, as the early and middle childhood years wane, the role of the secondary identifying figures customarily increases in importance, and for many children quickly exceeds that of the primary ones.

As reading, televion, and community contacts broaden his knowledge of people, usually by the time the child is eight-year-old his choices of identifying figures increase markedly. It is possible for him to establish strong identification with fictional characters, historical personages, or famous athletes. In some instances, these "tertiary identifying figures" exert critical control of and make vital contribution to the molding of the child's self concept at this stage of his development.

Identification is a complex way of perceiving another person—partly rational and partly emotional. At this time, psychological theory cannot adequately identify the totality of the process whereby a child selects his chief models. Sometimes the child himself does not know whose example he follows. It is believed that in some instances a veritable human *pasticcio* has been constructed by the child from which he emulates salient traits. It is vitally important that the teacher of minority group children understand the development of self concept, for the self concept in the fully-functioning personality dictates the outcome of the teaching-learning interplay.

The Role of Bibliotherapy in Developing Concept of Self

Bibliotherapy is based on the belief that a person is affected by what he reads. This belief is as old as literate society and has been remarked upon in some of the literature of antiquity.[5] While bibliotherapy is formally defined as "the use of selected reading materials as therapeutic adjuvants in medi-

4 Lee J. Cronbach, *Educational Psychology,* 2nd ed. (New York: Harcourt, Brace, and World, Inc., 1963).

5 William K. Beatty, "An Historical Review of Bibliotherapy", *Library Trends, IX* (October 1962), 107–117.

cine and psychiatry," for teachers and other educators bibliotherapy is simply the directed reading of books to aid in modifying the attitudes and behavior of children and youth. The effect of reading upon the young has been studied widely and has been, also, the subject of provocative speculation and heated debate.

While direct personal influence of the child's primary and secondary identifying figures is paramout in the formation of self-concept, it has been long appreciated that models in literature may make a positive contribution. The fact that a literary figure may arouse such close empathy that significant influences upon the reader result is of ancient acceptance. In classical times, the the library was often called "the healing place of the soul,"[6] and the curriculum of both past and present educational institutions has included the study of literature as a valuable source of vicarious interaction in the human experience. The possibility of the learner following examples of successful living and avoiding the errors others have made is widely endorsed by educators as reasonable expectations of directed reading.

It is accepted by theorists in the field of bibliotherapy that books may be the sources of significant models only to the extent that the learner's psycho-social needs are being met.[7] It has been suggested that "wish fulfillment" may be the determining module in identifying with a literary character or notable personage. The child's wishes, dreams, or desires may be gratified through "putting himself in the model's shoes" where he may find the role satisfying and fulfilling to his needs. Stated another way, in the evolvement of literary identifying figures, there is an inextricably interdependent relationship between the nature of the reader and the nature of the reading material. For the educator, in its highest level of conception, bibliotherapy is guided reading which takes the learner beyond literal comprehension to discovery through identification of new and personal values. At this level of reading comprehension the learner approaches Roger's[8] conceptualization of "pervasive learning"—learning that affects the individual's present and future behavior, his attitudes, and his personality. This is the kind of learning in which there is a change in self in the direction of self-enhancement.

Bibliotherapeutic Methods for Teachers of Minority Group Learners

Teachers of minority group children and youth may introduce them to the "world of books" in the expectation that a sense of self-discovery may result from discovering the common elements in human experience. A dual role is required of these teachers: they must be cartographers of the map of the "world of books" as well as skillful guides able to lead their students through the peaks, valley, plains, and rivers of the accumulated record of the culture of man.

In earlier sections of this paper, the theoretical bases were established for the processes whereby concepts of self are developed and for the role of bibliotherapy in self-identification. At this point, guidelines for teachers of minority-group children and youth will be presented which may be used in guided reading for the development of self-concept. While the principal materials, presented in the ensuing part of the paper will be limited specifically to the Afro-American minority, the guidelines have broad applicability to Puerto Rican, American Indian, Mexican, Appalachian White, and Cuban groups.

Directed Reading of Afro-American Content. Within recent years as an adjunct to the Afro-American's new, vigorous thrusts for comprehensive inclusion in the American way of life, there has been published a body of biographical and autobiographical liter-

6 International Reading Association Bibliography #16, *Bibliotherapy: An Annotated Bibliography* (Newark, Delaware, IRA, 1968).

7 American Council on Education, *Reading Ladders for Human Relations,* 4th ed., (Washington, D. C.: The Council, 1963).

8 Carl Rogers, *Client-Centered Theory* (Boston: Houghton-Mifflin Company, 1951).

ature about distinguished personalities of African antecendents who have made signal contributions to America. In addition to the foregoing, several historical works and historical fiction have appeared which purport to present the story of the Afro-American in America, both past and present. These literary efforts which have appeared in hitherto unprecedented volume are of a wide range in format, age appeal, and standards; but for the most part, they represent sincere efforts to fill in a long neglected area in American history.

Unlike the teacher of a few decades ago, the teacher of Afro-American children today finds a dearth of works of fiction and nonfiction which abound in easily identifiable racial and ethnic characters, plots, settings, and themes. The volume and diversity of this recent literature, however, poses a critical problem concerning its most profitable use in today's schools. In addition to the customary problems of book selection with works of varying literary standards, there is a new problem complicating book selection caused by ambiguous and paradoxical educational objectives currently besetting the Afro-American community. The teacher of Afro-American children is called upon today to decide *which* models in literature possessing *which* societal values shall the students be encouraged to emulate in the realization of *which* educational goals for living in *which* "world"—integrated or separated.

Within the framework of his school's objectives, the teacher of Afro-American children must plan and execute his bibliotherapy program through 1. selecting and utilizing appropriate guidelines for matching children and books, 2. establishing criteria for book selection, and 3. developing guided reading activities which ensure maximum literary identification.

1. *Guidelines for Matching Learners and Books*: From research in human growth and development, learning theory, and children's interests, the teacher of minority group children and youth may secure significant information about the characteristics and needs of the young at different ages and stages of development. It should be noted that the findings of these researches transcend racial and ethnic vagaries and as such have broad applicability. A few generalizations with pertinent bibliotherapeutic implications from these fields of study will be presented at this point. Through understandings such as the following the teacher may secure increased competence in bringing together the right book and the right child.

(a) From child development theory is garnered the pivotal premise concerning the uniqueness of the individual. Inherent in this principle is the fact that since one's biological heritage cannot be replicated, each person's life has its own story, and its own particular themes and continuity. Thus, one's experiences and aspirations help mold the individuality of one's present and future behavior. Closely allied with this primary concept are theories of the dynamic unity of the human organism, the sequential unfolding and development of phylogenetic characteristics from conception to maturity, the universality of human needs, and the important role of the environment in shaping the quality and quantity of intellectual development. Theories of the multi-dimensional and multi-determined nature of behavior, also, have special merit for the teacher of minority group children. *It may be implied from the foregoing that the literary needs of children would be infinitely diverse and highly specialized, and that the environmental opportunities and the child's needs at different ages of development should be continually considered in guided reading activities.*

(b) From learning theory the teacher of minority groups may find the following generalizations helpful. Learning may be conceived of as problem solving behavior resulting from goal seeking motives. The degree of relevance of the learning activity to the student's life style, and the magnitude of the personal involvement and interaction with the environment will all contribute to the success of the learning. Approval, recognition, and reward—especially from an identifying figure whom the learner holds in high regard—will similarly enhance learning. *It may be implied from the foregoing that guided reading should be an integral part of the in-school and out-of-school life of the child, and that book selection should utilize the student's goals, preferences and interests as primary motivational and orientational forces.*

(c) Finally, from researches of children's interests, the teacher of minority group children may find the following guides of help in matching books and children: Interests are determined by a multiplicity of factors—physiological structure and needs, culture-based sex roles, experiences, and level of psycho-socio development. Interests are learned and are needs satisfying. To a great extent, interests depend upon the child's environmental opportunities for experiencing and learning. The child who feels adequate for the task at hand because of cumulative success is able to explore new areas of living—whether through real or vicarious activities. *It may be implied from the foregoing that directed reading which satisfies psycho-socio needs should be capitalized upon and used to extend the child's interests.*

2. *Criteria for Book Selection*: For the teacher who wishes to assist students in the selection of books which are expected to supply Afro-American identifying figures and situations, a thorough knowledge of this field of literature is required. Knowing the individual needs, interests, and abilities of children and knowing the world of books are the two sides of the coin of effective book selection. Since there is no shortage of tools to assist in the selection of books, the possibility of eliminating unwise choices can today be minimized.

The criteria in general acceptance today for evaluating books transcend racial and ethnic themes and characterization.[9] The essentials of effective writing upon which books are judged include the nature of (a) the plot, (b) the quality of content, (c) the theme, (d) the characterization, and (e) the style. While surveying the book or a qualified resumé, the teacher should read with the following questions in mind: Does the book tell a good story, or in the case of non-fiction, are the factual sources reliable? Is the content worth the presentation? Is there meaning or significance behind the story? Are the characters credible, viable, consistent in their portrayal? Is the style appropriate to the plot, subject, theme, and characters? In addition to the preceding criteria, the format of the book should be evaluated; for it has been found that illustrations, typography, and even the quality of the paper as well as the jacket design can all attract or repel a potential reader.

Without the help which the teacher may secure from specialized book selection aids, it would be almost impossible for him to cover the current field of Afro-American literature. The catalogs, book lists, and periodicals that follow are a few of the distinguished publications in this field.

Adventuring With Books, National Council of Teachers of English. Champaign, Illinois, 1968. (This is a carefully selected list of old favorites and books of recent publication which are classified and annotated.)

Books About Negro Life for Children, Augusta Baker, New York: New York Public Library, 1967. (Selected titles which are submitted to stringent criteria as to themes, language, and format. The entries are briefly annotated and classified as to age groupings.)

Children's Catalog, Marion L. McConnel and Dorothy H. West. New York: H. W. Wilson Company, 11th ed., 1966 (Classified list giving titles, author, publisher, date, price, approximate grade level, and brief synopsis.)

Council on Interracial Books for Children, Inc. ₩9 E. 40th Street, New York 10016 (A list of "recommended" books of fiction and non-fiction that present fairly and constructively the pluralistic society in America—as to color, economic level, religion, urban and nonurban.)

The Horn Book, The Horn Book, Inc. Boston: Published six times yearly. (It

9 Charlotte S. Huck and Doris Y. Kuhn, *Children's Literature in the Elementary School*, 2nd ed. (Holt, Rinehart, and Winston, Inc., 1968).

includes current reviews of books for children and youth classified by subject and age level. Reproductions of many illustrations from newest books are incorporated as well as articles about authors and illustrators.)

The International Library of Negro Life and History, New York: Publishers Company under the auspices of the Association for the Study of Negro Life and History, 1967. (Five comprehensive volumes which treat the history of the Negro in medicine, music and art, the theatre, the Civil War, and historical biography.)

The Negro in Schoolroom Literature, Minnie W. Koblitz, ed., New York: Center for Urban Education, 33 W. 42nd Street, 1967. (A comprehensive bibliography of over 350 books about the Negro American heritage. Listings include full bibliographic information, grade levels, critical annotations for kindergarten through sixth grade.)

We Build Together, 3rd Rev., Charlemae Rollings, ed., Champaign, Illinois: National Council of Teachers of English, 1967. (A reader's guide to Negro life and literature for elementary and high school use. This new edition contains perceptive and complete annotations of books about the Negro in various avenues and levels of life in America.)

3. *An Approach for Directed Reading Activities*: At its highest level of conception, the reading process is a virtual dialogue between the reader and the author which involves subtle interaction with the mood, tone, and plot of the story. In order for children and youth to secure the most from literature, it has been long-established that they must learn the skills of interpreting what is read even as they must master the learning-to-read skills. It has been assumed, and research has substantiated it, that the greater the degree of reader comprehension, the greater are the chances for meaningful identification.

For a number of years teachers have used a variety of activities in an attempt to get students personally and deeply involved in comprehending literature. Book reports, books reviews, teacher directed discussions, and book fairs and displays have been used most frequently to stimulate interest in and understanding of recreatory and therapeutic reading. To a lesser extent have been used the graphic arts, music, the dance, and informal drama. It is the position of this paper that in this age of profuse auditory and simultaneous visual-auditory communication, it would be wise to incorporate these modes of expression as the dominant part of literary interpretation.

The image of the minority group child portrays him as generally favoring concrete, stimulus-bound learning situations and possesing perceptual styles uncomplementary to isolated, abstract, visual stimuli. In addition, this child is reported as responding most effectively to learning situations in which the goals are easily recognizable and readily attainable.[10] For these reasons it would seem profitable to have the directed reading activities for the minority group child utilize such promising instructional innovations as:

(1) *Peer directed reading discussions*—Encourage students to "do their own thing" when communicating their feelings, views, and understanding of the author's theme, mood, perspective. Let the students select the classmate whose "style" would probably be best for interpreting or sharing a particular book.

(2) *Relating popular music and dances to literary works*—Why not allow students to find popular "soul" records for classroom presentation which reflect their views of a character's traits, predicament, or role? Why not encourage the creation of or display of current dances which in the student's view are expressive of critical moments of a story?

(3) *Open-ended book reviewing*—Students should not necessarily have to agree with an established view as to the motives of a character. As long as a student can present a

10 Martin Deutsch, "The Disadvantaged Child and the Learning Process", *Education in Depressed Areas* (New York: Bureau of Publications, T. C., Columbia University, 1963).

rationale for his view which is defensible from some aspect of reality, the class should be able to accept it.

(4) *Informal dramatics and role playing*—Singly or in small groups students may participate in charades, pantomimes, or a form of the TV Game, "Password" in order to get their classmates to guess the names of characters in stories read by the entire group. Students may review a story up to the climax and then act-out the most exciting part. The tape-recorder may be used by individual students or small groups to record unstructured reactions to stories for sharing with classmates or other classes.

(5) *Graphic arts to interpret literary reactions*—In the spirit of the current vogue of free expression in tempera, oils, clay, wood, *et al.*, there is no reason why students should not be encouraged to use these media for literary interpretation. The author's mood, theme, or central plot could all be expressed as well as specific characters' dominant traits in non-realistic reactions. Unhampered oral explanations of the choice of certain colors to express ones view of a literary episode or tone should prove a fertile source of catharislike therapy.

A Final Word

In America today, with a sense of urgency perhaps never before witnessed in any literate society, we are striving to ensure the maximum development of all the children of all of the people. We are consciously attempting to bring into fruitful participation in our culture the ablebodied and able-minded from all segments of our society. Functional literacy is essential for even marginal participation in our way of life, and the higher level skills of comprehending beyond literal meanings are now required of the citizen who aspires to a place in our world in the upper socio-economic strata.

It is the thesis of this paper that despite the philosophy of Marshall McLuhan, understanding the printed word will be pivotal to full participation in our culture during the lifetime of those alive today. Especially for the minority group child it is important that literacy be developed commensurate with his potential. It is submitted herein that bibliotherapy may be an effective medium through which the dual goals of the development of a positive self-concept and increased literary involvement and interpretation are realized.

Questions and Projects Related to Bibliotherapy in Development of Minority Group Self Concept

1. Do you think religious minority groups should be mentioned? Why?
2. What are the effects of a poor self-concept at an early age? How do you know?
3. Who were your secondary identifying figures?
4. What fictional historical or famous characters did you identify with?
   a. Compare your selection of figures to that of your neighbor's.
5. Does anyone ever totally identify with another person? Explain.
6. What kinds of reading affect you most? Why?
   a. Do you think values and attitudes can be changed by selective reading? Why?
7. What books had the most influence when you were a child and an adolescent? Why?
8. How does one discover a sense of self through reading?
9. Which societal values, models in literature, educational goals would you select for Afro-American studies? Why?
10. How would you go about matching the "right" book for a child you know?
11. How does a teacher learn about a "Student's goals, preferences, and interests"?
12. What factors determine interests according to Newton?
    a. What are the interests that most involve you?
13. What do you look for when you choose a book? Explain and qualify.
14. What have you learned about yourself in reference to this article?

Mary (II): The Question of Skin Color

Physically she was more mature than the rest of her group, her body indented and curved around the hips with the beginnings of breasts. Despite this new maturity her coordination was better than her contemporaries; she was more agile than her classmates in running, jumping, and climbing, as well as in her ability to articulate her hand movements. There was a certain deftness about her. She moved smoothly and was as strong as the strongest boy.[1]

Emotionally she vacillated from outbursts of curses, tears, to a withdrawn, sullen watchful expression. Her mood fluctuated momentarily as if the depths of her feelings were on the surface, easily erased and replaced by another set.[2]

Her language was simple with as few words to express her thoughts as she considered necessary. The children feared her verbal gibes. She used phrases such as "Stop bullshitting me, you mother f. . . ."[3]

She had created a special world in which she permitted few to enter. There were certain rules that she abided by: one was that she could trust no one beyond a certain limit. Her wariness seldom broke down—except toward the younger children who leaned on her as a kind of substitute older sister and, Cynthia, her "best friend," as she called her.[4] Another rule was that if her teacher, or any of the darker-skinned children came to her she shrugged her shoulder, turned her head, grunted some words about wanting to be alone, then retreated to another part of the room. Her eyes had that certain kind of hungry look of one starved for love. Her desire to make human contact was restrained behind bars of mistrust. It was such a look of wanting affection and yet refusing it that marked her.[5] There were other rules that governed her behavior. Sometimes she violently attacked the children whose skins were darker than hers; she called them blackass-bastards, or hit them or scowled at or cursed them. This assault and violation was paralleled by a gentleness and submissive behavior toward the white-skinned children. She was particularly friendly with Cynthia, a tall blonde, blue-eyed child who, among many other things, loved to paint.[6] One day Cynthia made a painting of a girl with an oval-shaped face, blonde braided hair, and blue eyes. As Cynthia unclipped the newspaper print-sized painting from the easel Mary rose from the puzzle she was piecing together and walked to one of the other easels, and began to paint a face: neck, eyes, nose, mouth in black careful strokes. She then filled the oval with brown strokes for skin color and then chose the yellow paint and painted yellow braids. She stood away from it for a few moments then grabbed the print and tore it apart to bits. She then removed herself from the area and went to the book corner and thumbed through the pages of a book furiously.[7]

Although it was not uncommon for the children to mark their hands and wrists with ink designs or current slogans Mary wrote curse words on her palms, used her hands as a means of drawing attention upon herself. The aggressive language was both a joke and a means of obtaining group acknowledgment. She also marked each one of her fingers with crosses. When one of the children asked her why she did it she said that whatever she touched died and proceeded to raise her hands defiantly impendingly toward the youngster who backed away.[8]

Behind the smiles, the words, and the gestures there was a small unhappy child who didn't know how to escape far enough from the world that threatened her existence, and yet who didn't know how to grasp some sustenance from it.[9] One day Mary pressed up against her teacher and said, "I loved you but you don't love me because I'm black." Before the teacher had an opportunity to answer Mary drew away and ran out of the classroom. A short time later the teacher received a message from the head office that Mary was home sick, and that she would not be in school. Three days passed before Mary returned. A certain passive type of behavior was now present. Formerly she had watched and carefully guided her actions according to the actions of others. Now she was oblivious of others. She was there in body but her spirit was somwhere else. No words, or actions from others brought forth any of her old ways of reacting. She was emotionally flat, expression frozen. It was at this point that the school authorities decided to look into the matter by first consulting with the parents, then with a psychologist.[10]

Case Questions

1. What's missing in the physical description of this child?
2. Can you imagine Mary as a real person or is she too objectively described? Explain.
3. Should this be included in describing a child? Why?
4. Why is she less wary with younger children?
5. Have you met children with this "hungry look"?
   a. How much subjectivity is indicated here?
6. Can you explain this approach to the children?
7. In what way are you familiar with this behavioral manifestation?
8. How do you think Mary perceived her body according to this episode?
9. Is this an objective statement or a subjective one?
10. In what way can you identify with Mary?
    a. Can you imagine why Mary said what she did to the teacher?
    b. What would you do to help Mary if she were in your class?
    c. Is Mary's predicament an uncommon one?
    d. What do you think might happen to Mary?

Cyril (21) : A Question of Being

I remember the skin bleaches used in my neighborhood. If the adolescents or grown-ups weren't damaging their skin they were straightening out their kinky hair with gadgets and oils. I remember the smell of dead rats, that sickening sharp caustic stench between the walls or under the floors. We lived in a railroad flat, in one of a series of family packed rooms, with every door padlocked, a community kitchen with an icebox sectioned off with provisions. The lack of privacy was overpowering. The younger kids were put to sleep while the older active children remained outdoors until it was their turn. Try to imagine one room, partitioned off with hanging drapes or curtains for privacy. My youngest brother slept in a bathtub, which was padded with cushions and blankets. Few days passed without crisis. We were drawn in to each other's squabbles, loves, and tragedies. I don't remember too many situations that I didn't stomach. Guess if you live on the precipice of a volcano you stop reacting to the eruptions.[1]

We had fun, sharing together, joking, watching my grandmother teach us piano. We all took turns learning. The piano was a precious object with candles, crosses, and our cherished pictures. We were told about our history. My father was a runaway who lived in shanty town, worked on work gangs, in mills, every kind of job long before he was old enough to know what was happening to him. Fortunately, he became an apprentice to a shoemaker and learned the trade well enough to stay in one place. My mother was the daughter of a preacher. She had an education and didn't suffer like my father. My two older sisters resented me because I was lighter than they were. Father especially favored me and that made it difficult for me. My sisters and I get along now. We have our own lives. I know I can accept myself better than I did but I have to fume when I think of how we have been brainwashed to feel inferior. It's like a pecking order among chickens, the darker the skin the more we feel we are not good. Our current fight for black power and emphasis that black is beautiful helps us but it will take time before we rid ourselves of our feelings of inferiority.[2]

I don't feel sorry for myself because I know it won't help but I know I'm going to do everything to fight hate and that's what we have around us, within our group and outside of it. Some powerful changes have to take place or there's going to be more trouble everywhere. My brothers look on my father and me as part of an out-group because he's an old time daddy Negro and I am a moderate compared to them. They want action and change now, not in the years to come.[3]

I have close friends, but I am suspicious of people in general. I know it. Can't help it. I have been hurt too much. But I try to take things in stride.

I hope to be a teacher someday. Children accept you for being a person and can unlearn their prejudice more easily than adults. Children have love and fun in them.

My grandmother ran a nursery school in a cellar apartment and I helped her before I was even in my teens. I remember her telling me one day, "Cyril, don't forget your people. We are dark flowers on this earth but our honey is as sweet and good as all others. Take care to nourish us."[4]

Case Questions

1. Explain what Cyril might mean by the statement, "Guess if you live on the precipice of a volcano you stop reacting to the cruptions."
   a. What meaning can you attribute to the body image of a person who uses skin bleaches and hair straightening materials?
   b. Who or what determines the values that are most desirable in regard to body image?
   c. What effect do cultural stereotypes have on individuals who don't fit them? Explain your answer in regard to the question of blacks and whites.
2. How many black males in the last generation had the opportunity of a formalized education?
   a. What are some of the effects of this state of affairs today?
   b. Do the girls in the black community seem to have a more stable model with whom they can identify? Explain.
   c. What did Cyril mean by her statement relating to brainwashing and feeling inferior?
3. Why do you think there is conflict of values between the members of Cyril's family?
4. In what way did you identify with Cyril's dilemma?
   a. Why does she want to be a teacher?

10

DRUGS

Are drugs a substitute for love, security, and meaning? "What love, security, and meaning?" might be raised as a counterquestion. "The family is becoming obsolete," trust a slogan, meaningful belief, a thing of the past." What is important is money, power, position, status, and "living it up" today. Gloom and catastrophe pollute our environment. Beauty is out. "Stop the World, I Want to get Off." A sad commentary for what a number of people believe is a reality for them. They feel alienated from the establishment and seek out their own meanings to counter the dehumanized, violence-ridden, unconcerned environment. As a countermeasure some of them learn to adapt to these perceived dangers by withdrawing from time to time to the drug world where personal-social meanings are enhanced by the use of chemistry.

In the article "Drug Abuse," G. W. Larimore presents the facts about the dangers of drug taking and makes some constructive suggestions concerning the role of the school in combatting the problem. This statement should act as an introduction to further reading and exploration into the area of drug addiction. Hal, in the episode, "Drug Hallucination," illustrates in some detail how the structure and content of his perceptions take on impending shapes and meanings in which the boundaries of self and the physical world collide.

Finally, Ernest Harms, in his article "Remedies for Drug Abuse—Right or Wrong," states among other considerations that "our present concepts of aid and prevention now applied do not touch upon the impulses underlying addiction," and that we must "first apply a psychology and psychotherapy that can explain the addictive impulse to the degree that the addict is able to reorient himself toward other avenues of experience." Addiction is his defense against disbelief, disillusionment, and failure to find enough meaning and purpose in everyday life.

Drug Abuse

Granville W. Larimore

Acid... speed... grass... Big D... horse. Are you turned on to this slang, the shorthand used to communicate in the world of drug abuse? The language may change from time to time and from one part of the country to another. The jargon may even become part of the speech of those who are not drug abusers. But the problem represented by these terms is a serious one, and being alert to the slang is hardly sufficient knowledge for the secondary school principal.

The problem of drug abuse has been with mankind for a long time. Opium is listed in Assyrian records dating back to the seventh century B.C. Egyptians numbered it among their remedies nine centuries earlier, and Sumerians had a word for it 6,000 years ago. In South America, natives of the Peruvian Andes reduce feelings of hunger and fatigue by chewing leaves of the coca tree—the source of cocaine. Mexican Indians pluck the buttons from peyote cactus to get mescaline for their religious rites.

In the United States, drug abuse as a problem of any significance dates back to the Civil War. The hypodermic syringe, introduced a few years before that war, made it possible to inject morphine into the body and relieve pain rapidly. So many wounded soldiers became addicted that their condition was known as "army disease." Civilian patients, too, were given morphine for various disorders and became addicted. A great variety of patent medicines containing opium or opiates were widely sold as cure-alls from the back of covered wagons and in general stores.

Chinese who were imported to build the great railroads of the West introduced the practice of opium smoking to the United States and the practice spread eastward among native adventurers. By 1900, this country had an estimated 264,000 narcotic addicts, more than five times the current estimate although the population was less than half as large as now.

The difference today is that there are many more drugs capable of exerting a powerful influence on the mind. Chemical research has added a great number of synthetic drugs to supplement those derived from natural sources. As scientific investigation in medicine and pharmacology continues, the number and types of drugs open to abuse will mushroom. Even with controls by government, manufacturers, physicians, and pharmacists, blocking off access to these drugs by our young people will not be a satisfactory solution to the problem of drug abuse. The dangers we face from the proliferation of drugs do not rise from the drugs themselves. Nearly all of them play a vital role in the advances of modern medicine. It is the misuse of these drugs which we must learn to control.

Dependence and Withdrawal

Among the problems resulting from drug abuse is "dependence," a phenomenon which accompanies the repeated use of narcotics and certain other "mood-modifying" drugs. Dependence can be either physical or psychological, or both. Physical dependence causes a user to have intense physiological disturbances or "withdrawal" symptoms, when the drug is discontinued abruptly. As long as an adequate supply of the drug is available, symptoms of physical dependence are not evident.

Psychological dependence can develop even though the body does not crave a drug physically. A psychologically dependent

"Drug Abuse," by Granville W. Larimore, M.D. From the *Bulletin of the National Association of Secondary School Principals,* Vol. 52, No. 326, pp. 30–38. Reprinted with their permission.

drug user requires continued use of the drug to remain contented. Because it is subjective, psychological dependence varies according to the individual and the drug involved. Some drugs cause a user to develop tolerance, which means an individual has to take increasingly large doses in order to get the same effect from the drug.

Psychological dependence, the cavity of need which drug abuse fills, is the important factor in the makeup of the drug user. Dr. Henry Brill, vice-chairman of the New York State Narcotics Commission and one of the nation's outstanding authorities in the drug field, has said that psychic dependence is the common denominator of drug dependence: "If it does not exist there is no dependence, and if it does there is dependence even if all the other features are absent."

The Opiates

Among all the drugs, those with the longest history of abuse are doubtless the opium derivatives. The more common of the opiates are morphine, heroin, and codeine, the last being an ingredient of many cough mixtures such as "elixir terpin hydrate with codeine," sometimes referred to as "GI gin."

There have been "waves" of the abuse of codeine-containing compounds in recent years; as the youth in a particular community were introduced to the drug, its abuse would become a "fad" for a time and then disappear from the scene only to reappear a few years later. Codeine itself is not considered physiologically addicting, although this point is sometimes disputed; the chief danger of the abuse of codeine cough mixtures (other than the problems caused by their high alcohol content) is that of psychological dependence and the introduction of susceptible youth to a "career" of drug abuse.

There is no question, however, about the addicting properties and the dangers of the two other opium constituents, morphine and heroin—sometimes referred to as the "hard drugs." Heroin, chemically di-acetyl morphine, is the more popular among hardcore drug addicts. The street terms for heroin are many and include "horse" and "H." Heroin addicts are known in the argot of addicts as "skin-poppers" or "main-liners," depending on their favored route of administering the drug, i.e. subcutaneously or intravenously.

Just as in any disease, drug addiction requires the presence of a susceptible individual, an available supply of the disease-producing agent (a drug in this case), and an environment which facilitates the introduction of the drug to the susceptible host. In the case of heroin addiction these conditions are most often found in the ghetto areas of our larger cities. It is in those areas, such an certain sections of New York City, that the highest incidence of narcotic addiction occurs in this country.

The ghetto or even those sections of our cities that have become "hippie" haunts are not, however, the sole site of all drug abuse. This is particularly true of drugs such as marijuana, LSD, the barbiturates and the amphetamines, all of which in recent years have increasingly invaded suburbia as well as the campuses of the nation's colleges and secondary schools.

Marijuana

Among these drugs marijuana has been receiving particular public attention recently. Appearing like fine, green tobacco, marijuana is most commonly smoked in pipes or in slender, homemade cigarettes with crimped ends. Nicknames for marijuana abound but the most common are pot, sticks, joints, reefers, grass, weed, tea, or Mary Jane.

Typical marijuana users buy the drug loose and roll their own cigarettes. Less frequent users may buy individual cigarettes. The "roach," or cigarette butt, is saved for emergencies when fresh marijuana is not available. Effects of marijuana are indicated by its nickname "joy stick." Euphoria, a confused lightheadedness and distorted spatial and time sensations and perceptions are among the effects of marijuana. Smokers may stare off into space and experience alcoholic-type effects, speaking freely, day-dreaming, feeling less inhibited and relaxing pleasurably. A person smoking marijuana is likely to exhale an odor like burning grass. His eyes are often red and his pupils dilated, and he may giggle or laugh for no obvious reason.

Marijuana use does not result in a physical dependence on the drug although psychological dependence may occur. The habit of escaping from reality when it is unpleasant or painful may have serious results. Some authorities tend to deprecate the hazards of marijuana. Loose statements that marijuana is no worse than tobacco and no more harmful than a cocktail have appeared in the press. These are without basis in fact, and at least one pharmacologist, Dr. Miras from the University of Athens, has reported that personality changes after chronic use of marijuana include slowed speech, lethargy, lowered inhibitions and loss of morality. He based his report on 20 years of observing chronic, long-time users of marijuana in Greece.

The Hallucinogens

Among the hallucinogens—the "mood-modifiers," which have recently captured the popular imagination—LSD is the most notorious. LSD, the initials for lysergic acid diethylamide, is also known as acid, cubes, and Big D. "Of all the drugs abused in this country today, LSD is the most dangerous," Dr. Donald B. Louria, president of the New York State Council on Drug Addiction, has stated. One experience with LSD can produce permanent personality changes or prolonged psychological damage. Psychotic results from the drug may return under stress even though the drug has been discontinued.

Under careful medical surveillance, LSD may be used to treat chronic alcoholics, schizophrenic children, psychoneurotics, psychopaths, the sexually abnormal, and as a pain-killer for terminal patients. But without proper surveillance, LSD can have devastating effects.

The Santa Barbara, California, Ophthalmological Society recently reported that four University of Santa Barbara students lost their vision completely and permanently because they gazed at the sun while under the influence of LSD. One of the four explained he was "holding a religious conversation with the sun."

Also in California, Dr. J. Thomas Ungerleider, one of the nation's foremost LSD researchers, has had to turn LSD patients away for lack of bed space. He said, "We've got an outpatient, huddled in his room near here, who thinks he's an orange, and that if anybody touches him he'll squirt juice." Four teenagers were arrested near Los Angeles after their car rammed a house, killing a three-year-old. The police reported the driver seemed to be in a trance and kept trying to climb the jail cell wall, yelling, "I'm a graham cracker—oops, my arm crumbled off."

Case Studies in LSD

Dr. Louria studied patients hospitalized in New York City with LSD-induced actute psychoses or with chronic schizophrenia complicated by LSD ingestion. A substantial number were clearly from middle- or upper-class economic groups and of average to above average intelligence. His study documented some reactions to LSD:

- A young man in a panic jumped from a fourth-floor window, fracturing many bones.
- A college student had a two-inch chunk of tissue taken out of his cheek by a friend also under the influence of LSD.
- A young man tried to kill the two-year-old child of his girl friend.
- A man jumped in front of a train because LSD-induced voices told him to do so.
- A young woman in a panic was found wandering naked, incoherent, and violent on the streets at night.

Of 114 cases studied by Dr. Louria, 13.1 percent suffered from profound terror; 12.3

percent exhibited uncontrolled violence; 8.6 percent attempted either homicide or suicide; 15.8 percent required extended hospitalization, half of whom had no prior history of mental illness. The overwhelming majority, 88.4 percent of whom were white, had taken LSD on only one to three occasions. He concluded:

> The deluge of uncritical, often specious publicity and the miraculous effects attributed to LSD use by its proponents are influencing susceptible, unstable individuals to seek their own psychological salvation by self-administration of LSD under uncontrolled or inadequately supervised conditions. There is . . . no evidence that taking LSD under such conditions is beneficial and, in some cases, this results in profound mental deterioration necessitating prolonged psychiatric hospitalization . . . only a single experience with LSD may be needed.

Testimony to LSD hazards continues to come in from many sources. Dr. Virginia Apgar, director of basic research for the National Foundation—March of Dimes, has warned that LSD users may be risking birth defects in their children and grandchildren as well as exposing themselves to increased risk of cancer.

An effect of LSD that compounds its dangers is that it creates a "missionary zeal" among its users, who will give away quantities of the drug in order to get others to join them. "Turn on . . . tune in . . . and drop out" is the slogan of the proselytizers.

At least three types of LSD users have been noted. One consists of narcotic drug-dependent persons who take LSD or other hallucinogens infrequently after a "fix" with narcotics. Another group includes users of other drugs, especially marijuana, who relish the more intense effects of hallucinogens. The third group is composed of persons who repeatedly take LSD only or in combination with other hallucinogens over a sustained period of two weeks to a month. Unlike those in the second group, these users take the drugs not for social purposes but to achieve some personal, esoteric goal.

"Speed" and "Goofballs"

"Speed kills" is a slogan that is making its way through the circles of drug abusers, and it's a warning that doesn't pertain to safe driving. "Speed" is one of the many nicknames for amphetamines, stimulants prescribed by physicians to reduce appetites and to relieve mild depressions. The initiated also refer to amphetamines as purple hearts, bennies, pep pills, footballs, or co-pilots.

Taken orally in tablets or capsules, amphetamines cause the abuser to appear unusually cheerful and active. He becomes prone to accidents because the drug boosts his "nerve." Always seeking new heights, amphetamine abusers have now taken to injecting the drug into their veins, a practice which may produce profound antisocial behavior, delusions, and hallucinations.

Barbiturates, commonly prescribed as sleeping pills, are another type of drug frequently abused by young people. As capsules and tablets, barbiturates travel through illicit drug circles under nicknames such as goofballs, yellow jackets, blue heavens, red birds, and various trade names.

Death from an overdose of barbiturates, either accidentally or with suicidal intent, ranks with carbon monoxide in frequency. Because an overdose of these drugs makes the user "drunk," he may lose track of the amount he has taken and unintentionally take an overdose. The symptoms of drunkenness, confusion, mental sluggishness, slurred speech, and lack of coordination make the abuser of barbiturates prone to accidents. Behind the wheel of a car, a barbiturate user can be a menace.

This list of drugs being abused by our young people is by no means exhaustive. "Sniffing" is another dangerous practice, and its habitués are remarkably resourceful in seeking new substances to sniff. A list of these substances reads like the inventory of a well-stocked hardware store; airplane glue, shoe polish, lacquer, tire patch cement, paint, and lighter fluid are a few. An 11-year-old girl from Greenwich, Connecticut, died this year after inhaling an aerosol spray intended to frost cocktail glasses. The coolant chilled or froze her larynx and she was asphyxiated.

A suggestion that manufacturers add unpleasant ingredients to glue to stop glue-sniffing caused one expert to reply, "Where social problems are concerned, pressure of this sort is often like pressure on a capped tube of the glue itself. When one squeezes down on a bluge in one part of the tube, the bulge instantly reappears in another part of the tube. When the solution to the problem comes, it will come not from what is in the tube but what is in the boy."

The Antidote

"What is in the boy" will be the most effective answer to the spread of drug abuse among our young people. Educators can be instrumental in providing this answer. The harsh, hazardous facts of the tragedy that drug abuse can bring should be clearly outlined for teenagers as part of their health education.

Educators need to be thoroughly informed about the dangers of drug abuse in order to cut through the myths and misconceptions that often accompany the sensational accounts of drug use that are appearing in all the media. And they will have to develop methods of communicating the facts about drugs to young people so that a resistance is built up to the impulse to try them, just as vaccines build up a resistance to disease. Cigarette-smoking, alcohol abuse, and other vital health problems should be a part of this comprehensive "educational vaccination." To be effective, the program should begin long before young people reach high school. Health education should start when a child starts to school and continue until he leaves.

Educators in constant contact with young people need to be continuously alert to signs of drug abuse and ready to take appropriate action. It's a contagion that will not go away if ignored. Case-finding and law enforcement can be only a partial solution to the problem, particularly as the debilitating fingers of drug abuse reach out from urban ghettos to the suburbs, from poor children to the well-off and even the rich.

Campaign Against Drugs

Louria's study of LSD abuse led him to conclude that "it is imperative to initiate a vigorous and impeccably honest campaign as to the potential dangers of uncontrolled LSD use." Such education at the high school and college levels should be included as an integral part of a sound, comprehensive program of health education. Films, lectures, discussions, and other educational techniques must be directed primarily at the large and educable group of those who are often confused about drugs. "If we can but provide them with facts, presented in scrupulously honest fashion, the number of young individuals susceptible to the blandishments of the proselytizers should decrease."

Developing fertile ground in which to plant these facts is also something educators can achieve. Medical authorities and educators agree that helping pupils to develop well-adjusted personalities is basic in preventing drug abuse. School health education should seek to establish sound health habits and attitudes to help students attain the stability they need for physical, mental and emotional development. The home, school, and local community each has a responsibility to aid in providing an environment that gives children opportunities for physical activity, mental stimulation, and social satisfaction. If we can provide these outlets and use sound health education to implant resistance to the temptations of drug abuse, the spreading abuse of drugs among our young people can be contained.

Questions and Projects Related to Drug Abuse

1. In what way did the Larimore article enlighten you to the dangers of drugs?
2. In outline form, list some of the misconceptions you had about drugs before you read the article.
3. What should educators do to set up a program to combat drug abuse?
4. In what respect is every citizen a contributing factor to the drug scene?
5. Defend or criticize the use of marijuana.
6. What kind of programs exist in your community to combat drug addiction and help drug abusers?
7. What are the psychological, sociological, economic, and political implications to the drug picture?
8. Visit a community program that deals with rehabilitating drug abusers, then report what you learned to your class.
9. Suppose you are a high school teacher and you discover than one of your students takes drugs, what do you do?
10. Under what circumstances might a youngster start to take drugs?

Hal (17) : Drug Hallucination

First it was a dot, then it took legs and I knew it was a spider. It worked itself from the corner of the room where the lamp stood. It became larger and larger. It kept weaving long strands of broken webs in its wake.[1] I felt the threads over my face, more like hair, and tried to push them away to no avail. Now the spider was spinning under my shirt so I took it off and ran to the mirror to see if I could find it. There were hundreds of them crawling over me. I yelled, I remember, but no one seemed to hear.[2] I started to pound at them with my hands. It helped. They were gone. I heard myself laughing. I was like two people. One listening to the other. I remember laughing at the laughter.[3] Someone played recorder music and I began to see color lines. The drum-beats looked like suspended gobs of jelly. I closed my eyes and felt that I was being combed by fingers from the head down, inside my body.[4] Then some of the beats were opening up. They were filled with sweet syrup. I could taste it. It made me sick. I asked for something to wash my mouth. I was gagging until someone turned the music off.[5] Then I saw the spider again. I tried to push it away but was aware that if I harmed it would harm me. The plaster was starting to disintegrate into faces, white pale faces. They were contorted, out of shape, inhuman. I was petrified because I knew the faces belonged to death.[6] I could hear myself calling for help. I screamed and knew it was me because when I stopped it stopped.[7] The vision of the scream still hung in the air. It looked like an iron bird made of strands of wire.[8] When I closed my eyes the face was still there. It kept growing in size. I knew if I squeezed my eyelids it would disappear but I couldn't do it. Something stopped me.[9] Next I remember the webs over my body. started to scratch. It was awful. The spider was crawling inside me. I couldn't get at him. I started to throw up. I was sick. I fell asleep, I guess, because I don't remember anything else.[10]

Case Questions

1. Is there anything frightening about the story at this point? Explain.
2. Is there a special kind of logic here? Explain.
3. Can you explain what might have happened to Hal's sense of self?
   a. Have you ever felt like two people? Explain.
4. Try to explain how a physiological experience is transformed into an image.
   a. Have you ever dreamed something only to awake and find a physiological explanation for the dream?
5. In what way might the music have affected him?
6. Where might the white-pale face image of death come from?
7. Does Hal have a problem of being displaced? Explain.
8. What images or experiences come to your mind when you think of an iron bird? In what way is it associated with a scream here?
9. In what way is the logic of Hal's thinking different than a person who is not under drugs?
10. What have you learned about the effects of drugs? How much more meaning does this episode have for you now that you have answered these questions?

Remedies for Drug Abuse—Right and Wrong

Ernest Harms

It is not a gratifying task to stand up to those who have control over official public acts.

In an article in the *New York State Journal of Medicine* of December 15, 1962, and in the introduction to *Drug Addiction in Juveniles,* published in 1965, this writer told the story of the efforts made by him and a group of friends to do something about the wave of drug addiction that exists in this country. Although governmental authorities and officials of some scientific bodies tried to sabotage its issuance and distribution, the book had a wider circulation than any book dealing with problems of addiction published in this century. Despite this approbation by the public of a realistic and practical approach, those in control of the radical programs that have been initiated in recent months in New York City and New York State have completely ignored the proposals set forth in that book. This disregard of a serious effort that has proved successful in dealing with juvenile addiction is accompanied by a confession that the plan of forcible incarceration of drug addicts now being applied in New York State is not based on any concept that has proved to be a path to cure. The administrators of these programs have, by way of the radio and otherwise, openly declared that the programs are experimental since, they say, no demonstrated means of cure of drug addiction has yet been found. Thus, officials with power as their only asset, will "take the addict from the street" and incarcerate him for from three to five years in what cannot be described otherwise than a medical prison. Imprisonment of any kind should follow only conviction by due legal process in an established court, with the handling of the prisoner prescribed by law. What we are facing, in the present procedure, is autocracy. Viewed sociologically, we are in a situation in which the authorities, unable to cope in a realistic way with drug addiction, are applying the brutal procedure of jailing addicts. They forget that they have been equally unable to cope with the increase in other forms of crime, which are surely not the result of drug addiction alone. Autocracy, however, does not think, and it especially avoids thinking along lines that might annul its power and position.

We must not be content, however, with accusations and complaints, which are of little constructive value. If we are to do something basic about the present paradoxical situation, we must first of all attempt to understand the problems of drug addiction on the social level. We might ask: why do our few present concepts of aid in prevention or reduction of drug abuse fail so completely? The most apparent explanation is that the ideas and concepts now applied do not touch on the impulses underlying addiction. Stated more simply, the theoretical concepts and the practical approaches have been false ones. And they are false down to their basic concepts of the constitution of the body, the mind, and the social impulses of man. We see, behind the punitive moves, the sociologist with his abstract theories regarding modern society, and the psychiatrist who administers the popular pills and psychoanalytic rubdowns. Remarkable theories and brushed-up case histories are employed to make us believe in a one-and-only wonder-cure. Robot images of "the patient" and "the drug addict" are constructed that are far from describing the real people who, for a multiplicity of reasons, desperately try to solve their problems by the use of drugs. So-called studies of thousands

"Remedies for Drug Abuse—Right or Wrong," by Ernest Harms, M.D. From *Adolescence,* Vol. II, No. 5, pp. I-IV, Spring 1967.

of addicts have appeared which have employed questionnaires based on previously established concepts, the validity of which the responses are intended to prove.

Drug addicts have hundreds of individual problems which account for their behavior in relation to drugs. Indeed, individualism is characteristic of the drug-abuse problem. Neither punitive nor medical incarceration, nor medication, nor religions and ethical instruction can change the life pattern of the addict or in any overall way relieve him of his addiction. The relief or cure of drug addiction requires the resolution of the individual problems of the addict, and the first step in any attempt at such resolution is psychological and psychotherapeutic care and social readjustment. To be able to help an addicted individual we must first apply a psychology and psychotherapy that can explain and influence the addictive impulse to a degree that the addict is able to reorient himself toward other avenues of experience. The therapist treating the addicted individual must be able to view his entire psychological personality, which in many instances has been destroyed, seriously injured, or misdirected in terms of motivation. If the addict has been properly reoriented and restored to meaningful psychological existence, he will find the use of drugs unnecessary and an obstacle to his sound and positive strivings. Such psychological or psychiatric reorientation cannot be accomplished by means of Freudian or behavioristic concepts of psychological human experience; it requires a more humanistic and anthropomorphically-oriented approach. Further, it cannot be accomplished by means of short-term psychotherapy, tranquilizers, or group therapy; it calls rather for intimate individual and long-term efforts. What is needed is the rebuilding of a sound, healthful environment.

What is offered today as a plan for fighting addiction would suppress rather than build up. Imprisonment will destroy whatever may still remain of the addict's desire to live in a sound, open atmosphere. We know how criminal and pathological impulses. multiply under incarceration, and what wonders by way of cure have been accomplished by the "open" treatment of even psychotic patients. The punitive approach does not take into consideration that in the ranks of those whom it is proposed to imprison are not only low-grade individuals but a larger percentage of able and even exceptionally intelligent youth. We know from history how many among the ranks of the great poets, artists, musicians, and scientists have resorted to the stimulation of drugs. Such individuals would surely not return more able from three years of imprisonment.

We know that some of the centers of our present wave of drug addiction are among adolescents in our so-called schools of higher learning. I doubt that any of our addiction "bailiffs" has spent a night in a college dormitory, youth hostel, or other gathering-place of young persons who indulge in serious narcotics abuse. I doubt that any has listened with an "inner ear" to the tragically disillusioned and negatively-directed attitudes toward life that have led to delusion instead of proper existence—disbelief in any honesty in social and political life, disbelief in the possibility of any acceptable religious doctrines, hatred, cynicism, and desire for revenge. In the face of the absence of any built-in non-ideological beliefs, the student must endure an endless series of pressuring examinations and the worker must suffer subordination by unions. A night a week for a year or so spent in silent listening to the goings-on in the world of youth today might yield some understanding of why so many of our youth harbor the desperate urge to lull their consciousness with narcotics.

Only when we understand the world of youth will we have the proper perspective on what must be done to eradicate the deep impulses that lead to abuse of drugs. Given a decent world to live in and a sound psychology to live with, the present wave of drug addiction among our youth will pass. Difficult to accomplish as this may seem, it is the only way of overcoming the horror.

Questions and Projects Related to Remedies for Drug Abuse—Right or Wrong

1. What agencies of drug rehabilitation exist in your community? List the federal, state, and local agencies available.
2. What would you do if one of your friends asked you to join him in taking drugs?
3. How would you help a drug-addicted friend?
4. What kind of legislation should be enacted in order to deal with the problem of drug abuse?

II

VALUES

How do we go about helping ourselves, and our children develop values to live by? Evidently, there are no fixed answers. Each man must develop own way of believing, or his own scale of ethics and morals, from the multidude available. But does he determine his values or are they already there, programmed for him to incorporate from the day of his birth from his parents, community, and culture? Is he a victim of the wishes of others, or does he make choices along the way? If so, what are his criteria? Although these questions cut across all disciplines, the answer to them is crucial to the well-being of each person, group, and society, for reasons that are obvious to the man who is aware of the conflict of purposes in every domain of existence.

Some of these questions are taken up by Charlotte Buhler in the first article of this section. She states that, "there are no ready-made set of values, with which we can identify," that authority patterns are now under scrutiny. As a result of this, "the central educational problems of our time is how the individual can be helped to develop most adequately as a human being." Then she proceeds to discuss the concept of self-realization from a humanistic point of view. It will become clear to the reader in the episode about Eliot that values are not developed primarily out of a rational logical consideration void of experience.

In the next vignette, "Dead Fish in Summertime," certain community ways of behaving merge together despite the individual differences within the neighborhood. In A. Maslow's article, the central theme of man transcending the environment is paradoxically related to man learning to listen to himself, to the inner reaches of what makes him feel whole and human. In the episode that ensures, Amos asks himself questions about God in a most personal way and at one point directly calls for his aid. In a much more abstract, impersonal manner, J. Dewey raises certain questions that are pressing to this very day. It will be clear to the reader that unless one has a clear understanding of the meaning of his words, the questions themselves will not be understood.

Values and Beliefs in Our Time

Charlotte Buhler

We live in a time in which values and beliefs have become highly problematic. There are many reasons for this. One is the experience of disillusionment regarding the validity of some of our ideals of humanity's progress, which the cruelties and wars of our century meant for many of us. Another is the discovery of the relative position of many values in different cultures which modern anthropology disclosed. Another reason is the skepticism with which science on the one hand, and psychoanalysis on the other have taught us to look at the religious teachings and moral traditions which we inherited from our forefathers.

The difficulties which we experience in our own thinking are further increased, when we find ourselves in the role of educators of youth. This role is, as we all know, more challenged and more challenging than it ever was. For similar reasons which invalidated our own beliefs, youths are weary of authority, they dislike and distrust it. Many studies show that, in Europe as well as in America, the youths of this generation prefer to consult their peers rather than adults and to put more store by peer acceptance than by adult approval.

In working with youths as well as with parents and teachers, I find that successful leadership of the older generation depends on certain basic requirements. First and foremost are: kindness, honesty, understanding and competence. These represent the responses to some main needs in the person we want to educate, the need for love, for trust, the willingness to cooperate and the interest to learn.

Developing Adequate Values

The problem of developing an adequate set of values in ourselves as well as in those entrusted to us is a double one.

To begin with, we do not get, as people in previous times did, a ready-made set of values, with which we can unquestionably identify. Although there still are many divergent groups of people who try to go on living by the religious and moral traditions of the past, which they were taught, an ever-increasing number feel that they have to think things through for themselves. They want to get to a new unbiased understanding of human existence. Yet when attempting this, most people find that they are not really equipped to do this job in an adequate manner. They do not have the training to think about principles of living in a logical and systematic way. Nor do they know all the facts that they should be informed about, to reach any kind of valid conclusions.

In fact the more they learn about the subject, they discover—and this is the second problem—how limited their freedom of choice is. The reasons for these limitations are manifold.

One is that at the time when we begin to think consciously and deliberately about our values and beliefs, we have already been influenced and formed in many directions. We have picked up from or have been taught or even been indoctrinated by our environment. That includes our family, our neighbors, friends and the whole subculture in which we grow up. From at least about four years of age on, children begin to form

"The Problem of Values and Beliefs in Our Time," by Charlotte Buhler. From EDUCATIONAL LEADERSHIP, **21** (8), pp. 520–523, 541, May 1964.

opinions on values. From five years on, they are known to identify with prejudices of their environment. After that time, it becomes increasingly difficult for an individual to think about values without bias. Besides being brought up within the confines of some subculture, an individual's situation of life may be such that he cannot possibly free himself. He may be economically too dependent, too restricted in social opportunities, too much hampered by poor education, to be able to work on his development as a person.

Other reasons lie in personality factors. Some people are more adaptive than creative, and adhere to some group's opinions so as to be accepted and to belong. They feel securer in this complete identification with a group. Some people lack the flexibility to completely adopt new ideas. They prefer to stick by what they always believed in. This inflexibility becomes particularly marked in certain types of neuroses. Persons who suffer from serious emotional predicaments, are rarely in the position of making free decisions about directions they want to take in life.

Personal aptitudes, abilities and gifts or lack of them also have an influence on a person's value system. The mechanically gifted individual is more inclined to value technical progress than the artist, who favors the aesthetic.

Assuming a person is free enough, courageous enough and informed enough to try to set up his own set of values, what are some of the choices he will have to make?

Values Under Scrutiny

There are certain values rooted in the Judeo-Christian tradition, which remain essentially unchanged despite any modern skepticism or ethical reorientation. The high value of love in its many aspects and facets, including giving of one's self, kindness, generosity, empathy, and extending to tolerance and understanding has remained our greatest heritage.

The values connected with what Erich Fromm called the "authoritarian conscience" have become suspect, if not even discredited. The feeling of our youths, that the claims of authority have become dubious and that certainly authority should not be set up and maintained for authority's sake is shared by many thoughtful people of our time. The value of blind obedience has become completely invalid and even the value of conformity, which up until recently was generally undisputed, is scorned by those who want to see an individual's personality maximally developed.

One of the central educational problems of our time is how the individual can be helped to develop most adequately as a human being. How the growing child and adolescent can be guided to discipline themselves and to accept responsibility without the pressure of threats and punishment; how they can be helped to bring out and to work at their best potential: to accomplish this is the goal of the modern educator.

In fact, the development of an individual's best potential is possibly that new value concept which many thinkers of our time would put at the top of a value rank order. Since Carl Jung's, Karen Horney's and Erich Fromm's first formulations, this concept has found increasing acceptance and validation in the work of Carl Rogers, Rollo May, Abraham Maslow, Victor Frankl, myself and others.

Requirements for Self-Realization

The question of how to find and how to realize one's best potential is however not easily answered. Many people seem to find it difficult to clarify for themselves what they want to live for. And many others encounter nearly insurmountable hindrances on their way. Those who are able to do what they feel is their "task of life," as V. Frankl calls it, are indeed lucky.

For clarifying one's own best potential and for understanding one's own inner self, a person needs to meet two requirements. A person needs to be honest with himself and must know how to go about understanding himself.

Honesty was always regarded as a high value in our Western Civilization. However, in spite of the great acclaim, it always received up until recently this quality was not applied in quite the rigorous way in which we have learned to apply it now. It is only since Freud's teachings about the unconscious that we have learned to detect certain dishonesties which we use in interpreting our own motivations.

In wanting very much to behave in such a way that we can morally approve of ourselves, we often bring sacrifices and do what we think to be good deeds. It is one of Freud's merits to have debunked many of those martyrs and heroes that were analyzed, as people who sacrificed themselves not for beliefs, but for the secondary gains of praise and fame.

In our time, we appraise motives with caution and with the help of analytic exploration.

Besides the new honesty with which we see ourselves, we also have learned to esteem the new knowledge which modern scientific development has brought to us. This applies to the psychological penetration into the depth of the human mind, and it also applies to the knowledge about the universe, which we obtained from modern physics. While this leaves questions about the universe open to speculation, it has certainly made us aware of creativity as one of its main factors.

The respect of knowledge and the acquisition of more knowledge for the understanding of our human existence within the laws of the universe seems to many a high value of our time.

In one of his recent books, Erich Fromm calls boredom one of the main problems of the meaningless life of our time. Victor Frankl speaks of an "existential vacuum" as of that existence in which people give no ultimate purpose or meaning to their lives.

The opposite tendency of the person who tries to develop his best potentials, is that of self-fulfillment. This person has given his existence a purpose and feels neither empty nor bored. He has enthusiasm and belief in what he is doing. And he feels that in giving his best, he is fulfilling himself.

Role of Psychology

The analytic exploration of our motives and the clarification of our best potentials are not easy to accomplish without psychological guidance. The growing awareness of this fact has recently led many responsible leaders among educators and ministers to organize "self-discovery" groups under psychological direction. These are groups of grown-ups as well as of adolescents who are interested in learning to understand themselves and the workings of their motivation. They also want to be aware of their own inclinations and best potentials, so as to be equipped to set up proper goals and values for themselves. Thus psychology seems to play an important role for adequate self-development of the person of our time.

Questions and Projects Related to Values and Beliefs in Our Time

1. Why is youth weary of authority?
2. In what way do the following words have a personal meaning to you? Explain each one.
   a. Self-assertion.
   b. Love.
   c. Kindness.
   d. Giving of yourself.
   e. Generosity.
   f. Tolerance.
   g. Understanding.
3. What are some of the most pressing problems of our times according to Buhler?
4. Discuss the following quote and relate it to yourself: "A person must be honest with himself and must know how to go about understanding himself."
5. In what way is boredom related to self-fulfillment and meaning?

Eliot (9) : The Fried Eggs and Grandmother

He stuck his tongue out at his grandmother because she wanted him to eat the fried eggs. He didn't expect her to cry. He didn't know of any other way of escaping her. She chased him around the large dining-room table and insisted that he eat the eggs. Finally, in desperation, he stuck his tongue out at her, and she began to cry, and now he didn't know what to do.[1] He was sorry he had stuck his tongue out. He told her so, but she continued to cry. He told her he'd eat the eggs that she had placed on the table, but she held her head in her hands and cried.[2] He ate the eggs next to her, but she didn't seem to see him. She left the room after he only ate a few bites. After he finished eating the eggs he brought the plate to the kitchen and washed it. Then went to her bedroom. The door was closed. He stood there and waited to hear some sounds but heard nothing[3]

He prepared his books and put his jacket on, and went to school. When he returned home, he found his mother on the phone. He put his books on the dresser, went to the refrigerator, took a glass of milk, gulped it down, and left the house. Outside he played ball with his friends. Later, hc returned home, ate supper and talked to his mother and his father.[4] After he completed his homework, he went to bed. In bed, he reconsidered the day's events.[5]

He hadn't seen his grandmother since the episode. Had she said anything to his mother? Why had she cried? He never remembered sticking his tongue out to any member of the family. It was the first time she had really shown strong emotions toward him.[6] She seemed to tolerate him. This was the only time he really affected her. He couldn't remember whether she had ever cried before.[7] He remembered her face just before she covered it with her hands. How beautiful and majestic. The skin on her face was smoother than his mother's, more polished although wrinkled, more intricate with folds, more tightly drawn with veins. Her dark lips seemed to have a pulse of their own. Her hair was pulled back into a bun. It covered her delicate ears, framed her high cheek bones and wide-spaced eyes.[8] Just before she covered her face with her hands, it was contorted. At first he didn't understand her reaction. He had never seen her act that way before. He would not have stuck his tongue out, if he had known that it would upset her the way it did.[9]

He wished he had just eaten the eggs without a fuss. If she had yelled at him or hit him, it would have been better.[10] He loved her and had hurt her. What must she think of him?[11] How she must have suffered. He tried to sleep, but he couldn't. He thought the same things over and over again. He'd never repair what he had done. From now on he'd be especially good to her but that would not change what he had done. How could she like him now?[12]

Case Questions

1. Can you remember an incident similar to this one in your own childhood?
2. How do you think youngsters feel when they witness a grandparent or parent cry?
3. What would you have done if you were in this situation?
4. What did you do when you returned from school at this age?
5. Is it unusual for a child to "reconsider the day's events" at bedtime? What purpose does this experience serve in helping the child learn more about himself and those about him?
6. Did you misjudge what an adult felt toward you at this age?
7. Why is it that certain incidents stand out while others are forgotten?
8. Does this fit? Do you think Eliot perceived his grandmother as beautiful and majestic as he ran from her around the table? Explain your answer.
9. What would you change about what you did when you were a child?
10. Why do you think Eliot said this to himself?
11. Why should he care?
12. Do you think this episode changed Eliot in any way? Explain your answer.

Dead Fish in Summertime

The stench of dead fish emanated from the garbage cans. This, together with the humid heat, gave little space to the already confined sidewalk on which mostly mothers with their children and some of the old and lonely people sat, each to his own deck chair or box. The house opposite was boarded up because it was condemned. The house next to it was used for the storage of large bags of flour with which matzos were made. A large trailer truck was parked in front of this warehouse. Two men dressed in the traditional Orthodox Jewish religious garb with the long black cloth coats that matched their beards and large-brimmed hats unloaded the truck of the heavy bags of flour. Both were dusted with the flour from the sacks—their coats blotched with white. One of the smaller men wore his beard slightly white at the bottom.[1]

It was on this street where old shoes were separated according to their age and usability. Next to these shoes were cardboard cartons filled with assorted clothes that were loosely piled onto each other. They were sold according to their condition and market value, which varied according to what the proprietor felt the customer could bear. The vegetable store next to this one sold lettuce according to the size, which was determined by the amount of days the lettuce had not been sold. In one box, there were three fistlike lettuces for ten cents. Yellow specks covered the outside leaves. The proprietor had had a serious operation some years earlier and could only whisper—he had no voice. Some of the young children smiled, giggled, or were embarrassed when he spoke, but these were the children of new customers—the others knew him and understood that he was just that way—he whispered, others spoke with a voice.[2]

Cakes and tea and the soup of the day with black bread were sold next door. There were few who entered, but those who did were the old customers who sat with a glass of hot tea, which they poured out of a hot samovar. A large bowl of small squares of sugar stood on one table for those customers who drank their tea by holding a sugar between their front teeth, as they sipped the drink. It was always sweeter that way. Then yams, large green bananas, and black beans were displayed at the window front of the grocery. The heat that emanated from this store was present even in the winter, which kept many customers from leaving the premises to the cold outside streets. In this store, the young men leaned against the counter and spoke of humorous and serious things. It seemed to be their gathering place. When young girls entered, they were sure to be perused carefully in appreciation without overstepping the propriety of the girls. These were the same boys who, on the outside of the store, in the street, puffed up their chests and made suggestive statements to the girls.[3]

Behind one glass window that was shrouded with translucent golden curtains, lived a family of gypsies. The young and older girls were dressed in shiny satin on certain days—the boys in rags, the father in a poor suit. It was Monday, and soon, about noontime, his next to the youngest son, who was four, would take his father through the streets. The blind father walked one pace behind his son, who held out a small cup. The noontime flow of people was nearly as numbered as those that emptied out into the area at five and six o'clock in the evening. The women at this hour called out to the men to have their fortunes told. Some bent low to give a prospective customer a clear vision of their breasts. The children looked as if they were playing dress-up for some dramatic play situation. Their bodies straight and lean, faces tired, eyes tremendous and hungry. The older children looked guardedly at the young ones.[4]

The stench of dead fish permeated the atmosphere. It was night and the heat in the apartment house was unbearable. The only possible place to find moving air was on the street. Men, women, and children bedecked the sidewalk. They sat on kitchen chairs, which they had dragged out from their homes. Others sat more comfortably on beach and deck chairs. The conversations were about marriages, cooking, dresses, and children. The men complained and joked about all things, while the children played nearby and laughed and cried, were yelled at or slapped or were kissed and hugged.[5]

One man sat off to the side and peered at a large leather-covered book and moved his lips ever so gently. The sound of metal against metal of knitting needles mingled with the sounds of night. The sound of cars, and other voices, the sudden loud noises of sirens that filled the air with their bloom and death.[6]

Still the dead fish scent penetrated the air. For those who came by from another less-scented area of the city, the odor was overwhelming. They held their breath, walked as quickly as they could to escape the stench. One man who was new to the apartment house volunteered to pour the contents of a bottle of clorax over the dead fish. There was a new scent of rotting fish and clorax. The stench was worse. Some of the neighbors started to complain that their eyes were beginning to tear. No one stirred, however. They continued to talk. Those who first wipe their eyes found it no longer necessary. The new neighbor was the immediate hero of the house. Even though the results of his effort made the situation worse, he had attempted to change the situation.[7]

It was another night, that very night of the dead fish, and they sat there in front of the house as if there would always be another night. The whole air reeked of dead fish and clorax, but they sat there, under the lamplight, on their chairs, talking, laughing, sharing the deep and simple secrets of everyday living with the wishes and fears that all men have shared in common.[8]

Case Questions

1. What images came to your mind after you read this paragraph? Describe them.
   a. Try to describe a highly populated area of a city. What characteristics would you want to depict?
2. Why do you think the children smiled, giggled, or were embarrassed?
   a. Why did the other children accept the man's disability as a matter of fact?
3. Describe the human atmosphere in a store in your community.
   a. Are there certain unwritten rules that govern the behavior of the customers? Explain.
4. Compare the role of these children to the children in your neighborhood.
   a. Compare the learning of children in one neighborhood to what is learned in another.
5. With what aspects of this description can you identify?
6. Did any one religious, ethnic, or racial group come to mind while you read this episode? Explain.
7. Can you identify with this part of the episode? Why?
8. Compare the immediate environment in front of your house to that described in the episode.
   a. What factors will determine how a person perceives a neighborhood? How do you know?
   b. Do political, economic, sociological, historical, as well as other factors enter into your consideration? Why?

Health as Transcendence of Environment[1]

Abraham H. Maslow

My purpose is to save one point that may get lost in the current wave of discussion of mental health. The danger that I see is the resurgence, in new and more sophisticated forms, of the old identification of psychological health with adjustment, adjustment to reality, adjustment to society, adjustment to other people. That is, the authentic or healthy person is being defined not in his own right, not in his autonomy, not by his own intra-psychic and non-environmental laws, not as *different* from the environment, independent of it or opposed to it, but rather in environment-centered terms; e.g., of ability to master the environment, to be capable, adequate, effective, competent in relation to *it,* to do a good job, to perceive *it* well, to be in good relations to *it,* to be successful in *its* terms. To say it in another way, the job-analysis, the requirements of the task, should not be the major criterion of worth or health of the individual. There is not only an orientation to the outer but also to the inner. An extrapsychic centering point cannot be used for the theoretical task of defining the healthy psyche. We must not fall into the trap of defining the good organism in terms of what he is "good for," as if he were an instrument rather than something in himself, as if he were only a means to some extrinsic purpose. (As I understand Marxist psychology, it also is a very blunt and unmistakable expression of the view that the psyche is a mirror to reality.)

I am thinking especially of Robert White's recent paper in the *Psychological Review,* "Motivation Reconsidered" (9), and Robert Woodworth's book, *Dynamics of Behavior* (10). I have chosen these because they are excellent jobs, highly sophisticated, and because they have carried motivation theory forward in a huge leap. As far as they go, I agree with them. But I feel they don't go far enough. I feel also that they contain in a hidden form the danger that I have referred to, that the mastery, effectance and competence may be active rather than passive styles of adjustment to reality, but that they are *still* variations of adjustment theory. I feel we must leap beyond these statements, admirable though they may be, to the clear recognition of transcendence[2] of the environment, independent of it, able to stand against it, to fight it, to neglect it, or to turn one's back on it, to refuse it or adapt to it. (I pass by the temptation to discuss the masculine Western and American character of these themes. Would a woman, a Hindu, or even a Frenchman, think primarily in terms of mastery or competence?) My point is that, for a theory of mental health, extra-psychic success is not enough; we must also include intra-psychic health.

Another example, which I wouldn't take seriously were it not that so many others *do* take it seriously, is the Harry Stack Sullivan type of effort to define a Self simply in

1 Read before Symposium on Research Implications of Positive Mental Health, Eastern Psychological Association, April 15, 1960. This paper was stimulated into existence by a series of discussions with Mr. Stephen Cohen.

2 The word "transcendence" is used for lack of a better one. "Independence of" implies too simple a dichotomizing of self and of environment, and therefore is incorrect. "Transcendence" unfortunately implies for some a "higher" which spurns and repudiates the "lower," i.e., again a false dichotomizing. In other contexts I have used it as a contrast with "dichotomous way of thinking." The hierarchical-integrative way of thinking, which implies simply that the higher is built upon, rests upon, but includes the lower. For instance, the central nervous system or the hierarchy of basic needs or an army is hierarchically integrated. I use the word "transcendence" here in the hierarchical-integrative sense, rather than in the dichotomous sense.

terms of what other people think of him, an extreme cultural relativity in which a healthy individuality gets lost altogether. Not that this isn't true for the immature personality. It is. But we are talking about the healthy, fully grown person. And *he* certainly is characterized by his transcendence of other people's opinions.

To substantiate my conviction that we must save the differentiation between self and not-self in order to understand the fully matured person (authentic, self-actualizing, individuated, productive, healthy), I call your attention to the following considerations.

1. First I mention some data I presented in a 1951 paper called "Resistance to Acculturation" (3). I reported my healthy subjects to be superficially accepting of conventions, but privately to be casual, perfunctory, and detached about them. That is, they could take them or leave them. In practically all of them, I found a rather calm, goodhumored rejection of the stupidities and imperfections of the culture with greater or lesser effort at improving it. They definitely showed an ability to fight it vigorously when they thought it necessary. To quote from this paper: "The mixture of varying proportions of affection or approval, and hostility and criticism indicated that they select from American culture what is good in it by their lights and reject what they think bad in it. In a word, they weigh it, and judge it (by their own inner criteria), and then make their own decisions."

They also showed a surprising amount of detachment from people in general and a strong liking for privacy, even a need for it (4).

"For these and other reasons they may be called autonomous; i.e., ruled by the laws of their own character rather than by the rules of society (in so far as these are different). It is in this sense that they are not only or merely Americans but also members at large of the human species." I then hypothesized that "these people should have less 'national character,' and that they should be more like each other across cultural lines than they are like the less-developed members of their own culture."[3]

The point I wish to stress here is the detachment, the independence, the self-governing character of these people, the tendency to look within for the guiding values and rules to live by.

2. Furthermore, only by such a differentiation can we leave a theoretical place for meditation, contemplation and for all other forms of going into the Self, of turning away from the outer world in order to listen to the inner voices. This includes all the processes of all insight therapies, in which turning away from the world is a *sine qua non,* in which the path to health is via turning into the fantasies, the dreams, the preconscious and conscious, the archaic, the unrealistic, the primary processes; that is, the recovery of the intra-psychic in general. The psychoanalytic couch is outside the culture to the extent that this is possible. (In any fuller discussion, I would certainly argue the case for an enjoyment of consciousness itself and for experience-values.) (2, 6, 8).

3. The recent interest in health, creativeness, art, play, and love has taught us much, I think, about *general* psychology. From among the various consequences of these explorations, I would pick out one to emphasize for our present purposes, and that is the change in attitude toward the depths of human nature, the unconscious, the primary

3 Examples of this kind of transcendence are Walt Whitman or William James, who were profoundly American, most *purely* American, and yet were also very purely supracultural, internationalist members of the whole human species. They were universal men not in *spite* of their being Americans, but just *because* they were such good Americans. So, too, Martin Buber, a Jewish philosopher, was also more than Jewish. Hobusai, profoundly Japanese, was a universal artist. Probably *any* universal art cannot be rootless. Merely regional art is different from the regionally rooted art that becomes broadly general—human. We may remind ourselves here also of Piaget's children who could not conceive of being simultaneously Genevan and Swiss until they matured to the point of being able to include one within the other and both simultaneously in a hierarchically-integrated way. This and other examples are given by Allport (1).

processes, the archaic, the mythological and the poetic. Because the roots of ill health were found in the unconscious, it has been our tendency to think of the unconscious as bad, evil, crazy, dirty or dangerous, and to think of the primary processes as *distorting* the truth. But now that we have found these depths to be also the source of creativeness, of art, of love, of humor and play, and even of certain kinds of truth and knowledge, we can begin to speak of a healthy unconscious, of healthy regressions. And especially we can begin to value primary process cognition and archaic or mythological thinking instead of considering them to be pathological. We can now go into primary process cognitions for certain kinds of knowledge, not only about the self but also about the world, to which secondary processes are blind. These primary processes are part of normal or healthy human nature and must be included in any comprehensive theory of healthy human nature.

If you agree with this, then you must wrestle with the fact that they are intra-psychic and have their own autochthonous laws and rules, that they are not adapted to external reality or shaped by it or equipped to cope with it. More superficial layers of the personality differentiate out to take care of this job. To identify the whole psyche with these tools for coping with the environment is to lose something which we no longer dare to lose. Adequacy, adjustment, adaptation, competence, mastery, coping, these are all environment-oriented words and are therefore inadequate to describe the *whole* psyche, part of which has nothing to do with the environment.

4. The distinction between the coping aspect of behavior and the expressive aspect is also important here. On various grounds I have challenged the axiom that all behavior is motivated. Here I would stress the fact that expressive behavior is either unmotivated or, anyway, less motivated than coping behavior (depending on what you mean by 'motivated'). In their purer form, expressive behaviors have little to do with environment and do not have the purpose of changing it or adapting to it. The words adaptation, adequacy, competence, or mastery do not apply to expressive behaviors but only to coping behaviors. A reality-centered theory of full human nature cannot manage or incorporate expression, unless with great difficulty. The natural and easy centering point from which to understand expressive behavior is intra-psychic.

5. Being focused on a task produces organization for efficiency both within the organism and in the environment. What is irrelevant is pushed aside and not noticed. The various relevant capacities and information arrange themselves under the hegemony of a goal, a purpose, which means that importance becomes defined in terms of that which helps to solve the problem; i.e., in terms of usefulness. What doesn't help to solve the problem becomes unimportant. Selection becomes necessary. So does abstraction, which means also blindness to some things, inattention, exclusion.

But we have learned that motivated perception, task-orientation, cognition in terms of usefulness, which are all involved in effectance and in competence (which White defines as "an organism's capacity to interact effectively with its environment") leaves out something, and therefore is a partial blindness. For cognition to be complete, I have shown that it must be detached, disinterested, desireless, unmotivated. Only thus are we able to perceive the object in its own nature with its own objective, intrinsic characteristics, rather than abstracting it down to "what is useful," "what is threatening," etc. (4).

My point is that, to the extent that we try to master the environment or be effective with it, to that extent do we cut the possibility of full, objective, detached, noninterfering cognition. Only if we let it be, can we perceive fully. Again, to cite psychotherapeutic experience, the more eager we are to make a diagnosis and a plan of action, the *less* helpful do we become. The more eager we are to cure, the longer it takes. Every psychiatric researcher has to learn not to *try* to cure, *not* to be impatient. In this and in many other situations, to give in is to overcome, to be humble is to succeed. The Taoists and Zen Buddhists taking this path were able a thousand years ago to see what we psychologists are only beginning to be aware of.

But most important is my preliminary finding that this kind of cognition of the Being (B-cognition) of the world is found more often in healthy people and may even turn out to be one of the defining characteristics of health (7). I have also found it in the peak-experience (transient self-actualizing) (6). This implies that even with regard to healthy relations with the environment the words mastery, competence, effectiveness suggest far more active purposefulness than is wise for a concept of health.

As a single example of the consequence of this change in attitude toward unconscious processes, I hypothesized that sensory deprivation, instead of being frightening, should for very healthy people be pleasing. That is, since cutting off the outer world seems to permit the inner world to come to consciousness, and since the inner world is more accepted and enjoyed by healthier people, then they should enjoy sensory deprivation. (I have recently heard of one experiment in which highly creative people reacted in just this way, but I don't have the details.)

Summary

What these considerations can teach us about the theory of health is:

1. We cannot obliterate the autonomous self or pure psyche. It must not be treated as *only* an adaptational instrument.

2. Even when we deal with our relations with environment, we must make a theoretical place for a receptive relation to the environment as well as a masterful one.

3. Psychology is in part a branch of biology, in part a branch of sociology. But it is not *only* that. It has its own unique jurisdiction as well, that portion of the psyche which is *not* a reflection of the outer world or a molding to it. There could be such a thing as a psychological psychology.

References

1. Allport, G. Normative compatibility in the light of social science. In A. H. Maslow (Ed.), *New Knowledge in Human Values*. New York: Harper, 1959.
2. Cantril, H., and Bumstead, C. *Reflections on the Human Venture*. New York: Univ. Press, 1960.
3. Maslow, A. H. Resistance to acculturation. *J. Soc. Issues*, 1951, **1,** 26–29.
4. Maslow, A. H. *Motivation and Personality*. New York: Harper, 1954.
5. Maslow, A. H. Deficiency motivation and growth motivation. In M. R. Jones (Ed.), *Nebraska Symposium on Motivation* 1955. *Lincoln*: Univ. Nebraska Press, 1955.
6. Maslow, A. H. The cognition of being in the peak-experience. *J. Genetic Psychol.*, 1959, **94,** 43–66.
7. Maslow, A. H. Critique of self-actualization. I. Somc dangers of being-cognition. *J. Indiv. Psychol.*, 1959, **15,** 24–32.
8. Murphy, G. *Human Potentialities*. New York: Basic Books, 1959.
9. White, R. Motivation reconsidered: the concept of competence. *Psychol. Rev.*, **66,** 5, September, 1959, 297–333.
10. Woodworth, R. *Dynamics of Behavior*. New York: Holt, 1958.

Questions and Projects Related to Health and Transcendence of Environment

1. Is there any relationship between thc person who conforms to the dictates of society and what Maslow says about adjustment to reality to society and to other people? Explain.
2. List some current conventional expectations that you feel have no significant meaning to you.
3. In what way are you ruled by "your character" rather than the "laws of society"?
4. How detached, self-governing, and independent are you compared to your closest friends?
5. In what way have you turned away from the "outer" world and listened to the inner voices?
6. What does Maslow mean when he says: "only if we let it be, can we perceive fully"?

Amos (16) : The Bird and the Fishbone

Six crows hobbled and hopped across a small road between the newly plowed field and a chicken house. The scent of the red earth, manure, and seed combined with chorus of cackles. The row of trees that bordered the road cast oblique shadows into the sunlight. "Is there something dead," he thought, as he watched the lustrous black birds broad jump into flight again.[1] A grey spiny lizard scuttled under a stone. The airborne beasts ripped the air with their harsh cries then settled on the clumps and clods of earth. There was nothing dead that he could see and he continued to walk past the chicken houses toward the dirt road that led to his school. He stopped to examine the area where they had alighted. "Then why were they here?" he asked himself. "What business did they have?" The voices of children, the mechanical chugging of a tractor was louder now as he strode towards the school buildings.[2] It was late. Class had begun, he knew the teacher would ask him to explain his tardiness. Should he tell her that he had watched crows and wondered whether birds of prey can smell death or can they only see it? Should he ask her why the crow of a cock has the same rhythm, or why some birds awake earlier than others? Are they influenced by sun or do they have a built-in alarm clock? He started to smile because he knew he'd say something like, I woke-up late."[3] It was the truth but he still could have made the walk from the bus stop to the school in less time had he not stopped to wonder, to imagine what it was like to be a man plowing up the earth and examining it for its richness or deprivation, or working and joking with other men. As he thought of these things he remembered that the creator of all was God. Was he also the creator of death?[4] Did he make fish and fishbones? One had caught in his throat; then his father told him to take hard bread but there wasn't any, his brother had tossed it to the geese. Amos caughed and choked, and said it hurt. "You shouldn't talk when your mouth is full of fish," his brother teased. "Quiet. Don't you see he's choking," his mother said, "Now where are those dry bisquits?" she asked in exasperation. "Here, take the crust of this bread." He was forcing himself to cough, trying to dislodge the fishbone from his throat. He had to gargle with salt water, then had ice cream. He still felt the memory of the bone in his throat. Maybe God helped him swallow that crust and free him of the pain, but it took some doing. Could God help him explain why he was late?[5]

He straightened his back took a deep breath and turned the knob of the door and pushed. "Oh, God," he said to himself, as all eyes stared at him: the children, the teacher, and to his supreme mortification, the principal.[6]

Case Questions

1. Can you imagine the children in your community responding to this environment? Explain.
   a. Do you think they might ask such a question?
2. What do children in a crowded city area observe?
3. Why does Amos plan to tell his teacher he awoke late?
4. Are these logical questions for Amos to ask about God?
5. What is Amos's relationship to God?
6. Can you identify with Amos's concerns throughout this episode? Explain.
   a. In what way did you feel alien to what was described here?
   b. Is there anything about the story that might be offensive to a reader?

The Problem of Values[1]

John Dewey

All members of the Philosophical Association owe a debt of gratitude to the executive committee for formulating the question to be discussed at the next meeting. I am aware of no better way of expressing my own gratitude than to comply promptly with the request of the committee for submission of additional formulations of the question.

I shall first make a few remarks upon the formulation by four members of the committee.[2] I assume that in the question, "Is value something which is ultimate and which attaches itself to 'things' independently of consciousness, or of an organic being with desires and aversions?" the "or" is to be understood as marking a genuine alternative between "consciousness" and an "organic being with desires and aversions," not as indicating that the latter clause is in apposition with consciousness or explanatory of it. The alternative is genuine and important: for some may be inclined to connect the existence of values with organic behavior and yet not be willing to equate desires and aversions with "consciousness"—in fact, they may go so far as to hold that "consciousness" (in whatever sense the term is here used) is itself dependent upon matters connected with the desires and aversions of an organic being. Since, however, unconscious desire and aversions may appear to some to involve a contradiction in language, it would seem better to substitute a more objective term, such as selections and rejections; or better yet, to generalize the matter and make the alternative in question to be simply that of connection with the *behavior* of organic beings.

When the question is thus understood, some doubt arises as to the force of the term "ultimate" in the first alternative. Are values if regarded as variables of organic behavior less ultimate than if regarded as things irrespective of connection with organic behavior? And if the answer should be in the affirmative, what is the ground upon which this answer rests?

I have no doubt a successful discussion may be had on the basis of the formulation already presented. In some respects, however, the formulation seems unnecessarily tied up with the idealistic-realistic controversy. I recognize that this complication has the advantage of preserving continuity in the discussions from year to year; yet it is possible that the questions at issue might, in the present juncture, be dealt with in the end more effectively if approached by a flank movement. At all events, I venture to submit the following list of questions:

1. Can the question of the status of values in philosophic discussion be approached apart from the question of the status of qualities?

2. Can values be separated from traits of organic behavior? If organic behavior has its own distinguishing traits, does the affirmation that values are traits of organic behavior imply their "subjectivity?" If so, in what sense? Does connection with organic behavior imply their dependence upon awareness?

3. Do values antecede, or do they depend upon valuation—understanding by valuation a process of reflective estimation or judgment?

4. If they antecede, does valuation merely

1 This paper is presented in response to the request of the committee that further formulations of this problem be submitted for publication.

2 *Journal of Philosophy, Psychology, and Scientific Methods,* Vol. X, No. 10, p. 168.

"The Problem of Values," by John Dewey. Published in the *Journal of Philosophy*, Vol. X, No. 10, pp. 268–269, May 8, 1913. Reprinted by permission.

bring them to light without change, or does it modify antecedent values? Does it produce new values? If the latter occur, are the modification and production merely incidental or are they essential?

5. Can the place of intelligence in behavior in general (and in moral conduct in particular) be understood without implying that reflection reorganizes antecedent natural values?

6. What is the meaning of appreciation? Is it a particular mode of apprehending (knowing) values, or is it a name for the direct presence of values in experience? How is it related to valuation and criticism?

7. Does the presence of values in experience in general (or say religious values in particular) have an evidential import? That is to say, does the existence of religious values, for example, prove the existence of any class of objects beyond the values themselves? Or, again, does the presence in experience of any type of values purport to make the mind aware of something in the environment, taking that world in its widest possible sense? [This question may profitably be considered in connection with the first question, regarding qualities.]

8. If the answers to these questions should be in the negative, is the significance of such values for experience and for philosophy thereby determined to be null or illusory? Can an affirmative answer to this question be maintained except on the assumption that all experience is, *ipso facto*, intended to be an awareness of objects?

Questions and Projects Related to the Problem of Values

1. What difficulty, if any, do you have in understanding the following words the Dewey uses:
   a. Ultimate.
   b. Organic behavior.
   c. Consciousness.
2. Rewrite one of the questions he poses at the end of his article in the kind of language you understand best.
3. How is appreciation related to valuation and criticism?
4. What kinds of definitions and understandings should you have in order to understand this article?

PART TWO

ROLE PLAYING

When we said, "You must be the mother, I'll be the father, and you (to another child) will be the baby," we were role playing. We played house, doctor, hospital, restaurant, caveman, superman, and a dozen other themes. That was a long time ago. Now, with space, electronics, and TV the role-playing boundaries for the young child are extended further. Notwithstanding, the least common denominator is still man, who usually is projected into the role of the hero or the villain, the hunted or the hunter, the discovered or the discoverer. Then we grew up, learned how to become aware of ourselves and others in a more mature way, how to adapt to a multitude of different cues in our environment, and how to project our private meanings in the roles that we assumed with others. It is these private or idiosyncratic meanings that become socialized during the role-playing situation. When these occur, what we think, feel, or do becomes part of a matrix of impressions that others pick up, incorporate, integrate, and project in the form of a response. Their reaction to what we do, in turn, affects us. The interplay of forces between people, and the interplay of the psychological life space of motives, fears, values, needs, expectations, and experiences within individuals makes role playing both a personal and social phenomenon.

If we make believe we are someone else, put ourselves in the place of another person, try to imagine what it feels like to be in his shoes, to feel the impact of his wish, hope, or disappointment, we still do not depart from ourselves, from our conception and understanding of that person we portray. The person is shaped into being by our own private-social-biological image. Like a sculptor, painter, musician, or scientist, we create him as Pygmalion was fashioned, by our own endeavors and the dictates of the limits of what we are given. It is during this process of defining, translating, and interpreting the role that we learn to perceive ourselves differently, learn to test the limits of who we are by assuming different parts of a human situation.

The full impact of the above ideas will be felt when given life in the classroom. Then these hypothetical considerations can be realistically and directly examined and related to the experience of discovery. Before we do this, however, let us turn our attention to the section, "What To Do When You Observe or Participate in Role-Playing Situations." This section sets the stage for Dr. Moreno's article. He discusses the significance of psychodrama and sociodrama in everyday life. He explains how the stage, patient, director, auxiliary egos, and audience interact and create a dynamic environment in which self-insight is spontaneously experienced.

Then there is a choice of fifty role-playing situations to choose from. In each episode there is a conflict to be dealt with by the players, the teacher, and the class. The dynamic push and pull of individuals reacting, interacting, and resisting will be appreciated once the role players are in action.

The "Short Case Study Presentations," although more structured and detailed in the former section, will allow the players to act out their needs in essentially a similar way. Special emphasis is directed in depicting a dynamic family-school setting. Among other considerations, learning difficulties, truancy, and troubled behavior are problems to be confronted. Here, too, the players are given latitude to express what is meaningful to them within the confines of the data presented.

During role playing it is acceptable procedure to switch parts. The father becomes the mother, the son the father, the mother the school counselor, if that is the agreed arrangement. The sudden switch permits each role player an opportunity to gain insight into another point of view. He gains a more comprehensive picture of how another person feels when he subjectively has to put himself into the other person's predicament.

A few words about the task of the observers during the role-playing sessions. Each student can write down what he sees and hears, and differentiate this aspect of the observation from what he thinks, feels, assumes, imagines, or guesses is taking place in front of him. In other words, if the student can learn how to record what is happening by denoting the objective aspects of the role-playing situation and separate them from the subjective impressions that come to mind while observing, he will do what a detective does—put down the facts and then react to them in terms of the implications. "What To Do When You Observe or Participate in Role-Playing Situations" is an invaluable guide here. The objective data can be separated from the subjective aspects of the observation by dividing the page down the middle, or by underlying only the subjective dimensions of the recordings.

In addition, the class can periodically comment on what it feels is happening, how it perceives the different roles and the problem, and what questions it has. The comments and questions should not interrupt the continuity of the role playing.

There is a third alternative for the class. The students can compare notes, impressions, and observations by breaking up into small discussion groups. Each one elects a temporary representative to report back what it wants to share with the total class. The creative and learning possibilities are unlimited.

What To Do When You Observe or Participate in a Role-Playing Situation

1. Each individual is expected to keep in mind the data that is related to his role and the roles of others.
   a. The information concerning him can be interpreted as he wishes.
   b. He can resit, submit to, be ambivalent to, distort, or transform the material given to him during the role-playing situation.

2. The role players should be prepared to accept criticisms or suggestions from the class or the teacher in charge. (This should occur only after one dimension of the role-playing situation has been completed. Too many interruptions will hinder the flow of movement, exchange, and interaction between the players.)

3. The teacher should try to encourage the role-playing members and class to define, analyze, discuss, raise hypotheses, make recommendations, look for concensus, or relate the roles or findings to the course material.

4. The following factors ought to be kept in mind when examining the role playing situations:
   a. Who is in the position of authority most of the time?
   b. Does he use it in a democratic, laissez-faire, or autocratic manner?
   c. Is there a hierarchy of authority in the group?
   d. Is there an equalitarian type of relationship between each member in the group? Explain.
   e. Are the roles clearly and definitively differentiated by each member in the group?
   f. How much exchange of information took place?

5. At what times during the role-playing situation did the following events take place?
   a. Anxiety.
   b. Initiative.
   c. Resistance.
   d. Rejection.
   e. Hostility.
   f. Humor.
   g. Assertion.
   h. Frustration.
   i. A lack of clarity.
   j. Clarity.
   k. Insight.
   l. Unrelatedness.
   m. Fantasy.
   n. Genuineness of response.
   o. Lack of genuineness of response.
   p. Inconsistency of thinking, feelings, or actions.
   q. Rationalizing.
   r. Attempt at decision making.

s. Attempt at investigating the existing data.
t. Attempt at comparing experiences, ideas, feelings, and actions.
u. Attempt at defining the problem.
v. Attempt at classifying values, attitudes, and experiences.
w. Attempt at interpreting data.
x. Attempt at imagining new ways of dealing with the problem.
y. Attempt at criticizing.
z. Attempt at synthesizing.

6. How can you relate the role-playing situation to self-discovery?

7. How can you relate the role-playing situation to awareness of others?

8. How would you have role-played each one of the roles?

9. What would have happened if each member of the role-playing situation had to change his part and play the corresponding role according to his own perceptions?

10. Which role player did you identify with most? Why?

11. Whom did you identify with least? Why?

12. What fears and anxieties were instigated during the role-playing situation?

13. What hopes and aspirations were instigated during the role-playing situation?

14. Which member in the group conformed most to the expectations of others?

15. Was there a lack of conformity on the part of any of the members?

16. How dependent were the role players on each other?

17. How did the players respond to the suggestions within the group?

18. Were the solutions related to the problems?
    a. How reality-orientated were the recommendations?
    b. How practical were the recommendations?

19. How much satisfaction did you receive while you observed or participated in the role-playing situation?

20. What suggestions can you offer in enhancing the value of the next role-playing situation?

Psychodrama and Group Psychotherapy*

J. L. Moreno

Two thousand years ago mankind underwent, as we do today, a crisis of the first magnitude. To the broad masses catharsis came from Christianity, due to the universality of its methods and the practicality of its instruments, love and confession, charity and hope, instead of from the philosophical schools of Egypt and Greece. In our time the social and mental sciences aim at a similar accomplishment as religion once attained. Mankind's masses suffer from social and mental unrest. Catharsis will probably come again from instruments which combine universality of method with great practicality. One of the most promising methods developed in the last twenty-five years and fulfilling these demands is the psychodramatic method.

Drama is a transliteration of the Greek δρᾶμα which means action, or a thing done. Psychodrama can be defined, therefore, as the science which explores the "truth" by dramatic methods.

The psychodramatic method uses mainly five instruments—the stage, the subject or patient, the director, the staff of therapeutic aides or auxiliary egos, and the audience. The first instrument is the stage. Why a stage? It provides the patient with a living space which is multi-dimensional and flexible to the maximum. The living space of reality is often narrow and restraining, he may easily lose his equilibrium. On the stage he may find it again due to its methodology of freedom—freedom from unbearable stress and freedom for experience and expression. The stage space is an extension of life beyond the reality tests of life itself. Reality and fantasy are not in conflict, but both are functions within a wider sphere—the psychodramatic world of objects, persons and events. In its logic the ghost of Hamlet's father is just as real and permitted to exist as Hamlet himself. Delusions and hallucinations are given flesh—embodiment on the stage—and an equality of status with normal sensory perceptions. The architectural design of the stage is made in accord with therapeutic requirements. Its circular forms and levels of the stage, levels of aspiration, pointing out the vertical dimension, stimulate relief from tensions and permit mobility and flexibility of action. The locus of a psychodrama, if necessary, may be designated everywhere, wherever the patients are, the field of battle, the classroom or the private home. But the ultimate resolution of deep mental conflicts requires an objective setting, the therapeutic theater. Like in religion, although the devout may pray to his God in his own chamber, it is in the church where the community of believers attain the most complete confirmation of their faith.

The second instrument is the subject or patient. He is asked to be himself on the stage, to portray his own private world. He is told to be himself, not an actor, as the actor is compelled to sacrifice his own private self to the role imposed upon him by a playwright. Once he is warmed up to the task it is comparatively easy for the patient to give an account of his daily life in action, as no one is as much of an authority on himself as himself. He has to act freely, as things rise up in his mind; that is why he has to be given freedom of expression, spontaneity. Next in importance to spontaneity comes the process of enactment. The verbal level is transcended and included in the level of action. There are several forms of enactment, pretending to be in a role, re-enactment or acting out a past scene, living out a problem presently pressing, creating like on the stage or testing oneself for the future. Further comes the principle of in-

* Read at the American Psychiatric Association Meeting, May 30, 1946, in Chicago.

"Psychodrama and Group Psychotherapy," by J. L. Moreno. From *Sociometry*, Vol. 9, No. 2–3, pp. 249–253, 1946.

volvement. We have been brought up with the idea that, in test as well as in treatment situations, a minimum of involvement with other persons and objects is a most desirable thing for the patient. An illustration of this is the "Rorschach." The Rorschach situation is reduced to ink blots. In the Rorschach the subjects change but the situation is always the same. It is thought to be its greatest virtue that it is pure and therefore offers an "objective" test. The psychoanalytic interview in its orthodox form too, tried to be pure and objective, by reducing the involvement with the analyst to a minimum. In the psychodramatic situation a maximum of involvement with other subjects and things is not only possible but expected. Reality is not only not feared but provoked. Indeed, in the psychodramatic situation all degrees of involvement take place, from a minimum to a maximum. In addition comes the principle of realization. The patient is enabled not only to meet parts of himself, but the other persons who partake in his mental conflicts. These persons may be real or illusions. The reality test which is a mere word in other therapies is thus actually made true on the stage. The warming up process of the subject to psychodramatic portrayal is stimulated by numerous techniques, only a few of which are mentioned here: self presentation, soliloquy, projection, interpolation of resistance, reversal of roles, double ego, mirror techniques, auxiliary world, realization and psycho-chemical techniques. The aim of these sundry techniques is not to turn the patients into actors, but rather to stir them up to be on the stage what they *are*, more deeply and explicitly than they appear to be in life reality.

The third instrument is the director. He has three functions: producer, therapist and analyst. As producer he has to be on the alert to turn every clue which the subject offers into dramatic action, to make the line of production one with the life line of the subject, and never to let the production lose rapport with the audience. As therapist attacking and shocking the subject is at times just as permissible as laughing and joking with him; at times he may become indirect and passive and for all practical purposes the session seems to be run by the patient. As analyst he may complement his own interpretation by responses coming from informants in the audience, husband, parents, children, friends or neighbors.

The fourth instrument is a staff of auxiliary egos. These auxiliary egos or therapeutic actors have a double significance. They are extensions of the director, exploratory and therapeutic, but they are also extensions of the patient, portraying the actual or imagined personae of their life drama. The functions of the auxiliary ego are threefold: the function of the actor, portraying roles required by the patient's world; the function of the therapeutic agent, guiding the subject; and the function of the social investigator.

The fifth instrument is the audience. The audience itself has a double purpose. It may serve to help the patient or, being itself helped by the subject on the stage the audience becomes the patient. In helping the patient it is a sounding board of public opinion. Its responses and comments are as extemporaneous as those of the patient, they may vary from laughter to violent protest. The more isolated the patient is, for instance because his drama on the stage is shaped by delusions and hallucinations, the more important becomes, to him, the presence of an audience which is willing to accept and understand him. When the audience is helped by the subject, thus becoming the patient itself, the situation is reversed. The audience sees itself, that is, one of its collective syndromes portrayed on the stage.

The stage portion of a psychodramatic session has opened the way to action research and action therapy, role test and role training, situation tests and situational interviews whereas the audience portion has become the common ground of the better known forms of group psychotherapy, as lecture methods, dramatic methods and film methods. Scientific foundations of group psychotherapy require as a prerequisite a basic science of human relations, widely known as sociometry. It is from "sociatry," a pathological counterpart of such a science that knowledge can be derived as to abnormal organization of groups, the diagnosis and prognosis, prophylaxis and control of deviate group behavior.

Now that we have described the five basic instruments required to run a psychodramatic session we may ask ourselves: to what effect? We will limit ourselves here to the description of a single phenomenon, mental catharsis (stems from the Greek, it means purging, purification).

Breuer and Freud were ignorant of the psychotherapeutic implications of the drama milieu to which Aristotle referred. It remained for psychodrama to rediscover and treat the idea of catharsis in its relation to psychotherapy. We picked up the trend of thought where Aristotle had left off. We too, began with the drama but *reversed* the procedure. It was not the end phase but the initial phase of the drama towards which we directed attention. *Mental* catharsis was when we entered the scene with our investigations to be found only in dramatic literature, in faded memories of Aristotle's old definition and the term itself practically out of circulation. The psychoanalysts, after a flare up in the early 1890's had pushed it aside. As practically every human activity can be the source of some degree of catharsis the problem is to determine in what catharsis consists, in which way it differs for instance, from happiness, contentment, ecstasy, need satisfaction, and so forth, and whether one source is superior in the production of catharsis to another source; indeed, whether there is an element common to all sources which operates in the production of catharsis. Therefore my aim has been to define catharsis in such a way that all forms of influence which have a demonstrable cathartic effect can be shown as positive steps within a single total process of operation. I discovered the common principle producing catharsis to be: spontaneity.

Because of the universality of the act and its primordial nature it engulfs all other forms of expression. They flow naturally out of it or can be encouraged to emerge, verbal associations, musical associations, visual associations, color associations, rhythmic and dance associations, and every other stimulus which might arouse or inhibit the emergence of one or another factor, for instance, the use of psychochemical starters like sedatives, as barbiturates, sodium amytal, sodium pentotal; or shock methods as insulin, metrazol or electricity; or endocrinological medications as thyroid are fully within the scheme of total catharsis; they may condition and prepare the organism for psychodramatic integration. The need for the drama can be temporarily choked, for instance, by sleep or shock therapies. But the fundamental need for the realization of certain fantastic imageries cannot be "shocked away." Unless the subject is reduced to a brain invalid by surgery or prolonged shock treatments, the temporarily scared patient is bound to relapse and reproduce the same type of mental syndrome he had before treatment began. It is into the stream of action catharsis that all the rivulets of partial catharsis flow.

The treatment of audiences has become an important alternative to individual treatment. The relationship of the audience to itself in a psychodramatic session, being treated by its own spokesman on the stage, gives us a clue as to the reasons of the cathartic effect of psychodrama. According to historians of the Greek drama the audience was there first, the chorus, musing about a common syndrome. There were "keynoters" among them but they remained within the chorus. Aeschylos is credited with having put the first actor upon a social space outside of the chorus, the stage, not speaking to them, but portraying the woes of their own hero. Euripedes is credited with having put the second actor on the stage, thus making possible the dialogue and interaction of roles. We may be credited to have put the psyche itself on the stage. The psyche which originally came from the group—after a process of reconversion on the stage—personified by an actor—returns to the group—in the form of the psychodrama. That which was most startling, new and spectacular to see and to feel on the stage appears to the participants after thorough exposure as a process which is familiar to them and intimately known—as their own selves. The psychodrama confirms their own identity as in a mirror.

ROLE-PLAYING SITUATIONS

1. You are a parent and your teenage son or daughter decides to buy a piece of clothing that you definitely do not like. He or she insists that it is what every one wears, but you say it is ridiculous and too expensive. What happens?

Roles: Mother, father, or both parents.
Teenage son or daughter.

2. You are a parent and your daughter wants to go to a party that only starts at 10.30 P.M. You insist that it is a ridiculous hour for a party to start and do not want her to go. She, on the other hand, states that it is a party she has been looking forward to for weeks. What happens?

Roles: Mother, father, or both parents.
Teenage daughter.

3. You are a parent and your eighteen-year-old daughter wants to stay home for the weekend with a boyfriend with whom she has been going out for three months. She claims she loves him and that you should trust her not to do anything wrong. You say no and she says yes. What happens?

Roles: Mother, father, or both parents.
Teenage daughter.

4. You are a parent and your teenage daughter or son of sixteen tells you something that he or she wants you to keep secret. He or she finds out that you have related the secret to one of your relatives. What is the secret and what happens?

Roles: Mother, father, or both parents.
Teenager.

5. You are a black, white, or yellow parent and your son or daughter goes on a date with someone from another color group. You are against it. Your youngster insists it is his right. What happens?

Roles: Mother, father, or both parents.
Teenager.

6. You are a parent who believes that one slap is worth a thousand words when it really is necessary. Your husband or wife disagrees strongly. You are a teenager or child in the family and are asked your opinion. Take sides in this controversy.

Roles: Father and mother.
Teenager or child.

7. You believe that it is best to be open and honest about whatever anger you feel or think. Your spouse disagrees and states that children should not be witness to their parents' anger. You are a teenager or child in the family and are asked your opinion. Take sides in this controversy.

Roles: Father and mother.
Teenager or child.

8. You are a parent of a retarded child and feel free about mentioning it to people if the subject of children and differences come to a discussion. Your spouse disagrees. One of your other children, an adolescent or child, is asked to give his opinion about the subject, that is, whether he feels free to mention the fact that his brother or sister is retarded. Take sides in the controversy.

Roles: Father and mother.
Adolescent or child.

9. You are a parent and you want to watch your favorite TV program, which is different than the one your son or daughter wishes. What happens?

Roles: Mother, father, or both parents.
Son or daughter.

10. You are a parent who strongly feels that sex is best dealt with in books. Your spouse disagrees. Your son or daughter is asked what he thinks about the subject. Everyone takes a side. What happens?

Roles: Father and mother.
Adolescent or child.

11. You are a parent and strongly feel that the facts of life or sex education should not be taught in school. On the contrary, the subject should be dealt with by parents alone. Your spouse is in disagreement. Your son or daughter is asked to submit his opinion. Take sides in this controversy.

Roles: Father and mother.
Son or daughter.

12. You are a parent who feels strongly that your child or teenager ought to be achieving much higher grades than he does because, for one reason, the reality of times dictates the fact that the person who succeeds gets ahead. Your spouse disagrees. Your son or daughter is asked to give his opinion. In addition, your neighbor, a teacher who is an honest, straightforward person is asked to comment. He is joined by a school administrator who is his friend. Take sides in this controversy.

Roles: Mother and father.
Son or daughter.
Neighbor who is a teacher.
School administrator (friend of teacher).

13. You are a parent who strongly feels that your son or daughter should arrange his own clothes, books, and bed in his room. Your teenager claims that he cannot for various reasons. You insist. There is conflict of ideas and feelings. What happens?

Roles: Mother, father, or both parents.
Adolescent.

14. You, as a parent, insist that your son and daughter should have their homework examined by you or your spouse. Your spouse disagrees with your point of view. Your children are asked to give their opinion. Each one takes a side. What happens?

Roles: Father and mother.
Son and daughter.

15. You are told by a number of medical specialists that you will die in twenty-four hours. What would you do?

Roles: Whomever you wish to include in this scene.

16. You are told that in one month you will die but that you will have the opportunity to do whatever you wish. How will that affect what you do?

Roles: The patient.
Anyone else you wish.

17. A meteorite will inevitably collide with our earth and we will all go up in smoke. This will occur in one year. How will this affect your way of life?

Roles: Yourself and anyone else you wish.

18. You are a teacher and you believe that one of the primary functions of the school is to develop young peoples' interest in each other. Now you are given a new class of students. How would you try to accomplish what you believe is one of the primary functions of the school?

Roles: Teacher.
A number of students who ought to react to your suggestions.

19. You are a teacher. Your junior high school students want to have a dance without being chaperoned by anyone from the staff. You are against this idea. Another teacher is on the side of the students. The parent group is on your side. What happens?

Roles: Two teachers.
Some students who want to have a dance.
Representative of the parents.

20. You are a parent who believes that girls should be submissive and not assert themselves. Your spouse disagrees with you. Your teenage son or daughter is asked to comment on what he or she believes. What happens?

Roles: Father and mother.
Son or daughter.

21. You are a teacher and you find out that two of your students are kissing each other in the back of the room. You are very upset and ask to see the adolescents after school. You contact the parents. The principal is asked to join in, as well. What happens?

Roles: Two teenagers.
Two sets of parents.
Teacher.
Principal.

22. You are a college student and your friend wants you to take some drugs. You tell him for numerous reasons you are afraid. He insists and makes the whole invitation an adventurous one. You are about to comply to his wishes when another friend comes by and insists that you should not submit to taking drugs. There is a back and forth exchange of ideas. What happens?

Roles: You.
Your friend who wants you to take drugs.
Your friend who doesn't want you to take drugs.

23. You are a teacher who believes that there is nothing wrong in taking drugs once in a while. Your colleague disagrees with you. A discussion ensues. What happens?

Roles: Teacher for taking drugs.
Teacher against taking drugs.

24. You are black and you feel that blacks should only associate with blacks and not with whites, unless necessary. Your black contemporaries disagree with you and feel that blacks ought to integrate as much as possible and not hold any barrier because of color. What happens?

Roles: Blacks against integration.
Blacks for integration.

25. You are white and feel that whites should only associate with whites and not with blacks, unless necessary. Your white contemporaries disagree with you and feel that whites ought to integrate as much as possible and not hold any barrier because of color. What happens?

Roles: Whites against integration.
Whites for integration.

26. You are white and feel that whites should integrate with blacks. The blacks, on the other hand, are split into two groups—half for and half against integration.

Roles: White.
Two blacks.

27. Half of the white group is for integration and the other half is against it. Half of the black group is for integration and half against it. You are the organizer of these four groups. You are either white or black. How would you go about dealing with the problem if you were asked to bring these four groups together and act as chairman.

Roles: You, as chairman.
White for integration.
White against integration.
Black against integration.
Black for integration.

28. You are a student and you feel that interfaith and interracial dating should be tabooed. You are confronted with someone who disagrees with you strongly. What happens?

Roles: You, who are against interfaith and interracial dating.
Someone who disagrees with you.

29. You feel you are ugly, that you have no appeal to the opposite sex. This is how you feel. You meet a member of the opposite sex who is very interested in you. This person finds out that you feel you are ugly and tries to convince you in his own way that you are not. What happens?

Roles: You.
Your interested pursuer.

30. You are a student who feels it is your right to participate in political demonstrations. A fellow student disagrees with you strongly. The pros and cons are discussed. A teacher walks in and is asked what he thinks. He is given the opportunity to participate. What happens?

Roles: Two students.
Teacher.

31. If a college student witnesses injustice he ought to learn to mind his own business, according to you. One of your fellow students disagrees with you and feels that people ought to speak up and act when there is injustice. Two teachers are asked to give their point of view. One agrees with the first student while the other disagrees with him. What happens?

Roles: Two students.
Two teachers.

32. It is your contention that a sensitive person should not offend the feelings of someone else. A fellow student disagrees. Two teachers are asked to comment on the issue. As it turns out, each opposes the other and takes an opposite point of view. What happens?

Roles: You and your fellow student.
Two teachers.

33. It is your contention that one should always think first before speaking in order to avoid trouble. Your fellow student disagrees with you. Two teachers are asked to join in. What happens?

Roles: Two students.
Two teachers.

34. You are a teacher and it is your contention that it is not enough for a child to just sit down and concentrate on what has to be done and do it; other considerations must be kept in mind in order for a child to study or do his homework. A number of parents disagree with you. Two teenagers are asked to comment on what they think. What happens?

Roles: Teacher.
Two parents.
Two students.

35. You are a teacher and believe that schoolwork is for the school, and homework is for the home. Your colleague disagrees with you. This develops into an argument in which two students are asked to give their opinions, which are in opposition to each other. What happens.

Roles: Two teachers.
Two students.

36. You are a teacher who believes that physical education and recreational activities have a place outside of the initial academic learning curriculum. Your colleague disagrees. Two students are asked to give their opinions. In each case their opinions are diametrically opposed to each other.

Roles: Two teachers.
Two students.

37. As a teacher you believe that much time is lost in allowing students an opportunity to discuss subject matter in class. Your

colleague disagrees with you. Two students with opposing points of view are asked to comment on the issue. What happens?

Roles: Two teachers.
Two students.

38. The student who does not verbally participate in class should not receive a grade equal to that of the student who does, according to you. Your colleague disagrees with you and presents his argument. Two students are asked to comment on the issue and each, as it turns out, takes a different position. What happens?

Roles: Two teachers.
Two students.

39. According to you, as a teacher, religious education has a definite place in the college curriculum as well as on all levels of learning from the elementary school and up. In addition, it is your contention that much understanding can come from the proper type of religious orientation that gives respect and understanding to all religons. Your colleague disagrees with you. He believes, among other things, that religion must be separated from public education. Two students are asked what they think and, as it turns out, each takes an opposing point of view. What happens?

Roles: Two teachers.
Two students.

40. As a teacher it is your contention that it is important for a student to learn how to memorize somethings even if he does not understand its meaning, because he may never know when he might need it. Also, it develops certain powers of thinking that will help him in his studies. Your colleague disagrees with you. Two students are asked to give their opinion, each of which is in opposition to the other. What happens?

Roles: Two teachers.
Two students.

41. As a student you strongly feel that students should be given a definite voice in what happens on all levels of university planning and decision making. A fellow student disagrees with you on the basis that students are inexperienced in the affairs of academic planning and decision making and therefore should play a minor role in these matters. Two university teachers with opposing points of view are asked to join in the controversy. What happens?

Roles: Two students.
Two teachers.

42. As a college student you believe that a liberal arts or science course of studies on the college level are more important than business education. This issue is brought to a discussion when a fellow student states that he disagrees with you strongly and develops a rationale to oppose you. Two teachers with different points of view are asked to comment on the matter. What happens?

Roles: Two students.
Two teachers.

43. You are a student and are unconditionally against war. One of your classmates takes the other side. Two teachers with opposing points of view are asked to join in. Two parents are also asked to participate. Finally, two political statesmen are also included in the group. Each represents an opposite point of view. What happens?

Roles: Two students.
Two teachers.
Two parents.
Two political statesmen.

44. As a parent you believe that sexual intercourse should not take place before marriage. Your contention is challenged by another parent. Two teachers and two students are asked to participate, each with a different point of view.

Roles: Two parents.
Two teachers.
Two students.

45. You are an elementary school teacher applying for a teaching position and your only experience is student teaching and some community work. The principal meets with you in his office, together with a master teacher, and interviews you.

Roles: New teacher.
Principal.
Master teacher.

46. You are a new teacher of American History or some other junior or high school subject. You are applying for a teaching position and are asked to meet with the principal and educational adviser for an interview in a school where the children are disadvantaged. You are interviewed.

Roles: New teacher.
Principal.
Educational adviser.

47. You are an elementary or nursery school teacher who has just graduated from college. You are applying for a job at a school in which the children are disadvantaged. The principal, educational adviser, and parent representative of the neighborhood interview you.

Roles: New teacher.
Parent.
Educational adviser.
Parent representative.

48. You are an elementary or high school teacher. One of your students is seen taking some money from the jacket of another student. You are informed of the matter and asked to deal with the problem. You call the student to you; he states, before you even question him, that he did not do anything. What do you do?

Roles: Teacher.
Students who inform.
Student who allegedly took the money.
Anyone else you might want to include in the role-playing situation.

49. You are a teacher and the problem of tattling is brought up. You believe that students should protect their interests and are justified if they inform on a student if he cheats on an examination or copies his homework or is dishonest in any way. A fellow colleague is asked to comment on the subject and disagrees with you. Two students with opposing points of view are also asked to contribute their thinking and feelings on the subject. What happens?

Roles: Two teachers.
Two students.

50. As a teacher you believe that children who continually upset the routines of their class, disturb their neighbors, talk continually, are always interrupting others, or do not do their homework should be punished in various ways so that they understand the importance of school. You colleague disagrees with you and makes his thinking and feelings known. Two students with opposing points of view contribute their ideas. Two parents with contrasting opinions are likewise included in the discussion.

Roles: Two teachers.
Two students.
Two parents.

SHORT CASE STUDY PRESENTATIONS

Case of Dorothy (13)

Role players: Dorothy, stepfather, mother, and school counselor.

Background: Father died when Dorothy was six. Mother remarried three years later.

Mother: After the death of your husband you had to struggle to support yourself and Dorothy. When you remarried you continued to work because your new husband, Anthony, was just starting out as an appliance salesman. As for Dorothy, you demanded that she behaved herself; you did not tolerate any misbehavior. From the very beginning of your second marriage Dorothy showed intense resentment to Anthony. She wanted only you but that was impossible. She also resented you because she felt that if you loved your first husband, her real father, you would not have remarried. You suspected that she had fantasies about her deceased father and as a result never fully accepted his death.

Anthony (stepfather): It is difficult for you to feel anything positive for your stepdaughter, Dorothy, because she seems to resent you continually. Despite your continual efforts in the first few years to establish contact with her she never seemed to respond to you with warmth. More than once she told you that you had no right to discipline her because you were not her real father. You have the feeling that Dorothy dislikes you intensely and uses every mental device to attack you. You wish she were a little softer, more feminine. You do not know how to help her.

Dorothy: You place great importance on cleverness, being smart, an achiever. You have managed to succeed in obtaining high grades. You have alienated other children by your contempt for any sign of weakness for failure. You cannot accept failure and do your utmost to avoid it. You are highly competitive in class discussions and are quick to sense what the teacher wants to hear; you respond accordingly. You devote much of your time to books. At night you have nightmares. The only person you really trust is your mother. You have a mental image of your real father; in fact, you carry about a picture of him. Secretly you feel that someone like your father will come by and take care of you, just like your real father should have. As a child you often dreamed he was alive and would return. You felt that he abandoned you; you were angry with him. Guilt usually followed. Because you felt your mother's new husband was an imposter in the house, you did everything possible to get rid of him.

You want to succeed in school, get a scholarship, and leave home. You are interested in history because it deals with what happened in the past, which always fascinated you. You asked the school nurse for some sleeping pills because you are lately awakened by terrible nightmares.

School counselor: You have asked to meet with the parents because Dorothy has approached the school nurse for sleeping pills.

Situation 1

Time: Evening
Place: Home
People: Stepfather, mother, and Dorothy
Problem: To be determined by the role-playing group

Situation 2

Time: Morning
Place: School office
People: Stepfather, mother, Dorothy, and school counselor
Problem: To be determined by the role-playing group

Case of Martin (14)

Role players: Martin, Alfred, mother, father, and school counselor.

Father: You are a hard-working machinist who manages to support your family of two children and a wife. Your own childhood was difficult because your father died when you were six and your mother was too ill to care for you, which meant that you lived with your unmarried aunt. When you were a teenager you left school and took an apprenticship in a shop where you learned your present trade. You waited until you were in your late thirties before you married.

Martin was born four years after your wife had three miscarriages. That was the beginning of a long series of hospital experiences for Martin. He was premature, although constitutionally healthy. Hormones and vitamins were administered to him periodically because of his below normal height.

You are affectionate with your children, although you do not know what to do when Martin fights with his younger brother, Alfred, who is four years younger, normal size, robust, and healthy. When it comes to making decisions in the home your wife takes the initiative. You seldom assert yourself, are generous in giving, and want only the best for your children. You get along well with your fellow workers and seldom boss anyone. You are skilled in your trade. You find it easier to relate to Alfred, who is easygoing and cheerful despite the rivalry with his older brother, Martin.

Mother: You only married in your early thirties and tried to have children for a number of years without success. You were delighted when Martin was born but extremely worried and concerned about his health and height. You were in constant contact with endocrinologists and other specialists because of Martin's body size. You had no trouble with the pregnancy and birth of Alfred who, from the very beginning, was a healthy and easy child to rear.

Martin: Physically, you feel inferior. You have learned to withdraw from situations and activities in which you feel your size is a stigma, such as playing in sports or in any of the boy-girl social functions. You feel that the children in class have cast you in the role as the "shrimp" or "shorty" or "pint size." You do not react outwardly to these remarks; inside, however, you reconfirm the fact that there is something wrong with you, and that you have to learn more strategic ways of avoiding criticism. Recently you have considered learning karate, but you are afraid to expose your puny body before others. You bought a book on body building. You are tired of going to the hospital, of having doctors poke about and examine you. You would prefer that the teachers did not call on you. You feel that they take pity on you because of your height and that infuriates you. You do not want pity, just to be left alone. You feel a kind of self-revulsion when you look at yourself in the mirror or when you mentally compare yourself to other boys. You like to read, although you have trouble concentrating and remembering. You are not supposed to eat too much but you cannot help it. At home you fight with your brother because he will not leave you alone. Alfred is nearly your size even though he is four years younger. This bothers you, but there is nothing you can do about it. You do not know why you fight with him. Whatever you do to Alfred does not seem to affect him. He comes back for more, usually with affection despite the fact that you give him a difficult time.

It bothers you when your father takes a passive role with your mother. You love him but are angry with him because he does not act as you want him to. On the other hand, you see your mother as the more active, decisive person and respect her for it, resent her because you wish she were more passive and your father were more the authority in the house. You are jealous of the affection your parents give to Alfred.

School counselor: Although Martin is a little above average intelligence his work is among the poorest in the class. He doesn't seem to have any desire to work, removes himself from all class activities unless forced to attend and then is extremely passive. He will not join in any of the recreational activities regardless of the pressure that is put on him by his physical education teacher. Whenever he is requested to answer questions that are posed to him he often states that he does not hear, or does not know the answer. At times his replies are unrelated to the lesson.

The other children leave him alone and he makes little attempt to socialize with them. He is a loner. The teachers find him passive, uncooperative, although not aggressive. Outside of the presence of the children he is responsive and capable.

He is failing most of his subjects except mathematics and English. Power and strength are the underlying themes in his compositions. The hero is usually the underdog who struggles against violent opposition. Most of the stories end with the hero surmounting all obstacles.

Situation 1

Time: Evening
Place: Home
People: Father, mother, Martin, and Alfred
Problem: To be determined by the role-playing group

Situation 2

Time: Morning
Place: School office
People: School counselor, father, mother, and Martin
Problem: To be determined by the role-playing group

Case of Bud (17)

Role players: Father, mother, Bud, school counselor.

Father: You are a successful lawyer and well-to-do economically. You are down-to-earth, a rock of the old establishment, and believe your only son ought to apply himself and study hard and spend less time running about with girls or borrowing your car and money. Whenever you refuse to comply to his wishes he turns to your wife, who finds a way of talking you into submitting to your son's request. Most of the time you succumb to her wishes in order to maintain peace. You are asked to come to school because Bud is having trouble passing his courses. You are naturally very upset about this.

Mother: You have always been childlike in regard to your husband. You and your son have a close relationship. You live vicariously through his exploits with his girl friends, whom he speaks to you about freely. In fact, you share most of his problems and seldom judge him severely. At times you find the seriousness at which your husband takes everyday living absurd; in this sense you also belittle him together with your son. You were never serious about school and therefore can sympathize with and understand your son's attitude to learning. You take your responsibilities at home seriously and devote your time to making your home a beautiful place. You especially enjoy material things, although you are not a snob. You also feel the need to keep in touch with the latest fashions and recipes.

You have been informed of Bud's school status and are expected to meet with the professional authorities.

Bud: You are having trouble passing most of your school subjects and have been warned that you will not advance to the next class unless you achieve better grades and take a different approach to learning. You like to double in many things and lose interest quickly. Few things really upset you. You have humor, are flighty in your thinking, like to have a good time, and find serious things a bore. You are tolerated by the boys, but not admired or really respected. You are outwardly very much at home with girls and their interests; you enjoy playing with them and teasing them.

You like to be a sport and treat your friends. You wish you could be a playboy. You do not really know what you like outside of fun with cars, sex, and dancing. You also like the latest fashions in clothes.

School counselor: According to the teacher's records, Bud is failing most of his courses. His ability to apply himself to subject content is limited to a superficial analysis that is generally to the point but void of insight and depth of understanding. He kids around playfully with the students, although he does not make himself into the class clown. He is able to see relationships and potentially has the makings of a passing student, but he cannot seem to take school seriously. He is polite, witty, and whimsical, and he knows it and makes the most of it in winning over his adversaries. He seems to have trouble empathizing with others. He is an egoist, according to the teachers, and is seldom curious about what happens to others when it does not directly apply to his welfare.

You are informed that you will represent the education dimension of Bud's case. You feel that you need a rounded picture of the case and therefore have requested that the parents be invited to discuss their son's dilemma.

Situation 1

Time:	Evening
Place:	Home
People:	Father, mother, and Bud
Problem:	To be determined by the role-playing group

Situation 2

Time:	Morning
Place:	School office
People:	Father, mother, Bud, and school counselor
Problem:	To be determined by the role-playing group

Case of Roberta (16) and Ned (14)

Role players: Father, mother, Roberta, Ned, and school counselor.

Father: You are middle-aged, and work as an accountant. You claim that Roberta has trouble applying herself to her studies because she feels the unhappiness at home where conflict and discord are daily occurrences between you and your wife. Your relationship to Roberta is very close. If it were not for her and your son, Ned, you would have separated and divorced years ago. You have never stated this thought to either of your children. Almost every discussion with your wife turns into a fight or an argument. You are aware that this does not help the children but there is nothing you can do. You are willing to cooperate in any way you can in order to help your children. You have been informed that Roberta is failing a number of her subjects and Ned has been truant. You have been asked to come to school.

Mother: You work as a secretary and feel the intense need to be away from home during the day even though you feel guilty about it because it means that you cannot be at home when your children return from school. You are aware that the problems of the children are not unrelated to the relationship between you and your husband. You gave up the idea of divorce because of the children. You are especially close to Ned, although you feel a deep concern for Roberta. You want to help the children in any way you can. You have been informed that Roberta is having trouble passing her studies and Ned has been truant. Consequently, you have been invited to speak to the authorities at school.

Roberta: You have little desire to do anything but read or sleep. You find it almost impossible to study at home when your parents argue with each other. You cry often out of desparation. You wish you could help your parents.

At school, you find it difficult to concentrate. Your thoughts stray from the subjects. You daydream very often. During the language-arts class you often find yourself living through the book. It takes a few seconds before you can turn your attention to the class lesson. You lack a sense of confidence and because of this you avoid being with others. You are painfully shy, but do not know how to overcome this. You usually hesitate to speak out in class because you are afraid that you might say the wrong thing. You lose your train of thought, or become flustered when someone is critical of you or disagrees with you. You feel at home with the teachers who make the least demand on you. When one of the children asks you to do something you comply out of fear of arousing their disapproval. You find it very difficult to assert yourself with others.

You are especially timid about undressing before the other girls during physical education. You have asked the family doctor for a note to give to the school so that you will be excused from swimming. You love to dance, but only in the confines of your own room with no one around. You enjoy the arts and love to draw. In art class you are thought of highly by the teacher but try to avoid having attention drawn to you for the work you do.

You wish you were in an art school or in a place where you did not have to use so much mental effort. You want to study art when you graduate high school. You realize that you are failing a number of subjects because you have little interest and motivation in most of your classes. You are moody and depressed, but try not to show it. You feel you can only talk to your dog, Bogo. Your relationship with Ned is a close one, but he is much younger. Besides, he has his own friends and life. You are also worried about him because you see he is playing hooky from school and having trouble with learning.

Ned: You are closer to your mother than

you are to your father. You feel your father is passive with you but active with your sister Roberta. You dislike it when you are told what to do and generally react negatively to any kind of adult authority. Although the subject matter in class is generally not difficult to comprehend, you find it uninteresting. Lately you have been truant from school and know that there is a danger that you might not be promoted to the next class. You rely on others to do your assignments. You feel best when it comes to physical activities. Outside of school you are the captain of the football and baseball teams. You try to be fair with your teammates. You are quick to argue with others in class. Once you were elected to be on the debating club but you refused.

You are especially close to the woodworking shop teacher, poor in history, mathematics, and science. You like social studies, although you cannot seem to find time enough to study.

School counselor: Both Roberta and Ned are failing students for the reasons mentioned above. You want to meet with the parents and find out from them what they feel can be done to help the children. You have never conferred with any member of the family and have only informed the children that their parents will be obliged to come to school. You have various teachers' reports at your disposal. Both youngsters have the potential to learn and succeed but for one reason or the other have little interest in pursuing their studies with earnestness.

Situation 1

Time: Evening
Place: Home
People: Roberta, Ned, mother, and father
Problem: To be determined by the role-playing group

Situation 2

Time: Morning
Place: School office
People: School counselor, father, mother, Roberta, and Ned
Problem: To be determined by the role-playing group

PART THREE

PROVERBS AND QUOTATIONS

The following sayings are generally recognized as statements of wisdom that express a dimension of truth about the ways of existence. They capture the well-known facts about experience and what has been observed in life. They ordinarily indicate a course of action or quality of judgment. Their terseness and meaningfulness are like a key to a whole range of ideas and events we have experienced. Their content is drawn from educational, poetic, medical, legal, and religious values. They suggest moral rules, lessons, or dictates. They signify a condensation of experience similar in impact to what is commonly found in an adage, maxim, witticism, byword, or epigram. The concisely formulated saying might give us a glimpse of the obvious. For some people, they are woven in the matrix of their everyday existence. They help to heighten comparisons and sometimes produce humorous effects. They represent the conventional thoughts and feelings that reach back to our historical heritage. They can be used as a type of formula to guide an individual in what he does.

Notwithstanding the value of proverbs and quotations in the everyday functioning and endeavors of human experience, our intent in presenting them is to evoke thoughts, feelings, and images that can be used for self-discovery and social awareness. These proverbs and quotations tap the psychological world of an individual. They can be used as a verbal instrument to evoke a range and depth of projections. Of course, the response to these sayings are not to be measured—this is not a test. They should, however, be defined, interpreted, compared to, and classified according to the criteria of the students themselves. In other words, the person who undertakes to respond to these quotes is his own investigator and diagnostician. He and his fellow students analyze their perceptions of the proverbs and quotations. The differences he finds between his interpretations and those of his neighbors ought to sharpen and broaden his awareness of how he tends to perceive certain phenomena.

Our needs, fears, wishes, and anxieties will be elicited by these quotes. They will evoke images, metaphors, and similes from us. Our reactions to these sayings will be no less inferior or superior to that of another person. On the other hand, the uniqueness of each perception should enlighten us to what is generally not available to us in our consciousness. Our own symbols and beliefs will be brought to the foreground of our awareness. The quotes that represent cultural and educational stereotypes, child-rearing practices, and the philosophy of life will be critically examined against our understanding and knowledge. What was appropriate yesterday in reference to these sayings might not necessarily be acceptable today.

The section entitled "How To Use These Proverbs and Quotations" provides us with numerous ways in which the forthcoming material can be used for self-discovery and social awareness. The degree of flexibility in complying to the suggestions offered in this outline ought to be determined by the students and the teacher. Imagination, creativity, and freedom of response should be encouraged at all times.

The format and some of the proverbs and quotations were essentially inspired by Alexander F. Chamberlaine, *The Child and Childhood in Folklore,* Macmillan, 1895. Other sources of material were obtained from Archer Taylor, *The Proverb,* Folklore Associates, Hatboro, P., 1962; G. L. Apperson, *English Proverbs and Proverbial Phrases,* London, 1929; Burton E. Stevenson, *The Home Book of Proverbs, Maxims and Familiar Phrases,* New York, 1948; and W. G. Smith and Janet Haseltine, *The Oxford Book of English Proverbs* (2nd edition), London, 1948.

How To Use These Proverbs and Quotations

1. First think about them.
2. Write a few sentences about the meaning of one of them.
3. Try to give as many interpretations to the quote as you can.
4. How would you rewrite the proverb or quotation so that it makes more sense to you.
5. What do you agree with or disagree with in the saying?
6. Write a theme using the meaning of the quote as the basis of its content.
7. Compare the meaning of the quote you selected with another one in this section.
   a. In what way are they different?
   b. In what way are they similar?
   c. In what way are they related to each other?
8. Choose a proverb or quotation in this section that best represents what you believe or disbelieve, then state your reason for your selection.
9. What type of picture would you choose that would best represent or illustrate the meaning of the quote.
   a. Describe in detail the content of this picture as you would create it.
   b. Compare your imaginary picture to your neighbor's.
10. Find a fiction or nonfiction story that you feel applies to the theme of this quote.
11. What films, TV and radio programs deal directly or indirectly with the themes of the quotes below?
12. How would you construct a dramatic scene for a play in which the underlying theme of it is related to the meaning of the proverb or quotation (time, place, situation, characters)?
13. Group the quotes and proverbs according to two or three underlying differences.
    a. What is the reason for your classification system?
14. What actual observations have you made in your immediate surroundings that confirm or invalidate the meaning or theme of the quote?
15. Relate the meaning of the quote to your own life.
16. List the images that come to your mind and discuss them with your neighbor.
17. Suppose the proverb or quote were a truth for everyone all the time; what problems would exist for you and for mankind?
    a. How would you go about solving these problems?
18. Ask your friend or someone in your immediate family to respond to any one of these questions and compare your thoughts to his.
19. Select one humorous and one beautiful saying from this section.
20. Devise another question about these proverbs that you feel ought to be asked.

PROVERBS AND QUOTATIONS ABOUT

FATHER AND CHILD

1. Bone does not let go flesh, nor father son.

—Angolese.

2. Happy is the child whose father went to the devil.

3. He is a chip off the old block.

4. He is cut out of his father's eyes (i.e., very like his father).

—Frisian.

5. Many a father might say . . . "I put in gold into the furnace, and there came out this calf."

—Spurgeon.

6. The child has a red tongue like its father.

7. The fathers have eaten sour grapes, and the children's teeth are set on edge.

—Bible.

8. The ungrateful son is a wart on his father's face; to leave it is a blemish, to cut it a pain.

—Afghan.

9. To a father, who is growing old, there is nothing dearer than a daughter.

—Euripides.

10. Vinegar the son of wine (i.e., an unpopular son of a popular father).

—Talmud.

PROVERBS AND
QUOTATIONS ABOUT

MOTHER AND CHILD

1. He that is born of a hen must scrape for a living.

2. It is not, as thy mother says, but as thy neighbors say.
   —Hebrew.

3. Mai agucosa, filha preguicosa. (Diligent mother, idle daughter.)
   —Portuguese.

4. Milk with water is still milk (i.e., although your mother is bad, she is nevertheless your mother).

5. No bones are broken by a mother's fist.
   —Russian.

6. One good mother is worth a hundred schoolmasters.

7. One scream of fear from a mother may respond through the whole life of her daughter.
   —Jean Paul.

8. The elephant does not find his trunk heavy, nor the mother her babe.
   —Angolese (Africa).

9. The nurse's bread is better than the mother's cake.
   —Frisian.

10. Though a mother be a wolf, she does not eat her cub's flesh.
    —Afghan.

PROVERBS AND QUOTATIONS ABOUT

THE CHILD AND CHILDHOOD

1. A growing youth has a wolf in his belly.

2. A hungry belly has no ears.

3. Bon sang ne peut mentir. Qui naquit chat court apres les souris. (Good blood cannot lie. The kitten will chase the mouse.)

   —French.

4. Children and chickens are always a-picking.

5. Children, like dogs, have so sharp and fine a scent, that they detect and hunt out everything—the bad before all the rest.

   —Goethe.

6. Children tell in the streets what they hear round the hearth.

   —Portuguese.

7. Dochders zijn broze waaren. (Daughters are brittle ware.)

   —Dutch.

8. Give a child till he craves, and a dog while his tail doth wag, and you'll have a fair dog, but a foul knave.

9. One chick keeps a hen busy.

10. Sores are not to be shown to flies, and children are not to be taught to lie.

    —Malay.

PROVERBS AND QUOTATIONS ABOUT

HOME

1. There are some others that account a wife and children but as bills of charges.

—Bacon, *Of Marriage and Single Life.*

2. Most of the persons whom I see in my own house I see across a gulf.

—Emerson, *Journals.*

3. It is a piece of luck to have relations scarce.

—Menander, *Thupopos.*

4. God gives us relatives; thank God, we can choose our friends.

—Addison Mizner, *The Cynics' Calendar.*

5. The family is one of Nature's Masterpieces.

—George Santayana, *The Life of Reason.*

6. He that loves not his wife and children, feeds a lioness at home, and broods a nest of sorrow.

—Jeremy Taylor, *Sermons.*

7. The earth is all the home I have;
The heavens my wide roof-tree.

—W. E. Aytoun, *The Wandering Jew.*

8. The largest part of mankind are nowhere greater strangers than at home.

—S. T. Coleridge, *Table Talk.*

9. Every spirit makes its house, but afterwards the house confines the spirit.

—Emerson, *Conduct Of Life.*

10. And homeless near a thousand homes I stood.

—Wordsworth, *Guilt and Sorrow.*

PROVERBS AND
QUOTATIONS ABOUT

PLAY AND WORK

1. Mingle your cares with pleasures now and then.
—Dionysius Cato.

2. The bow that's always bent will quickly break;
But if unstrung will serve you at your need.
So let the mind some relaxation take
To come back to its task with fresher heed.
—Phaedrus, *Fables.*

3. Think of ease, but work on.
—George Herbert, *Jacula Prudentum.*

4. I go on working for the same reason that a hen goes on laying eggs.
—H. L. Mencken.

5. Work is a grand cure for all the maladies and miseries that ever beset mankind—honest work which you intend getting done!
—T. Carlyle, *Inaugural Address.*

6. . . . too busy with the crowded hour to fear to live or die . . .
—Emerson, *Quatrains.*

7. In war, hunting and love,
Men for one pleasure a thousand griefs prove.
—George Herbert.

8. Curiosity is little more than another name for hope.
—J. C. and A. W. Hare, *Guesses at Truth.*

9. Talk to him of Jacob's ladder, and he would ask the number of steps.
—Douglas Jerrold, *A Matter-Of-Fact Man*

10. I only ask for information.
—Dickens, *David Copperfield.*

PROVERBS AND QUOTATIONS ABOUT

PREJUDICE

1. A prejudice is a vagrant opinion without visible means of support.
—Ambrose Bierce, *The Devil's Dictionary.*

2. What extravagancy is not man capable of entertaining, when once his shackled reason is led in triumph by fancy and prejudice.
—Lord Chesterfield, *Letters.*

3. Prejudice is never easy unless it can pass itself off for reason.
—William Hazlitt, *Sketches and Essays.*

4. Prejudice is the child of ignorance.
—William Hazlitt, *Sketches And Essays.*

5. To be prejudiced is always to be weak.
—Samuel Johnson, *Taxation No Tyranny.*

6. All prejudices take their origin in the intestines.
—F. Nietzsche, *Ecce Homo.*

7. And much he hated all, but most the best.
—Homer, *Iliad.*

8. Folks never understand the folks they hate.
—J. R. Lowell, *Biglow Papers.*

9. Whom men fear they hate, and whom they hate, they wish dead.
—Cicero.

10. In time we hate that which we often fear.
—Shakespeare, *Anthony And Cleopatra.*

PROVERBS AND QUOTATIONS ABOUT

ANGER AND WAR

1. The flame of anger, bright and brief,
Sharpens the bark of love.
—W. S. Landor, *Miscellaneous Poems.*

2. However weak the hand, anger gives it strength.
—Ovid, *Amores.*

3. He that strives not to stem his anger's tide,
Does a wild horse without a bridle ride.
—Colley Cibber, *Love's Last Shift.*

4. A man in a passion rides a mad horse.
—Benjamin Franklin, *Poor Richard.*

5. When angry, count four; when very angry, swear.
—Mark Twain, *Pudd'nhead Wilson's Calendar.*

6. War is the only sport that is genuinely amusing. And it is the only sport that has any intelligible use.
—H. L. Mencken, *Prejudices.*

7. How that red rain hath made the harvest grow.
—Byron, *Childe Harold.*

8. War is death's feast.
—George Herbert, *Jacula Prudentum.*

9. The first casualty when ware comes is truth.
—Hiram Johnson, *Speech.*

10. The children born of thee are sword and fire,
Red ruin, and the breaking up of laws.
—Tennyson, *Guinevere.*

PROVERBS AND QUOTATIONS ABOUT

NATURE

1. Nature never did betray
The heart that loved her.
—Wordsworth, *Lines Composed A Few Miles Above Tintern Abbey.*

2. There are no grotesques in nature.
—Sir Thomas Browne, *Religio Medici.*

3. He that can draw a charm
From rocks, or woods or weeds, or things that seem
All mute, and does it—is wise.
—Bryan Waller Procter, *A Haunted Stream.*

4. Which of us is sometimes affected, almost to despair, by the splendid vision of earth and sky?
—John Keble, *Lectures on Poetry.*

5. We are what suns and winds and waters make us.
—Walter Savage Landor, *Hellenics.*

6. Nature is cruel, man is sick of blood;
Nature is stubborn, man would fain adorn;
Nature is fickle, man hath need of rest;
Nature forgives no debt, and fears no grave.
—Matthew Arnold, *Man and Nature.*

7. Nature's rules have no exceptions.
—Herbert Spencer, *Social Statics.*

8. Everything unnatural is imperfect.
—Napoleon, *Sayings of Napoleon.*

9. One touch of nature makes the whole world kin.
—Shakespeare, *Troilus and Cressida.*

10. Man is not content to take nature as he finds her. He insists on making her over.
—F. J. E. Woodbridge, *Contrasts in Education.*

PROVERBS AND QUOTATIONS ABOUT

SOLITUDE

1. Woe unto him that is never alone, and cannot bear to be alone.
—P. G. Hamerton, *The Intellecutal Life.*

2. The strongest man in the world is he who stands most alone.
—Henrik Ibsen, *An Enemy of The People.*

3. Solitude vivifies; isolation kills.
—Joseph Roux.

4. I never found the companion that was so companionable as solitude.
—Thoreau, *Walden.*

5. How lonely we are in the world!. . . You and I are but a pair of infinite isolations with some fellow islands a little more or less near to us.
—Thackeray, *Pendennis.*

6. Solitude affects some people like wine; they must not take too much of it, for it flies to their head.

7. I am as one who is left alone at a banquet, the lights dead and the flowers faded.
—Buliver-Lytton, *Last Days of Pompeii.*

8. He travels the fastest who travels alone.
—Rudyard Kipling, *The Winners.*

9. Alone, alone, all, all, alone,
Alone on a wide wide sea!
—S. T. Coleridge, *The Ancient Mariner.*

10. And nobody with me at sea but myself.
—Goldsmith, *The Haunch of Venison.*

PROVERBS AND QUOTATIONS ABOUT

CHILDREN—THEIR BEHAVIOR

1. Oh the idea was childish, but divinely beautiful.

—Schiller.

2. Fear made her bold.

—Luc.

3. Under a show of daring, great fear is concealed.

—Luc.

4. But take away the danger, in a thrice
Nature unbridled plunges into vice.

—Conington.

5. Pain has its limits, apprehension none.

—Plin.

6. Cowards die many times before their death
The valiant never taste of death but once.

—Shakespeare.

7. Besides, they always smell of bread and butter.

—Byron.

8. How sharper than a serpent's tooth it is to have a thankless child.

—Shakespeare, *King Lear.*

9. Children learn to creep ere they can learn to go.

—John Heywood, *Proverbs.*

10. Children have more need of models than of critics.

—Joubert.

PROVERBS AND
QUOTATIONS ABOUT

LOVE

1. Love is a fiend, a fire, a heaven, a hell,
   Where pleasure, pain, and sad repentance dwell.
   —Richard Barnfield, *The Shepherd's Content.*

2. Love is only one of many passions . . . and has no great influence on the sum of life.
   —Samuel Johnson, *Works.*

3. Love keeps the cold out better than a clock.
   It serves for food and raiment.
   —Longfellow, *The Spanish Student.*

4. But love is blind, and lovers cannot see the pretty follies that themselves commit.
   —Shakespeare, *The Merchant of Venice.*

5. What is love? Two souls and one flesh.
   Friendship? Two bodies and one soul.
   —Joseph Roux.

6. With all thy faults, I love thee still.
   —Cowper, *The Task.*

7. It adds a precious seeing to the eye.
   —Shakespeare, *Love's Labour's Lost.*

8. We learn only from those we love.
   —Goethe.

9. Love and a cough cannot be hid.
   —George Herbert, *Jacula Prudentum.*

10. Love is like the measles—all the worse when it comes late in life.
    —Douglas Jerrold, *Table Talk.*

PROVERBS AND QUOTATIONS ABOUT

STREETS AND CITIES

1. Cities should be walled with the courage of their inhabitants.

   —Plutarch.

2. . . . the people are the city . . .

   —Shakespeare, *Coriolanus.*

3. Midst the crowd, the hum, the shock of men.

   —Byron, *Childe Harold.*

4. All cities are mad; but the madness is gallant.
   All cities are beautiful: but the beauty is grim.

   —Christopher Morley, *Where The Blue Begins.*

5. High mountains are a feeling, but the hum of human cities torture.

   —Byron, *Childe Harold.*

6. In cities vice is hidden with most ease,
   Or seen with least reproach.

   —Cowper, *The Task.*

7. Cities give not the human senses room enough.

   —Emerson, *Essays.*

8. Cities force growth and make men talkative and entertaining, but they make them artificial.

   —Emerson, *Society and Solitude.*

9. The gloom and glare of towns.

   —Andrew Lang, *Ballade of the Midnight Forest.*

10. As one who long in populous city pent,
    Where houses thick and sewers annoy the air.

    —Milton, *Paradise Lost.*

PROVERBS AND QUOTATIONS ABOUT

FANTASY AND IMAGINATION

1. Imagination is not the talent of some men but is the health of every man.
—Emerson, *Letters and Social Aims.*

2. Imagination is the eye of the soul.
—Joubert, *Pensees.*

3. Imagination is more important than knowledge.
—Albert Einstein, *On Science.*

4. Imagination is a poor substitute for experience.
—Havelock Ellis, *The New Spirit.*

5. . . . them that build castles in the air . . .
—Sir Philip Sidney, *Apology for Poetry.*

6. Fancy may kill or cure.
—Thomas Fuller.

7. But lay on fancy's neck the reins.
—Matthew Green, *The Spleen.*

8. Aggressive Fancy working spells
Upon a mind o'erwrought.
—Thomas Hardy, *The Dynasts.*

9. In midway flight imagination tires;
Yet soon re-prunes her wing to soar anew.
—Young, *Night Thoughts.*

10. Imagination frames events unknown,
In wild, fantastic shapes of hideous ruin,
And what it fears creates.
—Hannah More, *Belshazzar.*

SUGGESTED READING: BOOKS

Adolescence

Aichhorn, August, *Wayward youth,* Viking, New York, 1965.

Alexander, Theron, *Children and adolescents: A biocultural approach to psychological development,* Atherton, New York, 1969.

Ausubel, D. P. *Theory and problems of adolescent development* Grune, New York, 1954.

Bandura, Albert, and Richard H. Walters, *Adolescent aggression,* Ronald, New York, 1959.

Blos, Peter, *On adolescence,* Macmillan, New York, 1961.

Caplan, Gerald, and Serge Lebovici, eds., *Adolescence: Psychosocial perspectives,* Basic Books, New York, 1968.

Deutsch, Helene, *Selected problems of adolescence,* Int. Univs., New York, 1967.

Friedenberg, Edgar Z., *Coming of age in America,* Random House, New York, 1965.

Friedenberg, Edgar Z., *Dignity of youth and other atavisms,* Beacon, New York, 1965.

Friedenberg, Edgar, *Vanishing adolescent,* Beacon, New York, 1959.

Garrison, Karl C., *Psychology of adolescence,* 6th ed., Prentice-Hall, New Jersey, 1965.

Gesell, Arnold, and others, *Youth: The years from ten to sixteen,* Harper, New York, 1956.

Grinder, Robert E., ed., *Studies in adolescence,* 2nd ed., Macmillan, New York, 1969.

Havighurst, Robert J., and others, *Growing up in River City,* Wiley, New York, 1962.

Jacobs, Jerry, *Adolescent Suicide,* Wiley, New York, 1970.

Joselyn, Irene M., *Adolescence Report from the Joint Commission on Mental Health of Children,* Harper & Row, New York, 1971.

McCandless, B. R., *Children: Behavior and development,* 2nd ed., Holt, New York, 1967.

Masserman, Jules H., ed., *Adolescence, dreams and training* (*Science and psychoanalysis,* Vol. 9), Grune, New York, 1966.

Medinnus, Gene R., and R. C. Johnson, *Child and adolescent psychology,* Wiley, New York, 1969.

Pearson, Gerald H. J., *Adolescence and the conflict of generations,* Norton, New York, 1958.

Rosenberg, Morris, *Society and the adolescent self-image,* Princeton, Pennsylvania, 1965.

Sebald, Hans, *Adolescence: A sociological analysis,* Meredith, New York, 1968.

Seldman, Jerome M., *Adolescent: A book of readings,* rev. ed., Holt, New York, 1960.

Stewart, Charles W., *Adolescent religion: A developmental study of the religion of youth,* Abingdon, New York, 1967.

Stone, L. Joseph, and Joseph Church, *Childhood and adolescence,* 2nd ed., Random House, New York, 1968.

Strang, Ruth, *Adolescent views himself: A psychology of adolescence,* McGraw, New York, 1957.

Wattenberg, William W., *Adolescent years,* text ed., Harcourt, New York, 1955.

Weiner, Irving B. *Psychological Disturbance in Adolescence.* Wiley, New York, 1970.

Confrontation and Aggression

Ashley Montagu, ed., *Man and Aggression.* Oxford University Press Fairlawn, New Jersey, 1968.

Berkowitz, Leonard, ed., *Roots of aggression,* Atherton, New York, 1969.

Buss, A. H., *Psychology of aggression,* Wiley, New York, 1961.

Daniels, David, N., et al., *Violence and the Struggle for Existence,* Little Brown, Boston, 1970.

Bron, Leonard D., et al., *Learning of Aggression in Children,* Little Brown, Boston, 1971.

Johnson, Roger N., *Aggression in Man and Animals,* Saunders, Philadelphia, 1972.
Lorenz, Konrad, *On aggression,* Harcourt, New York, 1966.
Storr, Anthony, *Human aggression,* Atheneum, New York, 1968.

Disadvantaged

Coles, Robert, *Dead End School,* Little Brown, Boston, 1968.
Coles, Robert, and Maria Piers, *Wages of Neglect: New Solutions for the Children of the Poor,* Quadrangle Books, New York, 1969.
Dennison, George, *Lives of Children,* Random House, New York, 1969.
Keniston, Kenneth, *Uncommitted: Alienated youth in American society,* Harcourt, New York, 1965.
Laing, Ronald D., *Politics of experience,* Pantheon, New York, 1967.
Sager, Clifford J. et al., *Black Ghetto Family in Therapy,* Grove Press, New York, 1970.

Belief

Buber, Martin, *Two types of faith,* Harper, New York, 1961.
Jaspers, Karl, *Philosophical faith and revelation,* Harper, New York, 1967.

Child Study

Ausubel, D. P., *Theory and problems of child development,* Grune, New York, 1958.
Axline, Virgina M., *Play therapy,* Ballantine, New York, 1969.
Baldwin, Alfred L., *Theories of child development,* Wiley, New York, 1967.
Breckenridge, Marian E., and Margaret N. Murphy, *Growth and development of the young child,* Saunders, Pennsylvania, 1969.
Carmichael, Leonard, *Manual of child psychology,* 2nd ed., Wiley, New York, 1954.
Clark, Kenneth B., *Prejudice and your child,* Beacon, New York, 1963.
Dennis, Wayne, ed., *Reading in child psychology,* 2nd ed., Prentice-Hall, New Jersey, 1963.
D'Evelyn, Katherine E., *Meeting children's emotional needs: A guide for teachers,* Prentice-Hall, New Jersey, 1957.
Erikson, Erik H., *Childhood and society,* rev. ed., Norton, New York, 1964.
Flavell, John H., and others, *Development of role-taking and communication skills in children,* Wiley, New York, 1968.
Frailberg, Selma, *Magic years,* Scribner, New York, 1959.
Havighurst, Robert J., and Bernice L. Neugarten, *American Indian and white children,* in prep. University of Chicago, Illinois, 1969.
Ilg, Frances L., and L. B. Ames, *Child behavior,* Harper, New York, 1955.
Inhelder, Barbel, and Jean Piaget, *Early growth of logic in the child,* Norton, New York, 1969.
Jersild, Arthur T., *Child psychology,* 6th ed., Prentice-Hall, New Jersey, 1968.
Landreth, Catherine, *Early childhood: Behavior and learning,* Knopf, New York, 1967.
Lowenfeld, Viktor, *Your child and his art,* Macmillan, New York, 1954.
McCandless, B. R., *Children: Behavior and development,* 2nd ed., Holt, New York, 1967.
Macfariane, Jean W., *Studies in child guidance,* Kraus, New York, 1938.
Millard, Cecil V., and J. W. M. Rothney, *Elementary school child: A book of cases,* Holy, New York, 1957.
Murchison, Carl A., ed., Handbook of child psychology, 2nd ed., rev. il., Russell, New York, 1933.
Murphy, Lois B., and others, *Personality in young children,* 2 volumes, Basic Books, New York, 1956.
Murphy, Lois, and others, *Widening world of childhood,* Basic Books, New York, 1962.
Mussen, Paul H., and others, *Child development and personality,* 3rd ed., Harper, New York, 1969.
Mussen, Paul H., *Handbook of research methods in child development,* Wiley, New York, 1960.
Ostrovsky, Everett, *Children without men,* rev. ed., Collier, New York, 1962.
Ostrovsky, Everett, *Sibling rivalry: A parent's guide,* Simon & Schuster, New York, 1970.
Piaget, Jean, *Child's conception of number,* Norton, New York, 1965.
Piaget, Jean, *Construction of reality in the child,* Basic Books, New York, 1954.
Piaget, Jean, *Origins of intelligence in children,* Int. Univs., New York, 1966.
Piaget, Jean, *Play, dreams, and imitation in childhood,* Norton, New York, 1962.
Redl, Rritz, and David Wineman, *Controls from within,* Free Press, New York, 1952.
Redl, Fritz, and D. Wineman, *When we deal with children,* Macmillan, New York, 1966.

Vavstelli, Celia S., *Piaget's Theory Applied to an Early Childhood Curriculum,* American Science & Engineering, Boston, 1970.
Vygotsky, Lev S., *Thought and Language,* Eugenia Hanfmann, and Gertude Vakar, trs. M. I. T. Press, Cambridge, Mass., 1962.
Wolff, Sula, *Children Under Stress,* Penguin Books, Baltimore.
Wright, Herbert F., *Recording and Analyzing Child Behavior,* Harper & Row, New York, 1967.

Creativity

Arieti, Silvano, *Intrapsychic self,* Basic Books, New York, 1967.
Koestler, Arthur, *Act of creation,* Dell, New York, 1966.
Lowenfeld, Viktor, and W. L. Brittain, *Creative and mental growth,* 4th ed., Macmillan, New York, 1964.

Drugs

Adelstein, Michael E., and Jean G., Pival, eds., *Drugs,* St. Martin Press, New York, 1972.
Andrews, Matthew, *Parents Guide to Drugs,* Doubleday, Garden City, New York, 1972.
Bennett, James C., and George D. Demes, *Drug Abuse and What We Can Do About It,* Charles C, Thomas, Springfield, Ill., 1972.
Brown, Wenzell, *Monkey on My Back,* Popular Library, New York, 1971.
Carey, James T., *College drug scene,* Prentice-Hall, New Jersey, 1968.
Hyde, Margaret O., ed., *Mind drugs,* McGraw, New York, 1968.
Maurer, David W., and V. H. Vogel, *Narcotics and narcotic addiction,* 3rd ed., Thomas, New York, 1967.
Nowlis, Helen H., *Drugs on the college campus,* Doubleday, New York, 1969.

The Family

Ackerman, Nathan W., *Psychodynamics of family life,* Basic Books, New York, 1958.
Billingsley, Andrew, *Black Families in White America,* Prentice-Hall, Englewood Cliffs, New Jersey, 1968.
Bossard, James H. S., and E. S. Boll, *Large family system,* University of Pennsylvania, Pennsylvania, 1956.
Delacato, Carl H., *Elementary School of the Future : A Guide for Parents.* Charles C, Thomas, Springfield, Ill., 1969.
Bracey, John H., Jr., et al., *Black Matriarchy. Myth or Reality,* Wadsworth, Belmont, Calif., 1971.
Farber B., *Family organization and crisis : Maintenance of integration in families with a severely mentally retarded child,* Kraus, New York, 1960.
Hess, Hannah S., *The Third Side of the Desk : How Parents Can Change the Schools,* Scribner's New York, 1972.

Learning by Discovery

Kuslan, Louis L., and A. Harris Stone, *Teaching children science,* Wadsworth, New York, 1968.
Lazarus, Arnold, and R. Knudson, *Selected objectives for the English language arts,* Houghton, New York, 1967.
McGavack, John, and Donald P. LaSalle, *Guppies, bubbles and vibrating objects,* Day, New York, 1969.
Massialas, Byron G., and J. Zevin, *Creative encounters in the classroom,* Wiley, New York, 1967.
Piltz, Albert, and Robert Sund, *Creative teaching of science in the elementary school,* Bacon, New York, 1968.

Play

Axline, Virginia M., *Play therapy,* Houghton, New York, 1947.
Piaget, Jean, *Play, dreams and imitation in childhood,* Norton, New York, 1962.
Piers, Maria W., ed., *Play and Development : A. Synposium,* Norton, New York, 1972.
Parent's Guide to Children's Play & Recreation, Macmillan, Riverside, New Jersey, 1965.
Smith, Anne M., *Play for Convalescent Children in Hospitals and at Home.* Barnes, A. S., Cranbury, New Jersey.
Winicott, D. W., *Playing and Reality,* Basic Books, New York, 1971.

Prejudice

Allport, Gordon W., *Nature of prejudice,* Doubleday, New York, 1958.

Baruch, Dorothy W., *Glass house of prejudice,* Morrow, New York, 1946.
Bettelheim, Bruno, and M. Janowitz, *Social change and prejudice,* Macmillan, New York, 1964.
Clark, Kenneth B., *Prejudice and your child,* Beacon, New York, 1963.
Powdermaker, Hortense, *Probing our prejudice,* Harper, New York, 1944.

Role Playing

Biddle, B. J., Thomas, *Role theory : Concepts and research,* Wiley, New York, 1966.
Boy, Angelo V., and Gerald J. Pine, *Counselor in the schools : A reconceptualization,* Houghton, New York, 1968.
Corsini, Raymond J., and others, *Roleplaying in business and industry,* Macmillan, New York, 1961.
Corsini, Raymond J., and Samuel, Cardone, *Roleplaying in Psycho-Therapy : A Manual,* Aldine Alberton, Chicago, 1966.
Gartner, Alan, et al., *Children Teach Children : Learning by Teaching,* Harper & Row, New York, 1971.
Horrocks, John E., and Dorothy Jackson, *Self and Role : A Theory of Self-Process and Role Behavior,* Houghton Mifflin, Boston, 1972.

Self

Gale, Raymond F., *Developmental behavior : A humanistic approach,* Macmillan, New York, 1969.
Gordon, Chad, and Kenneth J. Gergen, eds., *Self in social interaction,* Vol. 1, Wiley, New York, 1968.
Moustakas, Clark E., *Self: Explorations in personal growth,* Harper, New York, 1956.

Self-Actualization

Association for Supervision and Curriculum Development, *Humanizing education : The person in the process,* N. E. A., 1967.
Gale, Raymond F., *Developmental behavior : A humanistic approach,* Macmillan, New York, 1969.
Hammachek, Don E., ed., *Self in growth, teaching and learning,* Prentice-Hall, New Jersey, 1965.

Thinking and Creativity

Aylesworth, Thomas G., and Reagon, Gerald M., *Teaching for Thinking,* Doubleday, Garden City, New York, 1969.
Baker, Samm S., *Your key to creative thinking,* Harper, New York, 1962.
Boelen, Bernard J., *Existential Thinking,* Herder & Herder, New York, 1971.
Bruner, Jerome S., et al., *Study of Thinking,* Wiley, New York, 1956.
Kagan, Jerome, ed., *Creativity and learning,* Houghton, New York, 1967.
Parnes, Sidney J., *Creative behavior guidebook,* Scribner, New York, 1967.
Smith, James A., *Creative teaching of the social studies in the elementary school,* Bacon, New York, 1967.

School and Harizons

Blaine, Graham B., and Charles C. McArthur, *Emotional Problems of the Student,* 2nd ed., Appleton-Century-Crafts, New York, 1971.
Bower, Eli M., *Early Identification of Emotionally Handicapped Children in School,* 2nd ed., Charles C, Thomas, Springfield, Ill. 1970.
Despert, J. Louis, *Emotionally Disturbed Child—Then and Now,* Doubleday, Garden City, New York, 1970.
Hannam, Charles, et al., *Young Teachers and Reluctant Learners,* Penguin Books, Baltimore, 1973.

Values

Fairfield, Roy P., *Humanistic Frontiers in American Education,* Prentice-Hall, Englewood Cliffs, New Jersey, 1971.
Schwartz, Sheila, *Teaching the Humanities : Selected Readings,* Macmillan, Riverside, New Jersey, 1970.
Weinberg, Carl, *Humanistic Humanistic Foundations of Education,* Prentice-Hall, Englewood Cliffs, New Jersey, 1972.
Berson, Lenora, *Negroes and the Jews,* Random House, New York, 1971.

Sex Awareness

Baruch, Dorothy W., *New Ways in Sex Education : A Guide for Parents and Teachers,* McGraw Hill, New York, 1959.

Berenstain, Stan and Jan Berenstain, *How to Teach Your Children About Sex*, New York, 1972.

Block, William A., *What Your Child Really Wants to Know About Sex and Why*, Prentice-Hall, Englewood Cliffs, New Jersey, 1972.

Fraser, Stewart, *Sex, School and Society : Foreign and Domestic Perspectives*, Aurora Publishers, Nashville, Tenn., 1971.

Proverbs

Pahk, Induk, *Wisdom of the Dragon : Asian Proverbs*, Harper & Row, New York, 1970.

Reid J. Calvin, ed., *Proverbs to Live by*, Kenneth N. Taylor, tr. Regal Books, Glendale, Calif., 1972.

Smith, Arthur H., ed., *Proverbs and Common Sayings from the Chinese*, Dover Publishing, New York, 1914.

Vaughn, Henry H., *Welsh Proverbs with English Translations*, Gale Research Co., Detroit, Mich., 1969.

SUGGESTED READING: PERIODICALS

World of Play

Actions instead of words: play therapy for the young child. J. C. Waterland. *Elementary School Guidance and Counseling,* **4**: 180–7, March 1970.

Attention, anxiety, and rules in resistance-to-deviation in children. J. A. Cheyne and others. Bibliography. *Journal of Experimental Child Psychology,* **8**: 127–39, August 1969.

Children's play in three American subcultures. M. V. Eeagoe. *Journal of School Psychology,* **92**: 167–72, 1971.

Creative learning in children's playgrounds. A. Grey. *Childhood Education,* **45**: 491–9, May 1969.

Descriptive analysis of the play of young blind children. P. Tait. *Education of the Visually Handicapped,* **4**: 12–15, March 1972.

Effect of aggressive cartoons on children's interpersonal play. W. G. Hapkiewicz and A. H. Roden. *Child Development,* **42**: 1583–5, November 1971.

Exploratory and play behaviors of infants reared in an institution and in lower and middle class homes. R. R. Collard. Bibliography. *Child Development,* **42**: 1003–15, October 1971.

Involvement of the total child. N. Larrick. *The Instructor,* **79**: 42–3, December 1969.

Role of play in cognitive development. B. Sutton-Smith. Bibliography. Illustration. *Young Children,* **22**: 360–70, September 1967.

Secret world of children. S. W. Tiedt and I. M. Tiedt. *Childhood Education,* **44**: 363–5, February 1968.

Spontaneous play: an avenue for intellectual development. M. Almy. Bibliography. Illustration. *Young Children,* **22**: 264–77, May 1967.

Stability of nursery school children's social perception. F. J. Estavan. *The Journal of Experimental Education,* **34**: 48–54, Summer 1966.

Structured puppet play therapy. D. Vittner. *Elementary School Guidance and Counseling,* **4**: 68–70, October 1969.

Family

Accuracy of emotional communication and interpersonal compatibility. M. G. Hornstein. Bibliography. *Journal of Personality,* **35**: 20–30, March 1967.

Can parent classes affect family communications? R. S. Larson. Bibliography. *The School Counselor,* **19**: 261–70, March 1972.

Changing role of the family. P. A. Cortese. Bibliography. *Journal of School Health,* **41**: 475–80, November 1971.

Children, reasoning and interpersonal relations. T. N. Deal. Bibliography. *Childhood Education,* **45**: 291–3, January 1969.

Conflicting parental goals. C. K. Lipsman. *Personnel and Guidance Journal,* **45**: 277, November 1966.

Dynamics of the self. D. E. Hamachek. Illustration. *Journal of Education,* **101**: 7–8, March 1969.

Family interaction and the activities of young children. J. W. B. Douglas and others. Bibliography. *Journal of Child Psychology, Psychiatry and Allied Disciplines,* **9**: 157–71, December 1968.

Family relations courses taught in high school in the United States. A. A. Allen and K. F. King. *Journal of Home Economics,* **62**: 19–22, January 1970.

Father absence, cross-sex identity, and field dependent behavior in male adolescents. A. Barclay and D. R. Cusumano. Bibliography. *Child Development,* **38**: 243–50, March 1967.

Father role as perceived by young children and their fathers. J. H. James. Bibliography. *Journal of Home Economics,* **59**: 428–32, June 1967.

Hippie communal movement: effects on child birth and development. D. E. Smith and J. Sternfield. Bibliography. *American Journal of Orthopsychiatry,* **40**: 527–30, April 1970.

Kibbutz life and the Israeli woman, P. Hanes. *Forecast for Home Economics,* **17**: F 17–19+, December 1971.

Impact of the women's liberation movement on child development books. Z. S. Klapper. Bibliography. *American Journal of Orthopsychiatry,* **41**: 725–32, October 1971.

Myth and matter in treating the disorganized family: review of families of the slums: an exploration of their structure and treatment, by S. Minuchin and others. N. A. Polansky. *Children,* **15**: 201–2, September 1968.

Origin of man and his dependency on technology. K. Guy and R. C. Schacht. Bibliography. *American Council on Industrial Arts Teacher Education Yearbook,* **17**: 31–58, 1968.

Our stake in international standards for family living. J. A. Hannah. *Journal of Home Economics,* **63**: 396–9, Spring 1971.

Parent-child relations, need-nurturance, and vocational orientation. G. M. Appleton and J. C. Hansen. *Personnel and Guidance Journal,* **47**: 794–9, April 1969.

Poverty culture. C. E. Bradshaw. Illustration. *Childhood Education,* **46**: 79–84, November 1969.

Parents' values, family networks, and family development: working with disadvantaged families. D. R. Scheinfeld and others. *American Journal of Orthopsychiatry,* **40**: 413–25, April 1970.

Role models for lower class Negro boys. G. Henderson. Bibliography. *Personnel and Guidance Journal,* **46**: 6–10, September 1967.

Young Children in a new situation with and without their mothers. F. N. Cox and D. Campbell. *Child Development,* **39**: 123–31, March 1968.

Sex Awareness

Adolescent sexuality and the schools. A. P. Bell. *The North Central Association Quarterly,* **43**: 342–7, Spring 1969.

Age and first sources of sex information as reported by 88 college women. H. D. Thornburg. *The Journal of School Health,* **40**: 156–8, March 1970.

Are you guilty of teaching sex bias? M. Sadker. *Instructor,* **82**: 80–1, August 1972.

Awakening of adolescent femininity. L. Carter and M. Ostendorf. *Journal of School Health,* **40**: 203–5, April 1970.

Birth order, sex of siblings and incidence of learning disabilities. E. L. Vockell and B. Bennett. *Exceptional Children,* **39**: 162–4, October 1972.

Changes in self-concepts during a physical development program. W. R. Johnson and others. Bibliography, **39**: 560–5, October 1968.

Contemporary sex education: attitudes and implications for childrearing. J. D. Woody. Bibliography. *Journal of School Health,* **43**: 241–6 April 1973.

Education for family planning. C. E. Richardson. Bibliography. *Journal of School Health,* **39**: 537–43, October 1969.

Feminine image factor in girls' attitudes to school subjects. F. W. Slee. *The British Journal of Educational Psychology,* **38**: 212–14, June 1968.

Influence of sex and socioethnic factors upon imitation of teachers by elementary school children. S. H. Portuges and N. D. Feshbach. Bibliography. *Child Development,* **43**: 981–9, Spring 1972.

Opinions about sex education held by low-income Negro mothers. I. K. Lee and M. Stith. *Journal of Home Economics,* **61**: 359–62, May 1969.

Pill, the sexual revolution, and the schools. A. Montagu. *Phi Delta Kappan,* **49**: 480–4, May 1968.

School desegregation, socioeconomic status, sex and the aspirations of southern Negro adolescents. K. White and J. H. Knight. Bibliography. *The Journal of Negro Education,* **42**: 71–8, Winter 1973.

Sex and family living education. C. E. Willgoose. *The Instructor,* **79**: 96–7, February 1970.

Sex and sexuality presentations to emotionally disturbed children in a residential treatment center. N. C. Elsass. *Child Welfare,* **49**: 212–19, April 1970.

Sex education and life in the black ghetto. T. E. Brown. *Religious Education,* **64**: 450–8, November 1969.

Sex education can start in kindergarten. E. J. Mah. Illustration. *The Instructor,* **79**: 136–7, October 1969

Sex, social class and student performance. R. L. Holder. *Universities Quarterly,* **24**: 166–72, Spring 1970.

Sex-role identification and parental perceptions of social competence. S. Levine. *American Journal of Mental Deficiency,* **70**: 822–4, May 1966.

Who should plan your district's sex education program? J. Potter and R. W. Libby. *The American School Board Journal* **157**: 19–22, December 1969.

School and Its Horizons

Adolescent identity and self-perception as perception as predictors of scholastic achievement; Who am I technique. J. G. Jones and R. W. Strowig. Bibliography. *The Journal of Educational Research,* **62**: 78–82, October 1968.

Anxiety in elementary school children. B. N. Phillips. *Childhood Education,* **44**: 340–2, January 1968.

Assessment of children with learning disabilities. T. C. Lovitt. Bibliography. *Exceptional Children,* **34**: 233–9, December 1967.

Characteristics of gifted children. S. Krippner. Bibliography. *Education,* **88**: 15–21, September 1967.

Crisis intervention technique with potential college dropouts. W. C. Garner. Bibliography. *Personnel and Guidance Journal,* **48**: 552–60, March 1970.

Developing the open teacher. R. E. Boyd. *Education,* **92**: 58–62, April 1972.

Development of time concepts by kindergarten children. L. Stephens and W. H. Dutton. Bibliography. *School Science and Mathematics,* **69**: 59–63, January 1969.

Developmental changes in the self-concept during adolescence; Self-social symbols tasks. B. H. Long and others. Bibliography. *The School Review,* **76**: 210–30, June 1968.

Disadvantaged child who is successful in school. A. B. Coleman. *The Educational Forum,* **34**: 95–7, November 1969.

Disturbed youngsters in the classroom. W. C. More. Illustration. *Today's Education,* **58**: 30–7, April 1969.

Do black studies make a difference in ghetto children's achievement and attitudes? A. H. Yee and M. J. Fruth. *Journal of Negro Education,* **42**: 33–8, Winter 1973.

Effect of a dieting program on emotionally disturbed children. M. A. Krueger. *Child Welfare,* **52**: 172–7, March 1973.

Effects of tutoring and practice teaching on self-concept and attitudes in education H. J. Walberg and others. Bibliography. *The Journal of Teacher Education,* **19**: 283–91, Fall 1968.

Facilitating meaningful verbal learning in the classroom. D. P. Ausubel. *The Arithmetic Teacher,* **15**: 126–32, February 1968.

Ghetto dropout: analysis and partial solution. S. Cohen. Bibliography. *The Clearing House,* **44**: 118–22, October 1969.

Headteachers' expectations and their pupils' self-concepts. C. F. Palfrey. *Educational Research,* **15**: 123–7, Fall 1973.

Helping gifted children through mental health information and concepts. E. P. Torrance. *The Education Digest,* **33**: 34–7, October 1967.

How accurate are student evaluations of the extent of their knowledge of human sexuality? A. McCreary-Juhasz. *The Journal of School Health,* **37**: 409–12, October 1967.

Married students or married dropouts? J. Huber. *Educational Leadership,* **27**: 804–7, May 1970.

Psychological costs of quality and equality in education. U. Bronfenbrenner. Bibliography. *Child Development,* **38**: 909–25, December 1967.

Rebellious school dropout. S. B. Brown and T. T. Peterson. *School and Society,* **97**: 437–9, November 1969.

Self-ratings on the semantic differential: content versus response set. B. H. Long and others. Bibliography. *Child Development,* **39**: 647–56, June 1968.

Slow-progress student in graded and non-graded programs. W. E. Walker. Bibliography. *Peabody Journal of Education,* **50**: 191–210, April 1973.

Store-front school: Community education center, Buffalo, N. Y. Illustration. *American Vocational Journal,* **45**: 78, March 1970.

Street academies: one step off the sidewalk. J. Black. Illustration. *Saturday Review,* **52**: 88–9+, November 15, 1969.

Values that defeat learning. J. C. Lafferty.

National Association of Secondary School Principals Bulletin, **52**: 201–12, May 1968.
Why we teach: confessions from the male minority. I. Levine. *Teacher,* **90**: 40–3, November 1972.
Youth's dilemma: to be or to become. E. G. Williamson. Bibliography. *Personnel and Guidance Journal,* **46**: 173–7, October 1967.

Thinking and Creativity

Bilingualism: its effect on emotional and social development. H. Levine. Bibliography. *Journal of Secondary Education,* **44**: 69–73, February 1969.
Cognitive complexity in person perception and nation perception: a developmental approach. K. A. Signell. Bibliography. *Journal of Personality,* **34**: 517–37, December 1966.
Concept attainment of culturally advantaged and disadvantaged children utilizing artificial and lifelike stimulus tasks. S. Securro, Jr., and R. R. Walls. Bibliography. *Journal of Educational Psychology,* **62**: 531–8, December 1971.
Concerning Piaget's view on thinking and symbol formation. H. C. Furth. Bibliography. *Child Development,* **38**: 819–26, September 1967.
Creative and cognitive abilities of white and Negro children. B. O. Richmond. *Journal of Negro Education,* **40**: 111–16, Spring 1971.
Divergent thinking in blind children. W. J. Tisdall and others. Bibliography. *Journal of Educational Psychology,* **62**: 468–73, December 1971.
Effects of a creative problem-solving workshop upon the cognitive operations of verbal classroom interaction in the primary school grades. F. Martin. Bibliography. *Psychology in the Schools,* **9**: 126–30, April 1972.
Language acquisition: basic issues. S. F. Wanat. *The Reading Teacher,* **25**: 142–7, November 1971.
Learning and self-discovery. R. K. Morton. *Improving College and University Teaching,* **16**: 84, Spring 1968.
Music in a dynamic society. A. C. Eurich. *Music Journal,* **27**: 32+, January 1969.
On creativity and teaching. C. B. Paulston. *The Record,* **69**: 369–77, January 1968.
Perceptual skill development, a possible resource for the intellectually handicapped. M. Doyle. Bibliography. *American Journal of Mental Deficiency,* **71**: 776–82, March 1967.
Reading and the self-concept. F. Fennimore. *Journal of Reading,* **11**: 447–51+, March 1968.
Relation of re-creative experience to ego-stage development. L. A. Colley. Bibliography. *Adult Education,* **19**: 30–51, Fall 1968.
Self-perception and interpersonal attraction as related to tolerance-intolerance of ambiguity. J. E. Crandall. Bibliography. *Journal of Personality,* **37**: 127–40, March 1969.
Studies in perceptual development: perception exploration. D. Elkind and J. Weiss. Illustration. *Child Development,* **38**: 553–61, June 1967.

Becoming and Being

Autonomy and inner freedom: skills of emotional management. B. Bettelheim. *Association for Supervision and Curriculum Development Yearbook,* 73–94, 1969.
Cognitive structure: learning to read. D. P. Ausubel. *Education,* **87**: 544–8, May 1967.
Egocentrism in adolescent. D. Elkind. Bibliography. *Child Development,* **38**: 1025–34, December 1967.
Encounter and education. Tr. by D. Vandenberg and C. M. Smith. O. F. Bollnow. *The Educational Forum,* **36**: 303–12, March 1972.
Explicit personality theories and accuracy in person perception. R. E. Fancher, Jr. *Journal of Personality,* **34**: 252–61, June 1966.
Extentialism and music, education. D. L. Foster. *Music Journal,* **29**: 36+, Summer 1971.
Maslow's theory of needs in relation to vocational choice by students from lower socio-economic levels. C. K. Lipsman. Bibliography. *The Vocational Guidance Quarterly,* **15**: 283–8, June 1967.
Negro youth and psychological motivation. A. F. Pousaint and C. O. Atkinson. Bibliography. *The Journal of Negro Education,* **37**: 241–51, Summer 1968.
Relation of conservation to emotional and environmental aspects of development.

M. L. Goldschmid. Bibliography. *Child Development,* **39** : 579–89, June 1968.

Sartre's existentialism and education. H. S. Broudy. Bibliography. *Educational Theory,* **21** : 155–77, Spring 1971.

Success and failure as determinants of the performance predictions of mentally retarded and nonretarded children. S. O. Schuster and G. E. Gruen. Bibliography. *American Journal of Mental Deficiency,* **76** : 190–6, Summer 1971.

Test anxiety and self-concept. G. T. Kowitz. Illustration. *Childhood Education,* **44** : 162–4, November 1967.

The Disadvantaged

Black militant as a counselor : with comment by W. M. Banks. C. E. Vontress. Bibliography. *The Personnel and Guidance Journal,* **50** : 574–84, March 1972.

Changes in self-perceptions of Head-start trainees. M. E. Durrett and A. S. Radov. *The Elementary School Journal,* **72** : 321–6, March 1972.

Cognitive and linguistic deficits in psychotic children. J. W. Hagen and others. Bibliography. *Child Development,* **39** : 1103–17, December 1968.

Counseling the culturally deprived : a survey of high school counselors' opinions and attitudes. J. Clarke and H. Waters. *The School Counselor,* **19** : 201–9, January 1972.

Developmental task achievement of disadvantaged adolescents. S. S. Lail. *The High School Journal,* **52** : 89–97, November 1968.

Education, the disadvantaged, and values. E. H. West. *The Journal of Negro Education,* **37** : 95–7, Spring 1968.

Educationally disadvantaged. W. W. Brickman. *School and Society,* **96** : 196, March 30, 1968.

Ghetto child's self image. H. Rader. Illustration. *Education,* **56** : 298–300+, March 1968.

Informational analysis of intersensory communication in children of different social class. C. K. Conners and others. Bibliography. Illustration. *Child Development,* **38** : 251–66, March 1967.

Language arts materials for teachers of the disadvantaged. M. V. Doyle. *School and Community,* **58** : 14–15, March 1972.

New directions in psychological services for children with mental, emotional and cultural handicaps. S. Sarason. *New York Society for the Experimental Study of Education Yearbook,* 1967 : 48–50.

Problem of the culturally deprived. K. Price. Illustration. *The Record,* **69** : 122–31, November 1967.

Respect for education and education for respect. M. Frostig. *Claremont Reading Conference Yearbook,* **32** : 43–52, 1968.

Self-concepts of some disadvantaged students at inner city high school. *Contemporary Education,* **39** : 299–32, March 1968.

Self-other orientations of Indian and American adolescents. R. C. Ziller and others. Bibliography. *Journal of Personality,* **36** : 315–30, June 1968.

Specialized teacher training for inner-city schools. *School and Soceity,* **100** : 214–16, April 1972.

Training teachers for ethnic minority youths. D. H. Smith. *Phi Delta Kappan,* **53** : 285–7, January 1972.

Visual expression : a creative advantage of the disadvantaged. D. W. Rogers. Illustration. *The Elementary School Journal,* **68** : 394–9, May 1968.

Confrontation and Aggression

Aggression as a function of the interaction of the sex of the aggressor and the sex of the victim. S. P. Taylor and S. Epstein. *Journal of Personality,* **35** : 474–86, September 1967.

Aggressive classroom behavior and school achievement. J. F. Feldhusen and others. Bibliography. *Journal of Special Education,* **4** : 431–9, Fall 1970.

Are law and order and individual freedom inevitably in conflict? C. E. Hurst. *School and Community,* **58** : 8–9, May 1972.

Children's aggression following competition and exposure to and aggressive model. J. D. Nelson and others. Bibliography. *Child Development,* **40** : 1085–97, December 1969.

College student rebellion : explanations and answers B. Bettelheim. *Phi Delta Kappan,* **50** : 511–14, May 1969.

Concept of death in early childhood. P. Childers and M. Wimmer. *Child Development,* **42** : 1299–301, October 1971.

Concerned citizens in the making. J. J. Volkers.

Childhood Education, **45**: 269–72, January 1969.

Conformity of children in an ambiguous perceptual situation. N. H. Hamm and K. L. Hoving. Bibliography. *Child Development,* **40**: 773–84, September 1969.

Conformity, rebellion, and learning: confrontation of youth with society. I. Phillips and S. A. Szurek. Bibliography. *American Journal of Orthopsychiatry,* **40**: 463–72, April 1970.

Contexts of role conflict. K. V. Jones. *Comparative Education Review,* **14**: 45–9, February 1970.

Development of fear in man and other animals. G. W. Bronson. Bibliography. *Child Development,* **39**: 409–31, June 1968.

Early identification of youth with potential mental health problems. N. Lambert. *The High School Journal,* **51**: 288–93, April 1968.

Effect of aggressive cartoons on children's interpersonal play. W. G. Hapkiewicz and A. H. Roden. *Child Development,* **42**: 1583–5, November 1971.

Effect of self-confrontation, role playing, and response feedback on the level of self-esteem. C. Roberts. Bibliography. *The Speech Teacher,* **21**: 22–38, January 1972.

Generation gap: a problem of values. S. L. Halleck. *The Education Digest,* **34**: 32–5, January 1969.

Modeling and environmental generalization by mentally retarded subjects of televised aggressive or friendly behavior. J. V. Fechter, Jr. American Journal of Mental Deficiency, **76**: 266–7, Spring 1971.

Perception of deviant behavior: a study of cheating. J. Q. Knowlton and L. A. Hamerlynck. *Journal of Educational Psychology,* **58**: 379–85, December 1967.

Problems of violence. D. P. Moynihan. *American Association of School Administrators Official Report,* 1968: 5–18.

Research and theory on aggression and violence. R. Ulrich and M. Wolfe. Bibliography. Illustration. *The Science Teacher,* **36**: 24–8, May 1969.

Self-concept of the young child as he learns to read. J. T. Kunz. Bibliography. *Claremont Reading Conference Yearbook* **32**: 114–22, 1968.

Sesame Street: magic or malevolence? A. R. Ratliff and R. G. Ratliff. *Young Child,* **27**: 199–204, April 1972.

Situational effects on justifiableness of aggression at three age levels. D. W. Shantz and T. Pentz. Bibliography. *Child Development,* **43**: 274–81, March 1972.

Televised aggression and the interpersonal aggression of preschool children. F. B. Steuer and others. *Journal of Experimental Child Psychology,* **11**: 442–7, June 1971.

Test anxiety, confidence, commitment, and conformity. B. G. Rule and M. L. Sandilands. *Journal of Personality,* **37**: 460–7, September 1969.

Prejudice

Adolescent morality: a comparison of white and Negro concepts of selves and others. F. Schab. *Contemporary Education,* **43**: 284–6, April 1972.

Better self images. W. Fisher. *The Instructor,* **78**: 95, August 1968.

Black and white: challenging perceptions. C. Ross and K. Swick. *Clearing House,* **46**: 482–6, April 1972.

Changing attitudes of black students. W. M. Banks. Bibliography. *Personnel and Guidance Journal,* **48**: 739–45, May 1970.

Classroom discussion of racial identity, or How can we make it without acting white? C. G. McArdle and N. F. Young. Bibliography. *American Journal of Orthopsychiatry,* **40**: 135–41, January 1970.

Current attitudes and socialization patterns of white and Negro students entering college. E. L. Gaier and W. A. Watts. Bibliography. *The Journal of Negro Education,* **38**: 342–50, Fall 1969.

Development of self concept in Negro and white welfare children. T. R. Carpenter and T. V. Busse. *Child Development,* **40**: 935–9, September 1969.

Effects of black studies on Negro fifth grade students. R. W. Roth. *The Journal of Negro Education,* **38**: 435–9, Fall 1969.

Exploratory study of the modification of color and racial concept attitudes in preschool children. J. E. Williams and C. D. Edwards. Bibliography. *Child Development,* **40**: 737–50, September 1969.

Friendships among students in desegregated schools. D. Sachdeva. *California Journal of Educational Research,* **23**: 45–51, January 1972.

Implication of prejudice. T. Kusserow. *Physical Education,* **27**: 32–3, March 1970.

Jensen controversy: symposium. *Measurement and Evaluation in Guidance,* **3**: 7–24, Spring 1970.

Negro-white difference in employability, self-concept, and related measures among adolescents classified as mentally handicapped. L. S. Shulman. *The Journal of Negro Education,* **37**: 227–40, Summer 1968.

On the function analysis of social class differences in modes of speech. F. Williams and R. C. Naremore. Bibliography. *Speech Monographs,* **36**: 77–102, June 1969.

Reactions to adverse and favorable evaluations of one's self. I. D. Steiner. *Journal of Personality,* **36**: 553–63, December 1968.

Relationship between race and perception of racially related stimuli in preschool children. J. R. Stabler and others. Bibliography. *Child Development,* **40**: 1233–9, December 1969.

Self-image: a black perspective. F. E. Means. *The Journal of General Education,* **24**: 51–8, April 1972.

Teaching styles in four-year-olds. N. D. Feshbach and G. Devor. Bibliography. *Child Development,* **40**: 183–90, March 1969.

Trust: a new approach to student unrest. I. Tribble. *Educational Leadership,* **27**: 392–6, January 1970.

White adult behavior toward black and white children. B. Coates. Bibliography. *Child Development,* **43**: 143–54, March 1972.

Drugs

Abuse of medicinal products. J. A. Thomas and G. R. Knotts. *Journal of School Health,* **41**: 235–8, May 1971.

Bad drug trips and flashbacks. J. L. Juve. *Child Welfare,* **51**: 41–50, January 1972.

Drugs and creativity: a negative relationship. A. Beck. *School Arts,* **71**: 38–9, June 1972.

Drugs and the learning process. M. Henry and C. Mustiful. *Audiovisual Instruction,* **16**: 88, June 1971.

Effects of certain drugs on phonation. B. V. Fishman and others. *Journal of Speech and Hearing Research,* **14**: 301–6, June 1971.

Self image and attitudes toward drugs. M. L. Brehm and K. W. Back. *Journal of Personality,* **36**: 299–314, June 1968.

Objectification of screening for early detection of emotional disorder. D. R. Beach and others. Bibliography. *Child Development,* **39**: 1177–88, December 1968.

Values

Adapting to other values: the role of the adjustment teacher. E. M. Dean. *Elementary English,* **46**: 169–71, February 1969.

Development of artistic expression. R. Henkes. Illustration. *Arts and Activities,* **63**: 26–8, February 1968.

Didactic, experiential, and modeling factors in the learning of empathy. P. A. Payne and others. Bibliography. *Journal of Counseling Psychology,* **19**: 425–9, Spring 1972.

Education and the self-concept of the mentally retarded. H. D. Krop. Bibliography. *The Training School Bulletin,* **65**: 57–64, August 1968.

Empathy and second language learning; Micro-momentary expression test. A. Z. Guiora and others. Bibliography. *Language Learning,* **22**: 111–30, June 1972.

Essential Values in a changing society. W. L. Stone. *Adult Leadership,* **17**: 89, June 1968.

Examining our values. V. Schonborg. *Childhood Education,* **45**: 15–16, September 1968.

Growing: with list of books and films. *Media and Methods,* **8**: 38–41, January 1972.

High, average, low: and what makes teachers think so. M. Haberman and J. D. Raths. *The Elementary School Journal,* **68**: 241–5, February 1968.

How children learn values. B. J. Paschal. *The Education Digest,* **33**: 49–51, May 1968.

Negative self-concept of Mexican-American students. T. P. Carter. Illustration. *School and Society,* **96**: 217–19, March 30, 1968.

Nonverbal components of empathic communication. R. F. Haase and D. T. Tepper, Jr. Bibliography. *Journal of Counseling Psychology,* **19**: 417–24, Spring 1972.

Reliability of the ideal-self-concept. G. H. Frank and D. S. Hiester. *Journal of Counseling Psychology,* **14**: 356–7, July 1967.

Role of self concept in achievement. B. J. Paschal. *The Journal of Negro Education,* **37**: 392–6, Fall 1968.

Self-discovery. S. Cherney. *Adult Leadership,* **16**: 7–8+, May 1967.

Self-discovery and the role of the counselor. J. W. Robb. *Personnel and Guidance Journal,* **45**: 1008–11, June 1967.

Self-discovery, self expression and the self image in the i. t. a. classroom. J. A. Downing. Bibliography. *Claremont Reading Conference Yearbook,* **32**: 123–30, 1968.

Today's values, choices for the pregnant girl. E. McConnell. *Forecast for Home Economics,* **17**: F60–1+, Fall 1972.

Values and the poems of Marianne Moore. C. H. Edsall. *English Journal.* **58**: 516–18, April 1969.

Value education in the social studies. J. R. Fraenkel. Bibliography. *Phi Delta Kappan,* **50**: 457–61, April 1969.

Value of not following the directions. S. Daniels. *Instructor,* **81**: 21, August 1971.

Values that defeat learning. J. C. Lafferty. *National Association of Secondary School Principals Bulletin,* **52**: 201–12, May 1968.

Role Playing

Books and role-playing. C. Rudolph. *Elementary English,* **47**: 46–8, January 1970.

Communicating with today's teenagers; an exercise between generations. E. Schindler-Rainman. Illustration. *Children,* **16**: 218–23, November 1969.

From confrontation to collaboration. I. N. Berlin. Bibliography. *American Journal of Orthopsychiatry,* **40**: 473–80, April 1970.

Developing sensitivity and concern in children. V. R. Rogers Bibliography. *Social Education,* **31**: 299–302, April 1967.

Effectiveness of sensitivity training on the perception of non-verbal communications. D. J. Delaney and R. A. Heimann. Bibliography. *Journal of Counseling Psychology,* **13**: 436–40, Winter 1966.

Effects of self-confrontation, role playing, and response feedback on the level of self-esteem, C. Roberts. Bibliography. *The Speech Teacher,* **21**: 22–38, January 1972.

Model for peer group counseling based on role-playing, L. Ettkin and L. Snyder. *The School Counselor,* **19**: 215–18, January 1972.

Need for approval, defensive denial, and sensitivity to cultural stereotypes. L. I. Jacobson and L. H. Ford, Jr. Bibliography. *Journal of Personality,* **34**: 596–609, December 1966.

On campus in a wheelchair, M. Sinclair. *American Education,* **8**: back cover, March 1972.

Personal encounter for social understanding. R. M. Thomas. *Educational Leadership,* **24**: 497–500, March 1967.

Role perception in teaching and learning, S. L. Guskin. Bibliography. *Viewpoints,* **47**: 143–57, July 1971.

Role play simulation activities as a teaching strategy: suggestions for new uses. D. W. Champagne and J. F. Hines. *Educational Technology,* **11**: 58–60, August 1971.

Role playing: an approach to meaningful social learning. F. R. Shaftel. *Social Education,* **34**: 556–9, May 1970.

Role playing: effective technique in the teaching of history. W. Dumas. *The Clearing House,* **44**: 468–70, April 1970.

Role playing with borderline and mildly retarded adolescents in an institutional setting. J. F. Taylor. *Exceptional Children,* **36**: 206–8, November 1969.

Child Study

Adoption trends: January-June 1971. M. J. Smith. *Child Welfare,* **50**: 510–11, November 1971.

Education and mental health: a need for interdisciplinary involvement. L. Cahn and R. Peterson. *Journal of School Health,* **43**: 218–20, April 1973.

Group Discussion with emotionally disturbed children: implications of the concept of causal orientation. D. A. Sobel. *Journal of School Health,* **43**: 122–5, Fall 1973.

Help for the hyperkinetic child in school. V. K. Harlin. *Journal of School Health,* **42**: 587–92, December 1973.

Reaching Children who withdraw. E. Bernstein. *Instructor,* **82**: 98+, April 1973.

Some opinions on finding families for black children. E. Herzog and others. *Children,* **18**: 143–8, July 1971.

Adolescence

Adolescents with learning problems: how long must they wait? with discussion. C. L. Kline. Bibliography. *Journal of Learning Disabilities,* **5**: 262–84, May 1972.

Dating patterns of black and white adolescents in a southern community. G. E. Dickinson. *Adolescence,* **6** : 285–98, Fall 1971.

Development of vocational decisions during adolescence. J. W. Hollender. Bibliography. *Journal of Counseling Psychology,* **18** : 244–8, May 1971.

Growing : with list of books and films. *Media and Methods,* **8** : 38–41, January 1972.

Role confusion in adolescence. L. Barinbaum. *Adolescence,* **7** : 121–7, Spring 1972.

Voices from the back of the classroom. N. A. Springthall and R. L. Mosher. Bibliography. *The Journal of Teacher Education,* **22** : 166–75, Summer 1971.

Proverbs

Proverb story. P. Curran. *English Language Teaching,* **26** : 54–6, October 1971.

AUTHOR INDEX

SUBJECT INDEX